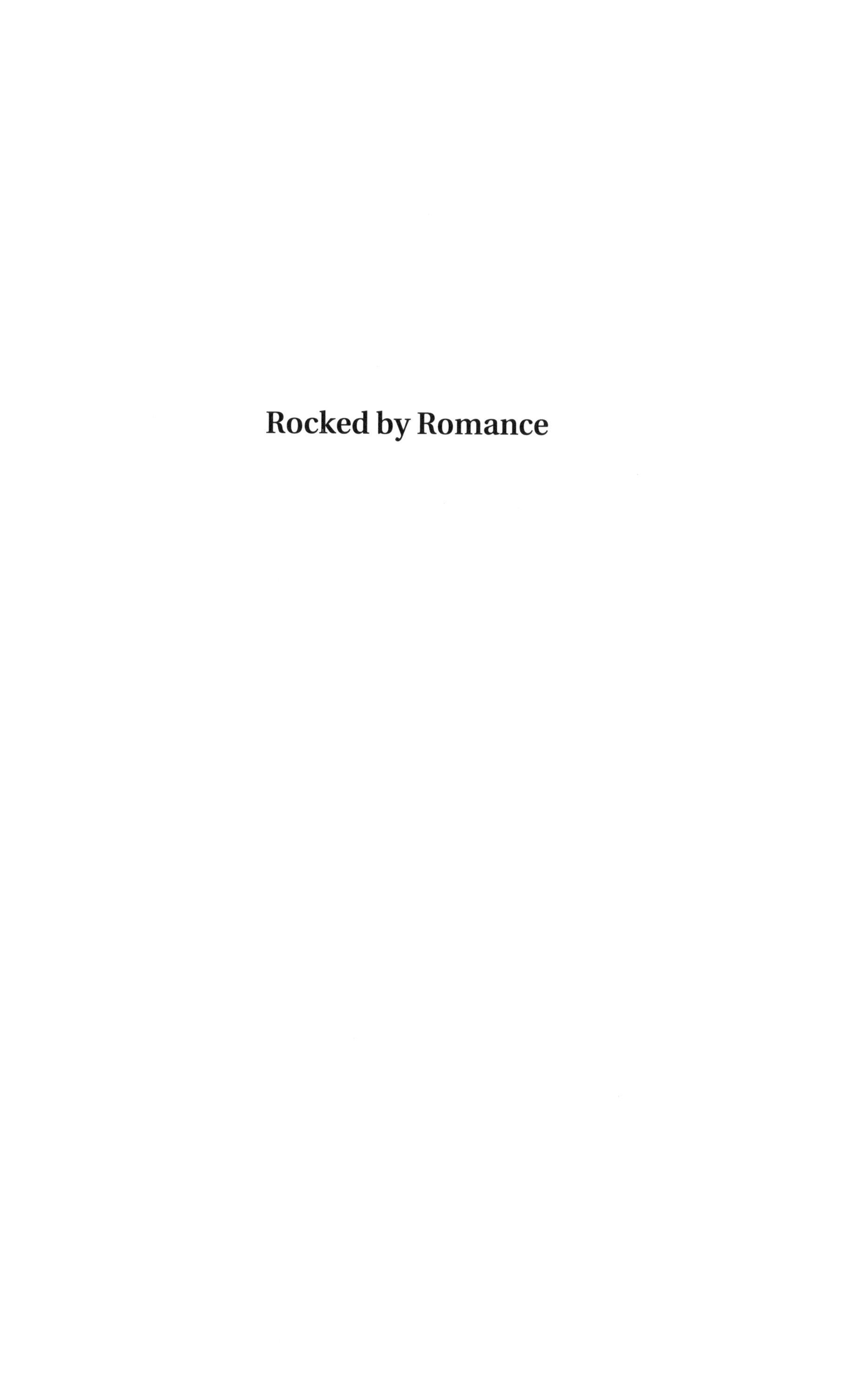

Rocked by Romance

Genreflecting Advisory Series

Diana T. Herald, Series Editor

Fluent in Fantasy: A Guide to Reading Interests
Diana Tixier Herald

Romance Fiction: A Guide to the Genre
Kristin Ramsdell

Now Read This: A Guide to Mainstream Fiction, 1978–1998
Nancy Pearl with assistance from Martha Knappe and Chris Higashi

Junior Genreflecting: A Guide to Good Reads and Series Fiction for Children
Bridget Dealy Volz, Cheryl Perkins Scheer, and Lynda Blackburn Welborn

Genreflecting: A Guide to Reading Interests in Genre Fiction, 5th Edition
Diana Tixier Herald

Now Read This II: A Guide to Mainstream Fiction, 1990–2001
Nancy Pearl

Christian Fiction: A Guide to the Genre
John Mort

Strictly Science Fiction: A Guide to Reading Interests
Diana Tixier Herald and Bonnie Kunzel

Hooked on Horror: A Guide to Reading Interests in Horror Fiction, 2d Edition
Anthony J. Fonseca and June Michele Pulliam

Make Mine a Mystery: A Reader's Guide to Mystery and Detective Fiction
Gary Warren Niebuhr

Teen Genreflecting: A Guide to Reading Interests, 2d Edition
Diana Tixier Herald

Blood, Bedlam, Bullets, and Badguys: A Reader's Guide to Adventure/Suspense Fiction
Michael B. Gannon

Rocked by Romance

A Guide to Teen Romance Fiction

Carolyn Carpan

Genreflecting Advisory Series

Diana T. Herald, Series Editor

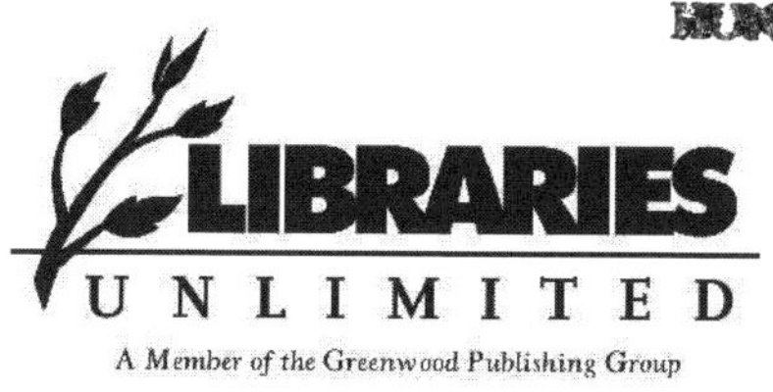

Westport, Connecticut • London

Library of Congress Cataloging-in-Publication Data

Carpan, A. Carolyn.
Rocked by romance : a guide to teen romance fiction / A. Carolyn Carpan.
p. cm. (Genreflecting advisory series)
Includes bibliographical references (p.) and index.
ISBN 1–59158–022–6
1. Young adult fiction, American—Stories, plots, etc. 2. Love stories, American—Stories, plots, etc. 3. Young adult fiction, American—Bibliography. 4. Love stories, American—Bibliography. I. Title. II. Series.
Z1231.L68C37 2004
[PS374.L6]
813.009'9283—dc22 2004040832

British Library Cataloguing in Publication Data is available.

Library of Congress Catalog Card Number: 2004040832
ISBN: 1–59158–022–6

First published in 2004

Libraries Unlimited, 88 Post Road West, Westport, CT 06881
A Member of the Greenwood Publishing Group, Inc.
www.lu.com

Printed in the United States of America

The paper used in this book complies with the Permanent Paper Standard issued by the National Information Standards Organization (Z39.48–1984).

10 9 8 7 6 5 4 3 2 1

In memory of my mother,
Eileen O'Connell
and
In memory of my godmother,
Joan Lynch

For my favorite young adults,
Sean O'Connell
and
Katie O'Connell

Contents

Foreword

Although stories exploring the newly discovered wonders of dating, first love, and blossoming sexuality have been consistently popular with teens and preteens for years, until now, there has been no single reference source devoted exclusively to this literature. Brief articles, bibliographies, and occasional chapters in guides covering broader topics were the only professional resources available, and it was clear to anyone who worked with young adults and understood the YA romance genre that something more was needed. Fortunately for readers and librarians alike, Carolyn Carpan has produced it. Well designed, comprehensive, and accessible, this guide does a beautiful job with this complex, multilayered genre and is a resource that fills a reference gap not only in the field of young adult literature but also in the larger Romance fiction genre.

We've needed a reference source like this for a long time; this excellent guide is well worth the wait.

Kristin Ramsdell
Author, *Romance Fiction: A Guide to the Genre*

Acknowledgments

I would like to thank Kristin Ramsdell for the inspiration for this book and also her encouragement to tackle the project. I also want to thank my editors, including Barbara Ittner, who provided much editorial assistance and encouragement along the way, and Diana Tixier Herald, for her contributions to the book. I also wish to acknowledge the assistance of my colleagues at Rollins College: Dorothy Mays, who showed me how to write a book proposal; Bill Svitavsky, who read early drafts; Patricia Grall and Shawne Keevan, who provided me with books and articles via interlibrary loan; and Donna Cohen, who gave me a research leave so I could write the book proposal and grant applications. Rollins College provided funding in the form of a Jack B. Critchfield Grant.

I want to thank the authors who are profiled here, who all graciously gave me some of their valuable time for interviews: Meg Cabot, Cheryl Zach, Lorraine Heath, Alex Sanchez, Robin Jones Gunn, Dian Curtis Regan, Megan McCafferty, Lurlene McDaniel, and Beverly Cleary. Editors and publicity staff at several publishing houses assisted me in obtaining book information, author interviews, and author photographs: Abigail McAden, HarperCollinsBooks; Josette Kurey, HarperCollins Books; Rebecca Grose, HarperCollins Books; Beth Mellow, Penguin; Wendy Loggia, Knopf/Delacorte; Christine Molito Labov, Random House; Victoria Stapleton, Simon & Schuster; and Kathy Dunn, Random House. I also wish to thank Charis Calhoon from the Romance Writers of America for helping arrange author interviews and providing me with a press pass for the 2002 Romance Writers of America conference.

I also want to thank Random House, Little, Brown, and Simon & Schuster for sending me review copies of many young adult novels; Linda Benson at *Voice of Youth Advocates*, who sent me a recent copy of the journal with a relevant article; and staff in the YALSA and *Booklist* offices at the American Library Association, who also provided copies of needed articles. Thanks also to authors Eileen Goudge, Cherie Bennett, and Katie MacAlister for romance series information. I also wish to thank the participants of the YALSA-BK listserv, especially Michael Cart, for suggestions regarding the book lists.

Last, but not least, I wish to thank my family and friends, who provided me with moral support in person and via telephone and e-mail, including Sally Cameron Jahncke, Katherine Patton, Anne Simms, Christy and Jamie MacArthur, Alison Creech, Leanne Chisholm, and Paula Clarke. I would also like to thank my aunt Colleen O'Connell for her support during this project.

Introduction

The teenage years are a time of tumult and change. The period is the transition time between childhood play and adult responsibilities. Teens today are diverse in their needs and interests, but they share certain basic characteristics and concerns. Two of the most important concerns for teens are the development of romantic relationships and coming to terms with their burgeoning sexuality. It makes sense, then, that fiction for teens would address these issues. In fact, it is difficult to find a young adult novel that does not somehow touch upon love and sex. Yet young adult novels are seldom classified as "romance fiction," and teen readers, unlike adult readers, do not specifically identify themselves as romance readers. So, although teens are highly interested in romance, and romance is rampant in young adult literature, permeating virtually every other young adult genre, readers' advisors and scholars have given little attention to young adult romance as a genre.

In her book *Romance Fiction: A Guide to the Genre*, Kristin Ramsdell explains that she did not include a chapter focusing on the young adult romance subgenre because "that subject is diverse enough to merit a separate guide of its own."[1] In a review of Ramsdell's book published in *Voice of Youth Advocates*, John Charles agrees: "[T]his topic deserves a whole book to itself."[2] These comments by my esteemed colleagues inspired me to tackle the task of putting together a guide and annotated bibliography of young adult romance fiction.

There are currently no other reference or readers' advisory guides specific to this genre, and only a few journal articles and scholarly studies have been published on the topic of young adult romance literature. Professionals who work with teen readers have been forced to rely on a handful of resources, hardly adequate for successfully serving teen readers. This book seeks to remedy that situation. I hope that librarians, teachers, and parents will use this guide to advise both girls and boys in the reading of young adult romance fiction.

Purpose, Scope, and Selection Criteria

This guide attempts to identify, organize, and describe stories of love and romance, drawing from a variety of other genres written for young adults, including fantasy, contemporary problem novels, Christian and historical fiction, and popular paperback series. It serves three purposes.

First, it provides public and school librarians, teachers, parents, and booksellers with a current and selective readers' advisory guide to the young adult romance genre. Second, it offers teen readers a guide to a favorite genre that is not clearly defined in the early twenty-first century. Third, the guide gives scholars information supporting research of the history, content, and reading of young adult romance novels. The book will also be of interest to publishers and writers of young adult fiction who wish to explore current publishing trends.

The bibliography covers current titles and young adult romance series novels written in English and available to American youth in public libraries, school libraries, and bookstores. Selections include award-winning titles written by critically acclaimed young adult authors, titles reviewed and recommended by young adult librarians, popular paperback series, and some adult romance fiction titles young adults might enjoy. They are appropriate for young adult readers aged eleven through sixteen.

Books selected for the title lists have generally been published since 1990, although books published prior to 1990 are included either because they are award-winning titles or because they are so popular with readers that they remain in print or are still available in libraries. Series selected for the bibliographies were popular, and therefore available, when the guide was compiled. The nature of young adult paperback series, however, is a continuously changing range of titles and series that suit the trends of the minute. If sales are sluggish, a series will disappear, only to be immediately replaced by another, more trendy, series. The twenty-year run of the Sweet Valley High series is highly unusual. (*Note:* If you are looking for a series book or a novel from this bibliography that has gone out of print, you might find it in the secondhand and out-of-print-book markets.)

Series written by various authors include a date range for publication of the series, rather than publication years for each title. Records are sketchy, and it is not always possible to identify the year of first publication of a paperback series book, particularly when popular series such as Sweet Valley High and Christy Miller were reprinted numerous times over many years. Wherever possible, authors' names were included, but when a series is written by numerous authors, it is not always easy to identify authors of all titles in a series.

Definition

So what exactly is teen romance fiction? When you hear the phrase "romance novel," you may automatically think of paperback books with covers showing scantily clad adult couples locked in passionate embraces. You might also think they are trashy books that you wouldn't recommend to any teenagers, especially since romance novels have sexual content that you think might not be appropriate for younger readers. And when you hear the phrase "young adult romance novels," you might envision something similar to adult romance novels, only with younger characters and perhaps tamer sexuality. While this notion applies to a portion of the young adult romance literature, young adult romance literature must be defined more broadly to include any book written for young adults that tells a love story.

In her book *Happily Ever After* (Libraries Unlimited, 1987), Kristin Ramsdell defines young adult romance novels as "romances or love stories written specifically for, and usually about, young adults or adolescents."[3] She states that the young adult romance "includes a definite emphasis on developing character, solving problems and growing up" and it is this feature that distinguishes the young adult romance from the other romance subgenres.[4] As characters in young adult romance literature grow and mature, they develop relationships with family, friends, and boyfriends or girlfriends.

Marc Aronson, an author and expert on young adult literature, contends:

> Y[oung] A[dult] novels seek to capture the intensity of adolescence, where truth is a pure value, exposure and secrecy are constant themes, and readers feel alienation with

> first force. . . . As characters measure the public world by the values of the family and reexamine the family in light of new truths found in the world, they begin to work out their individual sense of identity; they "come of age."[5]

In fact, for teens, love and sex are integral parts of becoming adults. Unlike adult readers, who often seek refuge or diversion in romance stories, teens usually see romance as uncharted territory, where they will have to make difficult choices and prove their worth. Thus, many romances for teens are framed within or coupled with other scenarios, such as coming of age, historical events, and so on.

Contemporary coming-of-age stories generally revolve around the social issues that young people are confronted with in their everyday lives, such as homosexuality, lesbianism, bisexuality, rape, incest, drugs, sex, HIV and AIDS, alcoholism, abortion, pregnancy, death, suicide, racial or religious prejudice, crime, or illness. These themes are often combined with stories of first love, crushes, unrequited love, first sexual encounters, and heartbreak.

Love and romance can also be found in historical fiction and Christian fiction written for young adults. Paperback romance series, which were popular in the 1980s, have been replaced with new series that combine romance with horror, paranormal phenomena, fantasy, and contemporary high school and family stories. Some of these series are tied to popular television shows, such as *Buffy the Vampire Slayer, Sabrina the Teenage Witch, Alias, Charmed, Smallville, Gilmore Girls*, and *7th Heaven.*

The Romance Writers of America claim the adult romance novel is a story comprised of two required elements: a central love story and an emotionally satisfying and optimistic ending.[6] They define young adult romance novels simply as "romantic novels for young adult readers," presumably with a central love story and a happy ending.[7] While this is a good beginning, contemporary young adult romance fiction requires a broader approach, one that accounts for both coming-of-age novels and series fiction. For purposes of this work, young adult romance fiction is comprised of various elements:

- A central love story that emphasizes the experience of love (usually first time, and which may be unrequited), sexual feelings, and/or sexual acts, such as kissing and/or sexual intercourse;
- A plot that includes problems related to these new emotions and experiences, such as unrequited love, pregnancy, abortion, adoption, or the possibility of sexually transmitted diseases such as HIV and AIDS;
- A plot that includes obstacles to the love relationship such as racism or religious prejudice, illness, war, incest, or rape; and
- Unlike adult romances, a story that does *not* always include an optimistic ending. Although many young adult romances have happy endings, some young adult authors want readers to know that real life does not always provide easy answers and inevitable resolutions to problems.

It is also important to note that with young adult romance fiction, other genre story elements are almost always present.

Organization and How to Use This Book

This work attempts to describe what comprises young adult romance fiction today, explain its appeal to readers, and map the genre according to subgenres and themes that reflect reader preferences. After a definition and a discussion of the characteristics and appeals of young adult romance fiction, this introduction offers a brief history of the genre, which lends further understanding to the genre and its appeals. General guidelines for advising readers and building a young adult library collection are given in Chapter 1.

Chapters 2 through 9 provide selected annotated bibliographies for the young adult romance genre, grouping titles according to types that reflect reader tastes. Chapters focus on the general subgenres of classic romance, contemporary romance, contemporary romance series, issues romance, alternative reality romance, romantic suspense, historical romance, and Christian romance, and each chapter is broken down into further subgenres and themes. Thus, the organization supports the search for read-alikes. If a reader says he or she particularly enjoyed a specific title or author, you can simply search for that author or title in the author/title index and turn to a page where titles with similar qualities or books by the same author are listed. A subject index provides further access to titles within particular topics.

Annotations are arranged alphabetically by author and book title. In the case of series, the series title is placed alphabetically, and individual titles within the series are organized chronologically. This exception is made because readers usually prefer to read series titles in this order.

Each entry in the bibliography includes the book title, publisher, and publication date. Each entry also includes an ISBN for the book. Whenever possible, these numbers refer to hardcover copies of the titles. If a book is only available in paperback, the ISBN for the paperback edition is listed. Where applicable, reissues are noted. The following grade levels are suggested for each title or series:

Middle School (MS) = grades 6–8 (ages 11–13)

Junior High School (JH) = grades 7–9 (ages 12–15)

High School (HS) = grades 9–12 (ages 14–18)

Grade levels are meant only as a general guide. The assignation of grade levels is based on reviews, catalog and book jacket copy, and the author's judgment. Thus, the levels are subjective, and users should not feel restricted by them.

Each annotated title ends with keywords that indicate significant themes in the book. Award-winning titles are denoted with an award symbol, with reference to the awards appearing at the end of the annotation. Stories that are sexually explicit are indicated by [Sexual Content]. Sexually explicit materials are indicated for informational purposes only; this guide is not intended as a censorship tool but instead seeks to describe features that readers may seek out or wish to avoid. Many teen readers enjoy reading books with sexual content, while others may feel uncomfortable with this type of material. It is the readers' advisor's role to determine what readers desire and to find titles that match those desires.

Books that are easy-to-read and are appropriate for reluctant readers are indicated by [Reluctant Readers]. Easy-to-read romances are short books with short sentences and simple vocabulary, while romances selected for reluctant readers provide exciting, fast-paced stories that will hold the readers' attention. Easy-to-read romances have short sentences and a simple vocabulary, and many of the romance series books included in the bibliography are appropriate for younger readers and reluctant readers.

Books written for adults, but enjoyed by teens, are indicated with [Adult]. These books often appeal to more mature teen readers. Books featuring male protagonists that may be appealing to boys as well as girls are indicated with [Male].

In addition, profiles of young adult romance authors are located in the bibliographic chapters to give users an idea of the type of person who writes within the subgenre. Readers can also get to know some of the authors by reading these profiles.

Chapter 10 provides an annotated list of research materials and information about young adult romance library research collections. Appendix A outlines a core collection, and Appendix B lists readers' advisor resources.

Awards

Young adult literature has gained some validation in recent years. Several awards for young adult fiction are now granted by the Young Adult Library Services Association (YALSA) of the American Library Association (ALA). These awards include the Michael L. Printz Award, which honors books chosen for excellence in young adult literature; the Margaret A. Edwards Award, which honors an author's lifetime achievement for writing books that have remained popular over time; and the Alex Awards, which are granted to adult books that will be enjoyed by young adults ages twelve through eighteen. Sometimes books written for young adults will be awarded the Newbery Medal or named a Newbery honor book, honors bestowed by the Association for Library Service to Children (ALSC) of the ALA for distinguished American children's books published the previous year.

Other awards for young adult fiction include Britain's Carnegie Medal granted by the Library Association, the Young Adult Canadian Book Award issued by the Canadian Library Association, and the National Book Foundation Award for Young People's Literature. The national award for the romance genre is the Romance Writers of America Rita Award. National and international awards for the fantasy genre include the Mythopoeic Award, the World Fantasy Award, the Locus Poll Award, and the William L. Crawford Memorial Award.

Award-winning titles are noted as such in this guide. In addition, titles selected by ALA and YALSA as Best Books for Young Adults, Popular Paperbacks, and selections of the Romance Genre List are designated as award winners.

Now, let's take a look at how young adult romance fiction has evolved.

History of Young Adult Romance Fiction

The Early Twentieth Century: A Touch of Romance

Although a special category of literature was not created for teen readers until the late 1960s, it has been suggested that books written in the early twentieth century, such as Lucy Maud Montgomery's Anne of Green Gables books, are early examples of coming-of-age stories that particularly appeal to teen readers. Although these books were originally intended for adult audiences, they are now considered classic stories for young adults. The Anne of Green Gables books are appealing to readers in part because they include love stories.

During the 1930s there was a shift in fiction publishing aimed at girls and young women. The Great Depression brought teen readers the Nancy Drew Mystery Series, created by Edward Stratemeyer, written by ghost writers, and published by the Stratemeyer Syndicate. The Nancy Drew of the 1930s was much too busy solving mysteries to be concerned with romance. Many imitators of the Nancy Drew Mystery Series followed, and the focus was on mystery rather than romance. Career stories were also popular with girls in the early and mid-twentieth century. Girls read about young career women who worked as nurses, such as *Sue Barton*, *Cherry Ames*, and *Penny Marsh*, or flight stewardesses, like *Vicki Barr* and *Dorothy Dixon.* Some girls' series books even focused on combining career, marriage, and mystery, such as the Ruth Fielding series. However, romance, love, and marriage were rarely a part of the mystery and career stories of the early and mid-twentieth century.

The 1940s: Young Adult Romance Blossoms

Although originally marketed as an adult title when it was published in 1942, it has been suggested that Maureen Daly's *Seventeenth Summer* was the first novel written for teen readers.[8] The love story of Angie Morrow and Jack Duluth is still in print and popular with young adult readers, despite the fact that elements of the story date the book in the 1940s. Daly was a teenager when she began writing the story, and she wrote from her own real-life experience. Young adult literature historian Michael Cart suggests the book is still popular with young adults because the theme of "first love offer[s] a timelessly appealing investigation of a universal rite of passage experience."[9]

From the 1940s through the 1960s, many authors copied the plot of *Seventeenth Summer* in a variety of light romance stories. Authors such as Rosamund du Jardin, Betty Cavanna, Anne Emery, Mary Stolz, Sally Bensen, and Beverly Cleary became very popular with teenage girls. Their innocent romance stories reflected the times, and the stories focused on middle-class girls who worried about getting dates for the prom, being accepted by the popular crowd, and being noticed by the most handsome boy in school. Several of these light romance stories are still in publication, including Maureen Daly's *Seventeenth Summer* and Beverly Cleary's *Fifteen, Jean and Johnny, The Luckiest Girl,* and *Sister of the Bride.*

The 1970s: Realistic Romance

In the late 1960s, with the debut of the teen "problem novel" (e.g., *The Outsiders* by S. E. Hinton and Paul Zindel's *The Pigman*), publishing for young adults turned away from pure and innocent romance. Stories focusing on real-life problems of ordinary teens dominated publishing and reading tastes in the 1970s. Such issues as abuse, sex, pregnancy, death, drugs, poverty, divorce, and prejudice became common themes in the newly created genre of young adult literature.

Some of these popular "problem novels" also included stories of love and romance, such as *Mr. and Mrs. Bo Jo Jones* by Ann Head, *My Darling, My Hamburger* by Paul Zindel, *Forever* by Judy Blume, and *Up in Seth's Room* by Norma Fox Mazer, but the focus of these stories was the mechanics of sexual intercourse, safe sex, and the emotional and physical consequences of sex. What made these novels remain popular with young adult readers for decades was the honest portrayal of the reality of love, romance, and sex in them.

The 1980s: The Contemporary Romance Boom

In 1979, the editors and publishers of Scholastic's Teenage Book Club (TAB), which was marketed in schools and libraries, realized that several light paperback romance titles were especially popular. A new marketing strategy was conceived to sell the romance books directly to teen readers in bookstores, and in January 1980, Scholastic introduced the Wildfire romance series. The series sold a whopping 1.8 million books in the first year, so Scholastic introduced the more serious Wishing Star romance series and a romantic suspense series called Windswept in 1981. Scholastic continued to expand their romance line through the mid-1980s, offering the critically acclaimed Sunfire historical series in 1984.

Other publishing houses saw an opportunity to take advantage of teens' interest in romance stories during the early 1980s, and they soon followed with more category romance series modeled on the romance series for adults, including Bantam's Sweet Dreams, Harlequin/Silhouette's First Love, Dell's Young Love, Tempo's Caprice, Dell Laurel Leaf's Heartlines, and Ballantine's Heart to Heart. Several series were introduced that allowed the reader to participate in the story by choosing the path of the heroine in Pocket's Follow Your Heart, Wanderer's Dream Your Own Romance, and Warner's Two by Two Romance. A significant feature of these early romance series for teens was the emphasis on the innocence of first love. Hand-holding and first kisses were as far as affections were allowed to go.

The romance series remained popular throughout the decade, and in 1983, Bantam introduced the first soap opera romance series, Sweet Valley High, with continuing characters, story lines, and cliff-hanger endings. Created by Francine Pascal, Sweet Valley High was originally conceived as a television soap opera for teens focusing on the lives and loves of identical twins Jessica and Elizabeth Wakefield. The series was written by various authors, including women's fiction author Eileen Goudge, under the pseudonym Kate William. The Sweet Valley High series became so popular that in 1985 *Perfect Summer*, a Super Edition book from the Sweet Valley High series, became the first young adult novel ever named to the *New York Times* paperback bestseller list.[10] Other Sweet Valley series followed, including Sweet Valley Kids, Sweet Valley Twins, and Sweet Valley University. The success of the series also spawned many imitators of the soap opera formula. In fact, ever since the 1980s, the soap opera format has been used in the publishing of genre fiction for children and young adults.

Throughout most of the 1980s, various romance series dominated the young adult publishing market. Several popular authors began their careers writing young adult romance series fiction during this time, including romance author Julie Garwood, young adult author Caroline B. Cooney, and mystery author Rhys Bowen, who wrote young adult romance under her real name, Janet Quin-Harkin.

The 1990s: The Return of Realistic Romance

The 1990s brought an end to the reign of the romance series. During the 1990s, horror series fiction, written by authors such as Christopher Pike and R. L. Stine, dominated the children's and young adult book markets. Bantam's Sweet Dreams romance series gave way to the similar Love Stories series in 1995, while the various Sweet Valley series for children and young adults, including the new Sweet Valley Junior High and SVH Senior Year, remained steady sellers with readers during the 1990s. A television show, *Francine Pascal's Sweet Valley High*, aired for four seasons in the mid-1990s and helped ensure the success of the series during the 1990s. Lurlene McDaniel's inspirational novels about teens facing life-threatening illnesses, which usually include romantic relationships, were also very popular. Several Christian teen romance series, like Robin Jones Gunn's Christy Miller series and Judy Baer's Cedar River Daydreams, joined the young adult romance boom late in the 1980s, and these series were in high demand throughout the 1990s. An article in *Publishers Weekly* in 1997 reported that "publishers are upbeat about the prospects for romance," especially since the popularity of horror series fiction was waning.[11]

Had romance disappeared? A careful examination of original titles and paperback series books published for young adult readers in the 1990s reveals that romance did not entirely disappear from young adult fiction. In fact, romance had always been a component of fiction written for young adults, and it remained an integral part of the contemporary literature. But in the 1990s, genre fiction began to cross boundaries, mixing elements and features of various genres together. Author Michael Cart suggested:

> Romance . . . seems to lend itself to bending and blending. Just consider some of the mix-and-match varieties: there are contemporary romances, multicultural or ethnic romances, humorous romances, gay and lesbian romances, suspense romances, western romances, Christian romances, science fiction/fantasy romances, gothic romances, period romances, bodice-ripping romances, soap-opera romances, weepies, [and] historical romances.[12]

Because of the phenomenon of bending and blending genres, fewer books written for teens are labeled "romance," but romance can be found in most literature written for young adults today. For instance, Francesca Lia Block's Weetzie Bat books mix fantasy with romance, while Caroline B. Cooney's Time Quartet blends romance, fantasy, and historical fiction. Lurlene McDaniel's inspirational novels, like *Don't Die My Love* and *Now I Lay Me Down to Sleep*, include romantic stories. In the 1990s, McDaniel's work became known among readers and librarians alike as romance fiction for the middle school and junior high set, and her books remain popular today.

Contemporary problem novels—or as they have been dubbed by the media, the "bleak books"—continued to dominate young adult fiction throughout the 1990s. While librarians know that the problem novel is not a new commodity in young adult publishing, Michael Cart reports that the "bleak books" are addressing important issues in the lives of youth directly by "acknowledging that bleakness is no stranger to many teenage lives today, and for sharing the sad news that not all endings are happy ones."[13]

As always, the contemporary problem novel includes themes of love, romance, sexuality, and all of the accompanying issues: crushes, first kisses, sex, homosexuality, bisexuality, lesbianism, pregnancy, abortion, incest, and rape, to name a few. But the problem novel of the 1990s is edgier than the problem novel of the 1970s, with or without love and romance, and Cart suggests that the cutting edge is sharper because today's teens are more sophisticated than teenagers of earlier generations.[14]

Not only are today's teens more sophisticated, there are more teenagers today than there were in previous generations, and the large numbers of teens are influencing the publishing industry. By 2000, there were more than 40 million young people between the ages of ten and nineteen in the United States.[15] Projections indicate that the teen population will continue to grow to 47 million by 2010, and by 2050 there will be 57.5 million teens in America.[16] In fact, the millennial generation, made up of people born between 1982 and 1998, "are well on their way to becoming America's first 100-million-person generation."[17]

With such a growth in the teen population, publishers are trying to find new and creative ways to reach more teenagers. Several of the major publishers of young adult fiction have recently reorganized, phasing out old imprints aimed at teen readers and introducing new imprints with more sophisticated cover art. For instance, HarperCollins introduced a line of trade paperbacks for teens called HarperTempest in 1999. Scholastic recently introduced a new teen imprint called Push. In 2001, Simon & Schuster replaced the old Archway, Pocket, and Minstrel imprints with Pulse, which publishes teen titles previously published under the old imprints and new original paperback fiction for teens.

Because book publishers are competing against various forms of entertainment media available to today's teens for their time and their money, many have started teaming up with other companies that produce entertainment media for teens. For instance, Simon & Schuster's Pocket Books began collaborating on books, like Stephen Chbosky's *Perks of Being a Wallflower,* with MTV in 1995. Penguin Putnam joined forces with Alloy Online, which bought the teen series book packager 17th Street Productions in 2000, to produce a new teen imprint called AlloyBooks. In 2000, AOL Time Warner created the Teen People Book Club, a partnership between *Teen People* magazine and Book-of-the-Month Club. In 2003, HarperCollins joined forces with Quicksilver's Roxy, a young women's action sports clothing brand, to produce a romance book series called Luna Bay: A Roxy Girl Series featuring teen surfers. And the HarperCollins Entertainment division continues its partnership with teen entertainment tycoons Mary-Kate and Ashley Olsen, publishing various paperback series such as The New Adventures of Mary-Kate & Ashley, So Little Time, Two of a Kind, and Mary-Kate and Ashley Sweet 16 in conjunction with the teens' production company, Dualstar Entertainment Group.

The Early Twenty-First Century: A Romance Revival

In the early twenty-first century, changes are taking place in the publishing of romance genre fiction for young adults. Random House recently ceased publication of all its romance series, including Love Stories, Clearwater Crossing, and SVH Senior Year. In a letter to readers of the final SVH Senior Year book, *Sweet 18*, Francine Pascal says, "I've decided to end the series now while it's still on top. Perhaps in a few years, I'll start again with a Sweet Valley for the twenty-first century."[18] In the meantime, Random House has no plans to publish new romance series for teen readers, although it continues to publish new titles by popular authors, like Lurlene McDaniel, who include love stories in their young adult novels.

Somewhat surprisingly, one publisher, HarperCollins/Avon, has shown an interest in reviving the popular formulaic paperback romance series for young adults. In May 2002, the company introduced a new line of historical romances for teen readers called Avon True Romance. This series offers readers "a 'sweet' introduction to romance novels" where "the characters don't go any further than kisses."[19] The publisher is relying on established authors of adult romance novels, such as Lorraine Heath, Kathryn Smith, Beverly Jenkins, and Elaine Barbieri, to help them get the series started. Meg Cabot, author of the popular young adult romantic comedy series The Princess Diaries, has also contributed two books to the series.

Unlike the romance series of the 1980s, the Avon True Romance titles use the adult historical angle for marketing. The cover art makes the series look like traditional adult historical romances, with covers featuring realistic drawings of couples staring into each other's eyes. Shiny embossed lettering is used for the authors' names and the titles of the books. The only indication that the series is meant for young adults is the words "For Teens" below the series name and the label "Teen Fiction" on the spine. While they are easy to read, the stories are lengthy and packed with accurate historical information, indicating the authors and publisher want to give young readers authentic stories of substance.

Will they catch on with teen readers? That remains to be seen, but other publishers are already following HarperCollins/Avon's lead. Dorchester Publishing launched a contemporary and paranormal romance series for teen readers called Smooch in 2003. Although it is too early to tell if romance series will go boom or bust in the early twenty-first century, if they do catch on, other light series romances will likely follow suit.

In the early twenty-first century, the teen book market continues to be dominated by the "bleak books" and paperback series fiction. In 2000, sales of hardcover and paperback juvenile books, which include young adult fiction, rose substantially compared to the previous year.[20] Stories of love and romance continue to be found mixed in with the various genres, including the "bleak books." The contemporary problem novel often includes stories of first love, romance, sex, and sexuality.

However, some new trends within this subgenre are noteworthy. For example, young adult authors are writing novels in verse, such as *Jinx* by Margaret Wild, *What My Mother Doesn't Know* by Sonya Sones, and *True Believer* by Virginia Euwer Wolff. Epistolary works using letters, e-mails, and diaries are also popular with teens. Cecily von Ziegesar's Gossip Girl uses e-mails to communicate with readers throughout the books in the series, while Sharon Draper's *Romiette and Julio* features the couple communicating via e-mail. Meg Cabot's The Princess Diaries books, Louise Rennison's Confessions of Georgia Nicolson series, and Catherine Clark's The Diaries of Courtney Von Dragen Smith use the diary format. The diary format allows these authors to use humor to lighten the awkward and embarrassing experiences of the teen years and provide an antidote to the heavy reality of the "bleak books."

Whether they are using humor or bleak reality, young adult authors of the early twenty-first century seem to have kept the focus on honest portrayals of the real emotions and experiences of first love. Meg Cabot offers readers accurate kissing instructions in *Princess in Love*, Alex Sanchez provides readers with a tale of young gay love in *Rainbow Boys*, and Michael Cart has edited a book of short stories covering the issues of abstinence, first sexual encounters, pregnancy, abortion, and obsessive teenage love in *Love and Sex: Ten Stories of Truth*.

Another trend to watch is that concerning teens and adult romance. Teens often read romance fiction written for adult audiences; 1 percent of romance readers are under the age of fourteen, while 7 percent are between the ages of fourteen and nineteen.[21] Romance fiction is a booming business in the early twenty-first century, with sales of $1.52 billion and 51.1 million romance readers in 2001.[22] These numbers will continue to grow, as teens from the millennial generation move from young adult romance fiction to adult romance fiction.

Recent trends in adult romance publishing, including the introduction of multicultural and alternative reality subgenres, are mirrored in young adult romance fiction publishing, although the young adult multicultural romance subgenre still has a lot of room for growth. It is likely teens who enjoy this subgenre are reading adult multicultural romances. In the meantime, the contemporary romance subgenre continues to dominate the adult and young adult romance publishing markets.

A way of looking at current young adult romance is to consider two distinct strands: a reality-based fiction featuring coming-of-age stories, including love, sex, romance, and related problems, like books in the "Issues Romance" chapter (Chapter 5); and a light, escapist romance fiction that purposely goes beyond the boundaries of reality, like books in the "Contemporary Romance" and "Contemporary Romance Series" and "Alternative Reality Romance" chapters (Chapters 3, 4, and 6, respectively). Young adult readers need access to both kinds of romance fiction. Young readers enjoy the lighter fare for times they want relief from the stress of their everyday lives; but they also like reading about the reality of teens' lives to learn how to survive the trials and tribulations of growing up. Today's young adult romance fiction offers readers harsh reality and, when they need it, an escape from this reality.

Notes

1. Kristin Ramsdell, *Romance Fiction: A Guide to the Genre* (Englewood, CO: Libraries Unlimited, 1999), xi.
2. John Charles, "Romance Fiction," *Voice of Youth Advocates* 22 (1999): 290–291.
3. Kristin Ramsdell, *Happily Ever After: A Guide to Reading Interests in Romance Fiction* (Englewood, CO: Libraries Unlimited, 1987), 208.
4. Ibid., 209.
5. Marc Aronson, *Exploding the Myths: The Truth about Teenagers and Reading* (Lanham, MD: Scarecrow Press, 2001), 20.
6. Romance Writers of America, *Romance Novels: What Are They?* 2002. Available: http://www.rwanational.org/romance.stm (accessed May 5, 2002).
7. Romance Writers of America, *Romance Writers of America Presents a Brief Guide to the Romance Genre.* 2002. Available: http://www.robynamos.com/Presskit/genre.htm (accessed May 5, 2002).
8. Michael Cart, *From Romance to Realism: Fifty Years of Growth and Change in Young Adult Literature* (New York: HarperCollins, 1996), 16.
9. Ibid., 18.
10. Mary M. Huntwork, "Why Girls Flock to Sweet Valley High," *School Library Journal* 36 (1990): 137–138.
11. Heather Vogel Frederick, "The Future Looks Bright for Teen Romance," *Publishers Weekly* 244 (November 10, 1997): 47.
12. Michael Cart, "After Many a Summer," *The Booklist* 99 (September 15, 2002): 223.
13. Michael Cart, "The Bleak Goes On," *The Booklist* 96 (September 15, 1999): 248.
14. Ibid., 248.

15. United States Census Bureau, *U. S. Summary: Census 2000 Profile.* n.d. Available: http://www.census.gov (accessed November 13, 2002).
16. Marc Aronson, "Coming of Age: One Editor's View of How Young Adult Publishing Developed in America," *Publisher's Weekly* 249 (February 11, 2002): 82.
17. Neil Howe and William Strauss, *Millennials Rising: The Next Great Generation* (New York: Vintage Books, 2000), 15.
18. Francine Pascal, "Dear Sweet Valley Reader," in *SVH Senior Year #48: Sweet 18* (New York: Bantam Books), 183–184.
19. Kathryn Smith, *Avon True Romance.* 2002. Available: http://www.kathryn-smith.com/YoungAdult/index.html (accessed May 4, 2002).
20. Association of American Publishers, *Juvenile Paperbound Sales Looking Up.* 2001. Available: http://www.publishers.org/press/releases.cfm?PressReleaseArticleID=72 (accessed November 13, 2002).
21. Romance Writers of America, *Romance Novels: Industry Statistics.* 2002. Available: http://www.rwanational.org/statistics.stm (accessed November 13, 2002).
22. Ibid.

Chapter 1

Serving the Teen Romance Reader

Serving young adult romance readers may seem a daunting task, but a few basic principles and guidelines can greatly aid you in this endeavor. In short, you need to know these readers and understand their reading preferences, understand the appeal of the genre, and have some familiarity with the titles.

Who Is the Young Adult Romance Reader?

Since I began this project, people have repeatedly asked me, "Do only girls read young adult romance novels?" When referring to pure romance fiction, the answer to this question is basically yes, because much of young adult romance fiction, especially the paperback romance series, is written for and marketed toward an audience of young teenage girls with money to spend on entertainment. Research suggests that girls read more than boys. The 2001 Teen Reading Survey, sponsored by the American Library Association (ALA) and Smartgirl, indicates that 35 percent of girls read for pleasure, while only 17 percent of boys read for fun.[1] In a study of teen reading habits spanning fifteen years, Lisa A. Hale and Chris Crowe found that romances and love stories continue to be girls' favorite genre for recreational reading, while boys prefer science fiction, fantasy, and sports stories.[2]

On the other hand, it is important for readers' advisors never to make assumptions about reader likes and dislikes. Because this guide defines the romance genre very broadly, it encompasses many titles that appeal to both sexes. For example, many of the titles in the "Issues Romance" chapter (Chapter 5) will appeal to male readers. However, male teens (as well as many female teens) will almost never identify themselves as "romance readers" or name "romance" as a genre they enjoy, so it is important to listen for other clues in the readers' advisory interview that might indicate interest. For example, if the reader mentions something about the boyfriend or girlfriend of the protagonist or comments on a relationship when describing a favorite book, this may suggest an interest in romance. Also, keep in mind that boys are more inclined to read and enjoy books with male protagonists. Look for [Male], indicating titles with male protagonists.

While recognizing that most readers of young adult romance fiction are preteen and teenage girls, this guide attempts to define the genre of young adult romance fiction in the early twenty-first century rather than define the reader of this fiction.

In a recent poll conducted by the National Education Association, teens said they "consider reading to be the most important skill a young person needs to be successful in life."[3] This guide uses a broad definition of young adult romance fiction, which includes award-winning titles from the fantasy, contemporary, historical, and Christian young adult fiction genres, and therefore, the guide provides reading material suitable for boys and girls who want to read for pleasure, for escape, or to learn about love, romance, sex, and sexuality. Teens can learn about kissing in Meg Cabot's *Princess in Love*, heterosexual sex in Judy Blume's *Forever*, or how to come to terms with being a young gay male in Alex Sanchez's *Rainbow Boys*.

By reading fiction, young adults learn about crushes, romance, first love, true love, heartbreak, unrequited love, sex, and sexuality. Young adults also read romance fiction for recreation.

Know Reader Preferences

When working with teen readers, you should be aware of which books they are reading and what they enjoy in a book. In the area of romance, you might want to find out if they like the new Avon True Romance series. Are particular titles popular with teens? Do they like adult romances? Talk to your regular customers about what they like to read. Also, if you catalog your romances, you will find it easier to answer these questions, as you will be able to tell how often certain titles circulate. Don't forget to check the return bins and the trucks of books waiting to be shelved, since the most popular titles usually circulate frequently. If you don't work at the circulation desk, talk to your circulation desk staff to find out what is popular.

Show your teen patrons that you respect them as people. Teens are put off by adults who clearly show their disrespect for or patronize them. You will lose your teen customers if you don't treat them with respect. Express deference for their reading choices, whether they want to read romances, horror fiction, or picture books. Show an appreciation of the romance genre, too, even if you are not a romance fan. Teens are not usually aware that romance fiction is generally regarded as trashy and unworthy of our recreational reading time. You might accidentally teach your patrons to be embarrassed about reading romance if you don't show romance the same respect you show other fiction genres.

The Appeal of the Young Adult Romance Genre

Why do young adults like to read romance fiction? Teens read romance fiction for several reasons. Joyce G. Saricks suggests that "romance appeals . . . to our emotions."[4] Teens want to know what it feels like to experience love and romance, and they may want confirmation of their own feelings. Teens often talk to each other about dating, kissing, and sex, but while they can learn a great deal from each other about these issues, they can also learn about love and romance by reading romance fiction.

In her study of young adult romance fiction reading, Linda Christian Smith found that teenage girls read romance fiction to learn how they should behave in relationships with boys.[5] Romance readers expect to be able to experience a first date, a first kiss, or a first sexual encounter vicariously through the experiences of the heroine. Teens want to learn how these experiences will feel physically, how these experiences will make them feel emotionally, and how to relate to their love interests in social situations. The age of the protagonist is also important to the appeal factor of young adult romances. Most teens want to read about their peers or teenagers who are a little older than they are, because they want to read about teens who have had experiences similar to their own, or they want to learn from the experiences of older teens.

1

Romantic feelings and love relationships are a part of growing up, and "emotions related to romantic relationships constitute a substantial part of adolescents' day-to-day emotional lives."[6] Psychologists have found that "[i]n addition to the emotion of love, the romantic emotions of American adolescents include anxiety, anger, jealousy, and despair."[7] Nevertheless, psychologists believe that the emotional growth that takes place when teenagers experience romantic emotions allows them to establish their identities as individuals and social beings, and as teens get older, they are better able to manage their romantic emotions. While teens often experience crushes during early adolescence, dating relationships are common as teens get older, and older teens are often involved in steady dating relationships. Because romantic relationships are an important part of teens' lives, teens want to learn more about love and romance, and they rely on their friends and the media to inform them about what it means to be involved in romantic relationships. Young adult romance literature is one medium through which teens can learn about love and romance.

Romance fiction also gives readers a brief break from their busy lives. Young adults, who are usually under a great deal of stress, may read romance fiction to escape from the reality of their everyday lives. Light romances and romance series fiction are particularly good at providing readers with entertaining diversions by using familiar—even formulaic—plots and a continuing cast of characters, settings, and stories. Light romances and romance series usually provide readers with a happily-ever-after ending.

As noted previously, not all young adult romance fiction novels provide happy endings. After all, can we really expect that teenage characters that always live happily ever after will be believable to today's sophisticated teens? Teens crave the truth and intensely dislike dishonesty. Teens want to know about real teen love relationships, and of course, many teen love relationships do not last. Furthermore, romantic relationships involving teens are often filled with conflict as teens learn how to relate to each other. So in order to be realistic, young adult romance fiction does not always provide happy endings. Single-title romance novels often give readers a more realistic look at teen romance than do series romances, and this is part of their appeal. But even without a happily-ever-after ending, authors usually find a way to let readers know that life goes on. For instance, in Judy Blume's *Forever*, after Katherine's relationship with Michael ends, Katherine is reminded that there are other young men out there waiting for her.

The characters of romance stories are also important to teen readers. Teens seek out characters with whom they can identify, and they generally look for protagonists who are the same age or slightly older than they are. Reading about characters of the same sex is more important to males than it is to females. Sexual orientation, ethnicity, and cultural background can also be factors. Sometimes teens look for role models, characters with attributes they admire (e.g., a witty way of expressing themselves, or moral strength). Teens also look for characters who get to experience important life events, experiences they wish to have, like a first date, a first kiss, or a long-term romantic relationship. And of course, the dynamics between characters and the love relationship, as expressed through dialogue and action, are very important to romance readers of all ages.

Pacing of romance stories can be an important factor for readers. The pacing of light young adult romance stories and romance series fiction is traditionally fast, which makes for a quick read. Many of the lighter paperback romances and romance series are intentionally shorter and easier to read than the young adult fiction published in hardcover. These titles are generally aimed at readers in middle and junior high school. Many teen readers are looking for a quick read because they are busy with school, homework, extracurricular activities, friends, and forms of entertainment media outside reading, such as television or the Internet. Series romances, particularly the soap opera variety, are easy to read because they usually contain short chapters, easy vocabulary, and a fast pacing that is driven by the story lines. After the first book in many soap opera romance series, little time is spent on characterization.

The pacing of some of the young adult romance novels can be slower than the lighter romances or series romances and may require a higher reading level. The slower pacing might be the result of a more complicated story line with several subplots, more characters, and more time spent on characterization. Since depicting the growth of the characters is often the motivation of young adult fiction, it is necessary for authors to spend time introducing the characters, showing how the characters deal with life's challenges, and informing readers how coping with challenges has helped the characters grow up.

Pacing of single-title young adult romance fiction also depends on the story line, however, because if the plot provides enough action and suspense to enthrall readers, readers will keep reading, no matter how long the book. For instance, readers just have to know the resolution to the romances in *Rainbow Boys* by Alex Sanchez, *Sloppy Firsts* and its sequel *Second Helpings* by Megan McCafferty, or Kate Cann's Love Trilogy, and so they just keep on reading. Reading a good story that is fast paced can help improve the reading abilities of teens.

Cover art is extremely important to the appeal of young adult romance novels. If teens think cover art is unappealing, they will not even pick up a book. Two different kinds of covers are trendy right now. One is bold, bright, and colorful. For instance, The Princess Diaries books feature a sparkly tiara on a hot pink, turquoise, bright red, or deep purple background. Garrett Freyman-Weyr's *My Heartbeat* features Keith Haring's signature stick people in bright red and green. Bright covers with comic-style drawings are also popular. Another kind of cover is dark and mysterious. For example, the cover of *Blood and Chocolate* by Annette Curtis Klause shows a young woman against a dark backdrop of trees, water, and fire. The cover of Francesca Lia Block's *Dangerous Angels: The Weetzie Bat Books* features a woman with wild blond hair and wings standing in front of dark green foliage, while the covers of Amelia Atwater-Rhodes's vampire stories, like *Demon in My View* and

Shattered Mirror, show dark images of young men with other objects such as trees, a rose, and broken glass, superimposed over the images of the boys. Whether they are bold and bright or dark and mysterious, both kinds of covers are meant to capture the attention of readers. Young adult romance cover art usually shows realistic drawings of contemporary teens or photographs of teen models. Unless the story is historical, whether they are drawings or models, teens on book covers must be dressed in current styles.

Sometimes images of people are not included as part of the cover art. Instead, objects relevant to the story are featured on young adult book covers, like the sparkly tiara on the covers of The Princess Diaries books and an upside-down baby chick on the cover of Wendelin Van Draanen's *Flipped.*

Another recent trend includes showing photographs of parts of young people's bodies, such as eyes, faces, legs, or torsos. Such art graces the covers of Kate Cann's Love Trilogy, Cecily von Ziegesar's Gossip Girls series, *Bringing Up the Bones* by Lara M. Zeises, and Tanuja Desai Hidier's *Born Confused.* This kind of art allows readers to visualize the characters as real people but also allows readers to imagine what the characters might look like—teens might even be able to visualize themselves as the characters.

The format is also an important factor in the appeal of young adult romance fiction. Young adult romance series are published in paperback format, with the series logo and book numbers prominently displayed on the books. Romance series are particularly appealing to teen readers because they are reasonably short in length. In contrast, single-title novels are often longer than series romance books, and they are usually published first in hardcover and then released later in paperback. Some single titles are only published in trade paper or paperback formats.

Setting and story elements can also be part of a romance novel's appeal. Since these elements are exclusive to specific subgenres, they are treated in some of the following chapters.

Although young adult romance fiction appeals to teens for many different reasons, the biggest appeal factor is emotional engagement. Romance readers experience emotions along with the characters in the stories. Other issues, such as age of the protagonist, pacing of the stories, cover art, and format, are also important factors that influence the appeal of young adult romance novels and series.

It seems clear that as long as there are teenagers, there will be a need for books about love and romance, but these books will only be read if authors and publishers can create stories that appeal to readers.

Tips for Advising the Young Adult Romance Reader

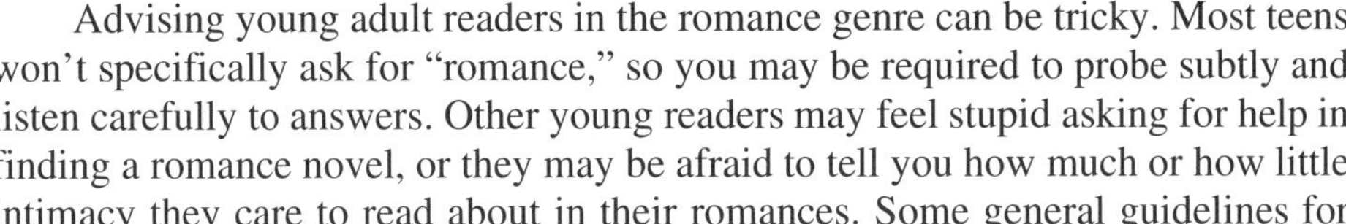

Advising young adult readers in the romance genre can be tricky. Most teens won't specifically ask for "romance," so you may be required to probe subtly and listen carefully to answers. Other young readers may feel stupid asking for help in finding a romance novel, or they may be afraid to tell you how much or how little intimacy they care to read about in their romances. Some general guidelines for working with teen readers can be found in Angelina Benedetti's "Leading the

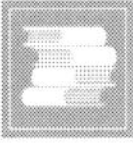

Horse to Water: Keeping Young People Reading in the Information Age," in *The Readers' Advisor's Companion,* edited by Kenneth D. Shearer and Robert Burgin (Libraries Unlimited, 2001). See Appendix B for a list of additional resources you can use to help identify romances to recommend to your patrons. Following are a few general tips for advising the young adult romance reader:

- Begin with a question your patron can easily answer, for example, ask, "What is the last great book you read?" or "Tell me about the last story you read that you enjoyed." Follow up with questions such as, "Why did you like that book?" or "What did you enjoy about that book?"
- Keep your questions as open-ended as possible to avoid yes or no answers. If the reader seems confused or reluctant to reply, ask whether he or she has read anything recently that he or she hated, or you might offer a few names of popular authors and titles and check the reader's response to these.
- If your patron has indicated an interest in themes of love or sex but hasn't named specific titles or authors, probe for further information. Find out which romance subgenres will be most appealing to a patron.
- Determine the age of your teenage patron. Angelina Benedetti suggests asking teen patrons their grade, as "asking their age might set up defenses you do not want to encounter."[8] The grade will give you a rough idea of your patron's age. Or ask which school the teen attends. Keep in mind that young readers like to read about characters who are their own age or a little older. Refer to the annotations and grade-level codes to help you identify which books will be appropriate for a particular reader.
- Find out if your patron wants to read for recreation or for a school assignment. If the book is needed for a book report, you might want to suggest a title from the "Classic Romance" chapter (Chapter 2), or a single title rather than a series book. Ask what the assignment is, and try to tie your suggestions into the curriculum area. For example, if the book is needed for a history assignment, check Chapter 7, "Historical Romance."
- Suggest romances published for adult audiences. If your patron has read all the young adult romances in your library, or is ready to move on to adult fiction, suggest some adult romances in a favorite romance subgenre. If your patron does not want to read stories containing sex, suggest books in the Inspirational or Regency subgenres. Refer to guides such as *Romance Fiction: A Guide to the Genre* by Kristin Ramsdell (Libraries Unlimited, 1999) and *Genreflecting: A Guide to Reading Interests in Genre Fiction*, 5th edition, by Diana Tixier Herald (Libraries Unlimited, 2000) to help you become familiar with the adult romance genre.
- Be honest with teens. If they ask you if you have read a particular book, answer truthfully. Teens will know if you are not being honest with them, and they won't seek your help again if you don't tell the truth. If you are asked about a book you have read, tell your patron what you thought about the book.
- Respect the reading choices of teens. Teens find it difficult enough to ask for help, and if they think you will laugh at or look down on them because they want to read about love, romance, and sex, they won't ask for your help. Reassure teens it is okay to read romances and series books, and that you are happy to help them find these books—word will spread that you are both receptive to working with teens and romance-friendly. If your patrons want to read series romances, show them where they

can find series in your library. Use the opportunity to suggest single romance titles that are similar to the series.

- Whenever you have the opportunity, promote young adult romances. (This may mean you don't call the books "romances," but be clear about the contents.) Include young adult romances in your booktalks and displays. Create young adult romance genre lists. Suggest a romance to the teen book club at your library. Invite young adult romance authors to speak at your library. Organize reviews of young adult romances in a binder and keep them at the reference desk for your patrons to read. Your customers will appreciate the fact that you know what teens (especially girls) like to read, and it will help build your reputation as a teen-romance-friendly librarian.

Selected Issues

Sex

In young adult romance fiction, sex is sometimes portrayed in explicit terms. Some teens may want to read about sex; others may not. Bouricius (2000) and Saricks (2001) acknowledge how difficult it can be to find out how much sex patrons expect in their romances.[9] Both authors suggest using terms such as "sweet," "gentle," or "innocent" to describe books that don't contain sex and using "spicy," "steamy," or "racy" to describe romance novels containing sex. Using these terms may not work with teen readers, especially younger teens, because they may not understand what you mean. And these terms are not as easily applied to young adult romances, because some sex may be found in all of the young adult romance subgenres, with the exception of some Christian young adult romance.

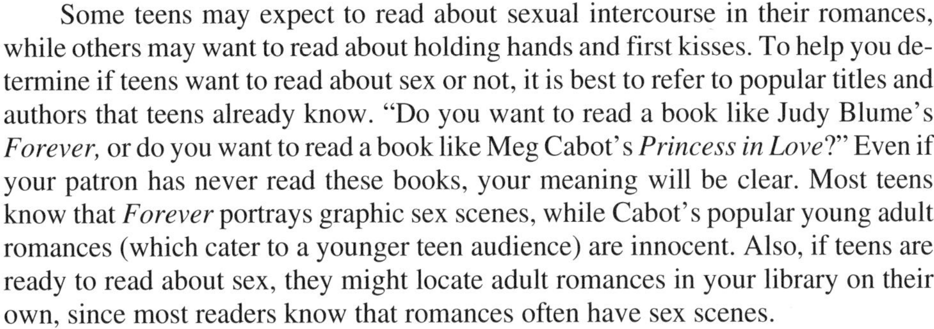

Some teens may expect to read about sexual intercourse in their romances, while others may want to read about holding hands and first kisses. To help you determine if teens want to read about sex or not, it is best to refer to popular titles and authors that teens already know. "Do you want to read a book like Judy Blume's *Forever,* or do you want to read a book like Meg Cabot's *Princess in Love*?" Even if your patron has never read these books, your meaning will be clear. Most teens know that *Forever* portrays graphic sex scenes, while Cabot's popular young adult romances (which cater to a younger teen audience) are innocent. Also, if teens are ready to read about sex, they might locate adult romances in your library on their own, since most readers know that romances often have sex scenes.

In assisting young readers on this issue, refer to the symbols that appear with the annotations. Romances with some sexual content are labeled [Sexual Content], even if the scenes are not very graphic. The annotation will contain further clues as to the level of sexuality. Another way to find out about the sexual content in young adult romances is to read reviews of young adult fiction. Reviewers of young adult books usually indicate if sex occurs in the story.

When you are advising readers, however, don't decide for your patrons if they are ready to read about sex. Teens have a right to read the books they enjoy, even if their parents don't want them reading about certain topics. Teens will censor themselves if

they encounter something that makes them uneasy or that they don't understand, or they will ask someone they trust to explain. To illustrate this point, consider the story Judy Blume told when she accepted the Margaret A. Edwards Award for *Forever* in 1996. Blume received a letter from a mother whose daughter wanted to read her novel *Forever*, a book that contains some explicit sex scenes. The mother thought her daughter was too young to read about sex at age ten, but she finally decided to let her daughter read the book only if she agreed to talk to her about it afterward. After her daughter finished reading the book, "[t]he mother looked at her and said 'Do you have any questions?' 'Yes, Mom . . . What's fondue?'."[10]

Censorship

Young adult romance fiction addresses controversial issues such as sex, homosexuality, teenage pregnancy, and date rape. You may find that some parents do not want their children reading books about topics the parents deem inappropriate or controversial, and parents may challenge the books you recommend to your teen patrons. For information on coping with censorship in your library, see Joni Richards Bodart's book *Radical Reads: 101 YA Novels on the Edge*. Bodart includes an appendix about censorship, with recommendations for how to deal with censorship in your library. A list of resources of support for resisting censorship is included. You can also find strategies for coping with censorship on the ALA's Office for Intellectual Freedom Web page at http://www.ala.org/Content/NavigationMenu/Our_Association/Offices/Intellectual_Freedom3/Default622.htm.

You may also find yourself wanting to censor certain books while helping your teen patrons find romances to read. Resist this urge! When helping teen readers find romance novels, remember it is not your job to decide whether a teenager is ready to read a story with graphic sex scenes, such as Judy Blume's *Forever* or a steamy adult romance. A patron who is not ready to read about sex likely won't read very much of *Forever* before putting the book down. Teens know when they are ready to read books with heavier topics or books written for adult audiences. Let teens judge for themselves what they are ready to read.

Know the Literature

To successfully advise young adult romance readers, you must familiarize yourself with young adult fiction in general and romance fiction written for teens. Romance permeates much of young adult fiction, and some books written for teens contain more romance than do others. Read a few books listed under each subgenre in this book to get a feel for the different kinds of romances available to teens. If you can get your hands on them, read the more popular romances so you can understand for yourself the appeal of the books and their authors.

As you sample titles from this genre, be sure not to overlook young adult series fiction, particularly young adult romance series. You don't have to read many. Since series titles feature the same settings, characters, and continuing story lines, one or two books in a series will give you a general sense of what that series has to offer. And series books are usually quick, easy reads, so you won't have to spend a lot of time reading them.

If you are not already familiar with romance fiction written for adult audiences, you will also want to learn about the genre, as you may find it necessary to recommend adult romances to teen readers. If you have time, read *Romance Fiction: A Guide to the Genre* by

Kristin Ramsdell (Libraries Unlimited, 1999). Ramsdell provides a complete guide that will help you learn everything you need to know about romance fiction, including extensive bibliographies organized by subgenres. Three other resources that contain information on romance fiction are Joyce G. Saricks's *The Readers' Advisory Guide to Genre Fiction* (American Library Association, 2001), Diana Tixier Herald's *Genreflecting: A Guide to Reading Interests in Genre Fiction*, 5th edition (Libraries Unlimited, 2000), and Diana Tixier Herald's *Teen Genreflecting*, 2d edition (Libraries Unlimited, 2003). Each of these books contains a chapter on the romance genre. Saricks explains the appeal of the romance genre fiction, while Herald provides lists of titles organized by subgenres. Herald's *Teen Genreflecting* covers romance in the "Contemporary" chapter of that book.

You can also rely on colleagues and library patrons to keep you informed about adult and young adult romance genres. Talk to your colleagues and patrons about what they are reading. Even if you are already a committed romance fan, you will discover that others have read different authors and series than you have. To keep up with new young adult fiction, or to learn about books and series that you haven't had a chance to read, join a listserv discussion group, such as YALSA_BK, where librarians, teens, and authors discuss teen fiction. Romance fiction is often a topic of discussion on the list, and you can pose questions to the list subscribers about anything related to young adult fiction. See Appendix B for instructions about joining listservs.

Building the Collection

To best serve young adult readers, it is essential to have a solid and balanced collection of young adult literature, including romance fiction. This chapter offers some guidelines for building a young adult romance collection. In addition, Appendix A, at the end of this book, includes a sample "core collection" list. It should be noted, however, that the demands and resources of each community vary widely. Thus, librarians are encouraged to adapt the guidelines and lists to fit their own libraries' particular needs.

Selection and Acquisition

Identifying young adult romances for your collection may be difficult because today romance is often mixed with other fiction genres, including fantasy, paranormal, horror, humor, adventure, mystery, contemporary issues, and historical fiction. Librarians often rely on book reviews to choose books for their young adult collections. Although hardcover young adult romance fiction is reviewed in a timely fashion, teen paperback romances are often not reviewed at all. When reviews of teen paperback fiction are published, it is often after a paperback book or series has been around for a while, and it may not be possible to purchase the books, or the complete series, by the time you find adequate reviews.

To keep apprised of new young adult romance, you may want to visit your local bookstore from time to time to have a look at the new books in the young adult or teen fiction section. Read the book jackets and book blurbs to learn about the

books. Of course, it is also useful to actually read young adult fiction, including hardcover fiction and teen series books. This can help you identify which books contain strong elements of romance. Checking to see what's new on bookstore shelves and reading teen fiction will keep you up to date with young adult fiction. More important, by reading young adult fiction, you will be able to determine genres covered by particular books and series.

Publishers' catalogs and jobber catalogs will also be helpful when you are selecting young adult romance fiction for your library. Publishers' catalogs are available by request from publishing companies. Many publishers also put their catalogs on their Web sites, where you can read, download, and print them. Jobbers, such as Baker & Taylor and Ingram, also produce monthly publications, available in print and on the Web, that announce new publications. Baker & Taylor's *Books and More for Growing Minds* includes young adult fiction, nonfiction, and audio books. Ingram's *Advance Magazine, Paperback Advance Magazine*, and *Children's Advance Magazine* list forthcoming young adult hardcover, paperback, and audio books.

Additional selection tools, including bibliographies and reviewing sources, can be found in Appendix B.

Selected Issues

When building a collection of young adult fiction, certain issues arise that must be considered. Following are some of the main issues you will encounter, as well as general advice on how to deal with them.

Format

Young adult romance fiction is available in a variety of formats, including hardcover, trade paperback, paperback, audio books, and e-books. Publishers have recently been experimenting with young adult novels published in the trade paperback format. Although the prices of the trade paperbacks are somewhere in between hardcovers and paperbacks, and therefore fairly reasonable, the covers on trade paperbacks are sometimes flimsy. In addition, I've found the larger size of trade paperbacks requires you to sit up while reading, which might not appeal to teens who like to read while lying in bed or lying on the beach. Libraries should consider binding their young adult trade paperbacks so they will have a longer shelf life.

Although this guide focuses on print books in hardcover, trade paper, and paperback, it is useful to know that young adult romances are also available in other formats. If your library can afford the higher costs of audio books and e-books, consider purchasing a few young adult romances in these formats. If your library is not yet interested in purchasing e-books, remember that teens are always on the cutting edge of technology, and teens will likely be interested in reading an e-book on their computers or palm pilots. Perhaps your library can test the viability of new formats for fiction, such as e-books, using the young adult collection.

Series

Young adult romance fiction is often published in paperback series, and librarians have traditionally had an aversion to series fiction. You may be surprised to learn that teens find paperback series fiction appealing because the books feature the same predictable characters, settings, and continuing story lines, allowing teens to experience a continuity they crave. Silk Makowski suggests that teen paperback series fiction has evolved into its own genre.[11] It is necessary for librarians to become knowledgeable about teen series fiction so they can make informed decisions about purchasing, cataloging, and recommending series fiction. If you plan to buy a series for your library, make a commitment to purchasing the entire series. Teens get frustrated when they can't find an entire series, and they will go elsewhere to find it.

To be knowledgeable of the full range of young adult romance fiction, familiarize yourself with the romance subgenre of teen series fiction. Reading teen romance series—just one book in each series—will help you to understand why teens find them appealing. Teens will look for romance series in your library, even if they don't ask you for them. Many won't return if you don't carry series books. And many teens won't return if you display your disdain for romances or series books when they seek your help finding books in these genres. Makowski asserts, "Make lifetime library users of these teens now by supplying what they want."[12]

Collection Control and Maintenance

Cataloging

Although libraries catalog hardcover young adult books, young adult paperbacks are not always cataloged. If paperbacks are cataloged, they are classified as a generic "paperback," making it impossible for teens to get information about them without seeing the books on the shelf and also making it impossible for you to tell which paperbacks circulate. For display purposes, paperbacks are sometimes separated out by genre, and stickers are often used to identify genre paperbacks. Genre displays and genre labels are helpful to all parties concerned. If your library does not catalog paperbacks, however, you are doing your teen patrons and yourself a disservice. Both you and your patrons probably have difficulty putting your hands on particular paperback romances quickly if they are not cataloged. You also have no way of knowing how often the books circulate. Cataloging young adult paperback books, including teen series, will help you and your patrons find books more easily. You can find out from the circulation records which paperbacks or series are popular, which may help you decide which paperbacks to replace when they become beat up. If your circulation statistics are high, you can use these numbers to argue for replacement of books or expansion of your young adult paperback area.

Display

Treat young adult romance fiction the same way you treat other genre fiction in the young adult section of your library. You may wish to display young adult books by genre. The young adult section of the library may be too small to have separate genre sections, but you can help distinguish romances from other genres by placing genre stickers on the books, including the hardcover and trade paperbacks. This will help teens who do not ask for your assistance when they are seeking romances to read, and it will help you find books more quickly, too.

Be creative in your approaches to promoting young adult romance fiction. Use exhibits, book lists, bookmarks, booktalks, and anything else you can dream up to promote young adult romance fiction. Design displays of young adult romances throughout the year, not just for Valentine's Day. For instance, you could put together a "Summer Love" display of young adult romances in the summer, when teens are likely to have more free time for recreational reading. Exhibit a new romance series to help sell the series to your readers. When setting up an exhibit, remember to take advantage of the cover art on the books to attract readers. Stay away from editions of classic books with old cover art, and never display a book that has outdated or ugly cover art. Instead, use books with bold and exciting cover art to grab the attention of your teen customers.

Weeding

While no one likes to remove books from the collection, it is a necessary task. Weeding books from the paperback collection should be fairly easy. Books that are falling apart can be removed, but check first to see if the books are still available (especially if they are part of a series), as you might want to replace them. Circulation statistics can help you determine which books to weed out of your young adult collection, so cataloging your paperbacks would also help you to deselect paperbacks from your collection. Get rid of books that are dated. Are teens really reading those old Sweet Dreams romances from the 1980s and 1990s that you still have on your shelves? If you can't tell from your circulation statistics, ask your circulation staff which young adult romances are circulating. Ask your patrons what they are reading. Weeding your hardback area will free up shelf space so you can display books with great cover art. You can also do temporary weeding projects, such as temporarily removing some duplicates, to create more space in your young adult area.

One thing to keep in mind when weeding young adult romances is the series phenomenon. It is important to keep series fiction intact because readers usually want to read every title in the series—in order.

Notes

1. Smartgirl, *Teen Read Week Survey*, 2001. Available: http://www.smartgirl.org/speakout/archives/trw/trw2001.html (accessed November 13, 2002).
2. Lisa A. Hale and Chris Crowe, " 'I Hate Reading If I Don't Have To': Results from a Longitudinal Study of High School Students' Reading Interests," *The Alan Review* 28 (2001): 49–57.
3. Pamela Paul, "Teen Book Club," *American Demographics* 23 (2001): 12–13.
4. Joyce G. Saricks, *The Readers' Advisory Guide to Genre Fiction* (Chicago: American Library Association, 2001), 203.
5. Linda Christian Smith, *Becoming a Woman through Romance* (New York: Routledge, 1990).
6. Reed W. Larson, Gerald L. Clore, and Gretchen A. Wood, "The Emotions of Romantic Relationships: Do They Wreak Havoc on Adolescents?," in *Development of Romantic Relationships in Adolescence*, eds. Wyndol Furman, B. Bradford Brown, and Candace Feiring (New York: Cambridge University Press, 1999), 19.

7. Ibid., 20.
8. Angelina Benedetti, "Leading the Horse to Water: Keeping Young People Reading in the Information Age," in *The Readers' Advisor's Companion*, eds. Kenneth D. Shearer and Robert Burgin (Englewood, CO: Libraries Unlimited, 2001), 243.

9. Anne Bouricius, *The Romance Readers' Advisory: The Librarian's Guide to Love in the Stacks* (Chicago: American Library Association, 2000); Joyce G. Saricks, *The Readers' Advisory Guide to Genre Fiction* (Chicago: American Library Association, 2001).

10. Judy Blume, "1996 Margaret A. Edwards Acceptance Speech — *Forever*: A Personal Story," *Journal of Youth Services in Libraries* 10 (1996): 153.
11. Silk Makowski, *Serious about Series: Evaluations and Annotations of Teen Fiction in Paperback Series* (Lanham, MD: Scarecrow Press, 1998), 2.

12. Ibid., 6.

Chapter 2

Classic Romance

Whether they were written 400 years ago or 20 years ago, some love stories hold universal appeal and are seemingly timeless, speaking to readers of all types over many generations. We call these classic romances. In classic romances the main focus of the story is on the romantic relationship and its development. These books address such universal themes as crushes, dating, first love, sex, pregnancy, marriage, and obstacles to love relationships. Often dated by their settings, classic romance stories usually evoke strong emotions and thus remain popular with readers for many years. Many classic romances were originally written as contemporary love stories, but since the books in this chapter are set anywhere from 20 to 400 years in the past, most of them may also be considered historical romances for today's teen readers.

Titles in this chapter are divided into two sections, "Historical Classics" and "Modern Classics." "Historical Classics" covers titles published in the nineteenth century and early twentieth century, like *Jane Eyre, Wuthering Heights,* and *Gone with the Wind*. The "Modern Classics" section includes novels published in the latter half of the twentieth century by popular authors such as Beverly Cleary, Judy Blume, and Paul Zindel. All titles selected for this chapter are still in print at the time of this writing.

Appeal

Although the settings of classic romance novels may seem dated by references to technology and popular culture, readers find the emotions of love and romance the same, no matter when the story was written or where the story is set. For instance, when I recently read Beverly Cleary's *Jean and Johnny*, I found I seemed to know the story, but I am honestly not sure if I read the book before, or if Jean's experiences were so similar to my own that I simply knew the story. The story reminded me of the pleasure and the embarrassment I felt when a popular boy in school nicknamed me "Penny" and flirted with me in science class. So I knew exactly how Jean felt when Johnny began paying attention to her and calling her "the cute girl." Classic romances elicit the many strong emotions related to love and romance, including embarrassment, despair, misery, joy, fear, pleasure, and heartache, and this is exactly why these classic love stories continue to speak to generations of teen readers.

The historical settings of classic romance novels also appeal to many teens. Teens regard anything written or set before they were born as historical, and though a few of the books listed in this chapter were written as late as the 1970s, even these books seem like ancient history to today's teen readers. The milieu of the 1960s is almost as strange and foreign to them as a setting in Victorian England. Details of the time period and geographic setting, from music to fashion to customs, can be fascinating—and they offer readers insights into history. Teens enjoy reading classic romances because they learn about what life was like before they were born and they learn important lessons about love and life.

Advising the Reader

Following are a few specific points to think about when advising readers of classic romances:

- Find out whether your patron is ready to read a classic romance by asking, "Have you read *Wuthering Heights* yet? Would you like to read something else similar?" If the answer is yes, then you can suggest other "Historical Classics," such as *Jane Eyre* or *Gone with the Wind.*
- Determine whether your patron enjoys historical fiction. Many of the classic young adult romance novels will seem like historical fiction to your patron, since they were written years ago. If the reader doesn't like historical fiction, suggest titles written by Beverly Cleary or Paul Zindel, where the focus is on the emotions of the hero or heroine.
- If your patron is not ready for "Historical Classics" but has already read all of the contemporary romances your library owns, suggest some "Modern Classics" he or she may have missed or passed over due to old cover art, such as Paul Zindel's *The Girl Who Wanted a Boy* or Beverly Cleary's *Sister of the Bride*. If your "Modern Classics" are older editions, consider replacing them with reissues that have new cover art. Younger teens will love the cover art on Beverly Cleary's books; the bright pastel covers with items such as hearts and flowers all over them are darling! Older teens, on the other hand, will be attracted to the very same titles by new cover art, introduced in 2003, showing illustrations of teen couples on dates. While the pictures have a fifties look, which reflects the rough time period of the stories, the bright colors and obvious dating scenes will attract romance readers. If replacement of books with old cover art is not an option, admit that the cover is old-fashioned, and direct teens to the charms of the story.
- Find out whether your patron wants to read a love story that includes sex. While the classics written prior to the 1960s do not mention sex directly, sex can be found in a few classics written after the 1950s, with varying degrees of description. Sometimes the sex takes place off-scene, such as in Paul Zindel's *My Darling, My Hamburger* or Ann Head's *Mr. and Mrs. Bo Jo Jones*, but the fact that sex has taken place is evident when the girl gets pregnant. In some classics, such as Paul Zindel's *I Never Loved Your Mind*, younger readers might miss the vague descriptions of sex altogether. In

some classic young adult romances, such as Judy Blume's *Forever,* sex is recognized as a significant part of teen love relationships. Find out if your patrons are ready to read about sex before suggesting *Forever.*

Historical Classics

Titles in this section have withstood the test of time and have proved to be popular with teens as well as adults. These are books written for a general audience, but they feature youthful characters. Like "Modern Classics," "Historical Classics" focus on the love story, and they feature strong characterization and maturing protagonists. Characters such as Jane Eyre, Elizabeth Bennet, and Heathcliff must prove they are worthy of love. As in "Modern Classics," these stories do not always have happy endings.

Themes in "Historical Classic" romance novels vary greatly. They include heroes and heroines who fall in love with the wrong person, deny their true love, and encounter obstacles to true love such as misunderstandings or lengthy separations. Family is also an important theme, especially in orphan stories such as *Jane Eyre* and *Wuthering Heights*, where the establishment of a loving family becomes paramount to the orphan protagonists.

Pacing in "Historical Classics" tends to be slower than in "Modern Classics." Remember, these books were written for adult readers, so they also tend to be longer than "Modern Classic" young adult romances. Because of the length, the story lines move along more slowly, and they often include detailed descriptions of people and places in between the action in the stories.

The tone of the "Historical Classic" romance is usually darker than that of "Modern Classic" young adult romance fiction—when the lovers are separated, the stories become saturated with misery, and supernatural events sometimes occur during periods of darkness.

Many of the classics in this section will be on required reading lists for school, but some teens will miss the opportunity to read some of these books for English class. Recommend these classics to your older teen patrons as well as those younger patrons who are clearly ready for them.

Austen, Jane

***Pride and Prejudice.* Cary & Lea, 1832. Reissued by Bantam Books in 1984. ISBN 0553213105. [Adult] JH/HS**

Elizabeth Bennet and her sisters, Jane, Mary, Catherine, and Lydia, are excited to meet their new neighbor, Mr. Bingley. The family is pleased when Bingley begins courting Jane, but Mr. and Mrs. Bennet worry that Elizabeth will remain a spinster when she turns down marriage proposals from Mr. Collins and Mr. Darcy. Elizabeth learns too late that she misjudged Darcy, and she yearns for a chance to make amends.

Keywords: dating, England, family, marriage

Brontë, Charlotte

Jane Eyre. **Harper & Bros., 1848. Reissued by Penguin Books in 1996. ISBN 0140434003. [Adult] JH/HS**

Orphan Jane Eyre is sent to boarding school after the death of her uncle. When she leaves school, Jane goes to work as a governess at Thornfield Hall, teaching Mr. Rochester's ward. Rochester and Jane fall in love, and they plan to marry. But on their wedding day, Jane learns that Rochester is already married to Bertha Mason, a madwoman who is hidden in his attic. Jane flees, planning never to return to Thornfield.

Keywords: careers, England, family, marriage, orphans

Brontë, Emily

Wuthering Heights. **Harper & Bros., 1848. Reissued by Penguin Books in 1996. ISBN 0140434186. [Adult] JH/HS**

Catherine Earnshaw loves Heathcliff, an orphan adopted by her family. But as she grows up, Catherine realizes her social status requires her to marry Edgar Linton rather than Heathcliff. When Heathcliff learns Catherine plans to marry Linton, he leaves Wuthering Heights. Several years later, he returns, and despite his marriage to Linton's sister Isabella, he remains devoted to Catherine.

Keywords: England, family, first love, marriage, orphans

Du Maurier, Daphne

Rebecca. **Doubleday, 1938. Reissued by William Morrow in 1997. ISBN 0380730405. [Adult] JH/HS**

The narrator, whose first name is unknown, falls in love and marries Maxim de Winter. The De Winters live on an English country estate called Manderley. Mrs. De Winter slowly learns about the life and death of her predecessor, Rebecca, and she fears Maxim will tire of her because she is nothing like the wonderful and beautiful Rebecca.

Keywords: death, England, marriage, mystery

Mitchell, Margaret

Gone with the Wind. **Macmillan, 1936. Reissued by Warner Books in 1999. ISBN 0446675539. [Adult] HS**

Seventeen-year-old Scarlett O'Hara, vivacious, pretty, and spoiled rotten, thinks she should have whatever she wants, but Ashley Wilkes has decided to marry Melanie Hamilton instead of Scarlett. Set against a vivid Civil War backdrop, this Pulitzer Prize winner chronicles Scarlett's loves and losses as she proves herself to be a true survivor.

Keywords: Civil War, family, marriage

Montgomery, Lucy Maud

Anne of Green Gables Series.

Anne Shirley, an outspoken orphan girl, is raised in the small fictional town of Avonlea on Prince Edward Island, Canada, during the early twentieth century. The series follows Anne as she grows up to become a teacher, a writer, a wife, and a mother.

Anne of Green Gables. **L. C. Page, 1908. Reissued by Bantam Books in 1998. ISBN 055321313X. MS/JH**

Anne Shirley, an orphan, arrives in Prince Edward Island to live with Marilla Cuthbert and her brother Matthew.

Keywords: Canada, family, orphans

Anne of Avonlea. **L. C. Page, 1909. Reissued by Bantam Books in 1998. ISBN 0553213148. MS/JH**

Sixteen-year-old Anne Shirley begins her job as the schoolteacher in Avonlea. Anne begins to meddle in the romances of her friends, while she wonders about Gilbert Blythe's strange behavior.

Keywords: Canada, careers, education

Anne of the Island. **L. C. Page, 1915. Reissued by Bantam Books in 1998. ISBN 0553213172. MS/JH**

Anne Shirley travels to Kingsport, Nova Scotia, to study at Redmond College. In Kingsport, Anne must choose between two suitors, Sam Tolliver and Gilbert Blythe.

Keywords: Canada, education, first love

Anne of Windy Poplars. **Fred A. Stokes, 1936. Reissued by Bantam Books in 1998. ISBN 0553213164. MS/JH**

Anne Shirley spends three years working as the principal of Summerside High School in Prince Edward Island.

Keywords: Canada, careers

Anne's House of Dreams. **Fred A. Stokes, 1917. Reissued by Bantam Books in 1998. ISBN 0553213180. MS/JH**

Anne Shirley prepares for her marriage to Dr. Gilbert Blythe.

Keywords: Canada, marriage, weddings

Anne of Ingleside. **Fred A. Stokes, 1939. Reissued by Bantam Books in 1998. ISBN 0553213156. MS/JH**

Anne Blythe, the mother of five children, worries that her husband Gilbert no longer loves her. She sets out to make her husband fall in love with her again!

Keywords: Canada, children, family, marriage

Rainbow Valley. **Fred A. Stokes, 1919. Reissued by Bantam Books in 1998. ISBN 0553269216. MS/JH**

Anne and Gilbert Blythe's children, Shirley, Jem, Walter, Nan, and Diana, play in a valley behind the maple grove with their new neighbors, the Merediths.

Keywords: Canada, children, family, marriage

Rilla of Ingleside. **Fred A. Stokes, 1921. Reissued by Bantam Books in 1998. ISBN 0553269224. MS/JH**

Fourteen-year-old Rilla Blythe's happy life, filled with first dances and first kisses with Kenneth Ford, is interrupted by World War I. Rilla's beau leaves Ingleside to fight in the war. Will Rilla ever see Kenneth again?

Keywords: family, first love, World War I

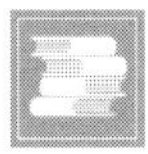

Montgomery, Lucy Maud

***The Blue Castle.* Fred A. Stokes, 1926. Reissued by Bantam Books in 1989. ISBN 0553280511. JH/HS**

At age twenty-nine, Valancy Stirling is considered an old maid, and she has given up hope of ever finding a husband. When Dr. Trent tells her she is dying, Valancy decides to enjoy what is left of her life, and she leaves her family to seek happiness. But Valancy never expected to find true love!

Keywords: Canada, family, first love, illness, marriage

Shakespeare, William

***Romeo and Juliet.* John Danter, 1597. Reissued by Oxford University Press in 2002. ISBN 0198320256. [Sexual Content, Adult] HS**

When Romeo Montague and Juliet Capulet meet at a masquerade, they fall passionately in love. But then they discover their families are rivals. Now Romeo and Juliet must decide how their love might survive.

Keywords: death, family, marriage

Modern Classics

"Modern Classic" romances are memorable for their powerful love stories and their strong protagonists. These novels fall into the various other young adult romance subgenres, including contemporary, historical, and alternative reality romance, so the pacing, setting, framework, and story lines differ from book to book. Characterization is important in the classics, however, and the protagonist of the classic young adult romance is usually an emotionally strong young woman who can learn and grow from her romantic experiences. For instance, Jean Jarrett in Beverly Cleary's *Jean and Johnny* grows as the result of her crush on Johnny, and Patty Bergen learns to grow up without Anton in Bette Greene's *Summer of My German Soldier* and its sequel *Morning Is a Long Time Coming*. Friends, family members, and boyfriends are usually secondary characters who help the protagonist grow up.

Classic young adult romances appeal to teens for several reasons. Teens can vicariously experience the emotions of love, romance, crushes, first dates, first kisses, and first sex by reading "Modern Classic" romances. While these emotions are important elements in all young adult romance stories, the books that stand out as classic young adult romance novels linger with readers because of their full descriptions of events and emotions. Teens won't forget Jane's first date in Beverly Cleary's *Fifteen*, Angie and Jack's first kiss in *Seventeenth Summer*, or the first time Katherine and Michael have sex in Judy Blume's *Forever*. Teen characters in "Modern Classics" mature as a result of their emotional romantic experiences.

Not all "Modern Classics" have happy endings, at least not the kind in which the couple lives happily ever after. Sometimes protagonists have to learn to live happily without their boyfriends, but these protagonists usually have optimistic futures where school, careers, and love relationships are concerned. Stories such as Judy Blume's *Forever,* Beverly

Cleary's *The Luckiest Girl,* and Madeleine L'Engle's *Camilla* help teens understand that young love may not last forever but that life goes on.

Blume, Judy

 *Forever.* **Bradbury Press, 1975. Reissued by Pocket Books, 1996. ISBN 0671695304. [Sexual Content] JH/HS**

High school seniors Katherine Danziger and Michael Wagner meet at a New Year's Eve party. Before long, they are involved in a committed sexual relationship that they believe will last forever. This controversial book has been banned from libraries frequently because of explicit sex. Winner of the 1996 Margaret A. Edwards Award.

Keywords: birth control, dating, first love, sex

Cleary, Beverly

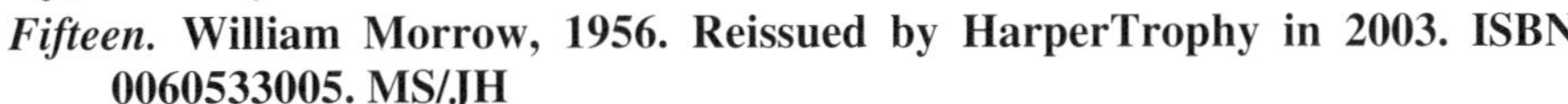

Fifteen. **William Morrow, 1956. Reissued by HarperTrophy in 2003. ISBN 0060533005. MS/JH**

Jane Purdy is ecstatic when Stan Crandall asks her out on her first date. After the date, Jane worries that Stan will never ask her out again, and she is heartbroken when Stan takes another girl to the first dance of the school year. Jane longs for another chance to let Stan know how much she likes him!

Keywords: dating, first love

Jean and Johnny. **William Morrow, 1959. Reissued by HarperTrophy in 2003. ISBN 0060533013. MS/JH**

Fifteen-year-old Jean Jarrett, who wears glasses and homemade clothes, is happy when Johnny Chessler, a popular boy at school, begins to pay attention to her. Will Johnny agree to go to the school dance with Jean?

Keywords: crushes, dating, first love

The Luckiest Girl. **William Morrow, 1958. Reissued by HarperTrophy in 2003. ISBN 0060532998. MS/JH**

Shelly Latham moves to southern California for her junior year of high school, where she falls in love with the star of the school basketball team. Shelly thinks she's the luckiest girl in the world!

Keywords: California, dating, first love

Sister of the Bride. **William Morrow, 1963. Reissued by HarperTrophy in 2003. ISBN 006053298X. MS/JH**

Sixteen-year-old Barbara seriously reconsiders her romantic dreams of love and marriage while watching her sister Rosemary prepare for her wedding day.

Keywords: dating, first love, marriage, weddings

Beverly Cleary, *Fifteen*

Beverly Cleary had already established a name for herself as a children's writer by the early 1950s with the publication of her highly popular Henry Huggins and Ramona books. But she became inspired to write teen romance novels after visiting a junior high school.

Beverly Cleary. Photo by Alan McEwen, 1999. Used with permission.

"I was talking to a group of junior high school girls about writing, and they said, 'Why don't you write books like you write, only about our age?' So that's what I did," Cleary explained in an interview in December 2002. The results were phenomenal, with blockbuster titles *Fifteen, The Luckiest Girl, Jean and Johnny,* and *Sister of the Bride*, originally published between 1956 and 1963, still popular with today's teen readers.

Although teen romance novels were popular during the 1950s, Cleary did not write her romantic novels simply because romances were trendy.

"I just don't pay any attention to that sort of thing," Cleary commented in the same interview. "I just write what I want to write." For her teen novels, Cleary also drew on her own experiences growing up, especially in writing *The Luckiest Girl*, which was published in 1958. "It's pretty much autobiographical," Cleary said. "But the boy in it was not modeled on the boy that I knew at that time. I was very careful to not make him be the boy I knew at the time. . . . Part of the fun of being an author is being able to rearrange life."

What does she hope readers will learn about romantic relationships from her books? "I don't think in terms of readers learning from my books, I concentrate on what I enjoy telling and hope that someone will enjoy reading what I have to say. If I find I'm beginning to teach, I throw that part of the book into the wastebasket," Cleary remarked. The author also noted that her favorite among her teen romances is the first she wrote, *Fifteen*. "I wrote it to keep busy when I was pregnant with twins. Writing was a pleasant way to pass the time," Cleary stated.

Cleary's romantic stories are set in the 1930s and 1940s, and while some say that the books seem dated today, the author believes they are simply true to the period. "The 1930s and 1940s were still a time when girls were protected, a time of innocence, at least in the society in which I grew up. I was struck by a recent letter from a girl who wondered why a girl in the story waited so anxiously for a telephone call from a boy, and she asked, 'Why didn't she just phone him?' Well, at the time I was writing about, that would not be considered appropriate. Girls waited for boys to call."

Later in the interview, Cleary observed, "[T]he world has changed so much since I wrote my teenage novels. Children grow up so much faster that I sometimes wonder if they have any childhood. When I travel around the country, I don't see

Beverly Cleary (*Cont.*)

children out playing on the lawns the way we used to play. It seems to me their lives are so programmed with lessons and soccer games and of course by television. . . . They don't have the childhood they used to and I think they're pushed into social life sooner than in my day. I learned to dance when I was fifteen, and now they have dancing classes after school in the fifth and sixth grades."

The author has also noticed from her fan mail that girls are reading her romance novels at a younger age. But readers still like her romantic stories for the same reason girls have enjoyed the stories for five decades. "They just love romance!," she declared. Although she never wrote another teen romance novel after *Sister of the Bride* in 1963, the sequel to Cleary's Newbery Award-winning *Dear Mr. Henshaw* includes a touch of romance. "In my book *Strider* . . . there is a teenage boy who has the beginnings of interest in a girl," the author remarked.

Beverly Cleary is one of the great pioneers of young adult fiction, and her work has endured for more than half a century. In her fifty-two-year career, Cleary has published more than forty books and earned numerous awards, including Newbery Honors for *Ramona and Her Father* and *Ramona Quimby, Age 8* and the American Library Association's Laura Ingalls Wilder Award. In 2000, the Library of Congress named Cleary a "Living Legend."

In 2002 the author reported that she continues to write articles, and she recently wrote an introduction to a new edition of Johanna Spyri's classic children's novel, *Heidi*. Despite her success, Cleary remains modest about her accomplishments: "I wrote my books and I was fortunate because readers like them. It's not been a very dramatic career. I've been exceptionally lucky. My writing life has always been happy."

For more information:

Cleary, Beverly. *A Girl from Yamhill: A Memoir.* New York: William Morrow, 1988.

Cleary, Beverly. *My Own Two Feet: A Memoir.* New York: William Morrow, 1995.

Beverly Cleary. n.d. Available: http://www.beverlycleary.com (accessed December 5, 2002).

Peacock, Scot, ed. "Beverly Cleary." In *Something about the Author.* Vol. 121. Detroit: Gale Research, 2001.

Daly, Maureen

***Seventeenth Summer.* Dodd, Mead, 1942. Reissued by Simon & Schuster in 2002. ISBN 0671619314. JH/HS**

High school graduate Angie Morrow experiences the joys and heartaches of summer love with her first boyfriend, Jack Duluth.

Keywords: dating, first love, vacations

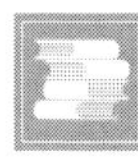

Greene, Bette

***Summer of My German Soldier*. Dial Books for Young Readers, 1973. Reissued by Penguin Putnam in 1999. ISBN 014130636X. MS/JH**

When Patty Bergen, a twelve-year-old Jewish-American girl, meets German prisoner-of-war Anton Reiker in her father's store, she knows she has found a friend. Patty hides Anton in her empty garage when he escapes from the military base, and as Patty takes care of Anton, she falls in love. Can Patty keep Anton safe forever?

Keywords: family, first love, religion, World War II

***Morning Is a Long Time Coming*. Dial Books for young Readers, 1978. Reissued by Penguin Putnam in 1999. ISBN 0141306351. [Sexual Content] JH**

High school graduate Patty Bergen travels to Europe with the intention of finding Anton Reiker's family. But while visiting Paris, Patty meets Roger Auberon, and she falls in love for the second time.

Keywords: dating, family, France

Head, Ann

***Mr. and Mrs. Bo Jo Jones*. G. P. Putnam's Sons, 1967. Reissued by New American Library in 1981. ISBN 0451163192. JH/HS**

July Greher and Bo Jo Jones only plan on dating until the end of senior year. But when July discovers she is pregnant, their plans change—they drop out of high school, get married, and move into a cheap apartment, and Bo Jo goes to work. July and Bo Jo know they will survive with the support of their families, but they are unsure if they can create a happy life for themselves.

Keywords: dating, marriage, pregnancy, sex

L'Engle, Madeleine

***And Both Were Young*. Lothrop, Lee & Shepard, 1949. Reissued by Bantam Books in 1983. ISBN 0440902290. JH/HS**

American teen Phillipa "Flip" Hunter attends a Swiss boarding school. When Flip meets Paul Laurens, a French boy who lives near her school, she falls in love. But Flip must keep her romance secret, because only seniors are allowed to date.

Keywords: education, first love, friendship, Switzerland

***Camilla*. Simon & Schuster, 1951. Reissued by Bantam Books in 1982. ISBN 0440911710. JH/HS**

Camilla Dickinson has always been protected from family problems, but now that she's fifteen, she is aware that her parents' marriage is in trouble. Camilla finds friendship, support, and first love from someone unexpected—her best friend's brother Frank.

Keywords: family, first love, friendship

Segal, Erich

***Love Story*. Harper & Row, 1970. Reissued by Avon Books in 2002. ISBN 0380017601. [Adult] HS**

Oliver Barrett, a wealthy law student, and Jenny Cavilleri, a music student from a working class family, fall in love. But can their love last? An ALA Best Book for Young Adults.

Keywords: dating, death, education, first love, illness

Smith, Betty

Joy in the Morning. **Harper & Row, 1963. Reissued by Harper Perennial in 2000. ISBN 0060956860. JH/HS**

Carl Brown and Annie McGairy meet in Brooklyn and they fall in love. When Carl moves to the Midwest to go to university, Annie follows him and the couple gets married. But married life is harder than Carl and Annie expected.

Keywords: first love, marriage, weddings

Zindel, Paul

The Girl Who Wanted a Boy. **Harper & Row, 1981. Reissued by Bantam Starfire in 1989. ISBN 9994911228. JH/HS**

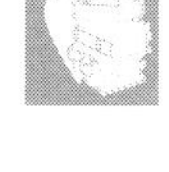

Sibella Cametta, a science and electronics genius, longs for a boyfriend. When Sibella spots Dan Douglas's photograph in the newspaper, she wants to meet him, and she finds him at the racetrack where he works. But Sibella is surprised to find out that Dan is not the handsome prince she believed him to be.

Keywords: crushes, first love

I Never Loved Your Mind. **Harper & Row, 1970. Reissued by Bantam Starfire in 1984. ISBN 055327323X. [Sexual Content] JH/HS**

High school dropout Dewey Daniels works as a hospital orderly, where he meets Yvette Goethals. Dewey brings Yvette presents until she agrees to go out with him, but Dewey is not prepared for Yvette's lifestyle as a vegetarian nudist. Can Dewey find a way to fit into Yvette's life?

Keywords: crushes, dating, first love

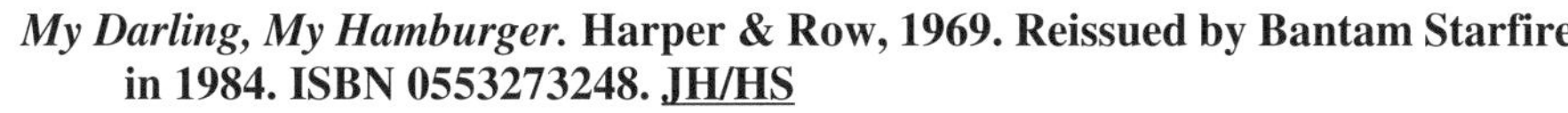

My Darling, My Hamburger. **Harper & Row, 1969. Reissued by Bantam Starfire in 1984. ISBN 0553273248. JH/HS**

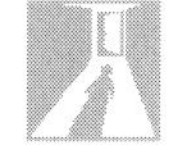

Maggie and Dennis doubledate with their friends Liz and Sean, but their relationship doesn't turn into anything serious. Liz and Sean, on the other hand, are involved in a serious relationship. Sean is always pressuring Liz to have sex, and when she finally agrees, she gets pregnant. Winner of the 2002 Margaret A. Edwards Award.

Keywords: abortion, dating, pregnancy, sex

Pardon Me, You're Stepping on My Eyeball. **Harper & Row, 1976. Reissued by Bantam Starfire in 1983. ISBN 055326690X. JH/HS**

Edna Shinglebox and Louis "Marsh" Mellow have a lot in common—they are both misfits with major parent problems. When Edna and Marsh begin dating, it is obvious that something is troubling Marsh, and he seems to want Edna's help. An ALA Best Book for Young Adults.

Keywords: dating, death, family, first love, grief

Chapter 3

Contemporary Romance

Young adult contemporary romance novels are light, innocent stories of teen crushes and first love. Emotions are the focus of these books. As teens fall in love for the first time, they experience a wide range of emotions—love, fear, jealousy, sadness, happiness, anger, and embarrassment. Contemporary romance fiction covers the range of emotions experienced by teens as they fall in love for the first time. Protagonists may fall in love with someone who doesn't love them back, or they may fall in love with someone who already loves another person, prompting them to feel sadness, anger, or jealousy. Teen characters might fall in love with someone who loves them back, and the characters may feel happiness and love while also feeling fearful and embarrassed about a first date or a first kiss. Contemporary romances include humorous stories of first love, portraying humor as a way of coping with all of these new and exciting emotions.

In contemporary romance, affections are usually limited to hand-holding and kisses, although sometimes books listed here include sex. Look for [Sexual Content] in the book listings, which indicates the portrayal of sex in a novel. Contemporary romance book lists included in this chapter are "Teen Love," "Humorous Romance," and "Multicultural Romance."

Appeal

The focus of contemporary romance fiction on emotions appeals to teens, who want to know how a first date or a first kiss will make them feel. Teens are curious about the emotions related to romance, and the lighter, more innocent contemporary romance stories can help teens learn about these emotions. Contemporary romance fiction can also help teens learn how to behave in certain social situations, such as a first date or a school dance, easing their fears about these events. Due to an emphasis on first experiences of love, including first dates and first kisses, contemporary romance fiction may be more appealing to younger teens.

Teens are drawn to fictional characters who seem like real people, and characters who experience real emotions appeal to teens. Contemporary romance fiction features strong, flawed characters who are believable because they display both strengths and weaknesses. Characters in contemporary romance fiction are not perfect, nor are their lives perfect, but they cope nevertheless. Humor is often used as a coping mechanism by teen characters in contemporary romance fiction. Humorous romances are particularly popular with teens because they show teens how humor can help them survive the horrible and embarrassing events that accompany teen love relationships and growing up.

Advising the Reader

Following are a few tips for advising the reader of contemporary young adult romance fiction:

- Find out if your patron wants to read about innocent first love before recommending books in the contemporary romance book list. The teen reader may wish to read a problem romance, a romantic suspense story, or a paranormal romance, all of which also feature modern-day settings. Contemporary romances are lighter and more innocent than these other romance subgenres, so be sure you know which subgenre is desired before making any suggestions.
- Ask if your patron wants to read a story with a happy ending. Many contemporary romances do not have traditional happily-ever-after endings, so you could end up suggesting a story with an ending that will not satisfy your patron. (*Note:* Because the summaries given do not give away endings, make sure you read some of the contemporary romances listed in the various book lists in this chapter, so you are aware of titles with both happy and not-so-happy endings.)
- Find out what grade your patron is in. This will give you a rough idea of age. Since contemporary romances focus on first love, suggest titles in these book lists to your younger patrons. But remember, today's teens are more sophisticated than young adults of earlier generations, so don't be surprised if your fourteen-year-old patron rolls his or her eyes if you suggest titles in the Mates and Dates series by Cathy Hopkins or Meg Cabot's The Princess Diaries series. Quickly suggest titles with a sophisticated sense of humor such as Megan McCafferty's The Diaries of Jessica Darling books or Gordon Korman's *Son of the Mob,* humorous revenge fantasy titles like *I Will Survive* by Kristin Kemp or *Burger Wuss* by M. T. Anderson, or my favorite story about jaded teens hurt by love, *David and Della* by Paul Zindel.
- Keep in mind that teens usually like to read stories about teens who are older than they are, so if it is possible to find out the age or grade of your customer, this will be helpful. Read the book summaries to find out the age or grade of protagonists, as characters of all ages are included in the contemporary romance book lists, and try to find books featuring characters older than your teen reader.

Teen Love

Themes included in "Teen Love" stories include crushes, unrequited love, dating, and first love. Titles included in the "Teen Love" book list include stories about the innocence and the intensity of the emotions of first love. Stories such as Avi's *Romeo and Juliet—Together (& Alive) at Last!* and Margaret Willey's *Finding David Delores* feature characters who are afraid to reveal their crushes to their love interests. Some titles feature obstacles to first love, such as parents who disapprove of their child's object of love, such as in C. S. Adler's *Not Just a Summer Crush,* or teens who meet on vacation and have only a short time together, like Melanie and Justin in *Just a Summer Romance* by Ann M. Martin. Other obstacles include jealous rivals, such as Harley in Ellen Wittlinger's *Razzle,* or a change of heart on behalf of one of the lovers, like Juli in Wendelin Van Draanen's *Flipped.*

The books in this category are primarily lighter stories about the emotions and experiences of crushes, first love, first kiss, and sometimes, first sex. Characterization is an important element of teen love stories. As teens learn who they are and gain confidence in themselves, they are ready to fall in love for the first time. For instance, in Julie Garwood's *A Girl Named Summer,* the protagonist lies to David about her athletic abilities, and when she discovers she is falling in love with him, she proves she is a real athlete and an honest person. In other stories, as the teen protagonists grow in their relationships, they sometimes decide to give up the safety of their love relationships to pursue their dreams. In *Send No Blessings* by Phyllis Reynolds Naylor, Beth decides to pursue her education and a career rather than marry her older boyfriend. And in Louise Plummer's *The Unlikely Romance of Kate Bjorkman,* Kate discovers that successful love relationships require hard work and forgiveness.

Because books in the "Teen Love" category focus on emotions and the innocence of first loves and first kisses, these stories will appeal particularly to younger teen readers. Younger teen readers find innocent stories of first love appealing because can they learn about how to behave in social situations such as first dates and first kisses. Stories such as Jacqueline Wilson's <u>The Girls Quartet</u>, Cathy Hopkins's <u>Mates and Dates</u> series, and Cherie Bennett's *Girls in Love* can help readers learn how to deal with the emotions of crushes and first love.

Adler, C. S.

Not Just a Summer Crush. **Houghton Mifflin, 1998. ISBN 0395885329. <u>MS/JH</u>**

When Hana's family travels to Cape Cod for the summer, she is surprised to bump into her favorite teacher Mr. Crane, and she spends time talking with him at the beach. Although Hana has a crush on Mr. Crane, nothing inappropriate occurs. But Hana's parents believe Mr. Crane is dangerous, and they forbid her to spend time with him.

Keywords: crushes, family, teachers, vacations

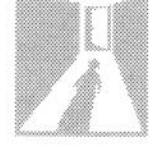

Appelt, Kathi A.

Kissing Tennessee: And Other Stories from the Stardust Dance. **Harcourt, 2000. ISBN 015202249X. <u>MS/JH</u>**

Eighth graders attend the Stardust Dance in honor of their graduation from Dogwood Junior High. Connected short stories provide details about the experiences of students attending the dance.

Keywords: dances, dating, sexuality, short stories

Avi

Romeo and Juliet—Together (& Alive) at Last! **Orchard, 1987. Reissued by Avon Books in 1997. ISBN 0380705257. [Male] MS/JH**

Pete Saltz has a crush on Anabell Stackpoole, but he is too shy to ask her out on a date. When Pete and Anabell are cast as the leads in the eighth-grade class production of *Romeo and Juliet*, a scheme organized by Pete's friend Ed, they will have to admit they like each other. Won't they?

Keywords: dating, first love, humor, kissing, theater

Bennett, Cherie

Girls in Love. **Scholastic, 1996. ISBN 0590880306. [Reluctant Readers] MS/JH**

High school seniors Tara Moore, Erin Kellerman, and Noelle LeBlanc are excited about Love, Michigan's annual Winterfest. While Tara tries to get the attention of handsome skier David Benjamin, Erin is confused about her feelings for ski jumper Luke Blakely and longtime boyfriend Pete Cole. Noelle, on the other hand, is busy practicing her figure skating and worrying about her health when she suddenly falls in love for the first time.

Keywords: crushes, dating, illness, sports, vacations

Brian, Kate

The Princess and the Pauper. **Simon & Schuster, 2003. ISBN 0689861737. [Reluctant Readers] MS/JH**

When Princess Carina of Vineland swaps places with ordinary sixteen-year-old Julia Johnson of Los Angeles for a night, she gives Julia explicit instructions to stay away from boring Markus Ingvaldsson during the ball. Instead, Julia falls in love with Markus, and when they escape the ball to eat a junk food dinner, the paparazzi catch them leaving the restaurant. Meanwhile, Carina goes to a club to see her e-mail pal Ribbit's band play. But Ribbit has girls falling all over him, and he barely has time for Carina. When Carina decides to stay after the concert to make out with Ribbit, she ends up on a bus to Texas, and there is no way she can make it back to L.A. in time to swap places with Julia.

Keywords: dating, family, first love, princesses

Bridgers, Sue Ellen

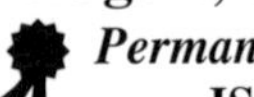

Permanent Connections. **HarperCollins, 1987. Reissued by Banks Channel Books in 1999. ISBN 1889199028. [Male] JH/HS**

High school student Rob Dickson moves to the family homestead in North Carolina to help take care of his Uncle Davis, who broke his leg. Rob meets Ellery and falls in love for the first time. An ALA Best Book for Young Adults and a selection of the YALSA Romance Genre List.

Keywords: family, first love

Burnham, Niki

Royally Jacked. **Pulse, 2004. ISBN 0689866682. [Reluctant Readers] JH/HS**

Valerie Winslow's parents are separating, and she must decide whether to stay in the United States with her mother and her mother's girlfriend, or move with her father to a castle in the small European country of Schwerinborg. Even though hottie David Anderson has finally noticed her, Val decides to move to Europe to avoid dealing with her mother's new life. When Val becomes friendly with Prince Georg, she is surprised to find herself thinking about the prince instead of David, and she is pleased when Georg asks her out on her first date.

Keywords: dating, divorce, family, first love, princes

Cann, Kate

Grecian Holiday. **Avon Books, 1999. ISBN 0064473023. [Sexual Content] JH/HS**

High school graduate Kelly joins her friends Jade and Sarah on a summer holiday in Greece, instead of traveling around Europe with her boyfriend Mike and his friends. Just as Kelly is getting used to life without Mike, he and his friends arrive in Greece. Kelly and Mike enjoy a few days together, but when they have another argument, Kelly is not sure she wants to continue her relationship with Mike.

Keywords: dating, friendship, vacations

Cann, Kate

The Richard Steele Trilogy.

College art student Richard Steele lands a graphics designer job at a local ad agency, and he hopes his newfound fortune will help him attract beautiful and snobby Portia, who hardly notices him. But his friend Bonny likes Rich just the way he is.

Hard Cash. **Pulse, 2003. ISBN 0689859058. [Male] JH/HS**

College student Rich Steele can't believe his luck—he has a new job working as a graphics designer for an ad agency. While Rich hopes his money and his new clothes will help him attract snobby classmate Portia, he doesn't notice his new friend Bonny is attracted to him.

Keywords: dating, education, employment, friendship

Shacked Up. **Pulse, 2004. ISBN 0689859066. [Male] JH/HS**

Rich's friend Bonny moves into his new flat to get away from her annoying mother. Rich is so busy lusting after the unattainable Portia that he doesn't even realize he's beginning to think of Bonny as more than a friend.

Keywords: dating, education, employment, friendship

Speeding. **Pulse, 2004. ISBN 0689859074. [Male] JH/HS**

Rich wants a real relationship with Bonny, but there are always obstacles. When Bonny's best friend needs rescuing from her scary boyfriend and a weird cult, Rich and Bonny travel to Scotland, with Bonny's mother close behind. Rich wonders if he and Bonny will ever have a normal relationship!

Keywords: dating, friendship

Cann, Kate

***Spanish Holiday.* Avon Books, 2004. ISBN 0060561602. JH/HS**

Laura and her best friends Yaz and Ruth travel to Spain for their summer vacation, but Laura is annoyed by Ruth's boyfriend, who joins them on their trip. Just when Laura thinks the whole vacation is ruined, they find a villa with a handsome neighbor.

Keywords: dating, friendship, vacations

Coville, Bruce, and Jane Yolen

***Armageddon Summer.* Harcourt, 1998. ISBN 0152017674. JH/HS**

Teens Marina and Jed, whose families belong to a religious cult called the Believers, fall in love while joining their families at the top of a mountain awaiting Armageddon.

Keywords: family, first love, religion, suspense

Dessen, Sarah

***Keeping the Moon.* Penguin Putnam, 1999. ISBN 0670885495. JH**

Fifteen-year-old Colie, who recently lost forty-five pounds, still suffers from the pain and rejection of her peers. While her fitness queen mother tours Europe, Colie spends the summer with her aunt Mira. After landing a summer job at the Last Chance Café, Colie finally meets some friends, Morgan and Isabel, and a boyfriend, Norman, who try to help her realize she is a beautiful and worthwhile person.

Keywords: body image, friendship, self-esteem, vacations

***This Lullaby.* Penguin Putnam, 2002. ISBN 0670035300. JH/HS**

Remy has one rule—keep your dating relationships casual. She is cynical about love, growing up with a hopelessly romantic mother who plans to marry for the fifth time. When Remy meets Dexter, a musician, she has trouble sticking to her rule. An ALA Best Book for Young Adults.

Keywords: dating, family, marriage

Dokey, Cameron

***How NOT to Spend Your Senior Year.* Pulse, 2004. ISBN 0689867034. JH/HS**

Jo O'Connor is enjoying her senior year and her relationship with her boyfriend Alex Crawford. Suddenly, Jo's life is turned upside down when her father tells her he is a witness in a murder trial, and they have to disappear. After Jo and her dad fake their deaths, Jo sneaks back to visit Alex, who believes she's a ghost. While Jo wants to spend time with Alex, she also likes Mark London, a boy at her new school. Jo manages to successfully lead two lives with two boyfriends, until her ghost is elected prom queen.

Keywords: crime, dances, dating, family, ghosts

Garwood, Julie

***A Girl Named Summer.* Scholastic, 1986. Reissued by Simon & Schuster in 1998. ISBN 067102342X. [Reluctant Readers] MS/JH**

Fifteen-year-old Summer falls in love with David. But Summer lies to David about her athletic abilities, and when he learns the truth, he dumps her for another girl. Can Summer win David's love again? Originally published as part of Scholastic's Wildfire romance series in 1986.

Keywords: dating, first love, sports

Graham, Rosemary

My Not-So-Terrible Time at the Hippie Hotel. **Viking, 2003. ISBN 0670036110. MS/JH**

Fourteen-year-old Tracy Forrester travels to Massachusetts with her father and siblings for a vacation, where they are expected to participate in a retreat for families of divorce. Tracy does not get along with the other teens at Farnsworth House, but things improve when perky Kelsey becomes her friend and Kevin, a teen who works at historic Plymouth, takes an interest in her. Tracy hopes to have her first summer romance with Kevin.

Keywords: dating, divorce, family, first love, friendship, vacations

Haddad, Charles

Calliope Day Falls . . . in Love. **Delacorte Press, 2003. ISBN 0385730705. MS**

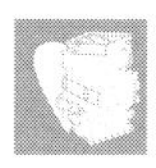

When fourth-grader Calliope Day finds a love poem intended for her best friend Noreen, she wants to know who wrote it. The poem sounds like something her father would have written, and Calliope intends to find the mystery boy who reminds her of her deceased father. A sequel to *Meet Calliope Day*.

Keywords: dating, first love, poetry

Hopkins, Cathy

The Mates and Dates Series.

Fourteen-year-old friends Lucy Lovering, Nesta Williams, and Izzie Foster help each other survive the ups and downs of friendship and dating.

Mates, Dates, and Inflatable Bras. **Pulse, 2003. ISBN 0689855443. [Reluctant Readers] MS/JH**

Lucy Lovering is upset when her best friend Izzie becomes friends with glamorous Nesta, the new girl in school. But Lucy forgets her troubles when she falls in love with Nesta's older brother Tony.

Keywords: dating, first love, friendship, kissing

Mates, Dates, and Cosmic Kisses. **Pulse, 2003. ISBN 0689855451. [Reluctant Readers] MS/JH**

Izzie Foster meets Mark while she is shopping for aromatherapy oils. When Izzie sits around at home, waiting for Mark to call and neglecting her friends, Lucy and Nesta take action.

Keywords: dating, first love, friendship

Mates, Dates, and Designer Divas. **Pulse, 2003. ISBN 068985546X. [Reluctant Readers] MS/JH**

Nesta Williams finds herself out of her league when she begins dating Simon Peddington Lee, a boy from a wealthy family, and she

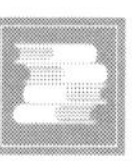

needs her friends Lucy and Izzie to help her survive her new relationship.

Keywords: dating, first love, friendship

Mates, Dates, and Sleepover Secrets. **Pulse, 2003. ISBN 0689859910. [Reluctant Readers] MS/JH**

When Lucy befriends lonely Theresa Joanne "T.J.," she hopes her friends Izzie and Nesta will accept T.J., too. T.J. hopes Lucy, Izzie, and Nesta will teach her how to attract boys.

Keywords: dating, friendship

Mates, Dates, and Sole Survivors. **Pulse, 2004. ISBN 0689859929. [Reluctant Readers] MS/JH**

Lucy decides she wants to start dating Tony, Nesta's older brother, but she is heartbroken to discover he has a new girlfriend. All her friends have boyfriends, so Lucy is on her own, until Izzie suggests a weekend away to cheer Lucy up. While they are away, Lucy meets Daniel, a boy who claims to love her. When Daniel's attention begins to smother her, Lucy wonders if the single life is right for her after all.

Keywords: dating, friendship

Mates, Dates, and Mad Mistakes. **Pulse, 2004. ISBN 0689867220. [Reluctant Readers] MS/JH**

Izzie wants to dazzle an older boy named Josh, so she creates a new image for herself, including a more independent attitude. Izzie can't understand why her family and friends don't like the new Izzie!

Keywords: dating, friendship

Mates, Dates, and Sequin Smiles. **Pulse, 2004. ISBN 0689867239. [Reluctant Readers] MS/JH**

Nesta is devastated when she gets braces on her teeth. She's convinced no boy will ever look at her again, even though her friends Lucy, Izzie, and T. J. tell her personality is more important than looks. Things are looking up for Nesta, however, when she meets Luke, who likes her for more than her good looks.

Keywords: body image, dating, friendship

Hopkins, Cathy

Truth or Dare.

Friends Cat, Becca, Squidge, and Lia play the game Truth or Dare.

White Lies and Barefaced Truths. **Pulse, 2004. ISBN 0689870035. [Reluctant Readers] MS/JH**

When best friends Cat and Becca play the game Truth or Dare, Cat has to admit that she wants to break up with her boyfriend Squidge. Cat and Becca discover they both have a crush on Ollie, and they must decide whether it is worth it to lose their friendship over a boy.

Keywords: crushes, dating, friendship

The Princess of Pop. **Pulse, 2004. ISBN 0689870027. [Reluctant Readers] <u>MS/JH</u>**

In another round of the game Truth or Dare, Squidge dares Becca to audition for the Pop Princess contest in London. Will Becca find the nerve to compete for the title of Pop Princess?

Keywords: dating, friendship

Teen Queens and Has Beens. **Pulse, 2004. ISBN 0689871295. [Reluctant Readers] <u>MS/JH</u>**

When Lia plays Truth or Dare, she attracts the attention of Jonno, the school hunk. Kaylie is upset that Jonno likes Lia, so she starts a bullying campaign against her, complete with rumors, threats, and exposed secrets.

Keywords: crushes, dating, friendship

Lane, Dakota

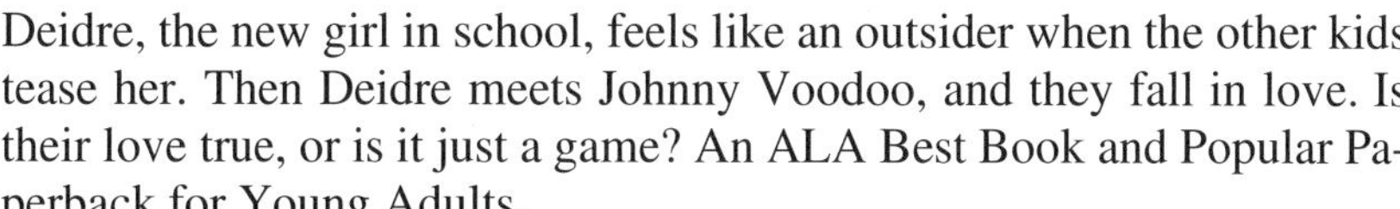

Johnny Voodoo. **Delacorte Press, 1996. ISBN 0385322305. <u>JH/HS</u>**

Deidre, the new girl in school, feels like an outsider when the other kids tease her. Then Deidre meets Johnny Voodoo, and they fall in love. Is their love true, or is it just a game? An ALA Best Book and Popular Paperback for Young Adults.

Keywords: bullying, dating, first love

Lantz, Frances Lin

Letters to Cupid. **Pleasant Company, 2001. ISBN 1584853743. <u>MS/JH</u>**

Thirteen-year-old Bridgette Carley wants to find true love, so she decides to do a report for school to learn the meaning of true love. Bridgette interviews her parents and her older siblings, writes letters to Cupid, learns about romantic films, and experiences a few crushes on boys at school. Will romantic Bridgette learn the secret of love?

Keywords: dating, family, letters

Mackler, Carolyn

The Earth, My Butt, and Other Big Round Things. **Candlewick, 2003. ISBN 0763619582. [Reluctant Readers] <u>MS/JH</u>**

Despite the fact that fifteen-year-old Virginia Shreves is overweight, Froggy Welsh enjoys making out with her after school. But Virginia adheres to the "Fat Girl Code of Conduct," which states sexual activity is a secret and "never . . . push the relationship thing." When her older brother Byron admits to committing date rape, Virginia is angry and disgusted with men, and she stops making out with Froggy. Virginia also stops eating and begins hurting herself on purpose. When Virginia realizes she is old enough to make decisions about her own life, she regains control and allows new friends, including Froggy, into her life. An ALA Best Book for Young Adults and a 2004 Michael L. Printz Honor Book.

Keywords: body image, date rape, dating, family, first love, friendship, self-esteem

Love and Other Four Letter Words. **Bantam Doubleday Dell, 2000. ISBN 0385327439. JH/HS**

When Sammie Davis's parents separate, fifteen-year-old Sammie and her mother move to a small apartment in New York City. Sammie meets new friends, including Eli, a boy who shares her love of folk music.

Keywords: dating, divorce, first love

Marchetta, Melina

Looking for Alibrandi. **Orchard, 1999. ISBN 0531301427. JH/HS**

Seventeen-year-old Italian-Australian Josie Alibrandi has family troubles: her single mother never told her father about Josie's birth, she hates her old-fashioned grandmother, and she is about to meet her absent father for the first time. Complicating her life further, Josie falls in love with two different boys, wealthy and unhappy John Barton and wild boy Jacob Coote.

Keywords: Australia, dating, family, first love, Italian Australians, suicide

Martin, Ann

Just a Summer Romance. **Holiday House, 1987. Reissued by Point in 1994. ISBN 0590439995. [Reluctant Readers] MS/JH**

Junior high school students Melanie Braderman and Justin Hart meet while vacationing for the summer on Fire Island. Justin insists that their love is "just a summer romance," and they part at the end of the summer. After returning home, Melanie learns that Justin is the star of a new television show. Now Melanie must find out what their summer romance meant to Justin.

Keywords: celebrities, first love, vacations

McPhee, Phoebe

The Alphabetical Hookup List Trilogy.

College roommates Jodi Stein, Celeste Alexander, and Ali Sheppard play a game requiring them to kiss a boy whose name begins with each letter of the alphabet.

The Alphabetical Hookup List A–J. **MTV/Pocket, 2002. ISBN 0743448421. [Reluctant Readers] JH/HS**

When college roommates Jodi Stein, Celeste Alexander, and Ali Sheppard all get dumped by their boyfriends, they begin a game that requires them to kiss one boy whose name begins with each letter of the alphabet.

Keywords: dating, friendship

The Alphabetical Hookup List K–Q. **MTV/Pocket, 2002. ISBN 074344843X. [Reluctant Readers] JH/HS**

Jodi, Celeste, and Ali take their kissing game to Paris, where their game gets them into trouble.

Keywords: dating, friendship

The Alphabetical Hookup List R–Z. **MTV/Pocket, 2002. ISBN 0743448448. [Reluctant Readers] JH/HS**

When someone threatens to expose their Alphabetical Hookup List game, Jodi, Celeste, and Ali could all be losers.

Keywords: dating, friendship

Naylor, Phyllis Reynolds

Send No Blessings. **Simon & Schuster, 1991. ISBN 0689315821. JH/HS**

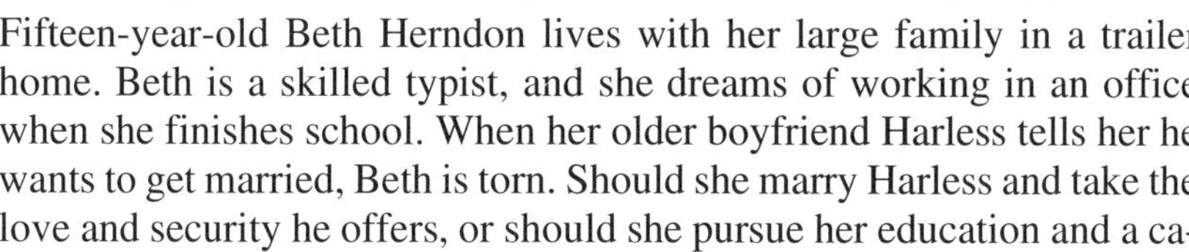

Fifteen-year-old Beth Herndon lives with her large family in a trailer home. Beth is a skilled typist, and she dreams of working in an office when she finishes school. When her older boyfriend Harless tells her he wants to get married, Beth is torn. Should she marry Harless and take the love and security he offers, or should she pursue her education and a career? An ALA Best Book for Young Adults.

Keywords: education, family, first love, poverty

O'Brien, Judith

Mary Jane. **Marvel Enterprises, 2003. ISBN 0785113088. MS/JH**

Ballet dancer Mary Jane Watson, the new girl at Midtown High School, falls in love with nerdy Peter Parker. Based on the Ultimate Spider-Man comics.

Keywords: dating, family, friendship, sports

Pearson, Mary E.

Scribbler of Dreams. **Harcourt, 2001. ISBN 0152023208. MS/JH**

The Malone and Crutchfield families have been feuding for generations. When Kaitlin Malone meets Bram Crutchfield at high school, they fall in love. Kait lies to Bram about her last name to hide her true identity. When Kait gets to know the Crutchfield family, she sees that they are not villains after all. What will Bram do when he finds out Kait is a Malone?

Keywords: dating, diaries, family, first love

Plummer, Louise

The Unlikely Romance of Kate Bjorkman. **Bantam Books, 1995. ISBN 0385320493. [Reluctant Readers] MS/JH**

Intelligent and gawky high school senior Kate Bjorkman dislikes popular romance novels, so she sets out to write the story of her own Christmas romance with Richard, her brother's best friend. In the process of writing her romance, Kate discovers relationships require hard work to be successful. An ALA Popular Paperback for Young Adults.

Keywords: dating, first love, friendship

Powell, Randy

Is Kissing a Girl Who Smokes Like Licking an Ashtray? **Farrar, Straus and Giroux, 1992. Reissued by Sunburst in 2003. ISBN 0374436282. [Male] JH/HS**

Biff, a shy high school senior who has never had a girlfriend, meets beautiful and wild Heidi. Biff and Heidi spend their spring break together, and Heidi brings Biff out of his shell. An ALA Best Book for Young Adults and a selection of the YALSA Romance Genre List.

Keywords: first love, vacations

Qualey, Marsha

***One Night.* Penguin Putnam, 2002. ISBN 0803726023. JH/HS**

Ex-heroin-addict Kelly Ray works for her aunt Kit, a radio talk show host. When she has a chance encounter with Prince Tomas Teronovich of Lakveria, she decides to try to keep him away from his bodyguards long enough to convince him to be a guest on her aunt's radio show. Kelly and Tom spend one night out together and during that time, they fall in love. Will their romance end before it begins?

Keywords: dating, princes

Ripslinger, Jon

***How I Fell in Love and Learned to Shoot Free Throws.* Millbrook Press, 2003. ISBN 0761318925. [Male] JH/HS**

Seventeen-year-old Danny Henderson is ecstatic when Angel McPherson, the star of the girl's basketball team, offers to help him with his free throws. Although Danny and Angel begin dating, Angel is distant and wants to keep their relationship a secret, and Danny wonders what other secrets she is hiding.

Keywords: dating, family, first love

Rostkowski, Margaret I.

***Moon Dancer.* Harcourt, 1995. ISBN 0152766383. JH/HS**

When fifteen-year-old Miranda goes hiking in southern Utah with her sister Jenny, her cousin Emily, and Emily's friend Max, the teens are supposed to help Emily find Native American rock art for a school project. But Mira finds herself falling in love with Max, and she is surprised to learn that he feels the same about her.

Keywords: adventure, first love, Utah

Sheldon, Dyan

***The Boy of My Dreams.* Candlewick, 1997. ISBN 0763600040. MS/JH**

Sixteen-year-old Michelle "Mike" Brindisi has found the boy of her dreams in college man Bill. With her efforts to attract Bill keeping her busy, she neglects her friends Hope and Bone. After a brief romance with Bill, Mike realizes her friendships are more important. Will Mike be able to see that Bone is really the boy of her dreams?

Keywords: crushes, friendship

Sones, Sonya

***What My Mother Doesn't Know.* Simon & Schuster, 2001. ISBN 0689841140. MS/JH**

In a novel written in verse, ninth-grader Sophie describes her search for Mr. Right. She has several romances with classmates and a cyber romance, but these romances don't last. Will Sophie ever find true love?

Keywords: dating, Internet, poetry

Spinelli, Jerry

***Stargirl.* Alfred A. Knopf, 2000. ISBN 0679886370. [Male] JH/HS**

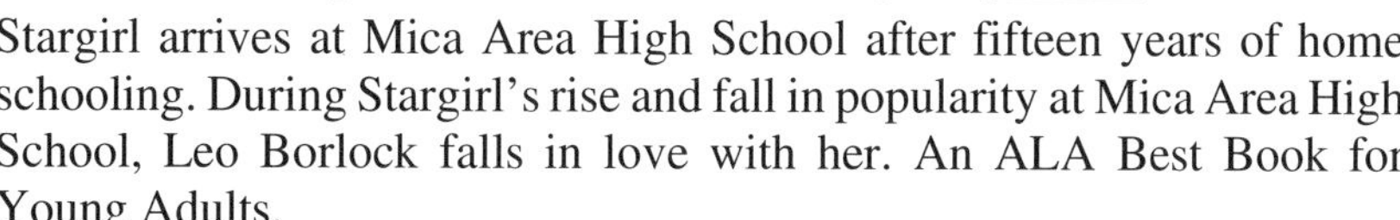

Stargirl arrives at Mica Area High School after fifteen years of home schooling. During Stargirl's rise and fall in popularity at Mica Area High School, Leo Borlock falls in love with her. An ALA Best Book for Young Adults.

Keywords: bullying, first love, popularity

Taniguchi, Tomoko

***Call Me Princess.* CPM Manga, 2000. ISBN 1562199242. JH**

When Mako's brother-in-law Ryo comes to visit, she is sure he is her dream man, the one who will call her "Princess." But Ryo rebuffs Mako's advances, and when her friend Yo confesses his love for her, Mako is forced to decide which boy she truly loves.

Keywords: first love, friendship, graphic novels

Thesman, Jean

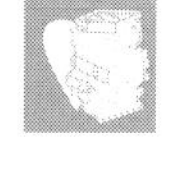

***Moonstones.* Viking, 1998. ISBN 0670879592. MS/JH**

Jane and her mother travel to Royal Bay to take care of business surrounding her grandmother's estate. They are joined by Jane's aunt Norma and cousin Ricki, and while their mothers deal with family disputes, Jane and Ricki sneak out of the house to meet boys. When Jane meets Carey, they fall madly in love. Can their love last?

Keywords: dating, family, first love, vacations

Trimble, Mary E.

***McClellan's Bluff.* Atlantic Bridge, 2003. ISBN 1931761485. JH/HS**

When seventeen-year-old Leslie Cahill falls in love with cowboy Sloan Stroh, who is eleven years older than Leslie, her family does not approve. Sequel to *Rosemount.*

Keywords: American West, family, first love

Van Draanen, Wendelin

***Flipped.* Alfred A. Knopf, 2001. ISBN 0375811745. MS/JH**

Juli Baker has had a crush on Bryce Loski since second grade, but Bryce has always thought Juli was weird. Now in the eighth grade, Bryce suddenly thinks Juli is cool, while Juli thinks Bryce might be a bit shallow. Will they ever agree on how they feel about each other? An ALA Best Book for Young Adults.

Keywords: crushes, first love

Voigt, Cynthia

***Bad Girls in Love.* Simon & Schuster, 2002. ISBN 0689824718. [Reluctant Readers] MS/JH**

In the fourth book in the Bad Girls Series, junior high school students Mikey Elsinger and Margalo Epps both experience love for the first time.

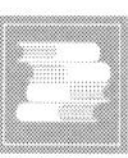

When Mikey develops a crush on Shawn Macavity, the star of the school play, she tries to attract Shawn's attention. Meanwhile, Margalo has a secret crush on her teacher. Will the girls ever find out the truth about love from firsthand experience? Previous titles in the series, which are not considered romances, include *Bad Girls, Bad, Badder, Baddest,* and *It's Not Easy Being Bad.*

Keywords: crushes, first love, theater

Wallace, Rich

Shots on Goal. **Alfred A. Knopf, 1997. ISBN 0619986707. [Male] MS/JH**

Best friends and soccer teammates Bones and Joey fight for the affections of sexy schoolmate Shannon.

Keywords: first love, friendship, jealousy, sports

Ware, Cheryl

Venola in Love. **Scholastic, 2000. ISBN 053133306X. MS/JH**

Seventh-grader Venola Cutright has a crush on the new boy in school, Nathan Racine. Venola tells her story of unrequited love and life in the seventh grade through her diary, e-mails to her best friend Sally, and letters to the editor of a teen magazine.

Keywords: crushes, diaries, first love

Willey, Margaret

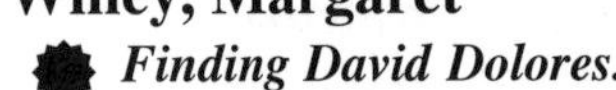

Finding David Dolores. **HarperCollins, 1986. Reissued by iUniverse.com in 2001. ISBN 0595196411. MS/JH**

Thirteen-year-old Arly's hobby is her obsession with David Dolores, an older boy. Her friend Regina wants to help make her fantasy become reality. But Arly is not sure she wants to know the real David Dolores. An ALA Best Book for Young Adults.

Keywords: crushes, friendship

Wilson, Jacqueline

The Girls Quartet.

British ninth-graders Ellie, Magda, and Nadine deal with peer pressure to find a boyfriend and to live up to a certain standard of beauty.

Girls in Love. **Delacorte Press, 2002. ISBN 038572974X. [Reluctant Readers] MS/JH**

Ellie is unlucky in love. Her friends Magda and Nadine both have boyfriends, and Ellie wants a boyfriend, too. When Ellie fantasizes a handsome boyfriend out of her geeky young pen pal Dan, she doesn't know the real Dan is better than any imaginary boy.

Keywords: dating, first love, friendship

Girls under Pressure. **Delacorte Press, 2002. ISBN 0385729758. [Reluctant Readers] MS/JH**

Ellie becomes obsessed about her weight after someone at a local modeling contest calls her fat. When Ellie begins bingeing and purging, she becomes so grouchy her friends don't want to have anything to do with her. And why has her boyfriend Dan stopped calling and writing her?

Keywords: body image, dating, eating disorders, friendship

Girls Out Late. **Delacorte Press, 2002. ISBN 0385729766. [Reluctant Readers] MS/JH**

When Ellie meets Russell, an older boy who shares her passion for art, they begin dating. Before long, Ellie is in love. In subplots, Magda has a crush on art teacher Mr. Windsor, and Nadine struggles to get over former boyfriend Liam.

Keywords: dating, friendship, kissing

Girls in Tears. **Delacorte Press, 2003. ISBN 0385730829. [Reluctant Readers] MS/JH**

3

Ellie and her friends are so unhappy! Ellie's romance with Russell is nearly finished; Magda's hamster died; and Nadine is lonely without a boyfriend. On top of all that, Nadine falls in love with a boy on the Internet, and she agrees to meet him in person—against the advice of her friends.

Keywords: dating, friendship, Internet

Wittlinger, Ellen

Lombardo's Law. **Houghton Mifflin, 1993. Reissued by Houghton Mifflin in 2003. ISBN 0618311084. JH/HS**

Fifteen-year-old Justine Trainor and new neighbor Mike Lombardo share a passion for avant-garde movies. While producing their own movie, Justine and Mike admit their attraction to each other.

Keywords: dating, first love

Razzle. **Simon & Schuster, 2001. ISBN 0689835655. [Male] JH/HS**

Kenyon Baker moves to Cape Cod for the summer with his retired parents. While Ken works to fix up the cottages at his parents' tourist resort, he meets eccentric Razzle, a young woman who becomes an instant friend and inspiration for his artistic photographs. Although Razzle has a huge crush on Ken, he doesn't even notice because he is busy dating Harley, Razzle's nemesis.

Keywords: crushes, dating, family, friendship, vacations

Wolff, Virginia Euwer

True Believer. **Simon & Schuster, 2001. ISBN 0689828276. JH/HS**

In the second book in the projected Make Lemonade Trilogy, LaVaughn still dreams of going to college, so she works hard at school. When a boy named Jody moves back to her neighborhood, LaVaughn falls in love for the first time. (*Note:* The first book in the trilogy, *Make Lemonade*, is not considered a romantic story.) An ALA Best Book for Young Adults, a 2002 Michael L. Printz Honor Book, and winner of the 2001 National Book Award.

Keywords: first love, homosexuality, poetry, poverty

Cheryl Zach (pseudonyms: Jennifer Cole, Jamie Suzanne, Nicole Byrd), *Runaway*

When Cheryl Zach began her writing career in the early 1980s, she never dreamed she would write young adult romance novels.

"I wanted to write adult historical romance. But my agent suggested I write a category romance for Harlequin, so I did," she said in an interview in April 2002. Zach's first novel, called *Twice a Fool,* was published in 1984 while she was working full-time as a teacher.

Cheryl Zach. Photo by Michelle Grisco. Used with permission.

After *Twice a Fool* was published, Zach said, "I wanted to write a story based on a student at school, about a shy girl who runs for class president, and my agent suggested we sell it as a young adult romance novel." *Frog Princess* was Zach's first young adult romance novel, written for the First Love from Silhouette line. The book won her a Rita Award in the young adult category from the Romance Writers of America. She wrote two more titles for the First Love series.

With the success of her first teen romances, it may have seemed Zach was onto something, but Zach found her luck beginning to wane.

"The market changed and many of the romance series ended. I wrote for the *Sweet Valley Twins* and *Sisters* series under pseudonyms. Then I changed agents so I could write under my own name and I was able to create a series about a blended family called *Smyth vs. Smith,*" Zach stated in the same interview. With Southern Angels, a historical romance series set during the Civil War, the author found herself moving into historical fiction, the genre in which she had originally intended to write.

"I prefer to write historicals because I enjoy the extensive research involved in historicals, but they are hard to market," she continued. Despite critical acclaim and a 1996 Virginia Romance Writers Holt Medallion Award for the first book in the series, *Hearts Divided,* the series ceased publishing after four titles.

Zach's other young adult romance novels are *Waiting for Amanda, Fortune's Child, Paradise, Kissing Caroline, Winds of Betrayal, A Dream of Freedom, Love's Rebellion, Runaway, Secret Admirer,* and *Carrie's Gold.* With three Rita Awards for *Frog Princess, Waiting for Amanda,* and *Runaway,* Zach was inducted into the Romance Writers of America Hall of Fame in 1996. She became the only young adult romance author to hold this honor.

Cheryl Zach (*Cont.*)

In the late 1990s, Zach finally began what she set out to do—write adult historical romance novels. She and her writing partner, daughter Michelle Place, use the pseudonym Nicole Byrd. Publications include *Robert's Lady, Dear Imposter, Lady in Waiting*, and *Widow in Scarlet.*

"I feel fortunate. This is what I used to dream about, I am doing what I love to do. I hope to keep writing until I die," Zach remarked.

Will Zach ever write young adult romance again? The author said she was writing a mystery novel for young adults, and she would like to write more young adult romances in the future. She said her young adult novels always contain an element of romance. In the author's words, "Romance may or may not be the principal plot, but it is always part of the story."

For further information:

Hedblad, Alan, ed. "Cheryl Zach." In *Something about the Author.* Vol. 98. Detroit: Gale Research, 1998.

McMahon, Thomas, ed. "Cheryl Zach." In *Authors and Artists for Young Adults.* Vol. 21. Detroit: Gale Research, 1997.

Nicole Byrd. 2003 Available:http://www.nicolebyrd.com/ (accessed January 15, 2003).

Senick, Gerard J., ed. "Cheryl Zach." In *Something about the Author Autobiography Series.* Vol. 24. Detroit: Gale Research, 1997.

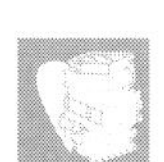

Young, Karen Romano

***The Beetle and Me: A Love Story.* William Morrow, 1999. ISBN 0688159222. MS/JH**

Daisy Pandolfi is not old enough to drive yet, but she spends her spare time fixing up a 1957 Volkswagen Beetle. Billy, a fellow stage crew member and auto shop class student, likes Daisy, but Daisy only likes Billy as a friend. An ALA Best Book for Young Adults.

Keywords: family, first love, friendship, theater

Zach, Cheryl

***Secret Admirer.* Berkley, 1999. ISBN 0425171140. [Reluctant Readers] JH/HS**

High school sophomore Brittany Parrish's life is far from perfect—her parents are getting divorced, and she thinks her relationship with her boyfriend Nate is boring. When Brittany seeks romance and excitement on the Internet, she believes she has found the man of her dreams. Then she decides to meet Randall in person. But instead of true love, Brittany finds herself in danger. Another title in Zach's Dear Diary Series, *Runaway*, can be found in the "Pregnancy and Parenting" book list in Chapter 5.

Keywords: dating, diaries, family, Internet

Humorous Romance

Contemporary teen romance fiction has traditionally taken the issues of love, romance, and sex very seriously. Recently, however, new authors of young adult fiction like Meg Cabot, Louise Rennison, and Megan McCafferty have created wonderful, amusing teen romance stories. These stories feature characters who face the embarrassing and agonizing events surrounding dating, first love, and growing up, and invite teens to use humor to cope with such events. For instance, the protagonist in Louise Rennison's Confessions of Georgia Nicolson series is always embarrassed by her little sister, her frightening cat, and her parents, but her relationships with Robbie Jennings and Dave the Laugh continue. In humorous romance stories, characters like Georgia learn and grow from their embarrassing experiences, making characterization a significant element of humorous romance. Being able to laugh at yourself shows strong character! The humorous romance subgenre is particularly appealing to teens because learning about love, romance, and related issues can be embarrassing. Humor helps to lighten the mood and show young readers that the embarrassing elements of love, romance, and growing up happen to everyone. These embarrassing events can even be funny! Judging from the popularity of these new authors, teens are enjoying humorous romance.

The diary format is popular in contemporary young adult romance fiction, whether in a series or a novel, but it is particularly prevalent in the humorous romance category. A diary style lends an air of reality and intimacy to the story, even if the story is actually fiction, and it makes a story appealing because it seems real. It's like talking to a friend. Letters and e-mails often accompany the diary format, allowing readers to see how the protagonist relates to family and friends. Since reality is fashionable in contemporary popular culture, with so-called reality television shows all the rage, it is not surprising that young adult fiction would follow this trend. Authors of humorous romance such as Meg Cabot, Louise Rennison, Megan McCafferty, and Catherine Clark are using the diary device with much success.

Anderson, M. T.

Burger Wuss. **Candlewick, 1999. ISBN 0763606804. [Male] JH**

Sixteen-year-old Anthony falls in love with Diana while he orders a meal from her at O'Dermott's, a popular fast-food chain, and they date for a short time. When Anthony loses Diana to an older O'Dermott's employee named Turner, he takes a job there so he can get revenge on Turner, with hilarious results. A subplot has Anthony's best friends, Rick and Jenn, madly in love.

Keywords: dating, first love, friendship, jealousy, revenge

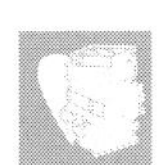

Meg Cabot (Pseudonyms: Jenny Carroll, Patricia Cabot, Meggin Cabot), *The Princess Diaries*

Meg Cabot finds inspiration for her popular young adult novels all around her. In fact, Cabot's popular The Princess Diaries series began as her own journal.

Meg Cabot, author of The Princess Diaries. Photo by Reven Wurman. Used with permission.

"Mom started dating my college teacher and I freaked out! I wrote a journal about it to get over my angst and then turned it into a story about a fourteen-year-old girl whose Mom was dating her teacher," Cabot reported in an interview in April 2002. The girl became an unlikely princess by the name of Mia Thermopolis, now known to millions of readers around the world.

Cabot's other young adult series were also inspired by real events. Cabot stated, "After my Dad died, me and my brother kept thinking we saw him everywhere, and I wondered, 'What if we could see everyone who is dead?' " This idea was the basis for The Mediator series, about a girl who can see and communicate with ghosts. The idea for Cabot's 1-800-WHERE-R-YOU quartet came to her after she and a friend were caught in a storm. Cabot said, "We hid under scaffolding. The scaffolding was struck by lightning, and afterwards we kept waiting for our psychic powers to appear."

Cabot may not be psychic, but she knows what life is like for today's teenagers. "I write about normal pressures of teen life," Cabot stated. But Cabot's female characters are not ordinary teenagers. Instead, they are princesses, ghost hunters, psychics, and reluctant national heroes. "Fans like this because they feel like freaks and the characters are actually freaks," Cabot said in 2002. As a result, Cabot's brief career as a young adult author has already been extremely successful. Her books *The Princess Diaries, Princess in the Spotlight, Princess in Love, Princess in Waiting,* and *All-American Girl* have all been *New York Times* bestsellers. *The Princess Diaries* was made into a feature film by Disney, and it was such a hit, a sequel is planned. Cabot reported in April 2002 that Disney will also produce a movie based on Samantha Madison's escapades in *All-American Girl.* In the meantime, fans of Cabot's 1-800-WHERE-R-YOU series can watch the Lifetime television show, called *1-800-Missing,* which is based on the books.

Meg Cabot (*Cont.*)

Like other young adult authors, Cabot didn't set out to become the author of popular young adult fiction. She began her writing career as a historical romance novelist, using the pen name Patricia Cabot. The author recently had an opportunity to combine her love of historical romance fiction and her talent for writing stories for teens. *Nicola and the Viscount* and *Victoria and the Rogue* were published in the Avon True Romance historical romance series for teen readers. In fact, all of Cabot's young adult novels include elements of love and romance.

"I wouldn't write anything without romance as part of the story," the author said in April 2002, then adding, "I like writing for young adults because of the innocent nature of the story lines."

Although Cabot's young adult novels are innocent, she has received letters from parents who object to the mention of sex in her books. But Cabot, who admitted that she is reliving her teen years, is writing for teens. "Kids are obsessed with talking about sex!" Cabot commented. Since her readers are interested in learning about love, romance, and everything that goes with the territory, the author said she tries to provide her readers with accurate information, and she draws on her own teenage experiences. For instance, a passage in *Princess in Love* instructing Mia in the art of kissing is copied word for word from a note a friend sent Cabot in high school. "Girls like the kissing instructions!," Cabot observed. "There are not enough guides to life for girls."

What advice does this author have for her readers? "Do not let boys know you like them!"

Cabot continues to write romance novels for adults, adding contemporary adult romance to her repertoire under her full name, Meggin Cabot, but she also plans to write more books in The Mediator and The Princess Diaries series. In April 2002, the author pronounced, "I hope to follow Mia to graduation!"

For more information:

Jenny Carroll. 2002. Available: http://www.jennycarroll.com (accessed September 12, 2002).

Meg Cabot. 2002. Available: http://www.megcabot.com (accessed September 12, 2002).

Peacock, Scot, ed. "Meg(gin) Cabot." In *Something about the Author.* Vol. 27. Detroit: Gale Research, 2002.

Peacock, Scot, ed. "Meg(gin) Cabot." In *Contemporary Authors.* Vol. 197. Detroit: Gale Research, 2002.

Cabot, Meg

All-American Girl. **HarperCollins, 2002. ISBN 0060294698. [Reluctant Readers] MS/JH**

Samantha Madison is an ordinary girl—she is madly in love with her sister's boyfriend Jack, she wears black clothes, she likes popular music, and she is a talented artist. Sam accidentally becomes a national hero when she saves the president's life during an attempted assassination, and suddenly Sam's new friendship with the president's son David is the hottest gossip in Washington. Can Sam give up her fantasy romance with Jack for a real romance with David?

Keywords: dating, family, first love, politics

Cabot, Meg

The Princess Diaries Series.

When fourteen-year-old misfit Mia Thermopolis discovers she is the heir to the throne of Genovia, a small European principality, she must learn how to act like a princess. Now Mia worries about ordinary teenage problems like school, boys, dating, kissing, and unusual problems like princess lessons, embarrassing herself in front of the media, and her debut in Genovian society.

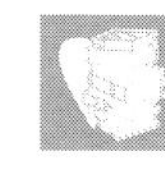

The Princess Diaries. **HarperCollins, 2000. ISBN 0380978482. [Reluctant Readers] MS/JH**

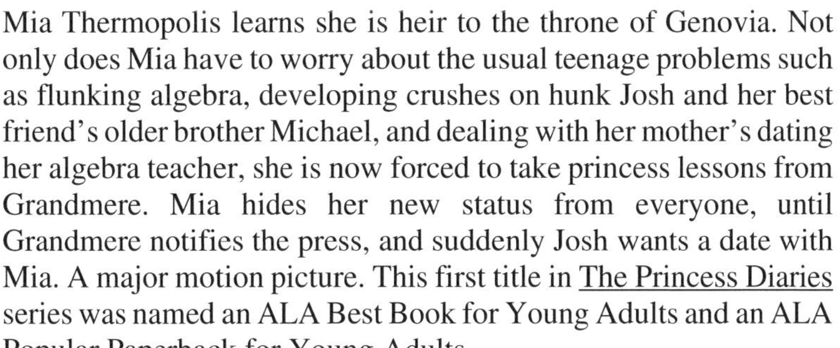

Mia Thermopolis learns she is heir to the throne of Genovia. Not only does Mia have to worry about the usual teenage problems such as flunking algebra, developing crushes on hunk Josh and her best friend's older brother Michael, and dealing with her mother's dating her algebra teacher, she is now forced to take princess lessons from Grandmere. Mia hides her new status from everyone, until Grandmere notifies the press, and suddenly Josh wants a date with Mia. A major motion picture. This first title in The Princess Diaries series was named an ALA Best Book for Young Adults and an ALA Popular Paperback for Young Adults.

Keywords: crushes, dating, diaries, princesses

The Princess Diaries Volume II: Princess in the Spotlight. **HarperCollins, 2001. ISBN 0060294655. [Reluctant Readers] MS/JH**

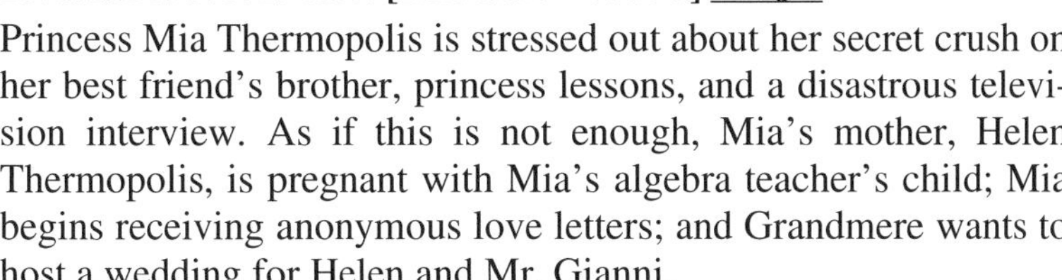

Princess Mia Thermopolis is stressed out about her secret crush on her best friend's brother, princess lessons, and a disastrous television interview. As if this is not enough, Mia's mother, Helen Thermopolis, is pregnant with Mia's algebra teacher's child; Mia begins receiving anonymous love letters; and Grandmere wants to host a wedding for Helen and Mr. Gianni.

Keywords: crushes, diaries, letters, princesses

The Princess Diaries Volume III: Princess in Love. **HarperCollins, 2002. ISBN 0060294671. [Reluctant Readers] MS/JH**

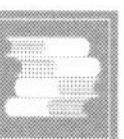

Mia finally has a boyfriend, but her boyfriend is her biology partner Kenny, not Michael, the boy she really likes. Out of desperation,

Mia starts sending anonymous love letters to Michael. Meanwhile, she gets kissing instructions from her friend Tina, and princess lessons with Grandmere continue as Mia prepares for her debut in Genovia.

Keywords: dating, diaries, kissing, letters, princesses

The Princess Diaries Volume IV: Princess in Waiting. **HarperCollins, 2003. ISBN 006009608X. [Reluctant Readers] MS/JH**

When Mia finishes her state visit to Genovia, she is excited to return home to her new boyfriend Michael. But Grandmere has big plans for Mia's love life, and Michael is not included!

Keywords: dating, diaries, princesses

The Princess Diaries Volume IV and a Half: Project Princess. **Harper Trophy, 2003. ISBN 0060571314. [Reluctant Readers] MS/JH**

Princess Mia and her friends are spending their spring break building houses for the less fortunate. While Mia clumsily works, causing some chaos and laughs, she hopes for opportunities to make out with her boyfriend Michael.

Keywords: dating, diaries, princesses

Princess in Pink. **HarperCollins, 2004. ISBN 0060096101. [Reluctant Readers] MS/JH**

Mia wants her boyfriend Michael to take her to the prom, but he does not like dances. Will Mia find a way to convince Michael to invite her to the prom?

Keywords: dances, dating, princesses

Clark, Catherine

The Diaries of Courtney Von Dragen Smith.

High school senior Courtney Von Dragen Smith begins writing in her journal as a way of coping when her boyfriend dumps her. Courtney continues writing in her diary about her long-distance romance when she goes away to college.

***Truth or Dairy*. William Morrow, 2000. ISBN 0380814439. JH/HS**

High school senior Courtney Von Dragen Smith begins her diary the day her college boyfriend, Dave, breaks up with her because he does not want a long-distance relationship. Courtney decides to run for student council and ignore boys for the rest of the school year. Will she be able to ignore Grant Superior?

Keywords: dating, diaries, family

Wurst Case Scenario. **HarperCollins, 2001. ISBN 0064472876. JH/HS**

Courtney recounts her trials and tribulations in her diary as she adjusts to life at college and a long-distance romance with boyfriend Grant. An ALA Popular Paperback for Young Adults.

Keywords: college, dating, diaries

Clark, Catherine

Maine Squeeze. **Avon Books, 2004. ISBN 0060567252. JH/HS**

Colleen lives on a boring island off the coast of Maine, but this summer she is having a great time. She has a job, a new boyfriend, and her parents have left her alone in the house. Everything is wonderful until her old boyfriend shows up and threatens to ruin Colleen's perfect summer.

Keywords: dating, vacations

Conford, Ellen

Crush: Stories. **HarperTrophy, 1998. ISBN 0064407780. [Reluctant Readers] MS/JH**

A collection of related stories about love and romance, *Crush* is about a group of high school students preparing for the Valentine's Day dance. Each story features a different character. Themes of the stories include peer pressure, respect, self-esteem, humor, and heartbreak.

Keywords: crushes, dances, short stories

Corbet, Robert

Fifteen Love. **Walker, 2003. ISBN 0080278513. [Reluctant Readers] MS/JH**

In a romantic comedy alternating between viewpoints, fifteen-year-olds Will, a tennis player, and Mia, a musician, like each other. Both Will and Mia are new to the dating game, and due to communication problems, their first date is a disaster. Both Will and Mia are ready to move on, but Will's brother and Mia's dog bring the couple together again.

Keywords: dating, family, first love

Eberhardt, Thom

Rat Boys: A Dating Experiment. **Hyperion, 2001. ISBN 0786806966. [Reluctant Readers] MS/JH**

Fourteen-year-olds Marci Kornbalm and Staci Weingarten do not have dates for the annual Spring Fling dance at school. When their boss finds a magic ring, the girls use it to turn two rats into two cute dates for the dance.

Keywords: dances, dating, magic

Frank, Lucy

Oy, Joy! **Dorling Kindersley, 1999. ISBN 0789425386. JH/HS**

As Joy begins her freshman year of high school, her Uncle Max moves in with her family to recover from a stroke. Joy and Uncle Max play matchmaker for each other, and Joy eventually finds a boyfriend named Max, while Uncle Max moves to Florida with Rose. A humorous story about family, friendship, and romance.

Keywords: dating, family, illness

Hawthorne, Rachel

Caribbean Cruising. **Avon Books, 2004. ISBN 0060596864. JH/HS**

Lindsay is going on her first cruise, and she has a list of things she wants to do, including meeting cute guys and finding a special boy for a summer fling. Her plans go awry, however, when she discovers she is falling in love.

Keywords: dating, friendship, vacations

Hayes, Daniel

No Effect. **Godine, 1993. ISBN 0879239891. MS/JH**

Eighth-grader Tyler McAlister and his best friend Lymie try out for the school wrestling team. Tyler falls in love with his science teacher, Miss Williams, and he invites her to his house for Thanksgiving dinner. Tyler is surprised, disappointed, and embarrassed when Miss Williams shows up with his wrestling coach as her date. An ALA Best Book for Young Adults.

Keywords: crushes, sports, teachers

Hite, Sid

Cecil in Space. **Henry Holt, 1999. ISBN 0805050558. JH/HS**

Seventeen-year-old Cecil Rowe pursues popular Ariel Crisp until he realizes that it is Isabel, his friend Isaac's sister, whom he really loves. Meanwhile, Cecil tries to help Isaac, who has been accused of vandalism. In this glimpse of the life of an ordinary teenage boy, we encounter Cecil's family, his friends, and his witty observations about life along the way.

Keywords: crime, crushes, first love

Keller, Beverly

The Amazon Papers. **Harcourt, 1996. ISBN 0152013458. JH/HS**

When Iris Hoving's mother goes away on vacation, Iris arranges to meet hunky Foster Prizer at the pool hall. But nothing happens the way Iris expects—her mother's car is damaged, her foot gets broken, Foster disappears, and Iris ends up going on a wild and comic adventure with Foster's ex-girlfriend Zelma. Along the way, Iris meets Byron, who suddenly seems more appealing than her missing date.

Keywords: dating, family

Kemp, Kristin

I Will Survive. **Push, 2002. ISBN 0439121957. [Reluctant Readers] JH/HS**

Ellen Hopkins learns her boyfriend Jack is having an affair with her best friend Melisha. Then her best friend Julian, who has always had a crush on her, begins dating her snobby, perfect younger sister Eve. Ellen and her new Goth friend Meg make comical plans for revenge on Melisha, Jack, Julian, and Eve that quickly turn nasty.

Keywords: dating, family, friendship, jealousy, revenge

Korman, Gordon

Son of the Mob. **Hyperion Books, 2002. ISBN 0786807695. [Male, Reluctant Readers] JH/HS**

High school senior Vince Luca is the son of a powerful Mob boss, and he tries not to let the family business complicate his own life. Despite Vince's efforts, his family's business often interferes in his love life, with hilarious results. When Vince begins dating Kendra, he doesn't realize that she is the daughter of the FBI agent who wants to capture his father. An ALA Best Book for Young Adults.

Keywords: crime, dating, family

Krulik, Nancy

Love & SK8. **Pulse, 2004. ISBN 0689870760.** **JH**

Angie is a skateboarder and a graffiti artist who spends her free time painting boards. Although lots of skater boys are interested in Angie, she's not interested in anyone, until she meets preppy Carter Morgan III. Despite the fact that Angie and Carter come from different worlds, they fall in love, but their differences make their relationship difficult.

Keywords: dating, sports

Ripped at the Seams. **Pulse, 2004. ISBN 0689867719.** **JH/HS**

Sami Granger moves to New York City to work for a fashion designer. Her boss steals her designs, and Sami loses her job when she tries to inform the public the designs belong to her. Sami ends up working in a lingerie store, where her designs win her a plus-size audience and the attentions of a photographer and a carpenter.

Keywords: dating, friendship

Lowry, Lois

Your Move, J. P.! **Houghton Mifflin, 1990. ISBN 0395536391. [Male]** **MS**

Twelve-year-old J. P. Tate falls in love with Angela Galsworthy, and to catch her attention, he tells her he has a rare and fatal illness. J. P.'s little white lie becomes a huge problem when he learns that Angela's father is a doctor and that he wants to help J. P. Soon J.P.'s humorous lies snowball out of control!

Keywords: crushes, illness

Lynch, Chris

Extreme Elvin. **HarperCollins, 1999. ISBN 0060280409. [Male]** **MS/JH**

Despite Elvin's sense of humor, he is not very popular at his new high school, and his friends Mike and Frank help him learn how to talk to girls and how to handle the school bully. Before long, Elvin is holding hands with Sally, resulting in a rumor that she gave him a sexually transmitted disease, and his popularity soars. Soon he is dating Barbara. Will Elvin's popularity last? The sequel to *Slot Machine*, which is not considered a romance novel.

Keywords: dating, first love, friendship

Martinet, Jeanne

Truer than True Romance: Classic Love Comics Retold. **Watson-Guptill, 2001. ISBN 0823084388.** **HS**

Martinet updates romance comics written during the 1950s through the 1970s, using the original illustrations with hilarious new captions.

Keywords: comics, graphic novels, short stories

Megan McCafferty, *Sloppy Firsts*

After working as an editor and writer for women's and teen magazines such as *YM, Cosmopolitan,* and *Fitness*, Megan McCafferty decided it was time to end her career in that business. "I knew it was time to get out of magazines when I realized that my boss's job seemed unbearable to me—I didn't want another promotion," McCafferty said in an interview in July 2002. "I wanted to write a book that I would enjoy reading. Because I had been an editor at *Cosmo*, quite a few people were surprised that I didn't write the type of novel publishers salivate over: a comic tale about a quirky, twenty-something's search for love in the big city. . . . I thought back to how I, like many teens before me, was blown away by *The Catcher in the Rye* when I was in seventh grade. . . . Since then I had devoured novels written from a first-person point of view, hoping that I'd finally find Holden Caulfield's female counterpart—a teenage protagonist that is highly-observant, hilarious, and wise beyond her years, yet still has a lot to learn about life."

Megan McCafferty. Photo © Christopher McCafferty. Used with permission.

Unable to find such a character, McCafferty decided to create such a character in her first novel, *Sloppy Firsts.* In the story, sixteen-year-old Jessica "Notso" Darling's best friend Hope has moved away, leaving Jessica to cope with high school by herself. McCafferty commented, "I knew that if I wrote honestly, *Sloppy Firsts* would relate to anyone who survived high school, a time when the tiniest event takes on the hugest significance, and a best friend moving away is nothing short of catastrophic. By refusing to dumb down or over dramatize her plight, Jessica Darling is both universally identifiable, yet unique. She's both insider and outsider, painfully inexperienced, yet sometimes too smart for her own good. Since no one in her world provides the model for who she wants to become, she has to experience the pain and pleasure of creating herself through trial-and-error."

McCafferty's fans tell her they enjoy reading her books because they like Jessica. "They appreciate how 'real' Jessica's world is, and accuse me of stealing pages from their own diaries! Jessica is such a relatable anti-heroine because she's not perfect and popular, but not a total loser either. They sympathize with her embarrassments and insecurities, and are inspired to be more like her when she stands up for herself. They also like that I didn't mince words, and brought out the humor in typical high school horrors. I wasn't afraid to use the foul language that can actually be heard in high school hallways across America. And they find it refreshing that I wrote about love, lust, and sex in the same frank way that they talk about it amongst themselves," McCafferty stated. "A lot of the emails I get start with 'I'm not a big fan of reading, but I LOVED your book.' To turn a non-booklover into a fan is seriously one of the best compliments I could ever get."

Megan McCafferty (*Cont.*)

Sloppy Firsts has also been well -received by critics and librarians. In the 2001 Smartgirl.com/American Library Association Teen Read Week survey, it was listed as one of the top ten books of the year and one of the best books of all time for readers ages seventeen and up. The book was also named one of the 2002 Books for the Teen Age by the New York Public Library, and it was selected as a Popular Paperback for Young Adults and a Quick Pick for Reluctant Readers by the American Library Association in 2003.

McCafferty's second book about Jessica, *Second Helpings,* focuses on Jessica's relationship with Marcus, the boy who became her new best friend and almost-boyfriend in *Sloppy Firsts.* McCafferty reported in July 2002 that she was writing her third novel. "It's about a twenty-nine year old singer in a wedding band who suffers from an identity crisis and is compelled to get in touch with people from her past. It will be marketed primarily to adults, but will definitely appeal to fans of my first two books because it has a lot of high school flashbacks." McCafferty remarked, "I hope to see more sophisticated books, TV shows, [and] movies for teens. They are a lot smarter than the pop culture powers-that-be give them credit for. And I hope that whatever efforts I make to this end are met with enthusiasm."

For more information:

Megan McCafferty. n.d. Available: http://www.meganmccafferty.com (accessed September 12, 2002).

McCafferty, Megan

The Diaries of Jessica Darling.

Sixteen-year-old Jessica Darling shares her deepest thoughts with her diary when her best friend Hope moves away. She continues writing her witty and sarcastic entries in her diary until the end of her senior year of high school.

 ***Sloppy Firsts.*** **Crown, 2001. ISBN 0609807900. [Reluctant Readers, Sexual Content] JH/HS**

Jessica "Notso" Darling's best friend Hope moves away, leaving her with only her journal to share her hilarious observations about life in high school. She becomes confused by her feelings for several boys, including class hunk Scotty Glazer, whom her friends and family think she should date; senior Paul Parlipiano, Jessica's secret crush who has his own secret; and class "Dreg" Marcus Flutie, who becomes more than a good friend. An ALA Popular Paperback for Young Adults.

Keywords: crushes, diaries, family, friendship

Second Helpings. **Crown, 2003. ISBN 0609807919. [Sexual Content, Reluctant Readers] JH/HS**

High school senior Jessica Darling is surprised to find herself dating the other class "brainiac," Len Levy, through the efforts of her former friend and almost-boyfriend, Marcus Flutie. But Jessica is confused by her lukewarm feelings for Len and her very strong feelings for Marcus, who doesn't seem to be interested in her anymore.

Keywords: dating, diaries, family, friendship

Okimoto, Jean Davies

Jason Kovak Series.

Jason's Women. **Little, Brown, 1986. Reissued by iUniverse.com in 2000. ISBN 059500797X. [Male] JH/HS**

Jason Kovak is lonely and unemployed, so he answers newspaper ads for blind dates and jobs. While the blind dates are a comical disaster, Jason gets a job gardening for Bertha Jane Fillmore and tutoring her adopted daughter, Thao Nguyen. An ALA Best Book for Young Adults.

Keywords: dating, employment

To Jaykae: Life Stinx. **Tom Doherty, 1999. ISBN 0312867328. [Reluctant Readers, Male] JH/HS**

In the sequel to *Jason's Women,* Jason Kovak's divorced father is getting remarried. Jason does not like his stepbrother, golden-boy Josh, who has it all: good looks, athletic ability, and popularity with girls. When Jason meets Allison in an Internet chat room, he pretends he is Josh. He even sends her Josh's picture. Finally, Jason realizes he should be honest with Allison about himself. But will Allison like him?

Keywords: dating, family, Internet

Pascal, Francine

The Victoria Martin Trilogy.

In sequels to the unromantic story *My Mother Was Never a Kid* (originally titled *Hangin' Out with Cici*), fourteen-year-old Victoria Martin experiences romance on her summer vacations.

My First Love and Other Disasters. **Penguin Putnam, 1979. Reissued by Pulse in 2003. ISBN 0689859899. MS/JH**

Victoria Martin works as an au pair on Fire Island, where she tries to catch the attention of Jim Freeman. But in a series of comedic mishaps, Victoria accidentally attracts the attention of Jim's friend Barry.

Keywords: dating, first love, friendship, vacations

Love & Betrayal & Hold the Mayo. **Penguin Putnam, 1985. Reissued by Pulse in 2003. ISBN 0689859902. MS/JH**

Fifteen-year-old Victoria Martin and her best friend Steffi work as waitresses at Camp Mohaph, where Steffi's boyfriend Robbie works as a counselor. When Victoria falls in love with Robbie, she tries to ignore her feelings, with hilarious results.

Keywords: dating, friendship, vacations

Paulsen, Gary

***The Boy Who Owned the School.* Orchard, 1990. Reissued by Bantam Doubleday Dell, 1991. ISBN 0440405246. [Male] MS/JH**

Clumsy Jacob Freisten tries to be invisible at school, but during gym class he literally bumps into popular Maria Tresser, and he falls in love. When Jacob's English teacher forces him to work on the school play for extra credit, Jacob gets to spend time with Maria. Will Maria ever notice Jacob?

Keywords: crushes, dating, theater

***The Schernoff Discoveries.* Bantam Doubleday Dell, 1997. ISBN 0385321945. [Male] MS/JH**

A humorous novel about the fourteen-year-old narrator and his best friend Harold Schernoff, social outcasts and nerds. The boys experience many firsts, including dating, kissing, driving, skiing, and fishing. An afterward informs readers what happened to the boys when they grew up. An ALA Best Book for Young Adults.

Keywords: dating, kissing, misfits

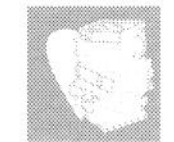

Payne, C. D.

The Journals of Nick Twisp.

Fourteen-year-old honor student Nick Twisp falls in love with beautiful Sheeni Saunders, gets into some trouble with the law, and becomes a fugitive.

***Youth in Revolt: The Journals of Nick Twisp.* Aviva, 1993. Reissued by Broadway in 1996. ISBN 0385481969. [Male] MS/JH**

Nick Twisp wants to win the love of Sheeni Saunders and lose his virginity with her. But Nick gets caught up in unexpected comic adventures, including faking his best friend's suicide and burning down half of Berkeley, and he is forced to enroll in high school in disguise to avoid being caught by the FBI. After all his hilarious adventures, will Nick get another chance with Sheeni?

Keywords: adventure, diaries, first love

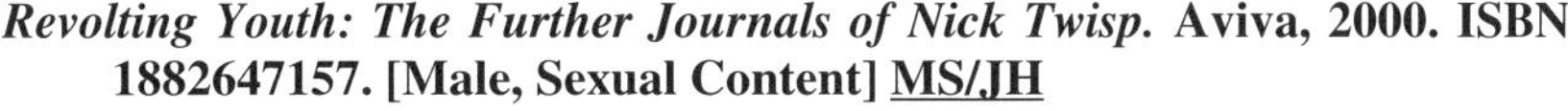

***Revolting Youth: The Further Journals of Nick Twisp.* Aviva, 2000. ISBN 1882647157. [Male, Sexual Content] MS/JH**

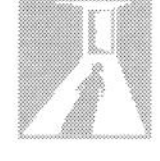

Nick Twisp is still hiding from his parents and the FBI, but thanks to his invention, the "Wart Watch," Nick is independently wealthy. Nick disguises himself as a woman, but his girlfriend Sheeni knows his true identity, and she visits him often. When the FBI finds Nick, he is on the run again.

Keywords: adventure, dating, diaries, first love

Rennison, Louise

The Confessions of Georgia Nicolson.

Georgia Nicolson, a fourteen-year-old British girl, has an annoying little sister, embarrassing parents, and a cat that terrorizes the neighborhood. Georgia and her friends spend their time worrying about boys and dating.

Angus, Thongs and Full Frontal Snogging: Confessions of Georgia Nicolson. **HarperCollins, 2000. ISBN 0060288140. [Reluctant Readers] MS/JH**

Georgia and her friends spend most of their time worrying about dating, boyfriends, and how to kiss properly. Before Georgia realizes it, she has a boyfriend, but it is not Sex God Robbie Jennings. Will Robbie ever notice her? An ALA Best Book for Young Adults, a 2001 Michael L. Printz Honor Book, and an ALA Popular Paperback for Young Adults.

Keywords: crushes, dating, diaries, kissing

On the Bright Side, I'm Now the Girlfriend of a Sex God: Further Confessions of Georgia Nicolson. **HarperCollins, 2001. ISBN 0060288132. [Reluctant Readers] MS/JH**

Georgia Nicolson is heartbroken at the thought of traveling with her family to New Zealand for the summer because Robbie Jennings (a.k.a. the Sex God) kissed her. When the family trip is canceled, Georgia and Robbie begin dating, but he breaks up with her because he is concerned about their age difference. Georgia spends the rest of the summer scheming to get him back, with hilarious results.

Keywords: crushes, dating, diaries, kissing

Knocked Out by My Nunga-Nungas: Further, Further Confessions of Georgia Nicolson. **HarperCollins, 2002. ISBN 0066236568. [Reluctant Readers] MS/JH**

Georgia Nicolson is finally dating Sex God Robbie Jennings. But when Robbie doesn't pay her enough attention one evening, Georgia's thoughts begin to travel to Dave the Laugh and her handsome French teacher Henri. Have Georgia's hormones gone crazy?

Keywords: crushes, dating, diaries

Dancing in My Nuddy-Pants: Even Further Confessions of Georgia Nicolson. **HarperCollins, 2003. ISBN 0060097477. [Reluctant Readers] MS/JH**

Georgia Nicolson wonders which boy is right for her, Sex God Robbie Jennings or Dave the Laugh.

Keywords: dating, diaries

Away Laughing on a Fast Camel. **HarperCollins, 2004. ISBN 0060599731. [Reluctant Readers] MS/JH**

Robbie the Sex God has gone to New Zealand, leaving Georgia without a boyfriend. Then Georgia meets Massimo, the new lead singer for the Stiff Dylans, and it's love at first sight. But Massimo does not feel the same about Georgia!

Keywords: dating, friendship

Scott, Kieran

Jingle Boy. **Delacorte Press, 2003. ISBN 0385731132. [Male] MS/JH**

Sixteen-year-old Paul Nicholas loves Christmas, and he has an enormous crush on Sarah, another Christmas nut. Suddenly everything goes wrong—Paul sees Sarah kissing Santa Claus at the mall, Christmas lights set the Nicholas family home on fire, and Paul's mother is fired from her job. Paul is ready to give up his hopes for a Christmas romance with Sarah and a happy Christmas with his family.

Keywords: Christmas, crushes, family, vacations

Soto, Gary

Nerdlandia: A Play. **Penguin Putnam, 1999. ISBN 0698117840. JH**

Martin, a Chicano nerd, tries to be like the homeboys with greased hair and tattoos to win his true love Ceci. Meanwhile, Ceci dumps her two-timing boyfriend and tries to become nerdy so Martin will like her. A slapstick Chicano version of the popular musical play and movie *Grease*.

Keywords: crushes, plays

Spinelli, Jerry

Jason Herkimer Series.

Junior high school student Jason Herkimer tells humorous stories of crushes and first love.

Space Station Seventh Grade. **Little, Brown, 1982. ISBN 0316808040. [Male] MS/JH**

Jason Herkimer humorously recounts his relationships with family, friends, and girls during his year in the seventh grade.

Keywords: crushes, family, school

Jason and Marceline. **Little, Brown, 1986. Reissued by Little, Brown, in 2000. ISBN 0316806625. [Male] MS/JH**

Ninth-grader Jason Herkimer falls in love with his friend Marceline McAllister. Jason and his classmates are obsessed with love, kissing, and sex, and Jason wants to do more than just kiss Marceline. But Marceline rejects him, and Jason must find a way to win back Marceline's love.

Keywords: dating, first love

Stine, R. L.

How I Broke Up with Ernie. **Archway, 1990. ISBN 0671694960. MS/JH**

Horror king R. L. Stine provides readers with a humorous look at teen romance. No matter how hard Amy tries to break up with Ernie, he does not get the message. He begins going along on her dates with her new boyfriend Colin. Will Ernie ever understand that Amy does not want to go out with him?

Keywords: dating, friendship

Phone Calls. **Pocket Books, 1990. ISBN 0671694979. [Reluctant Readers] MS/JH**

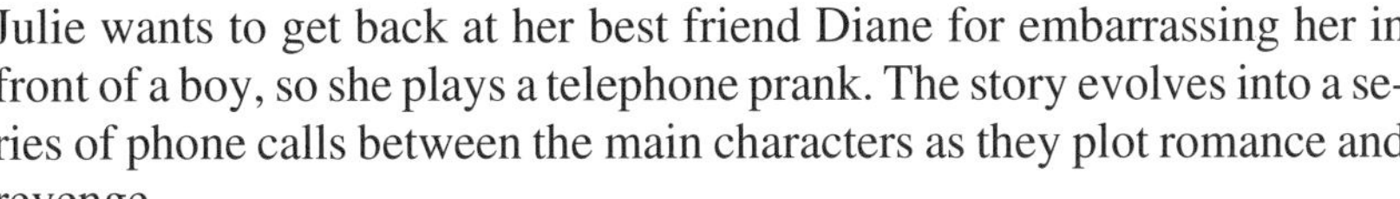

Julie wants to get back at her best friend Diane for embarrassing her in front of a boy, so she plays a telephone prank. The story evolves into a series of phone calls between the main characters as they plot romance and revenge.

Keywords: crushes, dating, revenge

Strasser, Todd

Time Zone High Series.

A series of interconnected romantic stories featuring students from Time Zone High.

How I Changed My Life. **Simon & Schuster, 1995. ISBN 0671884158. [Reluctant Readers] MS/JH**

Bolita Vine, called Bo, is overweight and introverted. Bo's social life consists of working as the stage manager of the school play. When Time Zone High football star Kyle Winthrop is injured, he takes a part in the school play opposite his girlfriend Chloe. Bo gives herself a makeover in order to win Kyle's love. Can Bo compete with Chloe for Kyle's affections?

Keywords: crushes, theater

How I Created My Perfect Prom Date. **Pocket Books, 1998. ISBN 0689820747. [Reluctant Readers] MS/JH**

Nicole, a senior at Time Zone High, is heartbroken when Brad asks someone else to the prom. In desperation, Nicole turns her friend Chase into the perfect prom date. When Chase becomes part of the popular clique, hilarious events threaten to change Nicole's prom plans, and she wonders if she will lose the perfect prom date and potential boyfriend. Originally published under the title *Girl Gives Birth to Own Prom Date* in 1996. Also a major motion picture called *Drive Me Crazy.*

Keywords: dances, dating, friendship

How I Spent My Last Night on Earth. **Simon & Schuster, 1998. ISBN 0689811136. [Reluctant Readers] MS/JH**

Allegra "Legs" Hanover learns of an Internet rumor indicating the earth will be destroyed the next day when it is hit by a giant asteroid called "Eros." Intellectual Legs realizes she has spent all her time worrying about her future, and she has never experienced true love, despite her crush on surfer Andros Bliss. While Legs, her friends, and the student body of Time Zone High spend the night at the beach waiting for the world to end, Andros finally notices Legs. With the world about to end, will Legs have the courage to follow her heart?

Keywords: crushes, Internet

Williams, Carol Lynch

My Angelica. **Delacorte Press, 1999. ISBN 038532622X. JH/HS**

High school sophomore Sage Oliver is writing a romance novel about a sexy and adventurous heroine named Angelica. Her best friend George Blandford, who is secretly in love with Sage, does not have the heart to tell Sage her story is terrible. Sage enters her story in the school's creative writing contest, and she ties George, a poet, for first place. But the judges think her funny story is a parody of a romance novel, and Sage is disappointed in her win.

Keywords: first love, friendship

Zindel, Paul

David and Della. **HarperCollins, 1993. Reissued by Bantam Books in 1995. ISBN 0553567276. JH/HS**

Sixteen-year-old David Mahooley, a teen playwright with a bad case of writer's block, hires teen writing coach and actress Della Jones to help him. In the process of writing a play about Della's tragic love affair with her ex-boyfriend, David falls in love with the hilarious and eccentric Della. Is Della too jaded to give David a chance?

Keywords: crushes, dating

Multicultural Romance

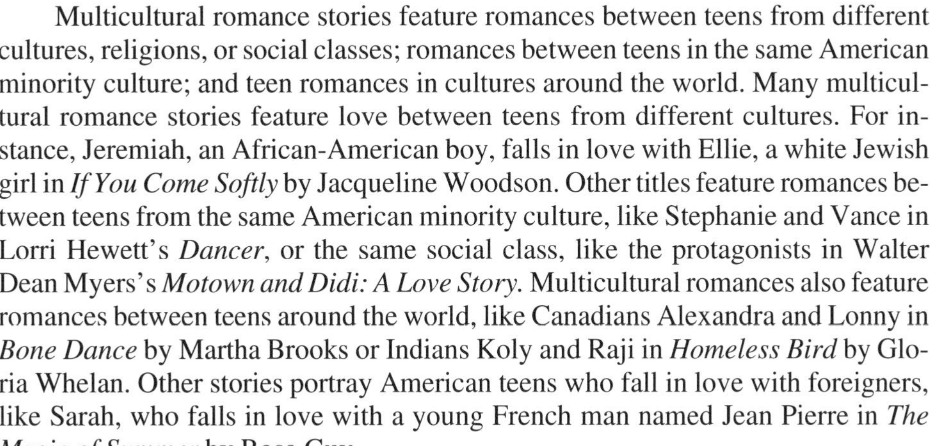

Multicultural romance stories feature romances between teens from different cultures, religions, or social classes; romances between teens in the same American minority culture; and teen romances in cultures around the world. Many multicultural romance stories feature love between teens from different cultures. For instance, Jeremiah, an African-American boy, falls in love with Ellie, a white Jewish girl in *If You Come Softly* by Jacqueline Woodson. Other titles feature romances between teens from the same American minority culture, like Stephanie and Vance in Lorri Hewett's *Dancer*, or the same social class, like the protagonists in Walter Dean Myers's *Motown and Didi: A Love Story.* Multicultural romances also feature romances between teens around the world, like Canadians Alexandra and Lonny in *Bone Dance* by Martha Brooks or Indians Koly and Raji in *Homeless Bird* by Gloria Whelan. Other stories portray American teens who fall in love with foreigners, like Sarah, who falls in love with a young French man named Jean Pierre in *The Music of Summer* by Rosa Guy.

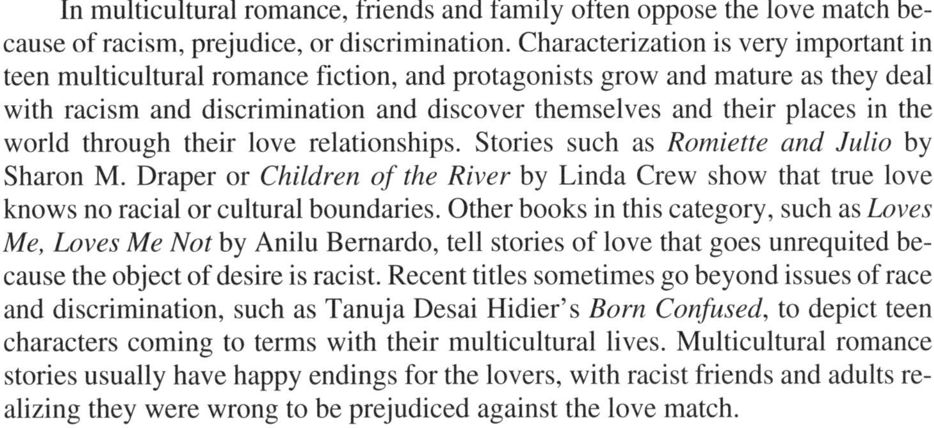

In multicultural romance, friends and family often oppose the love match because of racism, prejudice, or discrimination. Characterization is very important in teen multicultural romance fiction, and protagonists grow and mature as they deal with racism and discrimination and discover themselves and their places in the world through their love relationships. Stories such as *Romiette and Julio* by Sharon M. Draper or *Children of the River* by Linda Crew show that true love knows no racial or cultural boundaries. Other books in this category, such as *Loves Me, Loves Me Not* by Anilu Bernardo, tell stories of love that goes unrequited because the object of desire is racist. Recent titles sometimes go beyond issues of race and discrimination, such as Tanuja Desai Hidier's *Born Confused*, to depict teen characters coming to terms with their multicultural lives. Multicultural romance stories usually have happy endings for the lovers, with racist friends and adults realizing they were wrong to be prejudiced against the love match.

Balgassi, Haemi

Tae's Sonata. **Houghton Mifflin, 1997. ISBN 0395843146. MS/JH**

Eighth-grader Korean-American teen Tae Kim is assigned to work on a school project with popular Josh Morgan, and before long, Tae is in love with Josh.

Keywords: crushes, first love, friendship, Korean Americans

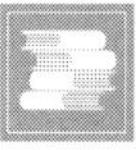

Bernardo, Anilu

***Loves Me, Loves Me Not.* Arte Publico, 1998. ISBN 155885259X. MS/JH**

Fifteen-year-old Cuban-American Maggie Castillo has a crush on handsome basketball player Zach. Maggie is excited when she learns Zach is the grandson of Mrs. Maxwell, the woman she helps out after school. But then Maggie discovers Zach is prejudiced against Latinos. Meanwhile, the new boy at school, Justin, has a crush on Maggie. An ALA Popular Paperback for Young Adults.

Keywords: crushes, Cuban Americans, dating, prejudice, racism

Brooks, Martha

***Bone Dance.* Orchard, 1997. ISBN 0531300218. JH/HS**

Seventeen-year-old Alexandra Sinclair inherits land and a cabin on the Canadian prairie from a father she never knew. When Alexandra visits her inheritance, she meets Lonny LaFreinere, a boy whose family used to own the land she has inherited. Together, Alexandra and Lonny learn about their Native Canadian heritage, grieve for their lost parents, and heal their loneliness with love. An ALA Popular Paperback for Young Adults and winner of the 1998 Young Adult Canadian Book Award.

Keywords: Canada, death, first love, grief, Native Canadians

Crew, Linda

***Children of the River.* Delacorte Press, 1989. Reissued by Laurel Leaf in 1991. ISBN 0440210224. JH/HS**

High school junior Sundara Sovann, a Cambodian refugee, is growing up in Oregon with her aunt and uncle. Sundara's family wants her to concentrate on her studies. After all, Cambodian girls do not date—they wait for arranged marriages to Cambodian boys. While Sundara struggles to balance her family's Cambodian customs with American traditions, she falls in love with popular football player Jonathan. An ALA Best Book for Young Adults and a 1987 Delacorte Press Contest Honor Book.

Keywords: Cambodia, Cambodian Americans, dating, first love

Draper, Sharon M.

***Romiette and Julio.* Simon & Schuster, 1999. ISBN 0689821808. [Reluctant Readers] MS/JH**

Sixteen-year-olds Romiette Capelle and Julio Montague meet on the Internet, and when they realize they attend the same high school, Romi and Julio meet in person and fall in love. But a local gang, the Devildogs, tries to keep Romi away from Julio because she is African American and he is Hispanic. When the couple ignores the gang's warnings, their lives become endangered.

Keywords: African Americans, crime, dating, Hispanics, Internet, racism

Ganesan, Indira

***Inheritance.* Alfred A. Knopf, 1998. ISBN 0679434429. JH/HS**

Fifteen-year-old Sonil, raised by her aunts in India, visits her mother and grandmother on an island off the coast of India. Although Sonil longs to know why her mother sent her away and who her American father is, her mother refuses to speak to her about it. Sonil gains some understanding of her mother when she, too, falls in love with an American man.

Keywords: dating, family, first love, India

Guy, Rosa

***The Music of Summer.* Delacorte Press, 1992. ISBN 0385305990. [Sexual Content] JH/HS**

Sarah, a student at Juilliard, joins her friend Cathy and her family in Cape Cod for a summer vacation. Cathy shuns Sarah in favor of her lighter-skinned friends, and Sarah is ostracized and bullied by Cathy and her friends. Madame Armand and her son join the house party, and Sarah becomes romantically and sexually involved with Jean Pierre. When the summer ends, Sarah has two choices, return to her musical studies at Juilliard or marry Jean Pierre. An ALA Best Book for Young Adults.

Keywords: African Americans, dating, vacations

Hamilton, Virginia

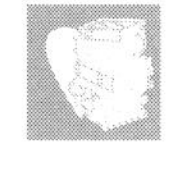
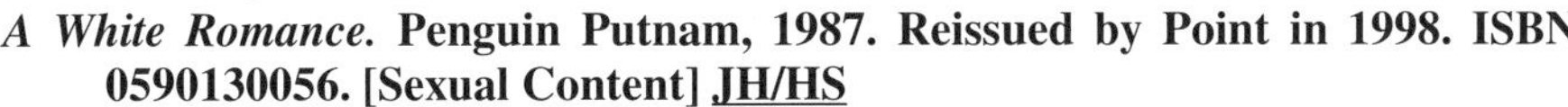

***A White Romance.* Penguin Putnam, 1987. Reissued by Point in 1998. ISBN 0590130056. [Sexual Content] JH/HS**

When Talley Barbour's inner-city high school becomes racially diverse, she struggles with racial prejudice, since her new best friend Didi and her new boyfriend David are both white. Didi and David show Talley a world of sex, drugs, and violence.

Keywords: African Americans, dating, drugs, friendship, racism, violence

Hewett, Lorri

***Dancer.* Penguin Putnam, 1999. ISBN 0525459685. JH/HS**

African-American ballet dancer Stephanie loses her self-confidence when she fails to win the lead role in the class performance of *Sleeping Beauty.* Stephanie regains her self-esteem with the help of her new dance teacher Winnie and her teacher's handsome nephew Vance, and Stephanie and Vance fall in love.

Keywords: African Americans, dating, first love, sports

Hidier, Tanuja Desai

***Born Confused.* Scholastic, 2002. ISBN 0439357624. JH/HS**

Seventeen-year-old Dimple Lala, photographer and daughter of Indian parents, secretly desires to be like her best friend, the beautiful and dynamic Gwyn. When Dimple's parents introduce her to a suitable young man, Karsh Kapoor, she immediately dislikes him. But when Dimple meets Karsh again in a club, sparks fly between them, and she is heartbroken when Gwyn begins dating her true love. An ALA Best Book for Young Adults.

Keywords: dating, family, first love, friendship, Indian Americans, photography

Lee, Marie G.

***Finding My Voice.* Houghton Mifflin, 1992. Reissued by HarperCollins in 2001. ISBN 0064472450. JH/HS**

Korean-American high school senior Ellen Sung, who spends all her time studying, doesn't have time for a boyfriend. But Ellen begins dating Tomper Sandel, and they fall in love. When racist taunts from other students begin to affect their relationship, Tomper pulls away from Ellen. Can Ellen and Tomper learn to deal with racism?

Keywords: dating, family, first love, Korean Americans, racism

Levoy, Myron

***Kelly 'N Me.* HarperCollins, 1992. ISBN 0060208384. JH/HS**

Fifteen-year-old Anthony Milano plays guitar in Central Park to help his mother pay the bills. In the park, Anthony meets Kelly Callahan, and they become a musical team. But Kelly is keeping a secret from Anthony.

Keywords: dating, first love, friendship, social class

Myers, Walter Dean

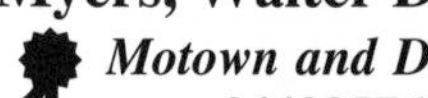

***Motown and Didi: A Love Story.* Viking, 1984. Reissued by Laurel Leaf in 1987. ISBN 0440957621. JH/HS**

Didi and Motown meet in Harlem, where they both dream of escape. Didi dreams of college, while Motown dreams of a steady job. They fall in love, making life in Harlem bearable, but can this love last? Winner of the 1994 Margaret A. Edwards Award.

Keywords: dating, poverty, social class

Namioka, Lensey

***Yang the Second and Her Secret Admirers.* Little, Brown, ISBN 0316597317. MS/JH**

Fifteen-year-old Chinese-American Yinglan Yang tries to resist assimilation into American culture, but her sister Yingtao and friend Kim decide to set her up with baseball player Paul Eng. The story turns into a romantic comedy of errors when Kim's brother Jason believes Yinglan has a crush on him. A companion to Namioka's titles *Yang the Youngest and His Terrible Ear* and *Yang the Third and Her Impossible Family.*

Keywords: Chinese Americans, crushes, dating

Qualey, Marsha

***Revolutions of the Heart.* Houghton Mifflin, 1993. ISBN 0395641683. JH/HS**

After her mother dies, seventeen-year-old Cory falls in love with Mac, a Native American boy. Their Wisconsin town struggles with racism in a disagreement about Native American fishing rights, and Cory is caught between Mac and her family.

Keywords: dating, family, first love, Native Americans, racism

Randle, Kristen D.

Breaking Rank. **William Morrow, 1999. ISBN 0688162436. JH/HS**

When seventeen-year-old Casey Willardson is asked to tutor Thomas "Baby" Fairbairn, a member of a reclusive gang unsupportive of traditional education called the Clan, she reluctantly agrees. Despite the fears of Clan members and Casey's family, Casey and Baby work well together. Soon the sparks are flying, and Casey and Baby are more than friends. Will their peers allow them to be together?

Keywords: dating, education, social class

Reynolds, Marilyn

Love Rules. **Morning Glory Press, 2001. ISBN 1885356765. JH/HS**

High school senior Lynn Wright begins dating Conan, an African-American football star, but Conan is afraid to tell his parents he is dating a white girl. Lynn helps her best friend Kit Dandridge, who has just revealed she is a lesbian, come out to her family and friends. Can Lynn and Kit help their families and friends overcome prejudice? A title in the True-to-Life Series from Hamilton High.

Keywords: dating, friendship, homosexuality, prejudice

Sweeney, Joyce

The Spirit Window. **Delacorte Press, 1998. ISBN 038532510X. JH/HS**

When fifteen-year-old Miranda's family travels to Florida to visit her grandmother, she does not expect to fall in love. But Miranda does fall in love—with Adam, her grandmother's half-Cherokee gardener. Conflict ensues when Miranda's father disapproves of the relationship, and further problems arise when Miranda's grandmother dies unexpectedly. An ALA Best Book for Young Adults.

Keywords: dating, death, family, first love, Native Americans, racism

Velasquez, Gloria

Ankiza. **Pinata, 2001. ISBN 155885309X. JH**

When high school students Ankiza and Hunter begin dating, their friends, classmates, and families do not approve because Ankiza is black and Hunter is white. Will Ankiza's friends and family support her when she receives anonymous hate mail? (*Note:* A book in The Roosevelt High School Series, this is the only title that focuses on multicultural romance.)

Keywords: African Americans, dating, family, prejudice, racism

Whelan, Gloria

Homeless Bird. **HarperCollins, 2000. ISBN 0064408191. JH/HS**

Koly, an Indian girl, marries a young, sickly man when she is just thirteen. When Koly's husband dies, her mother-in-law abandons her in the city. As Koly makes a life for herself, she hopes she has found true love

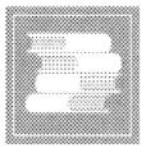

with Raji, a young rickshaw driver who wants to marry her. Includes a glossary of Hindi terms. Winner of the 2000 National Book Award.

Keywords: dating, family, India, marriage

Woodson, Jacqueline

***If You Come Softly*. Putnam, 1998. ISBN 0399231129. JH/HS**

High school students Jeremiah, an African-American boy, and Ellie, a white Jewish girl, meet and fall in love at a Manhattan prep school. Narrated by Jeremiah and Ellie in alternating chapters, the book tells their story of the prejudice they experience as a result of their love. An ALA Best Book for Young Adults.

Keywords: dating, death, first love, prejudice, racism, religion

Chapter 4

Contemporary Romance Series

Contemporary young adult romance series are light, innocent stories about dating, friendship, and first love. Affections are usually limited to hand-holding and kissing, since these series are written for younger teen readers in middle school and junior high school. Contemporary romance series generally fall into one of two categories—"Contemporary Soap Opera Romance Series" or "Contemporary Category Romance Series." "Contemporary Soap Opera Romance Series," such as Sweet Valley High or Making Out, feature the same characters, continuing story lines, and familiar settings. Although the books in the series usually appear to be written by one author, they are often written anonymously by different authors who are essentially hired ghost writers. For instance, the Sweet Valley High series was created by Francine Pascal and written by Kate William. Kate William is a pseudonym for various authors hired to write the series, including women's fiction author Eileen Goudge, who wrote five of the early titles in the series.

Books in the "Contemporary Category Romance Series," such as Love Stories or Smooch, are more likely written by the authors whose names are listed on the book covers. "Contemporary Category Romance Series" titles feature new characters and stories under a series name and logo. They are characterized by the familiar formulaic plot where girl meets boy, girl loses boy, girl gets boy back. Unlike the "Issues Romance" novels included in Chapter 5, happy endings are usually required. "Graphic Novel Romance Series" are also included in this chapter.

Additional romance series titles appear in "Historical Romance" (Chapter 8), "Christian Romance" (Chapter 9), and "Alternative Reality Romance" (Chapter 6).

Appeal

Contemporary romance series feature mostly female protagonists, so romance series will appeal to teen girls. Books in these series are quick, easy reads, and therefore, they are good suggestions for reluctant readers. More advanced teen readers will enjoy reading romance series simply for their entertainment value. Romance series are meant to entertain, not teach life lessons. Contemporary romance series readers know they will get familiar plots, characters, and settings from their favorite series. Teen readers enjoy the sense of continuity they know they will get from series romances. Those readers who find a series they like are usually hooked.

Series romance novels are published in paperback, making them inexpensive to buy, but they may not last long. While paperback romances are cheap enough for teens to buy themselves, some teens will look for these books in your library, so you will have to buy some of the more popular romance series. (*Note:* See Appendix A for the essential romance series.) You may need to replace the more popular titles as they become tattered. Paperback romances are popular because they are smaller than hardcover or trade paperback books, and they can be carried to school or the beach in a purse or backpack. You might want to consider binding the paperback romance series to help them last longer.

Advising the Reader

Following are a few tips to think about when advising readers of contemporary young adult romance series fiction:

- Find out whether your patron wants to read a book from a soap opera or a category romance series. This should be pretty easy, as the reader will likely ask for a title from a specific series by series name, such as Mary-Kate and Ashley Sweet 16. It's important to understand the difference between soap opera or category romance series, however, because if you don't have the book your reader wants, you can suggest another similar series the teen may not know.
- If you don't have the series your teen reader wants, suggest a single title with similar themes. Because contemporary romance series are light and innocent stories of first love, you can suggest books found in Chapter 3, which lists books focusing on lighter stories of first love and humorous romance.
- Become familiar with the romance series included in the "Historical Romance," "Christian Romance," and "Alternative Reality Romance" chapters of this book, since your patrons will ask for these series, too. If a patron is disappointed that you don't have the next book in the series he or she wants, you may be able to interest the reader in a series from another romance subgenre, such as the historical Avon True Romance series.
- If you invest in a young adult romance series for your library, make sure your library purchases all books in the series. Readers will expect to find the complete run of a series on your shelves. Your customers will be disappointed if you don't have the whole series, and they may not return.

Contemporary Soap Opera Romance Series

"Contemporary Soap Opera Romance Series" feature the same characters and continuing stories of love and friendship, often in a high school setting. The Sweet Valley High series, which began publishing in 1983, was the first "Contemporary Soap Opera Romance Series." Many other series have been modeled on it. Teen readers enjoy the continuity of reading about the same characters as they experience different challenges. A group of characters functions somewhat like a social group, and the reader becomes a part of this social group. Twins are a common theme, featured first in the various Sweet Valley series and, more recently, the books featuring film and television characters portrayed by Mary-Kate and Ashley Olsen.

It is important to many readers that they read these titles in order, and often they will request a number in the series, rather than a title. Thus, the numbers are listed here.

Elizabeth. Bantam Books, 2001. JH/HS

Created by Francine Pascal; Written by Laurie John (Pseudonym for Various Authors).

Introduced in January 2001, this romance series features the adventures of college student Elizabeth Wakefield, a main character from the Sweet Valley University series. Elizabeth leaves Sweet Valley for England after a fight with her twin sister Jessica, where she falls in love with Max, the son of an earl.

Keywords: dating, friendship, sisters, twins

1. *University, Interrupted*
2. *London Calling*
3. *Royal Pain*
4. *Downstairs, Upstairs*
5. *Max's Choice*
6. *I Need You*

Heart Beats. Simon & Schuster, 1998 to 1999. JH/HS

Written by Elizabeth M. Rees.

The students of Dance Tech, a ballet and ballroom dancing school, include Carlos, Sophy, and Roxanna, a multicultural cast of characters. Romance develops between Carlos and Sophy, and jealous Roxanna frequently plots revenge against Sophy.

Keywords: dancing, dating, friendship, sports

1. *Moving as One*
2. *Body Lines*
3. *In the Spotlight*
4. *Latin Nights*
5. *Face the Music*
6. *Last Dance*

Luna Bay. Harper Entertainment, 2003 to Present. MS/JH
Written by Fran Lantz.

Best friends Luna, Rae, Kanani, Isobel, and Cricket are surfers. While competing in exotic locations like California, Florida, and Hawaii, the girls encounter adventure and romance.

Keywords: dating, family, first love, friendship, sports

1. *Pier Pressure*
2. *Wave Good-Bye*
3. *Weather or Not*
4. *Oh Buoy!*
5. *Hawaii Five Go!*
6. *Heart Breakers*
7. *Board Games*
8. *Sea for Yourself*
9. *Current Affairs*

Making Out. Avon Books, 1998 to 2000. JH/HS
Written by Katherine Applegate.

From the author of the popular Animorphs series, Making Out was originally published by Harper Paperbacks as the Boyfriends, Girlfriends series. The series focuses on a group of friends, including Zoey, Jake, Nina, Claire, Lucas, and Benjamin, growing up and falling in love on an island off the coast of Maine.

Keywords: dating, friendship

1. *Zoey Fools Around*
2. *Jake Finds Out*
3. *Nina Won't Tell*
4. *Ben's in Love*
5. *Claire Gets Caught*
6. *What Zoey Saw*
7. *Lucas Gets Hurt*
8. *Aisha Goes Wild*
9. *Zoey Plays Games*
10. *Nina Shapes Up*
11. *Ben Takes a Chance*
12. *Claire Can't Lose*
13. *Don't Tell Zoey*
14. *Aaron Lets Go*
15. *Who Loves Kate?*
16. *Lara Gets Even*
17. *Two-Timing Aisha*

18. *Zoey Speaks Out*
19. *Kate Finds Love*
20. *Never Trust Lara*
21. *Trouble with Aaron*
22. *Always Loving Zoey*
23. *Lara Gets Lucky*
24. *Now Zoey's Alone*
25. *Don't Forget Lara*
26. *Zoey's Broken Heart*
27. *Falling for Claire*
28. *Zoey Comes Home*

Making Waves. 17th Street Press, 2001 to 2002. JH/HS
Written by Katherine Applegate.

Kate and Chelsea are high school graduates sharing a beach house with some new friends, while their former boyfriends reappear on the scene. Originally published by HarperCollins in 1993 as the Ocean City series.

Keywords: dating, friendship

1. *Making Waves*
2. *Tease*
3. *Sweet*
4. *Thrill*
5. *Heat*
6. *Secret*
7. *Attitude*
8. *Burn*
9. *Wild*
10. *Chill*
11. *Last Splash*

Mary-Kate and Ashley Sweet 16. Harper Entertainment, 2002 to the Present. MS/JH
Written by Various Authors.

Sixteen-year-old twins Mary-Kate and Ashley have a fabulous summer full of new friends and new boyfriends. When it's time to return to Bayside High in the fall, Mary-Kate, Ashley, and friends continue their adventures and romances.

Keywords: friendship, dating, sisters, twins

1. *Never Been Kissed*
2. *Wishes and Dreams*
3. *The Perfect Summer*

4. *Getting There*
5. *Starring You and Me*
6. *My Best Friend's Boyfriend*
7. *Playing Games*
8. *Truth or Dare*
9. *All That Glitters*
10. *Keeping Secrets*
11. *Little White Lies*
12. *Dream Holiday*
13. *Love and Kisses*
14. *Spring Into Style*
15. *California Dreams*

One Last Wish. Bantam Books, 1992 to 1998. MS/JH/HS
Written by Lurlene McDaniel.

Lurlene McDaniel presents a series of stories about young people coping with illness and death. The stories are connected through gifts to the protagonists from the One Last Wish Foundation, and several of the books in the series follow the same characters. As in McDaniel's other books, many of the stories in the series feature themes of love and romance.

Keywords: dating, death, friendship, illness

1. *A Time to Die*
2. *Mourning Song*
3. *Mother, Help Me Live*
4. *Someone Dies, Someone Lives*
5. *Sixteen and Dying*
6. *Let Him Live*
7. *The Legacy: Making Wishes Come True*
8. *Please Don't Die*
9. *She Died Too Young*
10. *All the Days of Her Life*
11. *A Season for Goodbye*
12. *Reach for Tomorrow*

Pine Hollow. Bantam Books, 1998 to 2001. MS/JH
Written by Bonnie Bryant.

The characters from Bonnie Bryant's Saddle Club series, Carole Hanson, Lisa Atwood, and Stevie Lake, start high school. The series focuses on friendship, first love, and horseback riding.

Keywords: animals, dating, first love, friendship, sports

1. *The Long Ride*
2. *The Trail Home*
3. *Reining In*
4. *Changing Leads*
5. *Conformation Faults*
6. *Shying at Trouble*
7. *Penalty Points*
8. *Course of Action*
9. *Riding to Win*
10. *Ground Training*
11. *Cross-Ties*
12. *Back in the Saddle*
13. *High Stakes*
14. *Headstrong*
15. *Setting the Pace*
16. *Track Record*
17. *Full Gallop*

<u>So Little Time</u>. Harper Entertainment, 2002 to Present. <u>MS</u>
Written by Various Authors.

Twins Chole and Riley Carlson experience the ups and downs of romance at West Malibu High, where Riley is constantly fighting off the love-struck Larry. Based on the television show *So Little Time* starring Mary-Kate and Ashley Olsen.

Keywords: crushes, dating, friendship, sisters, twins

1. *How to Train a Boy*
2. *Instant Boyfriend*
3. *Too Good to Be True*
4. *Just between Us*
5. *Tell Me about It*
6. *Secret Crush*
7. *Girl Talk*
8. *The Love Factor*
9. *Dating Game*
10. *A Girl's Guide to Guys*
11. *Boy Crazy*
12. *Best Friends Forever*
13. *Love Is in the Air*
14. *Spring Breakup*

Sunset Island. Berkley, 1991 to 1997. MS/JH
Written by Cherie Bennett.

Emma, Carrie, and Sam take summer jobs as au pairs on Sunset Island, where they encounter adventure and romance. Two spin-off series, Sunset after Dark and Club Sunset Island, are also listed here.

Keywords: dating, friendship, vacations

1. *Sunset Island*
2. *Sunset Kiss*
3. *Sunset Dreams*
4. *Sunset Farewell*
5. *Sunset Reunion*
6. *Sunset Secrets*
7. *Sunset Heat*
8. *Sunset Promises*
9. *Sunset Scandal*
10. *Sunset Whispers*
11. *Sunset Paradise*
12. *Sunset Surf*
13. *Sunset Deceptions*
14. *Sunset on the Road*
15. *Sunset Embrace*
16. *Sunset Wishes*
17. *Sunset Touch*
18. *Sunset Wedding*
19. *Sunset Glitter*
20. *Sunset Stranger*
21. *Sunset Heart*
22. *Sunset Revenge*
23. *Sunset Sensation*
24. *Sunset Magic*
25. *Sunset Illusions*
26. *Sunset Fire*
27. *Sunset Fantasy*
28. *Sunset Passion*
29. *Sunset Love*
30. *Sunset Fling*
31. *Sunset Tears*
32. *Sunset Spirit*
33. *Sunset Holiday*
34. *Sunset Forever*

Club Sunset Island.

Too Many Boys!

Dixie's First Kiss

Tori's Crush

Sunset after Dark (Darcy Laken Series).

Sunset after Dark

Sunset after Midnight

Sunset after Hours

SVH Senior Year. Bantam Books, 1999 to 2003. MS/JH
Created by Francine Pascal; Written by Various Authors.

Introduced in January 1999, SVH Senior Year recounts the adventures of Jessica and Elizabeth Wakefield as they recover from an earthquake and begin senior year at Sweet Valley High with new classmates. New characters are introduced, plots include heavier topics, and Jessica and Elizabeth appear to have swapped personalities. The series ceased publishing in 2003, ending the Sweet Valley series dynasty after twenty years.

Keywords: dating, friendship, sisters, twins

1. *Can't Stay Away*
2. *Say It to My Face*
3. *So Cool*
4. *I've Got a Secret*
5. *If Only You Knew*
6. *Your Basic Nightmare*
7. *Boy Meets Girl*
8. *Maria Who?*
9. *The One That Got Away*
10. *Broken Angel*
11. *Take Me On*
12. *Bad Girl*
13. *All about Love*
14. *Split Decision*
15. *On My Own*
16. *Three Girls and a Guy*
17. *Backstabber*
18. *As If I Care*
19. *It's My Life*
20. *Nothing Is Forever*
21. *The It Guy*
22. *So Not Me*

23. *Falling Apart*
24. *Never Let Go*
25. *Straight Up*
26. *Too Late*
27. *Playing Dirty*
28. *Meant to Be*
29 *Where We Belong*
30. *Close to You*
31. *Stay or Go*
32. *Road Trip*
33. *Me, Me, Me*
34. *Troublemaker*
35. *Control Freak*
36. *Tearing Me Apart*
37. *Be Mine*
38. *Get a Clue*
39. *Best of Enemies*
40. *Never Give Up*
41. *He's Back*
42. *Touch and Go*
43. *It Takes Two*
44. *Cruise Control*
45. *Tia in the Middle*
46. *Prom Night*
47. *Senior Cut Day*
48. *Sweet 18*

Sweet Valley Jr. High. Bantam Books, 1999 to 2001. MS/JH

Created by Francine Pascal; Written by Jamie Suzanne (Pseudonym for Various Authors).

The Sweet Valley school districts have been rezoned, and eighth-graders Elizabeth and Jessica Wakefield are being moved from Sweet Valley Middle School to Sweet Valley Jr. High School, where they meet new friends and first loves.

Keywords: crushes, first love, friendship, sisters, twins

1. *Get Real*
2. *One 2 Many*
3. *Soulmates*
4. *The Cool Crowd*
5. *Boy. Friend.*
6. *Lacey's Crush*

7. *How to Ruin a Friendship*
8. *Cheating on Anna*
9. *Too Popular*
10. *Twin Switch*
11. *Got a Problem?*
12. *Third Wheel*
13. *Three Days, Two Nights*
14. *My Perfect Guy*
15. *Hands Off!*
16. *Keepin' It Real*
17. *Whatever*
18. *True Blue*
19. *She Loves Me . . . Not*
20. *Wild Child*
21. *I'm So outta Here*
22. *What You Don't Know*
23. *Invisible Me*
24. *Clueless*
25. *Drama Queen*
26. *No More Mr. Nice Guy*
27. *She's Back*
28. *Dance Fever*
29. *He's the One*
30. *Too Many Good-Byes*

Sweet Valley High. Bantam Books, 1983 to 1998. MS/JH/HS
Created by Francine Pascal; Written by Kate William (Pseudonym for Various Authors).

The phenomenally popular Sweet Valley High series introduced teens to soap opera romance in 1983. The series features the lives and loves of identical twins Jessica and Elizabeth Wakefield and their high school friends. This series came to a close in 1998, after 184 titles, several spin-off book series, and a television show. In the *Last Wish, Earthquake,* and *Aftershock* trilogy, the lives of twins Jessica and Elizabeth Wakefield are turned upside down by an earthquake during their seventeenth birthday party, setting the stage for a revamped series called SVH Senior Year. The Sweet Valley High books have been reprinted many times, and they are still available in libraries and the out-of-print-book market. (*Note:* Super Editions, Super Thrillers, Super Stars, and Magna Editions (historical romances about *Sweet Valley* families) are listed at the end of the series, and although there are no numbers attached to these

books, numbers are included here to inform readers of the order in which these books were published.)

Keywords: adventure, dating, friendship, sisters, twins

1. *Double Love*
2. *Secrets*
3. *Playing with Fire*
4. *Power Play*
5. *All Night Long*
6. *Dangerous Love*
7. *Sister Dear*
8. *Heartbreaker*
9. *Racing Hearts*
10. *Wrong Kind of Girl*
11. *Too Good to Be True*
12. *When Love Dies*
13. *Kidnapped*
14. *Deceptions*
15. *Promises*
16. *Rags to Riches*
17. *Love Letters*
18. *Head over Heels*
19. *Showdown*
20. *Crash Landing!*
21. *Runaway*
22. *Too Much in Love*
23. *Say Goodbye*
24. *Memories*
25. *Nowhere to Run*
26. *Hostage*
27. *Lovestruck*
28. *Alone in the Crowd*
29. *Bitter Rivals*
30. *Jealous Lies*
31. *Taking Sides*
32. *The New Jessica*
33. *Starting Over*
34. *Forbidden Love*
35. *Out of Control*

36. *Last Chance*
37. *Rumors*
38. *Leaving Home*
39. *Secret Admirer*
40. *On the Edge*
41. *Outcast*
42. *Caught in the Middle*
43. *Hard Choices*
44. *Pretenses*
45. *Family Secrets*
46. *Decisions*
47. *Troublemaker*
48. *Slam Book Fever*
49. *Playing for Keeps*
50. *Out of Reach*
51. *Against the Odds*
52. *White Lies*
53. *Second Chance*
54. *Two-Boyfriend Weekend*
55. *Perfect Shot*
56. *Lost at Sea*
57. *Teacher Crush*
58. *Brokenhearted*
59. *In Love Again*
60. *That Fatal Night*
61. *Boy Trouble*
62. *Who's Who?*
63. *The New Elizabeth*
64. *The Ghost of Tricia Martin*
65. *Trouble at Home*
66. *Who's to Blame?*
67. *The Parent Plot*
68. *The Love Bet*
69. *Friend against Friend*
70. *Ms. Quarterback*
71. *Starring Jessica!*
72. *Rock Star's Girl*
73. *Regina's Legacy*

74. *The Perfect Girl*
75. *Amy's True Love*
76. *Miss Teen Sweet Valley*
77. *Cheating to Win*
78. *The Dating Game*
79. *The Long-Lost Brother*
80. *The Girl They Both Loved*
81. *Rosa's Lie*
82. *Kidnapped by the Cult!*
83. *Steven's Bride*
84. *The Stolen Diary*
85. *Soap Star*
86. *Jessica against Bruce*
87. *My Best Friend's Boyfriend*
88. *Love Letters for Sale*
89. *Elizabeth Betrayed*
90. *Don't Go Home with John*
91. *In Love with a Prince*
92. *She's Not What She Seems*
93. *Stepsisters*
94. *Are We in Love?*
95. *The Morning After*
96. *The Arrest*
97. *The Verdict*
98. *The Wedding*
99. *Beware the Baby-Sitter*
100. *The Evil Twin* (Magna Edition)
101. *The Boyfriend War*
102. *Almost Married*
103. *Operation Love Match*
104. *Love and Death in London*
105. *A Date with a Werewolf*
106. *Beware the Wolfman* (Super Thriller)
107. *Jessica's Secret Love*
108. *Left at the Altar*
109. *Double-Crossed*
110. *Death Threat*
111. *A Deadly Christmas* (Super Thriller)

112. *Jessica Quits the Squad*
113. *The Pom-Pom Wars*
114. *"V" for Victory*
115. *The Treasure of Death Valley*
116. *Nightmare in Death Valley*
117. *Jessica the Genius*
118. *College Weekend*
119. *Jessica's Older Guy*
120. *In Love with the Enemy*
121. *The High School War*
122. *A Kiss before Dying*
123. *Elizabeth's Rival*
124. *Meet Me at Midnight*
125. *Camp Killer*
126. *Tall, Dark, and Deadly*
127. *Dance of Death*
128. *Kiss of a Killer*
129. *Cover Girls*
130. *Model Flirt*
131. *Fashion Victim*
132. *Once upon a Time*
133. *To Catch a Thief*
134. *Happily Ever After*
135. *Lila's New Flame*
136. *Too Hot to Handle*
137. *Fight Fire with Fire*
138. *What Jessica Wants*
139. *Elizabeth Is Mine*
140. *Please Forgive Me*
141. *A Picture-Perfect Prom?*
142. *The Big Night*
143. *Party Weekend!*

Sweet Valley High: Super Editions

1. *Perfect Summer*
2. *Special Christmas*
3. *Spring Break*
4. *Malibu Summer*
5. *Winter Carnival*

6. *Spring Fever*
7. *Falling for Lucas*
8. *Jessica Takes Manhattan*
9. *Mystery Date*
10. *Last Wish*
11. *Earthquake*
12. *Aftershock*

Sweet Valley High: Super Thrillers

1. *Double Jeopardy*
2. *On the Run*
3. *No Place to Hide*
4. *Deadly Summer*
5. *Murder on the Line*
6. *Beware the Wolfman*
7. *A Deadly Christmas*
8. *Murder in Paradise*
9. *A Stranger in the House*
10. *A Killer on Board*
11. *"R" for Revenge*

Sweet Valley High: Super Stars

1. *Lila's Story*
2. *Bruce's Story*
3. *Enid's Story*
4. *Olivia's Story*
5. *Todd's Story*

Sweet Valley High: Magna Editions

1. *The Wakefields of Sweet Valley*
2. *The Wakefield Legacy: The Untold Story*
3. *A Night to Remember*
4. *The Evil Twin*
5. *Elizabeth's Secret Diary*
6. *Jessica's Secret Diary*
7. *Return of the Evil Twin*
8. *Elizabeth's Secret Diary Volume II*
9. *Jessica's Secret Diary Volume II*

10. *The Fowlers of Sweet Valley*
11. *The Patmans of Sweet Valley*
12. *Elizabeth's Secret Diary Volume III*
13. *Jessica's Secret Diary Volume III*

Sweet Valley University. Bantam Books, 1993 to 2000. [Sexual Content] JH/HS
Created by Francine Pascal; Written by Laurie John (Pseudonym for Various Authors).

In a spin-off from the Sweet Valley High series introduced in 1983, Elizabeth, Jessica, and the gang go off to college, make new friends, and deal with more serious issues.

Keywords: dating, friendship, sisters, twins

1. *College Girls*
2. *Love, Lies, and Jessica Wakefield*
3. *What Your Parents Don't Know*
4. *Anything for Love*
5. *A Married Woman*
6. *The Love of Her Life*
7. *Good-Bye to Love*
8. *Home for Christmas*
9. *Sorority Scandal*
10. *No Means No*
11. *Take Back the Night*
12. *College Cruise*
13. *SS Heartbreak*
14. *Shipboard Wedding*
15. *Behind Closed Doors*
16. *The Other Woman*
17. *Deadly Attraction*
18. *Billie's Secret*
19. *Broken Promises, Shattered Dreams*
20. *Here Comes the Bride*
21. *For the Love of Ryan*
22. *Elizabeth's Summer Love*
23. *Sweet Kiss of Summer*
24. *His Secret Past*
25. *Busted!*
26. *The Trial of Jessica Wakefield*
27. *Elizabeth and Todd Forever*
28. *Elizabeth's Heartbreak*

29. *One Last Kiss*
30. *Beauty and the Beach*
31. *The Truth about Ryan*
32. *The Boys of Summer*
33. *Out of the Picture*
34. *Spy Girl*
35. *Undercover Angels*
36. *Have You Heard about Elizabeth?*
37. *Breaking Away*
38. *Good-Bye, Elizabeth*
39. *Elizabeth Loves New York*
40. *Private Jessica*
41. *Escape to New York*
42. *Sneaking In*
43. *The Price of Love*
44. *Love Me Always*
45. *Don't Let Go*
46. *I'll Never Love Again*
47. *You're Not My Sister*
48. *No Rules*
49. *Stranded*
50. *Summer of Love*
51. *Living Together*
52. *Fooling Around*
53. *Truth or Dare*
54. *Rush Week*
55. *The First Time*
56. *Dropping Out*
57. *Who Knew?*
58. *The Dreaded Ex*
59. *Elizabeth in Love*
60. *Secret Love Diaries: Elizabeth*
61. *Secret Love Diaries: Jessica*
62. *Secret Love Diaries: Sam*
63. *Secret Love Diaries: Chloe*

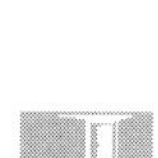

Sweet Valley University Thriller Editions

1. *Wanted for Murder*
2. *He's Watching You*
3. *Kiss of the Vampire*
4. *The House of Death*
5. *Running for Her Life*
6. *The Roommate*
7. *What Winston Saw*
8. *Dead before Dawn*
9. *Killer at Sea*
10. *Channel X*
11. *Love and Murder*
12. *Don't Answer the Phone*
13. *Cyberstalker: The Return of William White, Part I*
14. *Deadly Terror: The Return of William White, Part II*
15. *Loving the Enemy*
16. *Killer Party*
17. *Very Bad Things*
18. *Face It*

Turning Seventeen. HarperTrophy, 2000 to 2001. JH/HS
Written by Various Authors.

Brought to you by the publishers of *Seventeen* magazine, Turning Seventeen features the friendships and romances of seventeen-year-olds Kerri, Jessica, Maya, and Erin.

Keywords: dating, friendship

1. *Any Guy You Want*
2. *More Than This*
3. *For Real*
4. *Show Me Love*
5. *Can't Let Go*
6. *This Boy Is Mine*
7. *Secrets and Lies*
8. *We Have to Talk*
9. *Just Trust Me*
10. *Reality Check*

Two of a Kind. Harper Entertainment, 1999. MS
Written by Various Authors.

Twelve-year-old twins Mary-Kate and Ashley Burke live with their father in Chicago, where college student Carrie becomes their new babysitter. The adventures, including crushes, first dates, and first boyfriends, continue when Mary-Kate and Ashley go to boarding school at White Oak Academy. Based on the television show *Two of a Kind* starring Mary-Kate and Ashley Olsen.

Keywords: dating, friendship, sisters, twins

1. *It's a Twin Thing*
2. *How to Flunk Your First Date*
3. *The Sleepover Secret*
4. *One Twin Too Many*
5. *To Snoop or Not to Snoop?*
6. *My Sister the Supermodel*
7. *Two's a Crowd*
8. *Let's Party*
9. *Calling All Boys*
10. *Winner Take All*
11. *P. S. Wish You Were Here*
12. *The Cool Club*
13. *War of the Wardrobes*
14. *Bye-Bye Boyfriend*
15. *It's Snow Problem*
16. *Likes Me, Likes Me Not*
17. *Shore Thing*
18. *Two for the Road*
19. *Surprise, Surprise!*
20. *Sealed with a Kiss*
21. *Now You See Him, Now You Don't*
22. *April Fools' Rules!*
23. *Island Girls*
24. *Surf, Sand, and Secrets*
25. *Closer Than Ever*
26. *The Perfect Gift*
27. *The Facts about Flirting*
28. *The Dream Date Debate*
29. *Love-Set-Match*
30. *Making a Splash*
31. *Dare to Scare*

32. *Santa Girls*
33. *Heart to Heart*
34. *Prom Princess*
35. *Camp Rock 'n' Roll*
36. *Twist and Shout*

Contemporary Category Romance Series

"Contemporary Category Romance Series," which were extremely popular in the 1980s, feature new characters and new stories under a familiar series name. "Contemporary Category Romance Series" are formulaic in nature, and happy endings are mandatory. The "Contemporary Category Romance Series" has fizzled in popularity, in favor of the "Contemporary Soap Opera Romance Series," but a few contemporary category romances are available. Bantam's popular Love Stories series, which is still available, is included here. A new series, called Smooch, features a mix of contemporary, soap opera, issues, humorous, and paranormal romances, continuing the trend of mixing romance subgenres together.

Love Stories. Bantam Books, 1994 to 2001. MS/JH
Written by Various Authors.

Books in the Love Stories series are innocent stories of first love. Originally published as single titles, the series also included several trilogies and books that tell his *and* her sides of the love stories.

Keywords: dating, first love

1. *My First Love.* Callie West
2. *Sharing Sam.* Katherine Applegate
3. *How to Kiss a Guy.* Elizabeth Bernard
4. *The Boy Next Door.* Janet Quin-Harkin
5. *The Day I Met Him.* Catherine Clark
6. *Love Changes Everything.* Arlynn Presser
7. *More than a Friend.* Elizabeth Winfrey
8. *The Language of Love.* Kate Emburg
9. *My So-Called Boyfriend.* Elizabeth Winfrey
10. *It Had to Be You.* Stephanie Doyon
11. *Some Girls Do.* Dahlia Kosinski
12. *Hot Summer Nights.* Elizabeth Chandler
13. *Who Do You Love?* Janet Quin-Harkin
14. *Three-Guy Weekend.* Alexis Page
15. *Never Tell Ben.* Diane Namm
16. *Together Forever.* Cameron Dokey
17. *Up All Night.* Karen Michaels

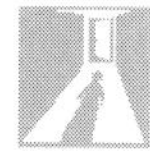

18. *24/7.* Amy S. Wilensky
19. *It's a Prom Thing.* Diane Schwemm
20. *The Guy I Left Behind.* Ali Brooke
21. *He's Not What You Think.* Randi Reisfeld
22. *A Kiss between Friends.* Erin Haft
23. *The Rumor about Julia.* Stephanie Sinclair
24. *Don't Say Good-Bye.* Diane Schwemm
25. *Crushing on You.* Wendy Loggia
26. *Our Secret Love.* Miranda Henry
27. *Trust Me.* Kieran Scott
28. *He's the One.* Nina Alexander
29. *Kiss and Tell.* Kieran Scott
30. *Falling for Ryan.* Julie Taylor
31. *Hard to Resist.* Wendy Loggia
32. *At First Sight.* Elizabeth Chandler
33. *What We Did Last Summer.* Elizabeth Craft
34. *As I Am.* Lynn Mason
35. *I Do.* Elizabeth Chandler
36. *While You Were Gone.* Kieran Scott
37. *Stolen Kisses.* Liesa Abrams
38. *Torn Apart.* Janet Quin-Harkin
39. *Behind His Back.* Diane Schwemm
40. *Playing for Keeps.* Nina Alexander
41. *How Do I Tell?* Kieran Scott
42. *His Other Girlfriend.* Liesa Abrams

Love Stories: Super Editions

1. *Listen to My Heart.* Katherine Applegate
2. *Kissing Caroline.* Cheryl Zach
3. *It's Different for Guys.* Stephanie Leighton
4. *My Best Friend's Girlfriend.* Wendy Loggia
5. *Love Happens.* Elizabeth Chandler
6. *Out of My League.* Everett Owens
7. *A Song for Caitlin.* J. E. Bright
8. *The "L" Word.* Lynn Mason
9. *Summer Love.* Wendy Loggia
10. *All That.* Lynn Mason
11. *The Dance.* Craig Hillman, Kieran Scott, and Elizabeth Skurnick
12. *Andy & Andie.* Malle Vallik

13. *Sweet Sixteen.* Allison Raine
14. *Three Princes.* Lynn Mason

Love Stories: Trilogies

1. *Max & Jane.* Elizabeth Craft
2. *Justin & Nicole.* Elizabeth Craft
3. *Jake & Christy.* Elizabeth Craft
4. *Danny.* Zoe Zimmerman
5. *Kevin.* Zoe Zimmerman
6. *Johnny.* Zoe Zimmerman
7. *London: Kit & Robin.* Rachel Hawthorne
8. *Paris: Alex & Dana.* Rachel Hawthorne
9. *Rome: Antonia & Carrie.* Rachel Hawthorne

Love Stories: His. Hers. Theirs.

1. *The Nine-Hour Date.* Emma Henry
2. *Snag Him!* Gretchen Greene
3. *Nick & the Nerd.* Rachel Hawthorne
4. *You're Dating Him?* A. Gersh
5. *The Popular One.* Lizzie Skurnick
6. *The Older Guy.* Rachel Hawthorne

Smooch. Dorchester, 2003 to Present. JH/HS
Written by Various Authors.

Smooch is a new contemporary and paranormal romance series. While the series begins with Katie Maxwell's Emily series, with four books planned, Smooch will also include single titles and other series.

Keywords: dating, friendship, humor

1. *The Year My Life Went Down the Loo.* Katie Maxwell
2. *A Girl, a Guy, and a Ghost.* Sherrie Rose
3. *The Real Deal: Focus on THIS!* Amy Kaye
4. *My Life as a Snowbunny.* Kaz Delaney
5. *They Wear WHAT under Their Kilts?* Katie Maxwell
6. *Putting Guys on the Ledge.* Stephie Davis
7. *You Are SO Cursed!* Naomi Nash
8. *The Real Deal: Unscripted.* Amy Kaye
9. *What's French for "Ew"?* Katie Maxwell

Graphic Novel Romance Series

Contemporary romance series are also available in graphic novel format, with text and illustrations included. The fast pacing and visual format of these series appeal to many teen readers. Since the graphic novels selected for this category were all first published in Japan, they feature Japanese characters and settings, which also fascinate many teens. Japanese comics, known as "manga," are becoming more popular in North America. Many manga feature stories of teen love and romance, such as *Mars* and *Kare Kano*. Ingram's standing order programs now include graphic novel series to help libraries stock popular graphic novels. "Graphic Novel Romance Series" listed here can also been found in the "Teen" sections of bookstores.

Kare Kano: His and Her Circumstances. Tokyopop, 2003 to Present. JH
Written by Masami Tsuda.

While top students Yukino Miyazawa and Soichiro Arima fight for the top seat in the class, they discover they are perfect for each other. Contains thirteen volumes.

Keywords: dating, education, first love, friendship, graphic novels

Marmalade Boy. Tokyopop, 2002 to 2003. JH
Written by Wataru Yoshizumi.

When Miki's parents swap partners with another family, the families decide to live together. Miki's life gets complicated when she falls in love with her new stepbrother Yuu. Contains eight volumes.

Keywords: dating, family, first love, graphic novels, humor

Mars. Tokyopop, 2002 to the Present. JH
Written by Fuyumi Soryo.

Kira, a shy artist, and Rei, a popular street-smart biker, surprise everyone when they begin dating. Although no one expects their love to last, Kira and Rei overcome many obstacles in their relationship. Contains fifteen volumes.

Keywords: dating, family, first love, graphic novels

Peach Girl. Tokyopop, 2001 to 2003. JH
Written by Miwa Ueda.

When Momo and Toji begin dating, Momo's best friend Sae begins scheming to break them up so she can date Toji. Contains eight volumes.

Keywords: dating, first love, graphic novels, humor

Peach Girl: Change of Heart. Tokyopop, 2003 to the Present. JH
Written by Miwa Ueda.

Momo and her new boyfriend Kiley are happy together. But Sae wants to break them up, Ryo wants to date Momo, and Kiley can't forget his ex-girlfriend Misao. Has Momo found true love with Kiley? Contains ten volumes.

Keywords: dating, graphic novels, humor

Video Girl Ai. Viz Communications, 2000 to the Present. [Sexual Content, Male] HS

Written by Masakazu Katsura.

The formerly dateless Yota Moteuchi gets tangled up in romances with Moemi, Nobuko, and video girl Ai, who popped out of Yota's television set. Contains five volumes.

Keywords: dating, friendship, graphic novels

Chapter 5

Issues Romance

Teens are growing up faster in the twenty-first century, and as young people become more sophisticated, the literature produced for them is also maturing. Young adult literature tackles tough issues facing modern teens, including sex, pregnancy, parenting, death, disease, and sexual identity. Young adult literature historian Michael Cart states, "Today's teens are more sophisticated than ever before."[1] In 2002, researchers discovered teens are "having sex at younger and younger ages—nearly 1 in 10 reports losing his or her virginity before the age of 13, a 15 percent increase since 1997, according to the Centers for Disease Control and Prevention."[2] "[M]ore than twice as many females ages 14, 15, and 16 are sexually active now, compared with young women of the same ages just 15 years ago."[3] Teen dating relationships have become more casual, and it is common for teens to hook up with friends to share sexual activities.[4] As younger teens become involved in romantic and sexual relationships, they are confronted with such serious issues as sexually transmitted diseases, pregnancy, adoption, abortion, parenting, sexual orientation, date rape, and physical abuse earlier than teenagers of previous generations.

Although contemporary young adult fiction has always addressed these difficult issues, Michael Cart suggests the contemporary teen problem novel has evolved in response to the experience of today's teens: "What is different . . . is the degree of candor with which these issues are being discussed, plus the editorial latitude being given to the author for expressing ambiguity, for maturely acknowledging that bleakness is no stranger to many teenage lives today, and for sharing the sad truth that not all endings are happy ones."[5] Much of today's realistic teen fiction offers a dark atmosphere and gritty realism. These stories, which reflect the complexities of society faced by teens today, can be disturbing and very emotionally compelling. Happy endings, therefore, are not necessarily the norm in issues romances.

Issues addressed in contemporary young adult romance fiction are no longer limited to crushes and innocent stories of first love and first kisses. Many contemporary young adult romance novels feature teens who are dealing with contemporary social problems related to romantic relationships—sex, pregnancy, abortion, adoption, racial or religious prejudice, incest, rape, crime, sexuality, suicide, illness, or death. In contemporary issues romance, the focus of the story line is a problem central to the lives of the teens in the story. Often the protagonist must learn how to deal with a particular problem in his or her life. Achieving romance, in spite of the problem, becomes one of the major challenges in these novels.

The issues addressed in the following book lists include "Sex"; "Pregnancy and Parenting"; "Date Rape and Physical Abuse"; "Disease, Death, and Grief"; and "Gay, Lesbian, and Bisexual Romance."

Appeal

Issues romances are appealing to teens because readers can learn important information about how to handle particular problems related to love and romance. For instance, teens who are curious about what a first sexual experience might be like can find out in graphic detail from Judy Blume's classic novel *Forever*. Or they might worry about what will happen if they get pregnant, as Emmy did in *Detour for Emmy* by Marilyn Reynolds. A teen might be confused about his or her sexual orientation like the characters in books by Nancy Garden, M. E. Kerr, and Alex Sanchez. A teenage girl might wonder why a boyfriend is physically abusive, as Caitlin wonders in Alex Flinn's *Breathing Underwater*.

By reading contemporary issues romance, young people can explore some of the issues related to problems teens face, and they can learn particular solutions to these problems. Characterization is a very important element in contemporary issues romance fiction. Young adult novels often feature teens who grapple with myriad problems and challenges as they grow up, and these issues are usually related to love, romance, sex, or sexual identity. These problems can also interfere with youths' search for love, romance, sex, or sexual identity. Protagonists in contemporary issues romances learn to deal with problems in their lives, and as a result, they mature or "come of age." Issues romances provide honest and realistic depictions of contemporary life, an approach that appeals to many teens, who often dislike phoniness and dishonest portrayals of teenage life. Because contemporary young adult romance stories address current social issues, young adults are also able to learn about important issues they may encounter in their own lives, while indulging their taste for realistic romance.

Character is an important factor in the appeal of these books. Readers are looking for protagonists with whom they can identify. They want to read about teens like them—in age, attitudes, interests, and other qualities, as well as in the worlds they inhabit. Thus, cover art is crucial. A dated cover can make or break the success of an issues romance novel.

Advising the Reader

Following are a few tips to think about when advising readers of issues romances:

- A patron who is interested in issues romances will usually ask for a book that is similar to another title he or she has already read. For instance, your patron may ask for books like Judy Blume's *Forever,* Alex Flinn's *Breathing Underwater,* Nancy Garden's *Annie on My Mind*, or anything similar to Lurlene McDaniel's books. Try to find out why the reader liked these books. Did he or she learn how to deal with a particular problem by reading how a fictional character solved a problem? If the topical book lists are not enough help, use the keywords at the ends of the entries to help you identify themes and issues covered in the books. Did your customer like the protagonist's spunky personality? Since characterization is an important element of issues romance fiction, character is also important to readers, and they may wish to read about characters with particular qualities or abilities that allow them to deal with the difficult issues they encounter in life. It is important to become familiar with issues romances, so you know what your patrons want when they ask for more books that include particular issues or characterization.

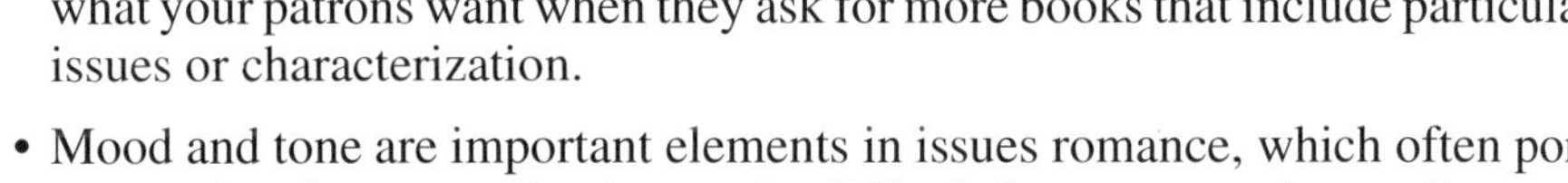

- Mood and tone are important elements in issues romance, which often portray a gritty, honest reality that can be difficult for young readers to discover. Ask whether your customer wants to read a story with a dark and honest take on reality, such as Kate Cann's Love Trilogy, Joanne Horniman's *Mahalia,* or Sarah Dessen's *Dreamland.* If so, issues romances are the right recommendations for this reader. If not, suggest he or she read books in the "Contemporary Romance" book lists found in Chapter 3 or "Contemporary Romance Series" book lists found in Chapter 4. Stories in these book lists offer a lighter, humorous look at life, and these stories are a stark contrast to issues romances.

- Find out if your patron wants to read a romance with a happy ending. If so, you may be better off suggesting he or she read "Contemporary Romance" books from Chapter 3, which are lighter in tone and more likely to have a happy ending.

Sex

Sex is often featured as an important issue in the lives of teens in contemporary romance fiction. Some teen protagonists are trying to decide whether or not to have sex for the first time, like Collette in Kate Cann's Love Trilogy, or they are experiencing sex for the first time with their first love, like Katherine and Michael in *Forever* by Judy Blume. Other characters are waiting until they are older to have sex, like Lauren in *If You Love Me* by Marilyn Reynolds, but the desire to wait for sex causes problems in their love relationships. Even when fictional teen characters are not sexually active, the topic of sex is almost always a part of their lives, directly or indirectly. Jujube Gelb is teased when a boy spreads a false rumor he had sex with her in Beth Goobie's *Sticks and Stones*; Jess's best friend Sari is obsessed with her sexual relationship with an older boy in Mariah Fredericks's *The True Meaning of Cleavage;* and the wealthy teens in the Gossip Girl series are always talking about sex, but they are actually getting very little action.

While sex is an element in much of contemporary young adult romance fiction, the books in this category focus on the tensions caused by sex in love relationships. Surprisingly, there is less emphasis on birth control and protection from sexually transmitted diseases than readers of issues romance might expect, although these issues are included in romances focusing on sex. (For more titles dealing with consequences of sex, see the next book list, "Pregnancy and Parenting.")

Teens find stories about sex appealing because they learn other young adults are struggling with the same very personal issues—whether or not they are ready for sex, the desire to know more about sex, and the wish to wait for sex. By reading issues romances, teens may learn useful information that will help them make decisions about sex that are right for them.

Block, Francesca Lia

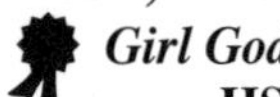 *Girl Goddess #9: Nine Stories.* **HarperCollins, 1998. ISBN 0060272112. [Sexual Content] HS**

A collection of short stories featuring themes of love and sex. An ALA Best Book for Young Adults.

Keywords: short stories

Blume, Judy

 *Forever.* **Bradbury Press, 1975. Reissued by Pocket Books, 1996. ISBN 0671695304. [Sexual Content] JH/HS**

When seniors Katherine and Michael fall in love, Katherine becomes involved in her first sexual relationship. Winner of the 1996 Margaret A. Edwards Award.

Keywords: birth control, dating, first love, sex

Cann, Kate

Love Trilogy.

Sixteen-year-old Colette and her best friend Val learn about the joys and heartaches of first love.

Ready? **HarperCollins, 2001. ISBN 0060289384. JH/HS**

When Colette meets Art at the local swimming pool, she falls in love at first sight. Colette is surprised when Art asks her out, and she is ecstatic when they begin dating. But Colette is a virgin, and Art expects their relationship to become sexual. Can Art wait until Colette is ready for sex?

Keywords: dating, first love, friendship

Sex? **HarperCollins, 2001. ISBN 0060289376. [Sexual Content] JH/HS**

Colette and Art begin dating again. Despite their agreement to take things slowly, their relationship quickly becomes sexual, and this time Colette is ready. In a subplot, Colette's best friend Val gets pregnant, and she must decide what she wants to do about it.

Keywords: abortion, dating, first love, friendship, pregnancy, sex

Go! **HarperCollins, 2001. ISBN 0060289392. [Sexual Content] JH/HS**

Colette is finally getting over her breakup with her first boyfriend Art when he reappears in her life. Although they try to be friends, Colette and Art are still attracted to each other. But Colette is more serious than Art about their relationship. Will Colette and Art have a future as friends or lovers?

Keywords: first love, friendship, sex

Cart, Michael (Editor)

Love and Sex: Ten Stories of Truth. **Simon & Schuster, 2001. ISBN 0689832036. [Sexual Content] JH/HS**

Editor Michael Cart has compiled ten stories about love and sex written by highly acclaimed young adult authors Joan Bauer, Louise Hawes, Garth Nix, Sonya Sones, Laurie Halse Anderson, Chris Lynch, Michael Lowenthal, Shelley Stoehr, Angela Johnson, and Emma Donoghue. Issues encountered in the stories include abstinence, pregnancy, abortion, obsessive teenage love, and confusion about sexual orientation and sexual identity. An ALA Best Book for Young Adults.

Keywords: short stories

Dean, Zoey

The A-List Series.

Anna Cabot Percy moves to Los Angeles, where she alienates A-list teens Cammie, Sam, and Dee by dating sexy college student Ben Birnbaum.

The A-List. **Little, Brown, 2003. ISBN 0316734357. [Reluctant Readers] JH/HS**

When Anna Cabot Percy travels to Los Angeles to visit her father, she meets sexy college student Ben Birnbaum, and they make out on the plane. Anna and Ben spend the next day together, attending a famous actor's wedding and a back-lot party, and Anna thinks she might be falling in love with Ben. Meanwhile, Ben's friends Cammie, Sam, and Dee are jealous because they are all in love with Ben.

Keywords: dating, family, friendship, wealth

Girls on Film. **Little, Brown, 2004. ISBN 0316734756. [Reluctant Readers] JH/HS**

Anna tells Ben to leave her alone, but he pursues her. Meanwhile, Anna wonders about her feelings for Adam. Anna joins her friend Sam for a spa weekend, where she learns Ben's real intentions.

Keywords: dating, family, friendship, wealth

Dessen, Sarah

Someone Like You. **Viking, 1998. ISBN 0670877786. [Sexual Content] JH/HS**

High school juniors Halley and Scarlett are best friends. While Halley is trying to decide whether to sleep with her first boyfriend, Scarlett is dealing with the death of her boyfriend and the discovery that she is pregnant. An ALA Best Book for Young Adults. The movie *How to Deal* is based on Dessen's novels *Someone Like You* and *That Summer.*

Keywords: first love, pregnancy, sex

Frank, Lucy

Will You Be My Brussels Sprout? **Holiday House, 1996. ISBN 0823412202. JH/HS**

Sixteen-year-old cellist Sarah meets David, her friend's brother, on her way to an audition. They begin dating, and soon Sarah and David fall in love. David pressures Sarah to have sex, but she decides she is not ready to have sex yet, and David becomes violent.

Keywords: abstinence, dating, first love, sex

Fredericks, Mariah

***The True Meaning of Cleavage.* Atheneum, 2003. ISBN 0689850921. JH/HS**

When best friends Jess and Sari begin high school, Sari becomes obsessed with senior David, who already has a girlfriend. Nevertheless, Sari becomes involved in a secret sexual affair with David, leaving Jess behind.

Keywords: dating, friendship, sex

Goobie, Beth

***Sticks and Stones.* Orca, 2002. ISBN 1551432137. [Reluctant Readers] MS/JH**

Jujube Gelb is happy to accompany Brent Floyd to the Valentine's dance. But when Jujube doesn't cooperate at the end of the date, Brent retaliates by telling his friends that he had sex with her. Soon everyone is calling Jujube a slut, and Jujube must stand up for herself.

Keywords: bullying, dances, dating

Kimmel, Eric A.

***One Good Tern Deserves Another.* Holiday House, 1994. ISBN 0823411389. [Male] MS/JH**

Fourteen-year-old P. B. Floyd and his mother move to Oregon after his stepfather is killed in the Persian Gulf War. P. B. and his mother spend time bird watching with Lani and her father, and P. B. and Lani fall in love. When the relationship between P. B. and Lani seems to be getting serious, P. B.'s mother explains the difference between having sex and making love, and P. B. and Lani must decide if they are ready for a serious relationship.

Keywords: dating, friendship, sex

Klein, Norma

***Just Friends.* Alfred A. Knopf, 1990. ISBN 0679802134. [Sexual Content] JH/HS**

In Klein's last young adult novel, high school seniors Isabel and Stuart are close friends. But Isabel harbors a secret crush on Stuart, and when her friend Ketti begins a sexual relationship with him, she is devastated. Isabel begins dating Gregory to try to make Stuart jealous, and before long, she is ready to have sex with Gregory. But Isabel knows she will miss Stuart, not Gregory, when she leaves for college.

Keywords: dating, first love, friendship, sex

McCants, William

***Much Ado about Prom Night.* Browndeer, 1995. ISBN 0152000836. [Reluctant Readers] JH/HS**

Peer counselor Becca Singleton has her hands full as her school's junior prom approaches. Everyone is worried about love and relationships! An ALA Best Book and Popular Paperback for Young Adults.

Keywords: abstinence, birth control, dances, dating, sex

Reynolds, Marilyn

If You Loved Me. **Morning Glory Press, 1999. ISBN 1885356552. [Sexual Content] JH/HS**

Seniors Lauren and Tyler are in love, and although Tyler pressures her to have sex, Lauren wants to wait until she is married. When Lauren discovers Tyler is sexually involved with another girl, Tyler explains he had sex with someone else out of respect for Lauren, but Lauren sees it as a betrayal of her love. A title in the True-to-Life Series from Hamilton High.

Keywords: abstinence, first love, friendship, sex

Werlin, Nancy

Are You Alone on Purpose? **Houghton Mifflin, 1994. ISBN 039567350X. [Sexual Content] MS/JH**

Thirteen-year-old Alison Shandling feels neglected by her parents, who center their lives on her autistic brother Adam. Bully Harry Roth is not coping well with his mother's death, and Alison becomes his latest target when her dysfunctional family joins Harry's temple. After Harry is paralyzed in a diving accident, Alison befriends him, and they fall in love.

Keywords: accidents, family, first love, religion

Whichter, Susan

The Fool Reversed. **Farrar, Straus & Giroux, 2000. ISBN 0374324468. [Sexual Content] HS**

When fifteen-year-old Anna Pavelk falls in love with twenty-nine-year-old Thorn, they begin a secret sexual affair. Anna's new friend Dylan, who has a crush on her, disapproves of her relationship with Thorn.

Keywords: crushes, dating, friendship, sex

Von Ziegesar, Cecily

Gossip Girl Series.

The anonymous Gossip Girl recounts teenage life in Upper East Side Manhattan via her Web site at www.gossipgirl.net. All of the stereotypical teen characters are found in this series: ringleader Blair Waldorf, her boyfriend Nate Archibald, and the beautiful girl all the girls envy and all the boys love, Serena van der Woodsen. Artsy misfits Dan Humphrey, his best friend Vanessa, and his naive younger sister Jenny, round out the cast of characters. Readers will be left wondering: Which character is Gossip Girl?

Gossip Girl. **Little, Brown, 2002. ISBN 0316910333. [Sexual Content, Reluctant Readers] JH/HS**

When Serena van der Woodsen returns to New York City from boarding school to complete her senior year, her former best friend Blair Waldorf is not happy. In Serena's absence, Blair has become the social ringleader of Constance Billard School for Girls and girlfriend of Nate Archibald. Serena's arrival interrupts Blair's plans to lose her virginity with Nate, and Blair worries that Nate will leave her for Serena.

Keywords: dating, wealth

You Know You Love Me: A Gossip Girl Novel. **Little, Brown, 2002. ISBN 0316911488. [Reluctant Readers] JH/HS**

Blair Waldorf has two goals: to do well in her Yale interview and to lose her virginity with her boyfriend, Nate. But Blair has been so busy preparing for her Yale interview and her role as maid of honor at her mother's wedding, she hasn't noticed that Nate has secretly been seeing another girl.

Keywords: dating, wealth

All I Want Is Everything: A Gossip Girl Novel. **Little, Brown, 2003. ISBN 0316912123. [Reluctant Readers] JH/HS**

Best friends Blair Waldorf and Serena van der Woodsen are spending Christmas vacation at a Caribbean resort, where Blair dates Miles and tries to forget her ex-boyfriend Nate and his new girlfriend Jenny. Meanwhile, Serena dodges the attentions of a lovesick rock star.

Keywords: dating, vacations, wealth

Because I'm Worth It. **Little, Brown, 2003. ISBN 0316909688. [Sexual Content, Reluctant Readers] JH/HS**

It's Valentine's Day, and everyone at Constance Billard School for Girls is having relationship problems. While Blair is seeing an older man who wants to help her get accepted to Yale, Serena is having too much fun at Fashion Week to notice her boyfriend Aaron has disappeared. Vanessa and Dan have sex for the first time, but their relationship is suddenly on the rocks when Dan gets mixed up with a young writer named Mystery Craze. Nate begins dating a troubled girl named Georgie he meets at drug rehab, and everyone wonders if Nate is in love.

Keywords: dating, drugs, sex, wealth

I Like It Like That. **Little, Brown, 2004. ISBN 0316735183. [Reluctant Readers] JH/HS**

Blair and Serena visit Sun Valley, Idaho, for spring break, where they meet up with Nate and his new girlfriend, Georgie. Meanwhile, in Manhattan, Dan is suffering from a broken heart and Jenny has a new boyfriend.

Keywords: dating, friendship, wealth

Pregnancy and Parenting

An unintended consequence of sex is pregnancy, and teens, whether or not they are involved in sexual relationships, need to be aware of how pregnancy can affect their lives. Teenage girls often wonder if they do have sex, what would happen if they became pregnant. The issues of sex, pregnancy, and parenting permeate young adult literature, and the novels selected for this category focus on the decisions made by teens about how to deal with a pregnancy, how a pregnancy affects their futures, and what they plan to do about their babies. Protagonists in some novels consider giving their babies up for adoption, like Valerie in *What Kind of Love?* by Sheila Cole or Emmy in *Detour for Emmy* by Marilyn Reynolds. Other protagonists decide to raise their babies, like Matt in Joanne Horniman's *Mahalia* or Bobby in Angela Johnson's *The First Part Last.* A popular theme features young men who choose to raise their children alone, like Sam in Margaret Bechard's *Hanging on to Max* and the main character in *Too Soon for Jeff* by Marilyn Reynolds. While abortion is sometimes considered an option by characters in young adult romance fiction, it is rarely chosen by protagonists, and if a character chooses abortion, it is often a secondary character, like Val in Kate Cann's Love Trilogy, found in the "Sex" book list. Although there are very few taboo topics in contemporary young adult literature, abortion still seems to be a topic few authors wish to tackle. Nevertheless, teen readers will discover how a pregnancy can affect their lives, and by reading books in the "Pregnancy and Parenting" book list, teens will discover they have options available to them if they, or their girlfriends, should become pregnant.

Bechard, Margaret

***Hanging on to Max*. Millbrook Press, 2002. ISBN 0761315799. [Reluctant Readers, Male] JH/HS**

When high school senior Sam Pettigrew's girlfriend Brittany decides to give up their baby for adoption, Sam decides he will care for their child himself. Sam finds love again with single parent Claire, a girl he has known since junior high school. Will Sam and Claire form a family? An ALA Best Book for Young Adults.

Keywords: adoption, children, parenting, pregnancy

Cole, Sheila

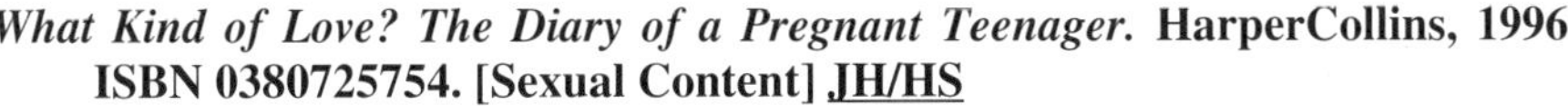

***What Kind of Love? The Diary of a Pregnant Teenager*. HarperCollins, 1996. ISBN 0380725754. [Sexual Content] JH/HS**

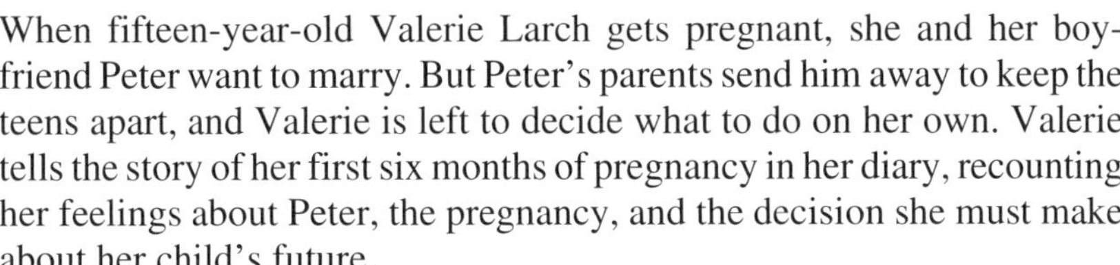

When fifteen-year-old Valerie Larch gets pregnant, she and her boyfriend Peter want to marry. But Peter's parents send him away to keep the teens apart, and Valerie is left to decide what to do on her own. Valerie tells the story of her first six months of pregnancy in her diary, recounting her feelings about Peter, the pregnancy, and the decision she must make about her child's future.

Keywords: adoption, diaries, pregnancy

Doherty, Berlie

***Dear Nobody*. Orchard, 1992. ISBN 0531054616. [Sexual Content, Male] JH/HS**

High school seniors Chris and Helen are making plans for college when Helen learns she is pregnant. As they struggle to decide what to do about the pregnancy and their relationship, readers see the story from both perspectives. While Chris narrates the story, we get Helen's story in letters addressed to their unborn child as "Dear Nobody." An ALA Best Book for Young Adults and winner of the 1991 Carnegie Medal.

Keywords: letters, pregnancy, sex

Fienberg, Anna

***Borrowed Light*. Delacorte Press, 2000. ISBN 0385327587. JH/HS**

Sixteen-year-old Callisto May, whose parents are distant and self-centered, yearns for a close relationship with someone older than her five-year-old

brother. Cally believes she has found comfort and security with boyfriend Tim, but he abandons her when she becomes pregnant. Where will Cally turn for help?

Keywords: abortion, family, first love, pregnancy, sex, siblings

Hobbs, Valerie

Get It While It's Hot—Or Not. **Orchard, 1996. ISBN 0531088901. JH/HS**

High school juniors Megan, Mia, and Elaine take care of their friend Kit, who becomes ill during her unplanned pregnancy. A wealthy couple plans to adopt Kit's baby, until Kit learns her former boyfriend is HIV positive. Meanwhile, Megan's relationship with boyfriend Joe is off again, as Megan becomes aware of the consequences of sex.

Keywords: adoption, dating, HIV, pregnancy, sex

Horniman, Joanne

Mahalia. **Alfred A. Knopf, 2003. ISBN 0375823255. [Sexual Content, Male] HS**

Seventeen-year-old Matt's girlfriend Emmy leaves, and he must take care of their daughter Mahalia on his own. The two survive with the help of Matt's mother, friends, and roommates Eliza and Virginia. Over time, Matt realizes he has a crush on Eliza, but he expects Emmy will be back, so he limits his relationship with Eliza to friendship. And just when Matt is ready to give up on Emmy, she returns.

Keywords: children, dating, parenting, pregnancy

Hrdlitschka, Shelley

Dancing Naked. **Orca Books, 2002. ISBN 1551432102. [Reluctant Readers] JH/HS**

Sixteen-year-old Kia discovers she is pregnant. Her unsupportive boyfriend wants her to have an abortion, but she can't go through with it. Kia's pregnancy progresses, as does her infatuation with her gay youth counselor, Justin. Although Kia wishes Justin would help her raise her baby, she knows she must decide whether to keep her baby or give the baby up for adoption.

Keywords: abortion, adoption, children, dating, pregnancy

Johnson, Angela

The First Part Last. **Simon & Schuster, 2003. ISBN 0689849222. [Male, Reluctant Readers] JH/HS**

Sixteen-year-old Bobby is shocked when he learns his girlfriend Nia is pregnant. Bobby and Nia's relationship ends, and they decide to give the baby up for adoption. But then tragedy strikes, and Bobby finds himself a single parent of a baby girl named Feather. A prequel to *Heaven*. An ALA Best Book for Young Adults, the 2004 Michael L. Printz Award Winner, and the 2004 Coretta Scott King Book Award Winner.

Keywords: adoption, dating, parenting, pregnancy

Reynolds, Marilyn

Detour for Emmy. **Morning Glory Press, 1993. ISBN 093093475X. [Sexual Content] JH/HS**

Ninth-grader Emmy meets Art and finds the love and attention she does not receive at home from her alcoholic mother, absent father, and criminal brother. The relationship between Emmy and Art quickly becomes sexual, and the one time they do not use birth control, Emmy gets pregnant. Art denies responsibility and breaks up with Emmy, leaving her to decide whether she wants to raise a child alone. A title in the True-to-Life Series from Hamilton High. An ALA Best Book for Young Adults.

Keywords: alcoholism, birth control, parenting, pregnancy, sex

Too Soon for Jeff. **Morning Glory Press, 1994. ISBN 0930934903. [Sexual Content, Male] JH/HS**

On the evening high school senior Jeff Browning was planning to break up with his girlfriend Christy, she informs him she is pregnant. Jeff plans to go to college on scholarship, and nothing will derail his plans, not even Christy's pregnancy. But Jeff's guilt, along with the disapproval of family and friends, force him to take responsibility for his son. A title in the True-to-Life Series from Hamilton High. An ALA Best Book for Young Adults.

Keywords: birth control, dating, parenting, pregnancy, sex

Ripslinger, Jon

Triangle. **Harcourt, 1994. ISBN 0152000488. [Sexual Content, Male] JH/HS**

High school graduates Jeremy, Darin, and Joy are friends. While Joy is officially dating Darin, she and Jeremy are involved in a sexual affair. Then Darin is paralyzed in an accident. Angry about his fate, he takes it out on his friends, and Jeremy and Joy decide to hide their affair until Joy discovers she is pregnant.

Keywords: accidents, dating, disabilities, friendship, pregnancy

Smith, Mary Ann Tirone

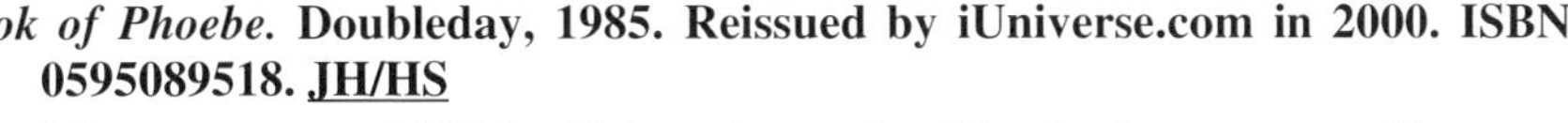

Book of Phoebe. **Doubleday, 1985. Reissued by iUniverse.com in 2000. ISBN 0595089518. JH/HS**

Nineteen-year-old Yale University senior Phoebe is pregnant. She travels to France, where she can have the baby and give it up for adoption. In Paris, Phoebe falls in love with wealthy artist Ben, and in a story within the story, Phoebe explains to Ben why she cannot have an abortion. An ALA Best Book for Young Adults.

Keywords: abortion, adoption, diaries, disabilities, pregnancy

Sparks, Beatrice

Annie's Baby: The Diary of Anonymous, a Pregnant Teenager. **William Morrow, 1998. ISBN 0380791412. [Sexual Content] JH**

High school freshman Annie falls in love with Danny, and despite his violent behavior and nasty temper, Annie becomes sexually involved with

him. After Danny rapes her, Annie discovers she is pregnant. Suddenly Danny rejects her, and Annie must turn to her mother for help.

Keywords: dating, diaries, physical abuse, pregnancy, rape

Velasquez, Gloria

***Teen Angel.* Pinata Books, 2003. ISBN 155885391X. [Sexual Content] JH/HS**

Latina teen Celia Chavez falls in love with Nicky, her friend's visiting cousin, and before long, Celia loses her virginity. After Nicky returns home, Celia discovers she is pregnant. Celia seeks help to decide what to do about her pregnancy. A title in the Roosevelt High Series.

Keywords: dating, family, pregnancy, sex

Zach, Cheryl

***Runaway.* Berkley, 1995. ISBN 042515047X. [Reluctant Readers] JH/HS**

When Cassie becomes pregnant, her father sends her to the McNaughton Home for Girls. But Cassie's boyfriend Seth finds her and convinces her to run away from the home, so they can raise their baby together. Another title in the Dear Diary Series, *Secret Admirer*, can be found in the "Teen Love" book list in Chapter 3. Winner of the 1996 Romance Writers of America Rita Award.

Keywords: adoption, dating, diaries, pregnancy

Date Rape and Physical Abuse

Physical abuse, incest, and rape are tough issues that young adults hear about in the media, and indeed, many teens deal with these issues in their daily lives. Young adult fiction tackles these issues, often in conjunction with themes of romance. The books in this category approach the issues from several angles and with different degrees of intensity. Sometimes the abuse is peripheral to the romance or provides a reason for fear of romance, as in Stephen Chbosky's *The Perks of Being a Wallflower,* while other stories focus on abuse within teen love relationships, such as Alex Flinn's *Breathing Underwater* and Sarah Dessen's *Dreamland.* Books in the "Date Rape and Physical Abuse" book list may appeal to teens who are questioning whether their relationship is abusive or trying to figure out what to do about an abusive relationship in their own life or the life of a friend. Other teens may just be curious about these issues and want to learn the warning signs so they will know what to do if they end up in a situation that could lead to date rape or physical abuse.

Chbosky, Stephen

***The Perks of Being a Wallflower.* MTV/Pocket Books, 1999. ISBN 0671027344. [Male] JH/HS**

Since the suicide of his best friend, high school freshman Charlie hangs out with Patrick and Samantha. Charlie likes Samantha, but she already has a boyfriend, so Charlie goes out with Mary Elizabeth for a while, but the relationship doesn't last. Charlie continues to have a crush on Samantha, but he panics when she decides she wants their friendship to include sex. An ALA Best Book for Young Adults.

Keywords: crushes, homosexuality, incest, sexual abuse

Clarke, Kathryn Ann

***The Breakable Vow*. Avon Books, 2004. ISBN 0060518219. [Sexual Content] HS**

High school senior Annie McGowan wants to wait until marriage, but her pushy boyfriend Kevin Griffin convinces her to have sex. When Annie discovers she is pregnant, she and Kevin decide to marry. The Griffins move to Texas, where Kevin attends university and Annie stays home with baby Mary. Kevin becomes violent, and Annie learns he fits the profile of a woman abuser. Will Annie find the courage to leave Kevin and make a life for herself and her daughter?

Keywords: dating, marriage, pregnancy, religion, sex, violence

Dessen, Sarah

***Dreamland.* Penguin Putnam, 2000. ISBN 0670891223. JH/HS**

When sixteen-year-old Caitlin O'Koren's older sister Cassandra runs away from home, Caitlin struggles to fill her sister's place in the family. She becomes a cheerleader, and one night at a football party, Caitlin meets bad boy Rogerson Briscoe. Suddenly Caitlin finds her first romance becoming dangerous, as Rogerson becomes more violent and abusive. But Caitlin isn't sure she wants to leave Rogerson. An ALA Popular Paperback for Young Adults.

Keywords: dating, first love, physical abuse

Draper, Sharon

***Darkness Before Dawn.* Simon & Schuster, 2001. ISBN 0689830807. JH/HS**

High school senior Keisha is mourning the loss of her ex-boyfriend Andy to suicide. Jonathan Hathaway, the new young track coach, comforts her. Keisha and Jonathan begin a secret romance, and Keisha is feeling happier than she has for a long time. When Jonathan tries to rape her at knifepoint, Keisha must find a way to survive her shame, fear, and heartbreak.

Keywords: dating, grief, rape, violence

Flinn, Alex

***Breathing Underwater.* HarperCollins, 2001. ISBN 0060291982. [Male] JH/HS**

Sixteen-year-old Nick Andreas tells his story of abuse, both as victim and perpetrator, in a story that moves back and forth in time. Nick's abusive father has taught him violence, and when he hits his girlfriend Caitlin, she files charges against him. Nick is ordered by the court to attend group counseling. Can counseling help Nick learn to control his violent temper? An ALA Popular Paperback for Young Adults.

Keywords: crime, dating, diaries, physical abuse

Hooper, Mary

***Amy.* Bloomsbury USA, 2002. ISBN 158234793X. MS/JH**

When fifteen-year-old Amy is abandoned by her best friends, she finds solace and romance on the Internet with a boy named Zed. But when

Amy meets Zed in person, he drugs her, rapes her, and takes photographs of her in the nude. When Amy remembers what happened, she and her new friend Beaky set a trap for Zed.

Keywords: crime, dating, drugs, Internet, rape

Miklowitz, Gloria

***Past Forgiving.* Simon & Schuster, 1995. ISBN 0671884425. JH/HS**

High school sophomore Alexandra begins dating Cliff, a senior, and she falls in love. She repeatedly excuses his jealousy, anger, and controlling behavior. Alex even forgives Cliff when he hits her, and she finds ways to blame herself for Cliff's violent behavior.

Keywords: date rape, first love, physical abuse, vacations

Randle, Kristen D.

***The Only Alien on the Planet.* Scholastic, 1995. ISBN 0590463098. JH/HS**

High school senior Ginny Christianson wants to know why Smitty Tibbs, a handsome and smart boy at her new school, never speaks to anyone. With the help of her friend Caulder, Ginny learns that Smitty has been physically abused by his older brother. After Smitty undergoes some therapy, he and Ginny begin a romance. An ALA Best Book for Young Adults.

Keywords: dating, family, physical abuse

Reynolds, Marilyn

***Baby Help.* Morning Glory Press, 1997. ISBN 1885356269. JH/HS**

Teen mother and high school senior Melissa Fisher can live with the physical and verbal abuse from her boyfriend Rudy. But when Rudy hits their daughter, Melissa realizes she must leave Rudy. A title in the True-to-Life Series from Hamilton High.

Keywords: children, dating, parenting, physical abuse

***But What about Me?* Morning Glory Press, 1996. ISBN 1885356102. [Sexual Content] JH/HS**

Eighteen-year-old Erica Arrendondo's relationship with Danny Lara becomes serious very quickly. Danny's mother recently died, and Danny is abusing alcohol in an attempt to deal with his grief. One night at a party, a friend of Danny's rapes Erica, and Danny is too drunk to help her. Erica must decide whether she wants to save Danny, or if she should just save herself from Danny's destructive lifestyle. A title in the True-to-Life Series from Hamilton High.

Keywords: alcoholism, dating, rape, sex

Rodowsky, Colby

***Lucy Peale.* Farrar, Straus and Giroux, 1992. ISBN 0374363811. JH/HS**

Seventeen-year-old Lucy Peale becomes pregnant when she is raped. Lucy's preacher father will not accept her pregnancy, and she leaves home to sleep under the boardwalk in Ocean City, Maryland. Lucy meets Jake, who gives her sanctuary. Lucy and Jake slowly fall in love and plan to marry and raise Lucy's baby. But Jake's work takes him away from Lucy for a time, and Lucy is not sure their relationship can survive the long separation. An ALA Popular Paperback for Young Adults.

Keywords: dating, family, marriage, pregnancy, rape

Rottman, S. L.

***Head above Water.* Peachtree, 1999. ISBN 1561451851. JH/HS**

High school junior Skye juggles her responsibilities of caring for her brother Sunny, who has Down's syndrome, with schoolwork, swimming, and her new boyfriend Mike. But when Skye starts neglecting her other responsibilities to spend more time with Mike, she heads for trouble.

Keywords: dating, disabilities, family, rape

Stratton, Allan

***Leslie's Journal.* Annick, 2000. ISBN 1550376659. [Sexual Content] JH/HS**

In a journal written for her sophomore English class, Leslie tells her teacher about her relationship with her first love, Jason. But Leslie is not prepared for the physical and verbal abuse Jason heaps on her, nor is she ready to talk about the abuse when a substitute teacher reads her journal. An ALA Popular Paperback for Young Adults.

Keywords: dating, diaries, first love, physical abuse, rape

Williams-Garcia, Rita

***Every Time a Rainbow Dies.* HarperCollins, 2000. ISBN 0688162452. [Sexual Content, Male] JH/HS**

Sixteen-year-old Thulani, a Jamaican immigrant, witnesses the rape of a Haitian girl, Ysa, in the alley next to his house in Brooklyn. He goes to her aid and helps her home, but when he seeks her out later, she rebuffs his offer of friendship. Thulani falls in love with Ysa, and eventually the couple begins a romantic and sexual relationship.

Keywords: crime, first love, multicultural romance, rape

Disease, Death, and Grief

A popular plot device in young adult romance literature involves the illness and resulting death or accidental death of a family member, friend, or lover. Many teens, whether or not they have experienced the illness or death of a loved one, are curious about how to deal with these issues, so books on these topics are very popular with teens. Teens particularly are drawn to the emotional drama that is involved when the story involves a boyfriend or girlfriend who is ill or dying. They can also learn a bit about diseases from these books. The reigning queen of the "Disease, Death, and Grief" category is Lurlene McDaniel, author of popular titles such as *Now I Lay Me Down to Sleep* and *A Rose for Melinda*, who is profiled in this section.

Arrick, Fran

***What You Don't Know Can Kill You.* Bantam Books, 1992. ISBN 0553074717. [Sexual Content] JH/HS**

When high school senior Ellen donates blood in the local blood drive, she is surprised her donation tests positive for HIV. She thought she had a monogamous relationship with her boyfriend Jack, but he admits he had sex with other girls while away at school. Jack and Ellen must find a way to face life with HIV and possibly AIDS. An ALA Best Book for Young Adults.

Keywords: dating, death, HIV, illness, sex, suicide

Crutcher, Chris

***Running Loose.* Greenwillow Books, 1983. Reissued by Laurel Leaf in 1986. ISBN 0440975700. [Male, Sexual Content] JH/HS**

High school senior Louie Banks has good friends, a position on the school football team, and a great girlfriend, Becky. When Louie argues with the football coach over an illegal play, he gets kicked off the team. Then Becky dies in a car accident. Can Louie put his life back together without Becky? An ALA Best Book for Young Adults.

Keywords: dating, death, grief, sports

Ferris, Jean

***Invincible Summer.* Farrar, Straus & Giroux, 1994. ISBN 0374336423. [Sexual Content] JH/HS**

Seventeen-year-old Robin Gregory meets Rick Winn at the hospital, where she is being tested for cancer. When Robin is diagnosed with leukemia, Rick provides her with love and support, despite his own battle with the disease. Shortly after they are both released from the hospital, Rick learns his cancer has spread and he will not survive the disease. Now Robin must support Rick. An ALA Best Book for Young Adults.

Keywords: dating, death, grief, illness

Freymann-Weyr, Garrett

***When I Was Older.* Houghton Mifflin, 2000. ISBN 0618055452. MS/JH**

Fifteen-year-old Sophie, who is grieving the loss of her younger brother, avoids boys. But Sophie is attracted to Francis, the son of her mother's new boyfriend. Francis has lost his mother, and he is grieving, too. Can Sophie and Francis find happiness together?

Keywords: dating, death, family, grief

Hahn, Mary Downing

***The Wind Blows Backward.* Houghton Mifflin, 1993. ISBN 0395629756. JH/HS**

High school senior Spencer turns to old friend Lauren for help in dealing with his depression over his father's suicide. Lauren and Spencer discover a shared interest in poetry, and they fall in love. But Lauren's love is not enough to help Spencer's depression, and when he is hurt in a motorcycle accident, Lauren fears Spencer wants to commit suicide.

Keywords: dating, death, depression, grief, suicide

Henson, Heather

Making the Run. **HarperCollins, 2002. ISBN 0060297964. [Sexual Content] JH/HS**

Lulu McClellan and her best friend Ginny are just passing time, waiting for graduation so they can leave their small Kentucky town. So Lu is surprised when she falls in love for the first time with Jay, her older brother's friend. While Lu and Jay begin a sexual relationship, it is Ginny who gets pregnant. Will Lu and Ginny survive their first love affairs?

Keywords: dating, death, family, first love, grief, pregnancy

Jenkins, Amanda

Damage. **HarperCollins, 2001. ISBN 0060290994. [Sexual Content, Male] JH/HS**

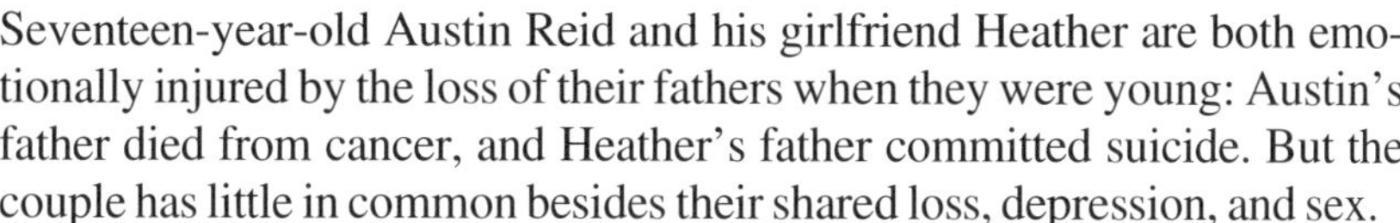

Seventeen-year-old Austin Reid and his girlfriend Heather are both emotionally injured by the loss of their fathers when they were young: Austin's father died from cancer, and Heather's father committed suicide. But the couple has little in common besides their shared loss, depression, and sex.

Keywords: dating, death, depression, grief

Kent, Deborah

Why Me? Trilogy.

Sick and injured teens in Hamilton Hospital's Adolescent Wing, who were already worried about normal problems like dating and boyfriends, learn to deal with their illnesses and injuries.

The Courage to Live. **Archway, 2001. ISBN 0743400313. MS/JH**

When high school junior Chloe Peterson is diagnosed with lupus, she thinks she would rather die than live with the disease. Chloe pushes everyone away, including Todd Bowers, a boy she recently met who wants to be her boyfriend.

Keywords: dating, illness, lupus

Living with a Secret. **Archway, 2001. ISBN 0743400321. MS/JH**

Fifteen-year-old Cassie Mullins is hired to work at Camp Caribou, a summer camp for kids with diabetes. But Cassie does not tell her employers that she is diabetic, and she hides her secret from Jason Moustakas, another camp counselor who likes her. When Cassie's mother and aunt arrive and reveal her secret, Jason is hurt that Cassie didn't trust him.

Keywords: dating, diabetes, illness, vacations

Don't Cry for Yesterday. **Pulse, 2002. ISBN 074340033X. MS/JH**

Amber Novak's date with Eric Moore ends when Eric loses control of his car. Amber's spinal cord is severed in the accident, and the doctors tell her she will never walk again, so Amber must get used to life in a wheelchair. Although Eric feels terrible about the accident, Amber is not sure if she can ever find it in her heart to forgive him.

Keywords: accidents, dating

Koertge, Ron

Stoner and Spaz. **Candlewick, 2002. ISBN 0763616087. [Sexual Content, Reluctant Readers, Male] JH/HS**

Sixteen-year-old Ben Bancroft, who has cerebral palsy, spends much of his free time alone at the movie theatre. When Ben meets Colleen Minou, a druggie from his high school, they become sexually involved. An ALA Best Book for Young Adults.

Keywords: dating, disabilities, drugs, friendship

Koss, Amy Goldman

Smoke Screen. **Pleasant Company, 2000. ISBN 158485202X. MS**

Sixth-grader Mitzi Burk has a crush on Mike Humphrey, who sits next to her in school; but Mike doesn't pay her any attention. In order to get Mike's attention, Mitzi tells him that her mother is suffering from a pretend disease called "stripitis." Soon the whole class knows Mitzi's mother is sick. How did Mitzi's lie, intended to attract a boy, turn into such a big deal?

Keywords: crushes, illness

McDaniel, Lurlene

As Long As We Both Shall Live. Bantam Books, 2003. ISBN 0553571087. [Reluctant Readers] MS/JH

Lovers April Lancaster and Mark Gianni are both sick—she has a brain tumor and he has cystic fibrosis. April is ecstatic when Mark proposes, and the couple plans to marry. When Mark dies, April must find a way to go on without him. Two books in one, including *Till Death Do Us Part* and *For Better, For Worse, Forever.* For more information, see the annotations immediately below.

Till Death Do Us Part. **Bantam Books, 1997. ISBN 0553570854. [Reluctant Readers] MS/JH**

When April Lancaster meets race car driver Mark Gianni, they fall in love. But they are both sick. April has a brain tumor, and Mark suffers from cystic fibrosis. When a racing accident exacerbates Mark's cystic fibrosis, April must decide if she will marry Mark, as they had planned.

Keywords: cancer, cystic fibrosis, dating, death, grief, illness

For Better, For Worse, Forever. **Bantam Books, 1997. ISBN 0553570889. [Reluctant Readers] MS/JH**

In the sequel to *Till Death Do Us Part*, April Lancaster and her parents are vacationing in St. Croix after the death of her fiancé Mark Gianni. April meets Brandon Benedict, a teenage boy who is coping with the loss of his mother. April and Brandon become close, but she does not tell him about her brain tumor. When April suddenly gets sick, she and her parents return to New York, leaving Brandon confused. Will April ever see Brandon again?

Keywords: cancer, dating, death, grief, illness, vacations

Lurlene McDaniel, *Now I Lay Me Down to Sleep*

Lurlene McDaniel became inspired to write stories about teens with chronic and terminal illness as she watched her son grow up coping with juvenile diabetes.

"Over time, as he grew, I saw that he (and all other sick kids) wanted pretty much the same thing—to be a regular kid, to not be different from their friends," McDaniel said in an interview in July 2002.

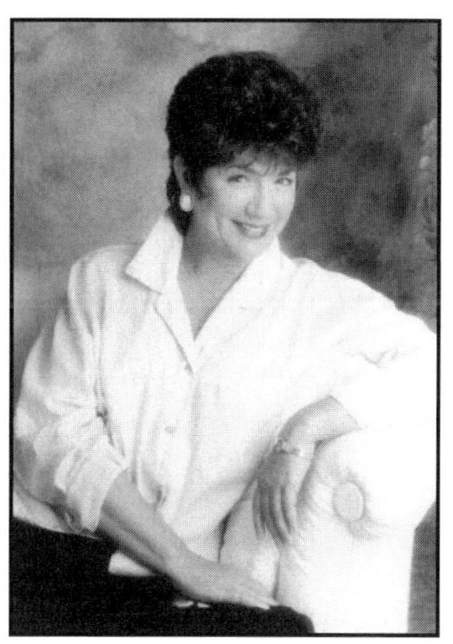

Lurlene McDaniel. Photo © Copeland Photography. Used with permission.

"The experience of raising a diabetic child gave my writing a direction I did not expect because once I entered the arena of illness, I learned plenty about various diseases. I found the kids, afflicted with various illnesses, awe-inspiring as they struggled to be 'normal' in their abnormal circumstances." Now that McDaniel's son is an adult, her young readers motivate her to continue writing her inspirational novels.

"I've met so many kids and teens in my work who are dealing with sickness and tragedy that they are my ultimate inspiration. I am consistently amazed by their maturity, wisdom, and courage," McDaniel stated in the same interview.

McDaniel's novels are renowned for their romantic story lines. Books such as *Don't Die, My Love, Now I Lay Me Down to Sleep, I'll Be Seeing You, Till Death Do Us Part, For Better, For Worse, Forever,* and *Time to Let Go* all feature romantic relationships.

In July 2002, McDaniel said, "I believe that the romantic element is very important in the stories. My readers are young and often on the brink of boy/girl relationships. To ignore the element of romance wouldn't be realistic. I think romance in the books adds a deeper poignancy and richness to the stories and characters. When a sixteen year old gets cancer, one of her main concerns is, 'What boy is going to date me when I'm bloated and bald from chemo treatments?' The boy who does becomes heroic to the reader."

McDaniel's latest novel, *A Rose for Melinda*, tells the story of a ballerina's battle with leukemia. A subplot portrays Melinda's experience of first love. A recent book of short stories, titled *How Do I Love Thee,* also focuses on romance. Of these short stories, McDaniel said, "I've always loved that poem and I wanted to illustrate that love has many aspects—romance, self-sacrifice, familial, selflessness, kindness, and generosity. Too often, people think of love as sex. That's only an aspect of love, not the total picture."

Lurlene McDaniel (*Cont.*)

McDaniel's stories are very popular with young readers. Fans report that her books represent reality for them. McDaniel stated, "Most often they write to say, 'Your books are real life.' Today's kids know the score about how fragile life can be. They lose friends in car accidents, parents divorce and/or die, friends vanish. They really know that 'happily ever after' is a fairy-tale concept. They like being addressed as intelligent beings, not kids without a clue about the real world. . . . I like to say my books are about learning to cope with what life deals you, which isn't always wonderful."

McDaniel's books have also been well received by teachers and librarians. Several of her books are included on the American Library Association's lists for Reluctant Readers, and some of her titles were selected for recommended reading lists to help young people cope with grief and death after the terrorist attacks on September 11, 2001. The author won a Romance Writers of America Rita Award in 1992 for *Now I Lay Me Down to Sleep*.

So what's next? McDaniel said her fans can expect something a bit different. In an interview in July 2002, McDaniel reported, "I've just finished a retro-style book called *Garden of Angels*. The novel is set in the South in 1974–75 and tells of a girl dealing with her mother's diagnosis of breast cancer, her family, a bad-boy whom she falls for, and the long shadow of the Vietnam War. It's also told in the first person, something I've not done before. I really enjoyed writing this book!"

For further information:

Drew, Bernard. "Lurlene McDaniel." In *The 100 Most Popular Young Adult Authors*. Englewood, CO: Libraries Unlimited, 1997.

Lodge, Sally. "Lurlene McDaniel." *Publisher's Weekly*, April 6, 1992.

Lurlene McDaniel. 2001. Available: http://www.eclectics.com/lurlenemcdaniel/ (accessed September 4, 2002).

Lurlene McDaniel. 2002. Available: http://www.randomhouse.com/features/lurlene/ (accessed September 4, 2002).

Podell, Tim. "A Talk with Lurlene McDaniel." Scarborough, NY: Educational Video Tapes, 1998.

Telgen, Diane, ed. "Lurlene McDaniel." In *Something about the Author*. Vol. 71. Detroit: Gale Research, 1993.

Verney, Sarah. "Lurlene McDaniel." In *Authors & Artists for Young Adults*, edited by E. A. DesChenes. Vol. 15. Detroit: Gale Research, 1995.

McDaniel, Lurlene

Don't Die, My Love. **Bantam Books, 1995. ISBN 0553567152. [Reluctant Readers] MS/JH**

The lives of high school sweethearts Julie Ellis and Luke Muldenhower are shattered when Luke is diagnosed with Hodgkin's lymphoma. Julie wants to help Luke get better, but he pushes her away after he discovers his illness is terminal. When Luke dies, Julie must come to terms with life without Luke.

Keywords: death, grief, illness

How Do I Love Thee: Three Stories. **Bantam Books, 2001. ISBN 0553571540. [Reluctant Readers] MS/JH**

A book of short stories centered on the famous poem by Elizabeth Barrett Browning. In "Night Vision," Brett tries to cheer up lonely Shayla, a teenager who is allergic to the sun. In "Bobby's Girl," Dana must choose between two brothers she loves, her boyfriend Bobby or her summer love Steve. "Laura's Heart" tells the story of Laura, a girl with heart problems, who learns important lessons about love and life when tragedy strikes the young man she loves.

Keywords: dating, death, grief, illness, short stories

I'll Be Seeing You. **Bantam Books, 1996. ISBN 0553567187. [Reluctant Readers] MS/JH**

Sixteen-year-old Carley Mattea meets Kyle Westin while she is in the hospital for surgery to remove a tumor from her face. Kyle was blinded when his chemistry experiment exploded, and the doctors don't know if his sight will return. Carley and Kyle fall in love, but Carley does not tell Kyle about the damage the cancer and the surgery did to her face. Will Kyle still like Carley when he can see her disfigured face? An ALA Popular Paperback for Young Adults.

Keywords: blindness, dating, illness

Now I Lay Me Down to Sleep. **Bantam Books, 1991. ISBN 0553288970. [Reluctant Readers] MS/JH**

Fifteen-year-old Carrie Blake, whose leukemia is in remission, meets Keith Gardner at a cancer support group. Carrie's life seems better for a time, despite her parents' divorce and the possibility that her cancer could return. When Keith's illness worsens, he participates in a hospice program that allows him to die at home, and Carrie has to face her future without Keith. Winner of the 1992 Romance Writers of America Rita Award.

Keywords: cancer, dating, death, illness

A Rose for Melinda. **Bantam Books, 2002. ISBN 0553570900. [Reluctant Readers] MS/JH**

Melinda Skye and Jesse Rose have remained best friends for many years, despite the fact that they live in different parts of the United States. When thirteen-year-old Melinda is diagnosed with leukemia, Jesse visits her

and the friends fall in love. Will Melinda and Jesse have a future together?

Keywords: cancer, dating, death, friendship, illness, letters

Saving Jessica. **Bantam Books, 1996. ISBN 0553567217. [Reluctant Readers] MS/JH**

Seventeen-year-old Jessica McMillian is diagnosed with kidney disease, and a kidney transplant is her only hope for a normal life. When her boyfriend Jeremy decides to donate one of his kidneys to Jessica, he is willing to take his parents to court to do it against their wishes.

Keywords: dating, illness

McDaniel, Lurlene

Somewhere between Life and Death Duo.

Somewhere between Life and Death. **Bantam Books, 1990. ISBN 0553283499. [Reluctant Readers] MS/JH**

When Erin Bennet's sister Amy is critically injured in a car accident, Erin and her family must accept the fact that Amy will die when she is removed from life support.

Keywords: accidents, death, grief

Time to Let Go. **Bantam Books, 1990. ISBN 0553283502. [Reluctant Readers] MS/JH**

In the companion novel to *Somewhere between Life and Death,* Erin Bennett experiences headaches, which started when her younger sister Amy died a year ago. When Erin is chosen to star opposite annoying and popular David Devlin in the school play, her headaches get worse. Will Erin be able to move on with a life that includes David?

Keywords: first love, grief, illness

McDaniel, Lurlene

Telling Christina Goodbye. **Bantam Books, 2002. ISBN 0553570870. [Reluctant Readers] MS/JH**

On their way home from a school basketball game, high school senior Trisha Thompson and her friends are in a terrible car accident. Trisha is injured, her best friend Christina is dead, and her boyfriend Cody is in a coma. When Cody wakes up, he has amnesia and does not remember Trisha.

Keywords: accidents, dating, death, grief

Pennebaker, Ruth

Conditions of Love. **Henry Holt, 1999. ISBN 0805061045. MS/JH**

Sarah Morgan's father died a year ago, and she is still coming to terms with her loss when she begins high school. Sarah and her best friend Ellie, both beset with family problems, spend gloomy weekends together. Sarah has a secret crush on Ben Cooper, a boy in her history class, and she constantly wonders about kissing and sex. Sarah decides to abandon her unhappy best friend in pursuit of love and fun.

Keywords: crushes, dating, death, family, friendship, grief

Rosenberg, Liz

***17: A Novel in Prose Poem.* Cricket, 2002. ISBN 081264915x. [Sexual Content] JH/HS**

When Stephanie falls in love with Denny, she is very happy to have a boyfriend. But Denny wonders if he might be gay, so their relationship ends, and Stephanie falls into a deep depression.

Keywords: dating, first love, illness, poetry, sex, sexual orientation

Wild, Margaret

***Jinx.* Walker, 2002. ISBN 0802788300. [Sexual Content] JH/HS**

After two of her former boyfriends die, seventeen-year-old Jen earns the nickname Jinx. Now Jinx believes their deaths were somehow her fault. How can Jinx ever love again?

Keywords: dating, death, grief, poetry

Willey, Margaret

***Saving Lenny.* Bantam Books, 1990. Reissued by iUniverse.com in 2002. ISBN 0595219306. MS/JH**

High school seniors Jesse Davis and Lenny Stevens fall in love. They decide not to go to college, and instead, they set up house in a cabin in the woods. Jesse discovers Lenny suffers from depression; and as the winter nears, Lenny becomes possessive of her. Told from the perspectives of Jesse and her friend Kay, who wants to rescue Jesse from her destructive relationship with Lenny.

Keywords: dating, illness, obsession

Williams, Carol Lynch

***Carolina Autumn.* Delacorte Press, 2000. ISBN 0385327161. JH/HS**

Carolina McKinney is grieving the loss of her father and sister, who died in a plane crash. High school is a fresh start for Carolina, and when she falls in love for the first time with Garrett, she is upset that her best friend Mara makes a play for her new boyfriend.

Keywords: dating, death, first love, friendship, grief

Zeises, Lara M.

***Bringing Up the Bones.* Delacorte Press, 2002. ISBN 0385730012. [Sexual Content] JH/HS**

While college freshman Bridget Edelstein mourns the loss of her best friend and ex-boyfriend Benji Gilbert, she falls in love with Jasper Douglas. But Bridget is not sure she is ready to love again so soon after Benji's death. A 2001 Delacorte Press Contest Honor Book.

Keywords: dating, death, friendship, grief

Gay, Lesbian, and Bisexual Romance

Many stories written for young adults feature young people who are exploring their sexual identities. The books in this section feature teens who are involved in their first romantic, dating, or sexual relationships. For instance, Kyle Meeks can no longer ignore his feelings for school jock Jason Carrillo in *Rainbow Boys* by Alex Sanchez, while the protagonist in Kate Walker's *Peter* questions his sexual orientation when he is attracted to a gay man. Some protagonists, like Aurin in Tea Benduhn's *Gravel Queen,* Nicola in Sarah Ryan's *Empress of the World,* and Eliza in Nancy Garden's classic novel *Annie on My Mind,* are surprised when they fall in love with another woman.

Books in the "Gay, Lesbian, and Bisexual Romance" book list reflect the problems teens encounter as they determine their sexual identities and enter their first same-sex relationships. Gay and lesbian teens often feel isolated, and reading about teens like them helps them understand their feelings and face the challenges of growing up gay, lesbian, or bisexual. Other teens may wonder if they are or a friend is gay or lesbian, or they may be curious about other sexual orientations and lifestyles. Whatever their reasons for reading books in the "Gay, Lesbian, and Bisexual Romance" list, teens will learn something about what it is like to be gay, lesbian, or bisexual in a society that often discriminates against people who are.

Benduhn, Tea

***Gravel Queen.* Simon & Schuster, 2003. ISBN 068984994X. JH/HS**

Seventeen-year-old Aurin is surprised when she falls in love with another girl, since she never considered she might be a lesbian. As Aurin and Neila experience the joys of first love, Aurin's friends Kenney and Fred feel neglected.

Keywords: crushes, dating, first love, friendship, homosexuality, sexual orientation

Boock, Paula

***Dare Truth or Promise.* Houghton Mifflin, 1999. ISBN 0395971179. [Sexual Content] JH/HS**

High school senior Louie Angelo never expected to fall in love with another girl. But when she meets Willa, the girls begin a physical relationship.

Keywords: dating, first love, homosexuality, lesbians, religion

Freymann-Weyr, Garret

***My Heartbeat.* Houghton Mifflin, 2002. ISBN 0618141812. [Sexual Content] JH/HS**

Fourteen-year-old Ellen has a crush on her brother Link's best friend James, but Ellen believes that Link and James may be involved in a homosexual relationship. When Ellen asks the boys about their relationship, Link denies that he is gay, and he stops seeing his friend. But James admits he is bisexual, and Ellen and James begin dating. An ALA Best Book for Young Adults and a 2003 Michael L. Printz Honor Book.

Keywords: bisexuality, crushes, dating, homosexuality

Garden, Nancy

Annie on My Mind. **Farrar, Straus & Giroux, 1982. ISBN 0374303665. JH/HS**

High school seniors Annie and Eliza meet at the Metropolitan Museum of Art, and they unexpectedly fall in love. Slowly, the girls learn to accept their new love for each other, but they choose to keep it a secret and pose as best friends. Nevertheless, Annie and Liza are not prepared for the events that unfold when their affair becomes public knowledge. This controversial book is frequently challenged in school and public libraries. An ALA Best Book for Young Adults, a selection of the YALSA Romance Genre List, and winner of the 2003 Margaret A. Edwards Award.

Keywords: dating, friendship, homosexuality, lesbians

Guy, Rosa

Ruby. **Viking, 1976. Reissued by Bantam Books in 1992. ISBN 0440211301. [Sexual Content] JH/HS**

High school seniors Ruby Cathy and Daphne Duprey become involved in a secret love affair.

An ALA Best Book for Young Adults.

Keywords: dating, first love, homosexuality, lesbians, multicultural romance

Hines, Sue

Out of the Shadows. **William Morrow, 1999. ISBN 0380811928. JH/HS**

High school freshman Rowanna is dealing with difficult issues, including her mother's death and the fact that she now has to live with her mother's partner, whom she dislikes. As if that's not enough, Rowanna's best friend Mark loves Jodie, the new girl at school, but Jodie secretly loves Rowanna. Rowanna suddenly finds herself part of a confusing love triangle.

Keywords: Australia, crushes, dating, death, homosexuality, lesbians, sexual orientation

Kerr, M. E.

Deliver Us from Evie. **HarperCollins, 1995. ISBN 0060244755. [Male] JH/HS**

Fifteen-year-old Parr Burrman tells the story of the discovery of his sister Evie's lesbianism. After Evie falls in love with Patty, the rich banker's daughter, Evie and Patty leave their small town to live together in New York City.

Keywords: dating, homosexuality, lesbians

"Hello," I Lied. **HarperCollins, 1997. ISBN 0060275294. [Sexual Content, Male] JH/HS**

Seventeen-year-old Lang Penner is spending the summer at the estate of former rock star Ben Nevada, where his mother works as housekeeper. Lang is a closeted gay, and his boyfriend Alex, whom Lang has left behind for the summer, wants to tell his friends about their relationship.

Lang is attracted to Huguette, a French girl he meets, and Lang wonders if it's possible to like both boys and girls.

Keywords: bisexuality, dating, homosexuality, sexual orientation, vacations

Levithan, David

***Boy Meets Boy.* Alfred A. Knopf, 2003. ISBN 0375824006. [Male, Reluctant Readers] JH/HS**

In a romantic comedy featuring a gay-straight alliance formed to help straight teens learn how to dance, high school sophomore Paul falls in love at first sight with Noah, and they begin dating. When Noah breaks up with him, Paul must find a way to win Noah back. An ALA Best Book for Young Adults.

Keywords: dating, friendship, homosexuality, sexual orientation

Myracle, Lauren

***Kissing Kate.* Dutton, 2003. ISBN 0525469176. JH/HS**

Lissa and Kate are best friends and high school sophomores. Their relationship changes forever when they share a passionate kiss, and while Kate won't have anything to do with Lissa, Lissa believes she is in love with her best friend. It seems Lissa and Kate may not be able to salvage their friendship. An ALA Best Book for Young Adults.

Keywords: crushes, first love, friendship, homosexuality, lesbians

Peters, Julie Anne

***Keeping You a Secret.* Little, Brown, 2003. ISBN 0316702757. JH/HS**

When high school senior Holland Jaeger falls in love with CeCe Goddard, she is very surprised. Holland breaks up with her boyfriend and begins an affair with CeCe, and despite her family's objections to the relationship, she makes plans to go to college with CeCe.

Keywords: bisexuality, dating, family, homophobia, lesbians

Ryan, Sarah

***Empress of the World.* Viking, 2001. ISBN 0670896888. JH/HS**

When Nicola enrolls in summer college courses, she never expects to fall in love with another girl. As Nicola and Southern belle Battle try to figure out their relationship and their sexuality, their relationship becomes very intense.

Keywords: bisexuality, dating, homosexuality, lesbians, sexual orientation

Alex Sanchez, *Rainbow Boys*

Alex Sanchez knows his subject well. He writes about teenage boys who are struggling to come to terms with themselves and their sexual identities, a conflict Sanchez learned about from personal experience. Sanchez's first book for young adults, *Rainbow Boys*, tells the stories of three teenage boys who are in different stages of accepting their homosexuality.

Alex Sanchez. Photo by Kevin Kerdash. Used with permission.

"The story grew out of my own struggle between wanting to accept myself and being afraid to do so. Our teenage years present such a defining time in our lives. It's the period when we're often struggling hardest to understand who we are," Sanchez said in an interview in June 2002. "The reason for having three central characters was to provide a panorama of experiences of what it's like to be a gay teen, so that readers could access the story through varying avenues."

Rainbow Boys touches on many burning issues—sexuality, homophobia, sex, and HIV. But romantic love is always a central theme in the story. Sanchez continued, "As I wrote the book, it became apparent that I was writing the book I desperately wanted and needed to read when I was a teenager—one that would have told me 'It's okay to be who you are. You don't have to hate yourself for it. It's okay to feel love for another boy.' My vision for *Rainbow Boys* was to write an upbeat and affirming love story that would inspire, help create empathy, and show readers that being gay is ultimately about love."

Sanchez, who works as a family and youth counselor, believes books offer young adults a way to understand themselves and their peers. In the same interview, he stated, "Young adults need to see images of themselves and their peers in literature—positive images and affirming stories to help guide them through the often painful and confusing terrain of adolescence. Books often hold a special place when you're gay or different, giving you hope for a world in which it's okay to be who you are. And for straight kids, books that address the issues of sexuality and homophobia can promote empathy, compassion, and understanding."

According to Sanchez, *Rainbow Boys* has been well received by teens, parents, critics, and librarians alike. The author said, "The emails I receive from teens are tremendously moving. Things like, 'In junior high, sex hardly ever gets addressed, especially homosexual issues, and yet we deal with homophobia every day . . . it's nice to know we're not alone.' "

Alex Sanchez (*Cont.*)

In 2002 *Rainbow Boys* was selected as a Best Book for Young Adults by the American Library Association and a Book for the Teen Age by the New York Public Library. The book was also a finalist for the Lambda Literary Award, and it received a Blue Ribbon of Dissent by the Bulletin of the Center for Children's Books.

After the smashing success of *Rainbow Boys,* Sanchez began writing a sequel called *Rainbow High.* "It continues to follow the lives of Jason, Kyle, Nelson, their families, and friends during the second half of senior year. The boys face new challenges, including romantic struggles, homophobia in sports, conflict with parents, and HIV," Sanchez remarked. He said he hoped to write a third book about the characters in *Rainbow Boys* to complete the trilogy. Sanchez also reported a short story he wrote about a thirteen-year-old gay Latino boy will be published in an anthology, edited by James Howe and published by Atheneum, called *13: Thirteen Stories That Capture the Agony and Ecstasy of Turning Thirteen.*

For further information:

Alex Sanchez. n.d. Available: http://www.alexsanchez.com/ (accessed September 12, 2002).

Emert, Toby. "An Interview with Alex Sanchez, Author of *Rainbow Boys.*" *The ALAN Review* 29, no. 3 (2002): 12–14.

Pavao, Kate. "Flying Starts: Alex Sanchez." *Publisher's Weekly,* December 24, 2001, 34–35.

Sanchez, Alex

<u>Rainbow Series.</u>

High school seniors Jason Carrillo, Kyle Meeks, and Nelson Glassman come to terms with their sexuality and their lives as gay men searching for love and acceptance.

Rainbow Boys. **Simon & Schuster, 2001. ISBN 0689841000. [Reluctant Readers, Sexual Content, Male] <u>JH/HS</u>**

Gay high school seniors Jason Carrillo, Kyle Meeks, and Nelson Glassman try to come to terms with their sexuality. While Nelson is out of the closet, he is secretly in love with his best friend Kyle. Kyle, on the other hand, is secretly in love with Jason, a popular jock who has a girlfriend but who dreams of sex with boys. An ALA Best Book for Young Adults.

Keywords: body image, dating, first love, HIV, homophobia, homosexuality, sex

Rainbow High. **Simon & Schuster, 2003. ISBN 0689854773. [Reluctant Readers, Sexual Content, Male] <u>JH/HS</u>**

As Jason, Nelson, and Kyle finish their senior year, they face familiar challenges. When Jason decides to reveal his homosexuality at school, he is surprised by the general acceptance of his classmates and basketball teammates. But he hurts Kyle's feelings by keeping their relationship a secret. Meanwhile, Nelson has fallen in love with college man Jeremy, who has AIDS.

Keywords: AIDS, dating, first love, HIV, homophobia, homosexuality, sex

Stoehr, Shelley

Tomorrow Wendy: A Love Story. **Bantam Books, 1998. ISBN 0385323395. [Sexual Content] JH/HS**

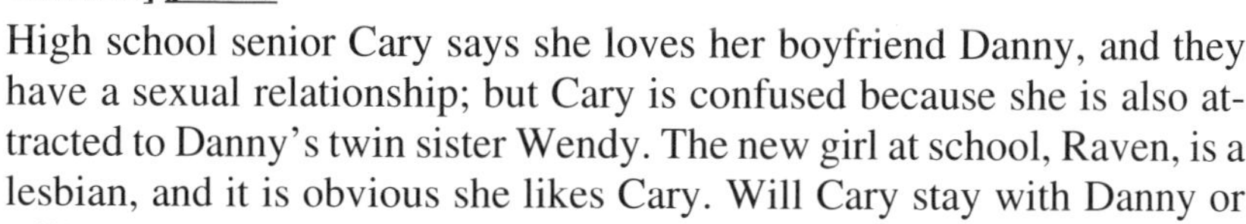

High school senior Cary says she loves her boyfriend Danny, and they have a sexual relationship; but Cary is confused because she is also attracted to Danny's twin sister Wendy. The new girl at school, Raven, is a lesbian, and it is obvious she likes Cary. Will Cary stay with Danny or will she take a chance with Raven?

Keywords: dating, drugs, homosexuality, lesbianism, sex

Taylor, William

The Blue Lawn. **Alyson, 1999. ISBN 1555834930. [Male] JH/HS**

Fifteen-year-old best friends David and Theo suddenly discover they are attracted to each other. David and Theo slowly learn to acknowledge their love with the help of the adults in their lives. An ALA Popular Paperback for Young Adults.

Keywords: first love, friendship, homosexuality

Walker, Kate

Peter. **Sandpiper, 2001. ISBN 0618111301. [Male] JH/HS**

When fifteen-year-old Peter starts feeling attracted to his brother's gay friend David, he questions his sexual orientation.

Keywords: Australia, crushes, homosexuality, sexuality

Wersba, Barbara

Whistle Me Home. **Henry Holt, 1997. ISBN 0805048502. JH/HS**

High school juniors Noli and T. J. fall in love, but T. J. is uncomfortable with their physical relationship. Despite the warning signs, Noli is shocked to discover that T. J. is gay. She reacts by drinking too much vodka and stalking T. J. as he begins a relationship with a boy. An ALA Best Book for Young Adults.

Keywords: alcoholism, first love, homosexuality, obsession

Williams, Bett

Girl Walking Backwards. **Tom Doherty, 1998. ISBN 0312194560. [Sexual Content] JH/HS**

Sixteen-year-old Skye passes the time masturbating and engaging in oral sex with her best friend Riley, but in her heart she knows she is a lesbian. When she meets Jessica, she develops a crush that borders on obsession, and Skye thinks one drunken kiss at a party makes them more than

friends. Then Jessica disappears to a psychiatric hospital, leaving Skye frantic with worry. Can a new friend and a new love help Skye understand the difference between casual friendship and real love?

Keywords: friendship, homosexuality, illness, lesbians

Wittlinger, Ellen

Hard Love. **Aladdin, 1999. ISBN 0689821344. [Male] JH/HS**

When high school junior John Galardi meets Marisol Guzman, they become fast friends over their shared love of zines. As time passes, John realizes he wants to be more than friends with Marisol and he believes their friendship could turn into love. There is one problem: Marisol is a lesbian. An ALA Best Book for Young Adults and a 2000 Michael L. Printz Honor Book.

Keywords: crushes, friendship, homosexuality, lesbians

Notes

1. Michael Cart, "The Bleak Goes On," *The Booklist* 96 (September 15, 1999): 248.
2. Anna Mulrine, "Risky Business," *U.S. News & World Report* 132 (May 27, 2002): 42–49.
3. Kristin A. Moore et al., *Beginning Too Soon: Adolescent Sexual Behavior, Pregnancy and Parenthood, A Review of Research and Interventions*.n.d. Available: http://aspe.os.dhhs.gov/hsp/cyp/xsteesex.htm (accessed February 5, 2003).
4. Laura Sessions Stepp, "The Buddy System: Sex in High School and College: What's Love Got to Do with It?," *Washington Post,* January 19, 2003, F01.
5. Cart, "Bleak Goes On," 248.

Chapter 6

Alternative Reality Romance

Alternative reality romance can be defined as "a collection of separate mini-subgenres linked by a common thread of fantasy or 'unreality.' "[1] This genre breaks the rules, or stretches the limits of reality, introducing into the romantic story elements of the fantastic and paranormal—ghosts, time travel, and shape-shifters, for example. Alternative reality romances are often set in other worlds—on other planets or in historical times, which may be described in detail. The stories are usually a blend of several genres, such as fantasy, myths, legends, fairy tales, paranormal, horror, and Gothic romance. The tone of these titles ranges from eerie and unsettling to downright scary. The books are often characterized by a battle that takes place between good and evil, which imposes mythological proportions on the stories, and also generates a great deal of excitement and suspense.

In this guide, the "Alternative Reality Romance" book list is separated into the following categories: "Paranormal Romance"; "Romantic Fantasy" (divided into "Contemporary Romantic Fantasy," "Historical Romantic Fantasy," and "Time Travel Romance") ; "Fairy Tales and Fables"; "Myths and Legends"; "Romantic Science Fiction"; and "Alternative Reality Romance Series."

Appeal

"Alternative Reality Romance" contains features of two favorite genres—romance and literature of the fantastic (i.e., fantasy, science fiction, and horror/suspense). These stories stretch the imagination and offer teen readers an escape from the reality of their everyday lives. Teens enjoy imagining what life might be like in another world or another time. They enjoy exploring possibilities.

Because alternate reality romance draws on so many different genres, it allows readers to experience a wide range of emotions—fear, suspense, hatred, compassion, love. As in stories of romantic mystery/suspense, conflicting emotions heighten the excitement. By providing adventure, suspense, strange creatures, and the like, while satisfying a craving for romance, these books offer teens a rich reading experience. Teens who enjoy reading fantasy, science fiction, paranormal, and romance will be especially happy to find stories combining these genres.

Advising the Reader

Following are a few points to keep in mind when advising young readers of alternate reality romance fiction:

- Remember that "Alternative Reality Romance" is an eclectic mix of several genres and readers may only like particular facets of this subgenre. Ask your patron, "What was the last good paranormal story or 'Romantic Fantasy' you read? Why did you like it?" Listen carefully to the response. There may be mention of characters who have magical powers, or stories based on familiar fairy tales, or that involve space travel. The fast pacing of adventurous "Romantic Fantasy" appeals to many readers, as do the mysterious qualities of paranormal romance stories. As you interview the reader, ask questions that arise naturally and that help you understand what your patron likes about the genre.
- It is also important to find out what readers don't like about this subgenre. For instance, many of the stories in the "Alternative Reality Romance" genre are darker in style, drawing on the horror and Gothic romance genres, and some readers may find these elements too frightening or gross. You might even ask your patron directly, "Do you like horror stories?" or "Do you like stories with werewolves or vampires?" Don't worry about why the reader likes or doesn't like these kinds of stories. If the reader doesn't like the darker stories, simply steer clear of paranormal stories and some of the darker fairy tales. Instead, suggest a "Romantic Fantasy" or a lighter fairy tale.
- Find out whether your patron likes stories set in contemporary or historical settings, since alternate reality romance includes stories of both types. Stories with historical settings can be found in the "Romantic Fantasy" section, under the categories "Historical Romantic Fantasy" and "Time Travel Romance." If the reader doesn't like historical stories, you will want to steer clear of the time travel stories, some of the "Romantic Fantasy," and stories based on fairy tales and myths. Instead, recommend stories from the paranormal romance subgenre.
- Find out if your patron likes popular television shows in this genre, such as *Buffy the Vampire Slayer* or *Charmed*. If so, then suggest books from these series. Novelizations of favorite television shows are very popular with teens who enjoy the shows.
- Don't forget that teens enjoy reading novels written for adult audiences. Suggest your patrons read adult titles similar to the young adult titles they enjoy. For instance, older teens who enjoy Caroline Cooney's Time Travel Quartet may also enjoy Diana Gabaldon's Outlander Series. Mature fans of Amelia Atwater-Rhodes's novels will enjoy Anne Rice's vampire stories. If teens aren't ready for adult titles, they will let you know, and if they are ready, you can help them expand their reading

horizons. For further information about the adult alternate reality romance genre, and suggestions for more adult titles, see Kristin Ramsdell's chapter "Alternative Reality Romance" in *Romance Fiction: A Guide to the Genre* (Libraries Unlimited, 1999) or the four-volume series *Enchanted Journeys beyond the Imagination: An Annotated Bibliography of Fantasy, Futuristic, Supernatural and Time Travel Romances* (Blue Diamond Publications, 1996, 1997) by Susan W. Bontley and Carol J. Sheridan.

Paranormal Romance

"Paranormal Romance" combines horror and romance, two popular genres in young adult fiction, appealing to our emotions on two basic levels. The suspense elements of paranormal romance appeal to the part of us that is frightened and intrigued by the unreal and the unexplained, while the romantic elements appeal to the part of us that wants to know what it feels like to be truly loved. "Paranormal Romance" stories often feature imaginary creatures, such as spooky and violent vampires, cute cupids, good witches, shape-shifters, guardian angels, or evil demons. Generally, the scenarios of these stories involve a young man who is some type of creature and a young woman who is human. Sometimes young women in the paranormal romance fall in love with young men, but the young women are more likely to fall in love with dangerous vampires, demons, and werewolves, temporary guardian angels, or ghosts from the past, and forbidden love is a common theme. The protagonist in the "Paranormal Romance" is usually, but not always, a young woman. Many of the protagonists in paranormal romances have special powers, such as psychic powers or the ability to communicate with ghosts or angels. These powers often place the young women in danger as they try to use their powers to solve problems and mysteries, but ultimately their powers enable them to escape from dangerous situations. Romance is both scary and empowering, so these stories reflect and accentuate feelings teens have about love and sex.

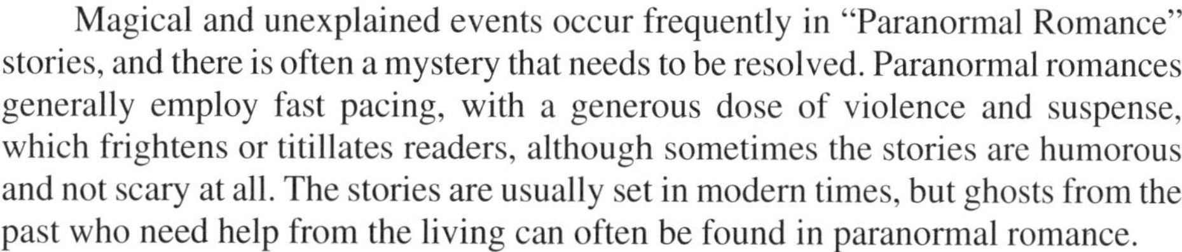

Magical and unexplained events occur frequently in "Paranormal Romance" stories, and there is often a mystery that needs to be resolved. Paranormal romances generally employ fast pacing, with a generous dose of violence and suspense, which frightens or titillates readers, although sometimes the stories are humorous and not scary at all. The stories are usually set in modern times, but ghosts from the past who need help from the living can often be found in paranormal romance.

The mood of the paranormal romance is usually dark and scary, and to ensure that mood, much of the action happens at night. Settings include large haunted houses and strange and unsettling alternate realities, and there is often the suggestion that the main characters may be trapped in these surroundings if they don't do what the vampires or ghosts want them to do. Dark stories about vampires, demons, or werewolves, such as *Demon in My View* by Amelia Atwater-Rhodes, *The Silver Kiss* by Annette Curtis Klause, and everything written by L. J. Smith, are very popular with teen readers.

Some lighter paranormal romances are still available for teens, although not as many as there were a few years ago. Light paranormal romances often include some humor, and the mood of light paranormal romance is not frightening, like the

darker paranormal romances. Readers who like lighter paranormal stories might enjoy Joan Bauer's *Thwonk*, which includes a cupid, and Laura Peyton Roberts's *Ghost of a Chance*, about a friendly ghost who falls in love with two best friends. Fans of lighter paranormal romance might also enjoy books in the Enchanted Hearts series, included in the romance series book list at the end of this chapter.

Whether young readers like the darker or lighter stories, they often have fun trying to imagine explanations for the strange creatures or events found in paranormal romance stories. Teens enjoy reading about unusual events that can't be explained, and when paranormal stories are combined with romance, readers will want to know how the paranormal love story can end happily ever after. While the ending of the teen paranormal romance does not always bring lovers together, young readers will still find paranormal romance novels satisfying because strange events in the stories come to an end and the mystery or problem driving the story is usually resolved.

Atwater-Rhodes, Amelia

***Demon in My View.* Delacorte Press, 2000. ISBN 038532720X. [Reluctant Readers] MS/JH**

Seventeen-year-old outcast Jessica Allodolah is a published author under the pen name of Ash Night. Jessica is surprised when Alex Remington, a new boy in school, reminds her of her vampire character Aubrey. Suddenly it seems Jessica's fantasy world might be real. As Jessica struggles to learn the truth, she tries to fight her attraction to Alex.

Keywords: Gothic romance, magic, suspense, vampires, witches

***Shattered Mirror.* Delacorte Press, 2001. ISBN 0385327935. [Reluctant Readers] MS/JH**

High school senior Sarah Vida is a teenage witch who hunts vampires, and her prey is Nikolas and Kaleo. Sarah meets Christopher, a vampire who is pretending to be a high school student, and they are attracted to each other despite the fact that they should not be together. The story gets complicated when Sarah learns Christopher is Nikolas's twin brother.

Keywords: Gothic romance, magic, suspense, vampires, witches

Bauer, Joan

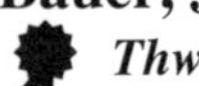

***Thwonk.* Delacorte Press, 1994. ISBN 0385320922. MS/JH**

A.J. McCreary, high school senior and photographer for the school newspaper, finds a stuffed cupid doll named Jonathan that comes to life and offers her assistance with romance. Suddenly Peter Terris, the school hunk, is madly in love with A.J. Now she finally has a date for the King of Hearts dance. But is lovesick Peter what A.J. really wants? An ALA Best Book for Young Adults.

Keywords: crushes, Cupid, humor

Cooney, Caroline B.

***The Stranger.* Scholastic, 1993. Reissued by Point in 1997. ISBN 0590456806. MS/JH**

High school student Nicoletta is forced to give up music class for an art appreciation class, where she meets Jethro, a mysterious boy. After Nicoletta and Jethro begin dating, she learns his secret: Jethro is part human, part monster. But

Nicoletta has fallen in love with Jethro, and now she must decide whether or not to stay with him.

Keywords: animals, dating, shape-shifters, suspense

Cusick, Richie Tankersley

***The House Next Door.* Pulse, 2002. ISBN 0743418387. MS/JH**

On a bet with her twin brother Charlie, seventeen-year-old Emma Donovan spends the night alone in the abandoned house next door. Emma finds herself living a night from the house's past, and she becomes involved in a passionate love affair with a familiar young man named Daniel. When Emma's night in the house ends, she continues to dream about the house and Daniel. Suddenly Emma is not sure if she is living in the past or in the present.

Keywords: dreams, ghosts, Gothic romance, twins

Deveraux, Jude

***An Angel for Emily.* Pocket Books, 1998. ISBN 0671003593. [Adult] HS**

Emily Jane Todd meets her guardian angel, Michael, when she runs into him with her car. Michael informs Emily he has been sent to rescue her from an ill-fated marriage to her fiancé, but Emily does not want to believe him.

Keywords: angels, marriage

***Wishes.* Pocket Books, 1989. ISBN 0671743856. [Adult] HS**

Nellie Grayson's sister, Terel, is the most beautiful and desirable girl in Chandler. But Jace Montgomery, a newcomer, likes Nellie.

Keywords: angels, magic

Goobie, Beth

***Before Wings.* Orca, 2001. ISBN 1551143610. JH/HS**

Fifteen-year-old Adrien spends the summer working as a counselor at Aunt Erin's summer camp, where she falls in love with Paul. Adrien and Paul both experience paranormal phenomena—Adrien sees the ghosts of five girls who died at the camp, while Paul dreams of his impending death. Can Adrien and Paul help each other understand the meaning of their visions?

Keywords: Canada, first love, friendship, ghosts, vacations

Hahn, Mary Downing

***Look for Me by Moonlight.* Houghton Mifflin, 1995. ISBN 039569843X. MS/JH**

Sixteen-year-old Cynda is spending six months with her father, stepmother, and half-brother Todd at an old haunted inn on the coast of Maine. Cynda likes Will, the housekeeper's grandson, until Vincent, a mysterious and charming guest, appears at the inn. But Todd is afraid of Vincent —and Cynda suspects Vincent is a vampire.

Keywords: first love, ghosts, vampires

Hawes, Louise

Rosey in the Present Tense. **Walker, 1999. ISBN 0802786855. JH/HS**

Six months after seventeen-year-old Franklin loses his girlfriend in a car accident, Rosey reappears to console her grieving boyfriend. Can Franklin ever get used to life without Rosey?

Keywords: death, ghosts, grief

Holder, Nancy, and Debbie Viguie

Wicked Series.

After Holly Cathers parents die, she moves in with her aunt and twin cousins Amanda and Nicole. The girls discover they are witches involved in an intergenerational feud with the Devereaux family, who are warlocks, and Holly is startled to realize that she and Jer Devereaux are soulmates.

Witch. **Pulse, 2002. ISBN 0743426967. JH/HS**

After her parents die, sixteen-year-old Holly Cathers is sent to live with her aunt and twin cousins Amanda and Nicole. Suddenly Holly develops magical powers, and she discovers she and her cousins are witches. When Holly falls in love with Jer Deveraux, a warlock from a rival family, she finds herself caught up in an intergenerational feud and a romance based on true love that has lasted for centuries.

Keywords: family, historical fiction, magic, witchcraft, witches

Curse. **Pulse, 2002. ISBN 0743426975. JH/HS**

While Nicole travels Europe trying to deny her magical heritage, Holly and Amanda try to find a way to rescue Jer, Holly's boyfriend, who has been kidnapped.

Keywords: family, historical fiction, magic, witchcraft, witches

Legacy. **Pulse, 2003. ISBN 0743426983. JH/HS**

Holly travels to England to rescue her soulmate Jer and her cousin Nicole.

Keywords: family, historical fiction, magic, witchcraft, witches

Spellbound. **Pulse, 2003. ISBN 0743426991. JH/HS**

Holly is under a powerful spell cast by Michael Devereaux, and her true love, Jer Devereaux, must find a way to rescue her. Warlock Alex Carruthers also poses a threat to the survival of Jer and Holly's love.

Keywords: family, historical fiction, magic, witchcraft, witches

Klause, Annette Curtis

Blood and Chocolate. **Bantam Doubleday Dell, 1997. ISBN 0385323050. [Sexual Content, Reluctant Readers] MS/JH**

Vivian is a teenage werewolf; Aiden is a teenage boy. When they meet and fall in love, they are forbidden to be together, because of their differences. Can Vivian and Aiden ever be together? An ALA Best Book for Young Adults and a YALSA Popular Paperback for Young Adults.

Keywords: Gothic romance, horror, suspense, violence, werewolves

The Silver Kiss. **Delacorte Press, 1991. ISBN 038530160X. [Reluctant Readers]** <u>MS/JH</u>

Seventeen-year-old Zoe is dealing with big problems, including her mother's imminent death from cancer, an overprotective father, and her best friend's move. While thinking about her problems in the park one evening, Zoe meets Simon. As their friendship progresses to romance, Zoe learns Simon is a vampire on a mission to kill his younger vampire brother. An ALA Best Book for Young Adults.

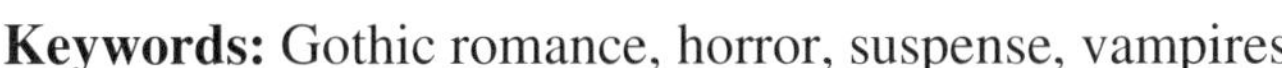

Keywords: Gothic romance, horror, suspense, vampires

Pike, Christopher

Witch. **Pocket Books, 2001. ISBN 0743427998.** <u>MS/JH</u>

High school student Julia is a clairvoyant witch. She sees in her future a young man she does not know get shot and die in her arms. Julia discovers the young man is her friend's new boyfriend, but she falls in love with him. Can she save him from his fate?

Keywords: clairvoyance, magic, witchcraft, witches

Roberts, Laura Peyton

Ghost of a Chance. **Bantam Doubleday Dell, 1999. ISBN 0440415349.** <u>MS/JH</u>

When her best friend Chloe introduces her to a ghost named James living in Chloe's mansion, sixteen-year-old Melissa falls in love with him. But she discovers Chloe is also in love with James. James likes both girls and involves them in a love triangle that could destroy their friendship.

Keywords: divorce, friendship, ghosts

Schreiber, Ellen

Vampire Kisses. **HarperCollins, 2003. ISBN 006009334X. [Reluctant Readers]** <u>MS/JH</u>

Raven, a teen Goth, is fascinated with vampires. When the mysterious Sterling family moves into the vacant mansion in town, Raven has to meet the handsome teenage son, Alexander. Soon Raven and Alexander are madly in love, but Raven must find out if Alexander is really a vampire.

Keywords: dating, first love, vampires

Smith, L. J.

<u>**Dark Visions Trilogy**</u>.

Psychically gifted students study their craft at the Zetes Institute, where adventure and romance abound.

The Strange Power. **Archway, 1994. ISBN 0671874543.** <u>JH/HS</u>

Kaitlyn Fairchild is offered a scholarship to study at the Zetes Institute with four other psychically gifted students. Kaitlyn is drawn to bad boy Gabriel and good boy Rob. But they soon discover someone is trying to steal their psychic powers.

Keywords: clairvoyance, vampires

The Possessed. **Archway, 1995. ISBN 0671874551. JH/HS**

The students at Zetes Institute continue working to learn who wants to steal their psychic powers.

Keywords: clairvoyance, vampires

The Passion. **Archway, 1995. ISBN 067187456X. JH/HS**

Kaitlyn must choose between good and evil, and this means she must decide if she will be with Rob or Gabriel.

Keywords: clairvoyance, vampires

Smith, L. J.

The Forbidden Game Trilogy.

Julian hopes to capture Jenny's love using games played in alternate worlds.

The Hunter. **Archway, 1994. ISBN 0671874519. JH/HS**

When Julian gives Jenny Thornton a game, she and her friends are thrust into The Shadow World, hunted by Julian, a.k.a. The Shadow Man. Julian hopes to win Jenny through the game.

Keywords: fantasy, games, horror

The Chase. **Archway, 1994. ISBN 0671874527. JH/HS**

Julian returns to win Jenny in a new game. Suddenly Jenny's friends begin disappearing, victims of the game, and Jenny must try to save them without being captured by Julian.

Keywords: fantasy, games, horror

The Kill. **Archway, 1994. ISBN 0671874535. JH/HS**

Jenny continues to hunt for her missing friends. But can she avoid becoming Julian's bride?

Keywords: fantasy, games, horror

Smith, L. J.

The Secret Circle Trilogy.

Witches Cassie and Diana struggle for control of the coven and the love of coven leader Adam.

The Initiation. **Harper Paperbacks, 1992. Reissued by Harper Paperbacks in 1999. ISBN 0061067121. JH/HS**

When Cassie arrives in New Salem for her junior year of high school, she joins the Secret Circle, a coven of young witches that rule the town. When Cassie falls in love with coven leader Adam, Cassie considers using dark magic to attract him, even though he is her best friend's boyfriend.

Keywords: magic, witchcraft, witches

The Captive. **Harper Paperbacks, 1992. Reissued by Harper Paperbacks in 1999. ISBN 0061067156. JH/HS**

Cassie is caught in a struggle for power of the coven between Faye and Diana. Faye uses Cassie's forbidden love for Adam to her advantage, and Cassie turns to Adam for help.

Keywords: magic, witchcraft, witches

The Power. **Harper Paperbacks, 1992. Reissued by Harper Paperbacks in 1999. ISBN 0061067199. JH/HS**

Cassie and Diana enter the final battle against the evil witch Faye. Will Cassie have to relinquish her love for Adam in order to save the coven and New Salem from evil?

Keywords: magic, witchcraft, witches

Smith, L. J.

The Vampire Diaries Quartet.

Elena falls in love with brother vampires Damon and Stefan.

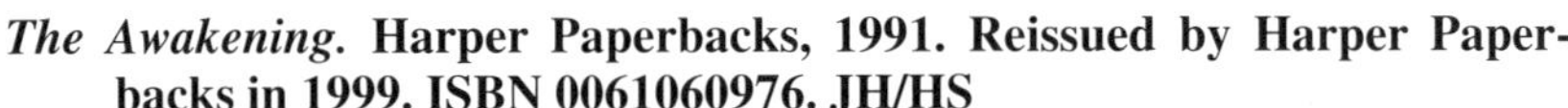

The Awakening. **Harper Paperbacks, 1991. Reissued by Harper Paperbacks in 1999. ISBN 0061060976. JH/HS**

Elena and Stefan meet at school and fall in love. When Stefan is accused of attacking people, he confesses to Elena that he is a vampire. But Stefan believes his brother Damon is responsible for the attacks, and he needs Elena's help to prove it.

Keywords: crime, family, Gothic romance, vampires

The Struggle. **Harper Paperbacks, 1991. Reissued by Harper Paperbacks in 1999. ISBN 006102001X. JH/HS**

Elena is caught in a love triangle between brothers and vampires Stefan and Damon.

Keywords: family, Gothic romance, vampires

The Fury. **Harper Paperbacks, 1991. Reissued by Harper Paperbacks in 1999. ISBN 0061059919. JH/HS**

Elena, now a vampire, must bring brothers Stefan and Damon together again.

Keywords: family, Gothic romance, vampires

Dark Reunion. **Harper Paperbacks, 1991. Reissued by Harper Paperbacks in 1999. ISBN 0061059927. JH/HS**

Elena, Stefan, and Damon must join forces to fight evil. When the fighting ends, which brother will Elena choose?

Keywords: family, Gothic romance, vampires

Vande Velde, Vivian

Companions of the Night. **Harcourt, 1995. Reissued by Magic Carpet in 2002. ISBN 0152166696. JH/HS**

Sixteen-year-old Kerry Nowicki finds herself on a dangerous adventure when she helps a young man, Ethan Byrne, escape from a group of men who claim Ethan is a vampire. The men chasing Ethan assume Kerry is also a vampire, and they kidnap her father and brother. Can Kerry trust Ethan not to harm her as they search for her family? An ALA Best Book for Young Adults and Popular Paperback for Young Adults.

Keywords: adventure, suspense, vampires

Romantic Fantasy

Fantasy invites readers to suspend their beliefs and realities. Fantasy stories usually involve the characters on quests and adventures that take place in alternate worlds, such as other planets or other historical times. It is this quest theme, in part, that differentiates "Romantic Fantasy" from "Paranormal Romance." The atmosphere is not usually as dark in these books. "Paranormal Romance" and "Romantic Fantasy" also feature alternate worlds, but in "Romantic Fantasy" the alternate worlds are very real for the characters. For example, "Romantic Fantasy" stories take place in imaginary worlds or planets, like Sherryl Jordan's *Secret Sacrament*, and the characters belong in these worlds. Often the characters travel between fantasy worlds as they pursue their quests, such as Princess Leonora and Prince Coren in Carol Matas's and Perry Nodelman's The Minds Sequence.

"Romantic Fantasy" stories are often set in quasi-historical times, allowing authors to create their vision of what life may have been like in the past. For instance, Patricia C. Wrede's *Magician's Ward* is a Regency romance that includes wizards and magic. Sometimes characters in "Romantic Fantasy" are transported backward through time, like the characters in Caroline B. Cooney's Time Travel Quartet or Judith O'Brien's *Timeless Love*. The historical settings also differentiate "Romantic Fantasy" from "Paranormal Romance," which focuses on paranormal phenomena and romance in contemporary settings.

Fantasy allows readers to stretch their imaginations beyond reality, and "Romantic Fantasy" stories follow this pattern. Not only does "Romantic Fantasy" include alternate worlds, it also contains imaginary creatures such as shape-shifters, witches, mermaids, or vampires. Creatures found in "Romantic Fantasy" include magical animals, such as wolves, cats, and pigs, while imaginary creatures such as mermaids and dragons are also featured in "Romantic Fantasy."

Teens have always been big fantasy fiction fans, and fantasy is especially popular now, with the Harry Potter series and the Lord of the Rings trilogy selling to millions. Many teens read fantasy fiction intended for adult audiences. Nevertheless, teens who read either romance or fantasy will be delighted to discover "Romantic Fantasy" written especially for them. For younger teens new to young adult genre fiction, "Romantic Fantasy" is a great way to introduce them to both the romance and the fantasy genres. The book lists in the "Romantic Fantasy" section have been divided into the following categories: Contemporary Romantic Fantasy; Historical Romantic Fantasy; and Time Travel Romance.

Contemporary Romantic Fantasy

Contemporary romantic fantasies feature modern-day settings, but unusual and fantastic events occur in these stories. For instance, Hailey and Claire find a brokenhearted mermaid in a swimming pool in Alice Hoffman's *Aquamarine*, while Owl Tycho is a shape-shifter with a crush on her ninth-grade teacher in Patrice Kindl's *Owl in Love*. Contemporary romantic fantasies are sometimes set in alternate modern worlds, like the "Downside" of New York City in Neal Schusterman's *Downsiders*. Characters are sometimes transported from alternate worlds into the contemporary world, like Princess Quinn in Dian Curtis Regan's *Princess Nevermore*. Whatever the setting, readers of "Contemporary Romantic Fantasy" must be prepared for incredible adventures to take place along with the love story.

Atwater-Rhodes, Amelia

Hawksong. **Delacorte Press, 2003. ISBN 0385730713. [Reluctant Readers] MS/JH**

Nineteen-year-old Danica Shardae, queen of the avian shape-shifters, joins forces with her enemy Zane Cobriana to end war between the avian and the serpiente. When they are in public, Danica and Zane pretend to be in love. Will Danica be able to trust Zane enough to make their union real?

Keywords: animals, marriage, shape-shifters

Block, Francesca Lia

Weetzie Bat Saga.

Dangerous Angels: The Weetzie Bat Books. **HarperCollins, 1998. ISBN 0064406970. [Sexual Content] JH/HS**

Weetzie Bat, her best friend Dirk, and her daughters Cherokee and Witch Baby search for love. The final book in the saga, *Baby-Be Bop,* is not considered a romantic story.

Keywords: family, first love, friendship

Weetzie Bat. **HarperCollins, 1989. ISBN 0060205342. [Sexual Content] JH/HS**

Weetzie Bat and her best friend Dirk, who is gay, search for love and happiness in urban Los Angeles. With the help of a genie, Weetzie finds My Secret Agent Lover Man, Dirk finds Duck, and they, along with babies Cherokee Bat and Witch Baby, live together as a family. An ALA Best Book for Young Adults.

Keywords: first love, genies

Witch Baby. **HarperCollins, 1991. ISBN 0060205482. [Reluctant Readers] JH/HS**

Witch Baby, the illegitimate child of My Secret Agent Lover Man, joins Weetzie Bat's family. As Witch Baby grows up, she falls in love with her friend Angel Juan Perez. She is heartbroken when Angel Juan and his family are deported to Mexico, and Witch Baby learns about love and loss.

Keywords: first love, friendship, grief

Cherokee Bat and the Goat Guys. **HarperCollins, 1992. ISBN 0060202696. [Sexual Content, Reluctant Readers] JH/HS**

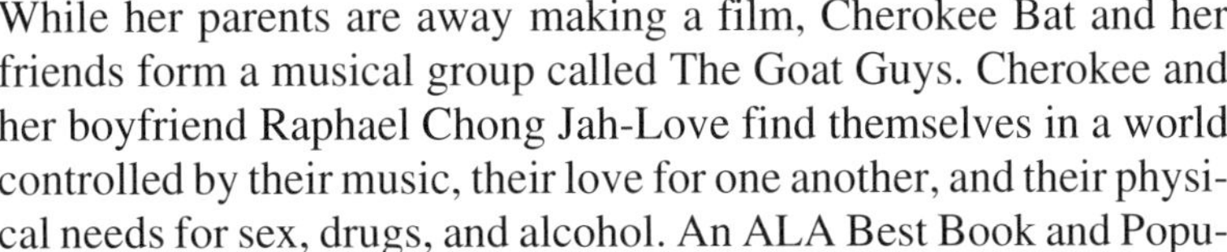

While her parents are away making a film, Cherokee Bat and her friends form a musical group called The Goat Guys. Cherokee and her boyfriend Raphael Chong Jah-Love find themselves in a world controlled by their music, their love for one another, and their physical needs for sex, drugs, and alcohol. An ALA Best Book and Popular Paperback for Young Adults.

Keywords: dating, drugs, first love, music, sex

Missing Angel Juan. **HarperCollins, 1993. ISBN 006023007X. [Sexual Content, Reluctant Readers] JH/HS**

Witch Baby is heartbroken when her boyfriend, Angel Juan, goes to New York City to play music, leaving her behind. Witch Baby follows him to New York City, where she meets the ghost of her grandfather, Charlie Bat. Witch Baby and Charlie search all over the city for Angel Juan. Will Witch Baby ever see her true love again? An ALA Best Book for Young Adults.

Keywords: dating, first love, friendship, ghosts

Hoffman, Alice

Aquamarine. **Scholastic, 2001. ISBN 0439098637. [Reluctant Readers] MS/JH**

Twelve-year-old best friends Hailey and Claire find a brokenhearted mermaid named Aquamarine stuck in a swimming pool at the deserted beach club. When Aquamarine falls in love with Raymond, the boy who works at the beach club's snack counter, she refuses to return to the ocean until Hailey and Claire help her win Raymond's love.

Keywords: friendship, mermaids

Jones, Diana Wynne

Fire and Hemlock. **Greenwillow Books, 1984. Reissued by Greenwillow Books, 2002. ISBN 006447352X. JH/HS**

Polly reminisces about her childhood as she packs for college. She remembers her parents' divorce, school days, and heroic adventures with her adult friend Thomas Lynn. Tom trains Polly to be a hero, and Polly develops a crush on Tom as she grows older.

Keywords: adventure, crushes, magic

Kindl, Patrice

Owl in Love. **Houghton Mifflin, 1993. ISBN 0395661625. MS/JH**

Ninth-grader Owl Tycho is a shape-shifter who can transform from human to owl at will. Owl has a crush on her science teacher, Mr. Lindstrom, and she sits outside his bedroom window at night. Near Mr. Lindstrom's house, Owl meets a shape-shifter boy named Houle, who is a young and incompetent owl, so Owl nurtures him and he becomes the object of her affections. An ALA Best Book for Young Adults and winner of the 1995 Mythopoeic Children's Book Award.

Keywords: animals, crushes, humor, shape-shifters, teachers

The Woman in the Wall. **Houghton Mifflin, 1997. ISBN 0395830141. MS/JH**

Fourteen-year-old Anna is extremely shy. When her family forgets about her existence, she disappears into a secret room she built in the family's library. When Anna finds a love letter meant for her sister Andrea, she thinks it was written for her and she begins corresponding with her sister's suitor.

Keywords: crushes, family, first love, letters

Matas, Carol, and Perry Nodelman

The Minds Sequence.

Princess Leonora and Prince Coren, a young couple engaged to be married, work together to fight evil.

Of Two Minds. **Scholastic, 1998. ISBN 0590394681.** **MS/JH**

Princess Leonora, who can make whatever she imagines real, is betrothed to Prince Coren, who can read minds. Leonora's parents hope that Coren will be able to help Leonora control her powers. But Leonora and Coren don't like each other. To escape their marriage, Leonora and Coren travel to another land, where the evil Havek steals their powers. Leonora and Coren must work together to restore their powers and return home. Will Leonora and Coren learn to like each other?

Keywords: marriage, princes, princesses

More Minds. **Scholastic, 1998. ISBN 059039469X.** **MS/JH**

In the middle of planning their wedding, Princess Leonora and Prince Coren set off to find a giant who is terrorizing Gepeth.

Keywords: marriage, princes, princesses

Out of Their Minds. **Simon & Schuster, 1998. ISBN 0689819463.** **MS/JH**

Princess Leonora and Prince Coren travel to Coren's homeland of Andilla for their marriage. But chaos ensues when something upsets The Balance, and Coren and Leonora must discover what is wrong.

Keywords: marriage, princes, princesses

A Meeting of Minds. **Simon & Schuster, 1999. ISBN 0689819471.** **MS/JH**

Princess Leonora and Prince Coren are transported to a science fiction convention in Winnipeg, Canada, where they meet the authors who created them. Will Leonora and Coren find their way back for their wedding?

Keywords: marriage, princes, princesses

Regan, Dian Curtis

Princess Nevermore. **Scholastic, 1995. ISBN 0590457586. [Reluctant Readers]** **MS/JH**

Princess Quinnella lives in Mandria, a world below earth. When Quinn turns sixteen, she will be married to a prince, but Quinn inadvertently travels to outer earth before her birthday. Quinn falls in love with fellow high school student Adam, and she is pursued by Zack the jock. Although she knows she should return to Mandria, Quinn is tempted to stay on earth.

Keywords: first love, magic, marriage, princesses

Dian Curtis Regan, *Princess Nevermore*

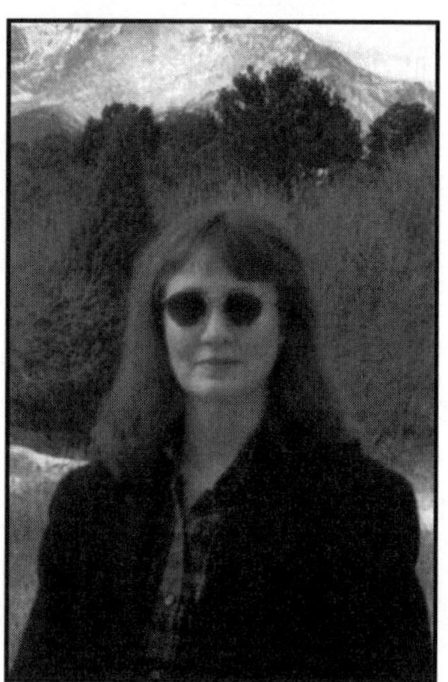

Dian Curtis Regan. Photo by John Regan. Used with permission.

Dian Curtis Regan loves her large collection of stuffed walruses. In an interview in May 2002, Regan said, "Early on in my career, I wrote a series of stories about a very outspoken walrus. Everyone who read the stories felt moved to give me a walrus . . . I have over 100 walruses." Regan's walrus collection is featured on her Web site, and walruses appear in many of the stories she has written for children and young adults, including the romantic fantasy *Princess Nevermore*.

Besides walruses, Regan's young adult stories include themes of love and romance. "When writing for young adults, love and romance are almost always part of the story simply because they're high on a teen's list of interests. This is such a bittersweet time of life, relationship-wise, I think the topic is endlessly intriguing," Regan noted. "Also, it's helpful for teens to note how book characters react to various scenarios that the reader has also faced or will face in the future. I think it helps them to make wise choices."

Regan, a former teacher, knows her audience and is aware that younger readers enjoy her young adult novels. In the same interview, she remarked, "I've always called my YA novels 'young, young adult.' I know from letters I receive that readers as young as eight are reading *Princess Nevermore*, but the story is 'young' and not graphic, so I'm not concerned. The young adult short stories I've recently published in *Shattered* and *Soul Stories* are for a slightly older audience and are more graphic."

Regan's books for young adults include *I've Got Your Number, The Perfect Age, Game of Survival, Jilly's Ghost, The Initiation,* and *Princess Nevermore*. She has also contributed short stories to the anthologies *Dirty Laundry, Shattered, Soul Stories*, *Period Pieces, Mysterious 13*, and *New Year, New Love*. The author's efforts have not gone unrecognized. Her books have won regional, national, and international awards, and in 1993, she was named "Member of the Year" by the Society of Children's Book Writers and Illustrators.

Responding to an editor's remark that the early twenty-first century is the "Golden Age of young adult literature," Regan commented, "I think it's an exciting time to be writing for teenagers. I think they're the best audience, and I love meeting young readers and hearing from them."

Working on two young adult books, a novel called *Adjusting to Midnight* about a thirteen-year-old girl who is blinded in an accident, and the much requested sequel to her popular book *Princess Nevermore*, Regan offered some hints about the sequel. "Book two opens with the king about to choose a husband for Quinn, who is stuck emotionally until she has some sort of closure in

Dian Curtis Regan (*Cont.*)

her relationship with Adam. And Cam can no longer live not knowing who he is and where he came from. The wizard, Melikar, allows Cam to leave Mandria in search of answers."

Who will the king choose to be Princess Quinn's husband? Will Cam learn his true heritage? Will Quinn and Cam find true love? Or perhaps more importantly, will the story feature a walrus? Fans of Regan's work will find answers to these questions in the sequel to *Princess Nevermore*.

For further information:

Dian Curtis Regan. 2002. Available: http://www.diancurtisregan.com/ (accessed September 12, 2002).

Olendorf, Donna, ed. "Dian Curtis Regan." In *Contemporary Authors*. Vol. 142. Detroit: Gale Research, 1994.

Peacock, Scott, ed. "Dian Curtis Regan." In *Something about the Author*. Vol. 133. Detroit: Gale Research, 2002.

Shusterman, Neal

***Downsiders*. Simon & Schuster, 1999. ISBN 0689803753. JH**

Talon lives in "the Downside," a world that exists in the sewers and subways of New York City. When Talon accidentally meets fourteen-year-old Lindsay, a "Topsider," they become friends. Despite the differences in their lifestyles, Talon and Lindsay fall in love. Can their love survive?

Keywords: family, first love, friendship

Historical Romantic Fantasy

"Historical Romantic Fantasy" stories are set during different historical time periods. Sometimes it is obvious that the love story is set during a certain time period, such as Patricia C. Wrede's *Magician's Ward*, set in the Regency Period between 1811 and 1820 when the Prince of Wales ruled England as Prince Regent. Sometimes historical romantic fantasies are set during vague time periods, such as Sherryl Jordan's *The Secret Sacrament*, which is set during the Middle Ages, or Judith Tarr's *Pride of Kings*, which is set during the Crusades. Usually, however, historical romantic fantasies do not clearly define the time period in which they are set. If your patron wants to read something set in a definite time period, suggest a title from Chapter 7, "Historical Romance." If readers are willing to suspend their beliefs and take a journey into a vague or unknown time period filled with adventure and romance, then historical romantic fantasies will please them.

Freisner, Esther M.

***Wishing Season.* Simon & Schuster, 1993. ISBN 0689315740. JH/HS**

The genie Khalid's master, Haroun, wishes for an infinite number of wishes, which means Khalid will serve Haroun forever. But genie maiden Tamar loves Khalid, and she teams up with an alley cat and a princess to try to rescue Khalid.

Keywords: genies, humor, magic

Hanley, Victoria

***The Seer and the Sword.* Holiday House, 2000. ISBN 0823415325. JH/HS**

When Princess Torina's father gives her a slave, she sets the slave free. Landen, Torina's former slave, becomes a member of the King's army and her good friend. Their friendship falters when Landen tells Torina that Vesputo pretends to be her lover only to further his political agenda. When Vesputo gets nasty, Torina and Landen flee the country and separate. Will Torina and Landen be able to thwart Vesputo and find their way back to each other?

Keywords: clairvoyance, politics, princesses

Jordan, Sherryl

***The Hunting of the Last Dragon.* HarperCollins, 2002. ISBN 0060289031. JH/HS**

When Jude returns home to find his village destroyed and his family dead, he joins a traveling fair, where he tends to Jing-wei. Jing-wei is a young Chinese woman with bound feet, and she is exhibited as a freak in the fair. Jing-wei convinces Jude to leave the fair to find the dragon that killed his family, and while they are on their quest, Jing-wei falls in love with Jude. An ALA Best Book for Young Adults.

Keywords: Britain, dragons, first love, Middle Ages, travel

***The Raging Quiet.* Simon & Schuster, 1999. ISBN 0689821409. JH/HS**

When Marnie's husband is killed in an accident two days after their wedding, the villagers blame Marnie. Marnie befriends Raven, a deaf man, but the villagers think Marnie is a witch because she can communicate with Raven using hand signs. While Marnie and Raven are falling in love, the villagers are planning Marnie's witch trial.

Keywords: disabilities, marriage, witches

***Secret Sacrament.* HarperCollins, 2001. ISBN 006028904X. [Sexual Content] JH/HS**

Gabriel Eskban Vala, a young Navoran student of physical and spiritual healing, is clairvoyant. His visions inform him that men are plotting his death, so he runs away to live with the Shinali, a farming clan. Gabriel falls in love with Ashila, a Shinali healer. Can Gabriel and Ashila unite the Navoran and the Shinali tribes, despite the political and historical differences between the clans?

Keywords: clairvoyance, farming, first love

***Wolf Woman.* Houghton Mifflin, 1994. ISBN 0395709326. MS/JH**

Tanith lived with a pack of wolves until the age of three, when Chief Ahearn found her and raised her as his daughter. An outsider in the clan, Tanith's only friend is Gibran, the son of a chieftain in a neighboring village. But Tanith is drawn to the wolves for comfort after the death of her adopted mother. Tanith must choose between Gibran, the boy who loves her, and the wolves. An ALA Best Book for Young Adults.

Keywords: animals, first love, historical fiction

Llwelyn, Morgan

"Lion of Ireland" Duo.

Brian Boru, king of Ireland, and his teenage sons Donough and Teigue fight Ireland's enemies. While they are not busy at war, they enjoy romance.

***Lion of Ireland.* Houghton Mifflin, 1980. Reissued by Tor in 2002. ISBN 0765302578. [Adult] HS**

Brian Boru, legendary king of Ireland, fights Ireland's enemies. He finds time for love and romance with Fiona, Deirdre, and Gormlaith.

Keywords: Ireland, war

***The Pride of Lions.* Tor, 1996. Reissued by Tor in 1997. ISBN 0812536509. [Adult] HS**

Brian Boru's fifteen-year-old son Donough battles his brother Teigue for the crown of Ireland. Donough finds happiness with a Druid girl named Cera, and though he loves her, he cannot marry her and become king. Donough must decide whether to give up Cera or the crown.

Keywords: Ireland, war

McKillip, Patricia A.

***The Forgotten Beasts of Eld.* Atheneum, 1974. Reissued by Magic Carpet Books in 1996. ISBN 0152008691. JH/HS**

Sixteen-year-old Sybel, who lives alone on Eld mountain with only her father's magical animals for company, is visited by Coren and presented with a baby. Sybel cares for baby Tam, her nephew, until Coren returns to take the child back. Sybel marries Coren, who truly loves her, to take revenge upon him. Will Sybel fall in love with Coren? Winner of the 1975 World Fantasy Award.

Keywords: animals, magic, wizards

McKinley, Robin

***The Blue Sword.* Greenwillow Books, 1982. Reissued by Ace Books in 1991. ISBN 0441068804. MS/JH**

In the sequel to *The Hero and the Crown,* Harry Crewe is kidnapped by the king of the Free Hillfolk. She learns she has magical powers, and with training, she will become a female warrior. Along the way, Harry falls in love with the handsome king who has kidnapped her. A 1983 Newbery Honor Book, an ALA Best Book and Popular Paperback for Young Adults.

Keywords: adventure, kidnapping, magic, warriors

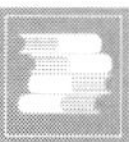

 ***The Hero and the Crown.* Greenwillow Books, 1985. Reissued by Penguin Putnam in 2000. ISBN 0141309814. MS/JH**

Aerin, daughter of the king of Damar, learns how to slay dragons using the Blue Sword. When Aerin is injured in a battle with an evil dragon, she finds the wizard healer Luthe, who helps her learn about her heritage and her destiny. On her adventures, Aerin falls in love with two different men, and she must choose between them. An ALA Best Book for Young Adults and winner of the 1985 Newbery Award.

Keywords: dragons, magic, princesses, witches, wizards

Pierce, Meredith Ann

 ***The Woman Who Loved Reindeer.* Atlantic Monthly Press, 1985. Reissued by Magic Carpet in 2000. ISBN 0152017992. [Sexual Content] JH/HS**

Caribou raises her sister-in-law's baby by a trangl, a being that is part human and part reindeer, but Reindeer never feels like her own child. When Reindeer grows up, he and Caribou become lovers, but Reindeer must also run with the wild deer. When the villagers ask for Caribou's help to escape a wildfire, Caribou and Reindeer take the villagers on a quest for safety. An ALA Best Book for Young Adults.

Keywords: animals, shape-shifters

Shinn, Sharon

 ***The Shape-Changer's Wife.* Ace Books, 1995. Reissued by Ace Books in 2003. ISBN 044101061X. HS**

A young wizardry student, Aubrey, seeks to learn shape-shifting from the master, Glyrender. But Aubrey does not expect to fall in love with the shape-changer's beautiful wife, Lillith.

Winner of the 1996 William L. Crawford Memorial Award.

Keywords: magic, shape-shifters, wizards

 ***Summers at Castle Auburn.* Ace Books, 2001. ISBN 0441008038. MS/JH**

Seventeen-year-old Coriel spends her summers at Castle Auburn with her half-sister Elisandra, who is engaged to Prince Bryan, the future king. Coriel spends the rest of the year with her maternal grandmother, who teaches her the magic of herbs, and she plans to succeed her grandmother as the village wise woman. Coriel has a crush on Prince Bryan, but her uncle has plans for a political marriage for Coriel. An ALA Best Book for Young Adults.

Keywords: crushes, magic, marriage, politics

Tarr, Judith

***Pride of Kings.* Roc, 2001. ISBN 0451458478. [Adult] HS**

In a historical fantasy story about King Richard the Lionhearted and his brother John, who succeeds Richard as King, the brothers rule over the two worlds of the humans and the fairies. The story is told from the perspective of John's squire Arslan, who falls in love with Eschiva, a fairy guardian of Britain.

Keywords: Britain, Crusades, fairies, family

Wrede, Patricia C.

Magician's Ward. **Tor, 1997. Reissued by Tor in 2002. ISBN 0765342480. HS**

The sequel to *Mairelon the Magician* finds Kim working as Mairelon's ward and apprentice. Kim's aunt, however, wants her to marry. When Mairelon's magical powers are stolen and several wizards have disappeared, Kim must find time to solve the mystery between visits with suitors, trips to the opera, and preparations for her coming-out ball.

Keywords: magic, mystery, Regency romance, wizards

Time Travel Romance

Time travel romances feature teens who travel backward or forward through time. For instance, the characters in Caroline B. Cooney's Time Travel Quartet travel between the late nineteenth and late twentieth centuries, while the teen goddesses in Clea Hantman's Goddesses Quartet travel from ancient Athens, Greece, to contemporary Athens, Georgia. Usually the time traveling occurs by accident, and the protagonist must find a way to travel through time again so she can return home. This problem generates a great deal of suspense because the protagonist may be trapped forever if she cannot find a way to travel home. Readers enjoy this suspense, along with the historical settings that are usually a part of time travel romances.

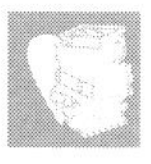

Although she is now a university student, my cousin Rose still speaks fondly of Caroline B. Cooney's Time Travel Quartet, which she enjoyed reading in her early teens. Mature teen readers of "Time Travel Romance" will also enjoy Diana Gabaldon's Outlander series. Judith O'Brien, author of *Timeless Love*, has also written time travel romances for adults. For more adult time travel romance titles, see the bibliography included in Kristin Ramsdell's *Romance Fiction* (Libraries Unlimited, 1999).

Cooney, Caroline B.

Time Travel Quartet.

Fifteen-year-old Annie Lockwood travels to the 1890s, where she falls in love with a teenage boy named Strat.

Both Sides of Time. **Delacorte Press, 1995. ISBN 0385321740. JH/HS**

Annie Lockwood accidentally time travels to the 1890s during a storm. In the Victorian era, Annie falls in love with Hiram Stratton Jr., a boy from a wealthy family. Will Annie return to the present, or will she stay with Strat?

Keywords: dating, historical fiction, time travel

Out of Time. **Bantam Books, 1995. ISBN 0385322267. JH/HS**

Annie Lockwood time travels to the Victorian era to find Strat. But Annie discovers Strat's family has placed him in an insane asylum because he truly believed Annie came from the future. Annie must find a way to rescue her true love.

Keywords: dating, historical fiction, time travel

Prisoner of Time. **Bantam Doubleday Dell, 1998. ISBN 0385322445. JH/HS**

Devonny Stratton, trapped in an engagement to an English lord and threatened with blackmail, calls out across time for help to the twentieth century, where her brother is living. But instead of locating Strat, Annie Lockwood's brother Todd comes to take Devonny into the future.

Keywords: dating, historical fiction, time travel

For All Time. **Delacorte Press, 2001. ISBN 0385327730. JH/HS**

When Annie Lockwood tries to travel back in time to see Strat, her true love, she accidentally ends up in ancient Egypt. Will the time-crossed lovers ever be together again?

Keywords: dating, Egypt, historical fiction, time travel

Curley, Marianne

Old Magic. **Pulse, 2002. ISBN 0743437691. MS/JH**

From the moment high school sophomore Kate Warren first sees Jarrod Thornton, she senses there is something special about him. When Kate discovers Jarrod has supernatural powers, he does not believe her. Kate convinces Jarrod that he is a witch, and while they travel back through time to solve the mystery of Jarrod's family history, Kate and Jarrod fall in love.

Keywords: Australia, dating, magic, Middle Ages, witches

Deveraux, Jude

Knight in Shining Armor. **Pocket Books, 1989. Reissued by Pocket Books in 2002. ISBN 0743439724. [Adult] HS**

Dougless Montgomery has been deserted by her lover, and in her despair, she finds herself in an old English church. To her surprise, Nicholas Stafford, Earl of Thornwyck and sixteenth-century knight, appears. Together Dougless and Nicholas embark on an adventure and a love affair that takes them to the sixteenth century.

Keywords: ghosts, historical fiction, knights, time travel

Gabaldon, Diana

Outlander Series.

Claire Randall time travels to eighteenth-century Scotland, where she falls in love with Jamie Fraser.

Outlander. **Bantam Doubleday Dell, 1991. ISBN 0385302304. [Adult, Sexual Content] HS**

Claire and Frank Randall travel to the Scottish highlands for a second honeymoon. While visiting standing stones, Claire is accidentally transported 200 years back in time to Scotland at the beginning of the second Jacobite rising. In the eighteenth century, Claire falls in love with Jamie Fraser. Winner of the 1992 Romance Writers of America Rita award.

Keywords: historical fiction, Scotland, time travel

Dragonfly in Amber. **Delacorte Press, 1992. ISBN 0385302312. [Adult, Sexual Content] HS**

Twenty years after Claire Randall accidentally traveled through time to eighteenth-century Scotland, she returns to Scotland with her daughter Brianna to show her the secret of the standing stones and to introduce her to her real father. Claire travels back in time again to help her husband James Fraser before the battle of Culloden Moor.

Keywords: France, historical fiction, Scotland, time travel

Voyager. **Delacorte Press, 1993. ISBN 0385302320. [Adult, Sexual Content] HS**

Voyager continues the story of Claire Randall and Jamie Fraser as they flee the battle of Culloden and travel to the West Indies.

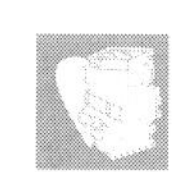

Keywords: historical fiction, Scotland, time travel, West Indies

Drums of Autumn. **Delacorte Press, 1997. ISBN 0385311400. [Adult, Sexual Content] HS**

Claire Randall travels through time again to be with her eighteenth-century husband Jamie Fraser. The Frasers travel to the American colonies on the eve of the American Revolution and attempt to settle in the Mountains. Little do they know that their daughter Brianna has time traveled from the twentieth century, with her boyfriend Roger Wakefield in pursuit, to find her mother.

Keywords: historical fiction, Revolutionary War, Scotland, time travel

The Fiery Cross. **Delacorte Press, 2001. ISBN 0385315279. [Adult, Sexual Content] HS**

The story of time travelers Claire and Brianna Randall continues as they prepare for the American Revolution with their husbands.

Keywords: historical fiction, Revolutionary War, time travel

Hantman, Clea

Goddesses Quartet.

Zeus accidentally banishes his daughters Polly, Era, and Thalia to contemporary Athens, Georgia, and he sends Thalia's boyfriend Appollo to find them.

Heaven Sent. **HarperTrophy/Avon, 2002. ISBN 0064408752. [Reluctant Readers] MS/JH**

When Zeus banishes daughters Polly, Era, and Thalia as punishment, he accidentally sends them to contemporary Athens, Georgia, instead of Athens in Ancient Greece. While the girls get used to life in America, Polly falls in love with Tom, and Thalia misses her boyfriend Appollo. The goddesses also have to deal with the Furies, who have followed them to Athens High.

Keywords: Ancient Greece, dating, myths, time travel

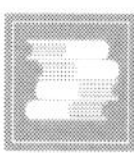

Three Girls and a God. **HarperTrophy/Avon, 2002. ISBN 0064408035. [Reluctant Readers] MS/JH**

Zeus sends Thalia's boyfriend Appollo, disguised as Dylan from Denver, to help the goddesses conquer challenges so they can return home. But Thalia doesn't recognize Appollo, due to his disguise, and she doesn't want to have anything to do with him.

Keywords: Ancient Greece, dating, myths, time travel

Muses on the Move. **HarperTrophy/Avon, 2002. ISBN 0064408043. [Reluctant Readers] MS/JH**

The goddesses go on a road trip with their friend Pocky. While Appollo keeps an eye on them, Thalia can't stop thinking about Dylan from Denver.

Keywords: Ancient Greece, dating, myths, time travel

Love or Fate. **HarperTrophy/Avon, 2002. ISBN 0064408051. [Reluctant Readers] MS/JH**

Polly, Thalia, and Era have been sent to Hades, where they are at the mercy of their rivals, the Furies. Will Appollo be able to rescue the goddesses?

Keywords: Ancient Greece, dating, myths, time travel

Montes, Marisa

A Circle of Time. **Harcourt, 2002. ISBN 0152026266. JH/HS**

When fourteen-year-old Allison Blair is injured in a car accident, she is transported to California in 1906, where she becomes Becky Thompson. As Allison tries to learn the reason for her time travels, she falls in love with Becky's boyfriend, Joshua. Suddenly Allison isn't sure she wants to return home.

Keywords: historical fiction, mystery, suspense, time travel

O'Brien, Judith

Timeless Love. **Pulse, 2002. ISBN 0743419219. MS/JH**

After receiving an antique necklace for her sixteenth birthday, Samantha accidentally time travels to Tudor England. Sam arrives in the bedchamber of the sickly King Edward VI. Sam also meets Sir Barnaby Fitzpatrick, with whom she falls in love. Sam and Barnaby run away when the Duke of Northumberland turns Edward against them. Will Sam ever find her way home?

Keywords: Britain, historical fiction, time travel

Vande Velde, Vivian

A Well-Timed Enchantment. **Harcourt, 1998. ISBN 0152017658. MS/JH**

Fifteen-year-old Deanna drops her watch in a well, and when she tries to retrieve it, she and her cat Oliver are transported to tenth-century France. Oliver arrives in human form. After an adventurous time searching for the watch, Deanna and Oliver return home, and Oliver turns back into a cat. There's only one problem—Deanna has fallen in love with the human version of Oliver!

Keywords: animals, historical fiction, shape-shifters, time travel

Fairy Tales and Fables

The "Fairy Tales and Fables" subgenre features revisions of romantic fairy tales, as well as reworkings, takeoffs, and even new romantic stories based on well-known fairy tales and fables. Like "Romantic Fantasy" and "Paranormal Romance" stories, "Fairy Tales and Fables" insist that readers leave reality behind. For instance, many of these stories include fairies that can perform magic. Retellings and reworkings of fairy tales and fables are appealing to teens because they are already familiar with many of the stories, such as *Cinderella, Beauty and the Beast,* and *Sleeping Beauty*. In their retellings of fairy tales and fables, authors introduce historical settings and sophisticated plots, appealing to readers who have outgrown children's picture books. Readers who like "Romantic Fantasy" will also enjoy the new and revised romantic fairy tales and fables, since quasi-historical settings, imagined worlds, and use of magic are found in both genres.

The titles in this section offer familiar elements of fairy tales, but with new twists and fresh perspectives. Teens enjoy looking at things from alternative viewpoints, and these stories satisfy that desire. Readers will be captivated by new romance stories based on familiar fairy tales and fables, such as Francesca Lia Block's short stories in *The Rose and the Beast*, Gail Carson Levine's *Ella Enchanted,* or Adele Geras's Edgarton Hall Trilogy. Readers will also enjoy new stories written in the fairy tale tradition, such as Francesca Lia Block's *I Was a Teenage Fairy* and Holly Black's *Tithe*. Some of these new and revised fairy tales, such as William Goldman's *The Princess Bride* and Robin McKinley's *Beauty,* are already considered classics. For more information about books providing retellings and reworkings of fairy tales, read Gail de Vos and Anna E. Altmann's *New Tales for Old* (Greenwood, 1999) and *Tales, Then and Now* (Greenwood, 2001).

Black, Holly

***Tithe: A Modern Faerie Tale.* Simon & Schuster, 2002. ISBN 0689849249. JH/HS**

When Kaye helps Roiben, an injured fairy she finds in the street late one night, she falls in love with him. Then Kaye learns that she is really a green pixie with wings, instead of a sixteen-year-old girl, and she is drawn into the fairy world. Roiben is surprised to discover that Kaye is a pixie. But other faeries think Kaye is mortal, and they plan to sacrifice her in a ritual ceremony. An ALA Best Book for Young Adults.

Keywords: fairies, fantasy, first love

Block, Francesca Lia

***I Was a Teenage Fairy.* HarperCollins, 1998. ISBN 0060277475. JH/HS**

Sixteen-year-old beauty queen Barbie Marks has a modeling career, a little fairy named Mab, and a first love named Todd. A dark side of the story involves the molestation of Barbie and Griffin, Todd's gay roommate, by a male fashion photographer.

Keywords: crime, fairies, first love, homosexuality, physical abuse

The Rose and the Beast: Fairy Tales Retold. **HarperCollins, 2000. ISBN 0060281294. JH/HS**

Block locates her revised fairy tales, such as *Snow White, Cinderella, Beauty and the Beast, Thumbelina,* and *Rose Red and Rose White*, in modern-day Los Angeles. Many of the nine stories in the book include romance.

Keywords: fairies, short stories

Conford, Ellen

The Frog Princess of Pelham. **Little, Brown, 1997. ISBN 0316152463. [Reluctant Readers] MS/JH**

When Danny Malone kisses fifteen-year-old Chandler, a wealthy orphan, she turns into a frog. While Danny tries to turn Chandler back into a girl, they become good friends. If Chandler turns back into a girl, will Danny and Chandler become more than friends? Based on *The Frog Prince*.

Keywords: animals, shape-shifters

Dokey, Cameron

Beauty Sleep. **Pulse, 2002. ISBN 074342221X. JH/HS**

When Princess Aurore is christened, she is cursed by her cousin Jane to fall asleep for 100 years after she pricks her finger on a sharp object. Aurore grows up protected by her parents and her older cousin Oswald. At age sixteen, Aurore runs away to the Forest, where she meets Prince Ironheart, who seeks to awaken a sleeping princess with the kiss of true love. Can Ironheart save Aurore from her fate? A retelling of *Sleeping Beauty*.

Keywords: family, princes, princesses

Storyteller's Daughter. **Pulse, 2002. ISBN 0743422201. JH/HS**

After King Shahrayar finds his wife with her lover, the queen dies by her own hand. Hurt by the betrayal, Shahrayar hardens his heart and he declares that any woman who becomes his bride will die the morning after the wedding. Shahrazad, the daughter of the king's trusted advisor, is determined to marry the king, in the hopes that she can thaw his cold heart. On their wedding night, Shahrazad begins to tell a story, and Shahrayar keeps her alive for many days and nights to hear the story. Can Shahrazad help Shahrayar find love again? Based on *The Arabian Nights*.

Keywords: kings, princes, princesses

Sunlight and Shadow. **Pulse, 2004. ISBN 0689869991. JH/HS**

Mina is born on the longest night of the darkest month of the year, and her father, who is Mage of the Day, fears she belongs to the Dark. When Mina is sixteen, her father brings her into sunlight, and in revenge, Mina's mother, who is Queen of the Night, makes a deal with a handsome prince. If he can free Mina from the sunlight, then Mina will marry him. Based on *The Magic Flute*.

Keywords: marriage, princes

Donoghue, Emma

***Kissing the Witch: Old Tales in New Skins.* HarperCollins, 1997. ISBN 0060275758. [Sexual Content] HS**

Retellings of familiar fairy tales, such as *Beauty and the Beast, Snow White, Cinderella,* and *Rapunzel*, focusing on women and their sexuality.

Keywords: homosexuality, lesbians

Ferris, Jean

***Once upon a Marigold.* Harcourt, 2002. ISBN 0152167919. MS/JH**

When Christian looks through his telescope at the nearby castle, he spots Princess Marigold and falls madly in love with her. Although Christian is a commoner, he begins secretly courting the princess, and she falls in love with him. Will Christian ever be allowed to marry his true love? An ALA Best Book for Young Adults.

Keywords: humor, princes, princesses

Gaiman, Neil, and Charles Vess

***Stardust: Being a Romance within the Realms of Faerie.* DC Comics, 1999. ISBN 156389470X. [Sexual Content] JH/HS**

In order to win the hand of his beloved Victoria, Tristan Thorn promises her the gift of a fallen star. The star landed just beyond the wall separating his town from the Faerie realm, requiring Tristan to venture into the land of Faerie. Will Tristan find the star and win Victoria's love?

Keywords: graphic novels, magic

Geras, Adele

Edgerton Hall Trilogy.

Teenage roommates attending Edgerton Hall, a boarding school, experience love and adventure in the 1960s.

***The Tower Room.* Harcourt, 1992. Reissued by Harcourt in1998. ISBN 0152015183. JH/HS**

Megan Thomas is a student at Edgerton Hall, a British boarding school, in the 1960s. Megan falls in love with Simon Findlay, the new young lab assistant at the school. Each night, Simon climbs up to the tower room Megan shares with her roommates, Alice and Bella. When the school's headmistress finds out about the lovers' secret meetings, their fate lies in her hands. Based on *Rapunzel.*

Keywords: diaries, education, first love, historical fiction

***Watching the Roses.* Harcourt, 1992. Reissued by Harcourt in 1998. ISBN 0152015175. [Sexual Content] JH/HS**

At her christening, Alice is cursed by Aunt Violette, who says she will be "snuffed out" on her eighteenth birthday. Alice is raped on the night of her eighteenth birthday party, and she withdraws from the world, lying in bed and refusing to speak. Instead, Alice writes

her story in a journal she finds. Will Jean Luc, the boy Alice loves, be able to help her? Based on *Sleeping Beauty.*

Keywords: diaries, first love, historical fiction, rape

Pictures of the Night. **Harcourt, 1993. Reissued by Harcourt in 1998. ISBN 0152015191. [Sexual Content] JH/HS**

Bella sings with a seven-member band that plays gigs in London and Paris. Although songwriter Greg has a crush on Bella, she falls in love at first sight with American medical student Mark across a crowded room, and she fears she will never see him again. Meanwhile, Bella's jealous stepmother Marjorie tries to kill her. Based on *Snow White.*

Keywords: family, first love, historical fiction, music

Goldman, William

The Princess Bride. **Harcourt, 1973. Reissued by Random House in 2003. ISBN 0345418263. HS**

Westley, a handsome farm boy, loves Buttercup, the most beautiful woman in the world. Westley encounters many villains on his quest to win his true love, including Prince Humperdinck, who plans to marry Buttercup. An abridgement of S. Morgenstern's original story. Also a popular motion picture.

Keywords: adventure, marriage, princes, weddings

Haddix, Margaret Peterson

Just Ella. **Simon & Schuster, 1999. ISBN 0689821867. [Reluctant Readers] MS/JH**

In a continuation of the *Cinderella* story, fifteen-year-old Ella has accepted Prince Charming's marriage proposal. When Ella tries to break off the engagement, after realizing Prince Charming is superficial, she is imprisoned in the dungeon. Will Ella ever escape?

Keywords: marriage, princes

Jukes, Mavis

Cinderella 2000. **Delacorte Press, 1999. ISBN 0385327110. MS/JH**

Fourteen-year-old Ashley Ella Toral wants to spend New Year's Eve 1999 at a country club party, where her crush Trevor Cranston will be ringing in the millennium. But her stepmother Phyllis has asked her to baby sit her twin stepsisters on New Year's Eve. Can Grammie, Phyllis's grandmother, save the day? Based on *Cinderella.*

Keywords: crushes, family, humor

Kindl, Patrice

Goose Chase. **Houghton Mifflin, 2001. ISBN 0618033777. MS/JH**

Fourteen-year-old Alexandria Aurora Fortunato gives bread to an old woman, who as thanks puts a spell on Alexandria, making her rich and beautiful. Alexandria attracts a king and a prince, neither of whom she wants to marry, so her suitors imprison her in a tower. Her geese help her escape and, on the run, Alexandria encounters many adventures. Based on the fairy tale *Goose Girl.*

Keywords: adventure, animals, marriage

Levine, Gail Carson

 *Ella Enchanted.* **HarperCollins, 1997. ISBN 0060275103. [Reluctant Readers] MS/JH**

Ella of Frell is given the gift of obedience by a fairy, but she discovers the gift is a curse because she must obey everyone's wishes, including the requests of stepmother Dame Olga and her daughters. Ella falls in love with Prince Char, but she renounces her feelings for him because she is afraid her curse might endanger Prince Char and the kingdom. Can Ella and Char ever be together? Based on *Cinderella.* An ALA Best Book for Young Adults and a 1998 Newbery Honor Book. Also a feature film.

Keywords: curses, fairies, family, princes

Levine, Gail Carson

The Princess Tales Series.

Several titles in Levine's Princess Tales series include retellings of romantic fairy tales.

The Princess Test. **HarperCollins, 1999. ISBN 0060280638. MS**

Prince Nicholas needs a bride, so his family searches all through the kingdom of Biddle for a princess. But Nicholas falls in love with Lorelei, a blacksmith's daughter. How will Lorelei pass the princess tests designed by King Humphrey? Based on *The Princess and the Pea.*

Keywords: marriage, princes, princesses

Princess Sonora and the Long Sleep. **HarperCollins, 1999. ISBN 0060280646. MS**

At her birth several fairies bring wishes for Princess Sonora, and she grows up ten times smarter than anyone else, knowing that she will one day be pricked by a spindle. Can Princess Sonora control her fate, or will she have to rely on a prince to rescue her? A revision of *Sleeping Beauty.*

Keywords: fairies, princes, princesses

Cinderellis and the Glass Hill. **HarperCollins, 2000. ISBN 006028336X. MS**

Cinderellis plans to use magic to climb the glass hill and win the love of Princess Marigold Charming. A revision of *Cinderella.*

Keywords: marriage, princes, princesses

For Biddle's Sake. **HarperCollins, 2002. ISBN 0060000945. MS**

Parsley loves Prince Tansy, the king's youngest son. When Bombina the fairy accidentally turns Parsley into a toad, Parsley needs Tansy to propose marriage to break the spell. Will Tansy ever be able to love a toad? A revision of the fairy tale *Puddocky.*

Keywords: fairies, princes, princesses

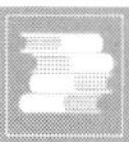

The Fairy's Return. **HarperCollins, 2002. ISBN 0066238005. MS**

When Princess Lark meets Robin, the baker's son, the pair falls madly in love. But their parents won't allow them to marry. Can Ethelinda the fairy help the lovebirds? Based on *The Golden Goose*.

Keywords: fairies, princes, princesses

Loggia, Wendy

Ever After: A Cinderella Story. **Laurel Leaf, 1998. ISBN 0440228158. MS/JH**

Danielle works as a servant for her stepmother, the Baroness Rodmilla of Ghent. A chance meeting with Prince Henry, who is in search of a wife, leads Danielle and the prince to true love. But the Baroness intends for her daughter Marguerite to marry Prince Henry. Based on the popular movie of the same name.

Keywords: dances, family, princes

Lynn, Tracy

Snow. **Pulse, 2003. ISBN 0689855567. MS/JH**

When Jessica, Duchess of Kenigh, learns her stepmother is planning to kill her, she runs away to London. A group of creatures called the Lonely Ones, who are half-animal and half-human, give Jessica a home and the new name Snow. Snow and Raven fall in love, but before they can admit their feelings, the Lonely Ones rally to protect Snow when her evil stepmother comes looking for her. Based on *Snow White*.

Keywords: family, first love, stepmothers

McKiernan, Dennis L.

Once upon a Winter's Night. **New American Library, 2001. ISBN 0451458400. JH/HS**

When a bear knocks on Camille's door, she is surprised to learn that Prince Alain of Summerwood wishes to marry her. Camille decides to go with Bear to Summerwood, where she falls in love with Prince Alain. But the prince is keeping a secret from Camille. A revision of *East o' the Sun and West o' the Moon*.

Keywords: animals, magic, marriage, princes, shape-shifters

McKillip, Patricia

Winter Rose. **Ace Books, 1996. ISBN 0441003346. HS**

Rois Melior discovers Corbett Lynn rebuilding his grandfather's house and is attracted to him, but her fairy senses warn her to stay away from him. When her sister Laurel breaks off her engagement due to an infatuation with Corbett, Rois tries to learn more about Corbett's mysterious family. Suddenly Corbett disappears, and Laurel wastes away with heartbreak. Only Rois can find Corbett and save her sister.

Keywords: curses, fairies

McKinley, Robin

***Beauty: A Retelling of the Story of Beauty and the Beast.* HarperCollins, 1978. Reissued by HarperCollins in 1993. ISBN 0064404773. MS/JH**

In exchange for his life, a man promises a beast his beautiful daughter. Although Beauty is held captive in a castle by Beast, she will not agree to marry him. An ALA Best Book for Young Adults.

Keywords: animals, magic, shape-shifters

***Rose Daughter.* Greenwillow Books, 1997. ISBN 0688154395. MS/JH/HS**

McKinley's second retelling of the *Beauty and the Beast* fairy tale. An ALA Best Book for Young Adults.

Keywords: animals, magic, shape-shifters

***The Stone Fey.* Harcourt, 1998. ISBN 0152000178. [Sexual Content] JH/HS**

While Maddy is waiting for her fiancé Donal to return so they can be married, she is drawn to the Stone Fey, who lives in the Hills. Maddy will have to choose between Donal and the Stone Fey.

Keywords: fairies, fantasy, marriage, picture books

Napoli, Donna Jo

***Beast.* Simon & Schuster, 2000. ISBN 0689835892. JH/HS**

Prince Orasmyn is transformed into a lion as punishment after he violates the Qur'an and his Muslim heritage. Orasmyn travels to Persia, India, and France, searching for roses. In France, he finds an abandoned castle and Belle, his true love. Based on *Beauty and the Beast.*

Keywords: animals, magic, shape-shifters

***Zel.* Penguin Putnam, 1996. ISBN 0525456120. [Sexual Content] JH/HS**

Mother locks her daughter Zel in the tower after she falls in love with Count Konrad. The characters of Zel, Count Konrad, and Mother tell the story of a mother desperate to keep her daughter to herself. Based on *Rapunzel.*

Keywords: historical fiction, witches

Osborne, Mary Pope

***Haunted Waters.* Candlewick, 1994. ISBN 156402119X. JH**

Lord Huldbrand, a knight, takes refuge with a fisherman's family. Huldbrand falls in love with the fisherman's foster daughter, a young sea creature named Undine, and they marry. Undine and Huldbrand live in his castle, but Undine is drawn back to the water. Will Undine and Huldbrand find a way to live together? Based on a nineteenth-century fable called *Undine.*

Keywords: fairies, marriage, travel

Schreiber, Ellen

***Teenage Mermaid.* HarperCollins, 2003. ISBN 0060082054. MS/JH**

Teen mermaid Lilly meets teen surfer Spencer while saving him from drowning. When a chance meeting brings Lilly and Spencer together again, they fall madly in love. Based on the *Little Mermaid*, this story is told from the perspectives of Lilly and Spencer.

Keywords: dating, mermaids, sports

Tepper, Sheri S.

***Beauty: A Novel.* Bantam Doubleday Dell, 1991. ISBN 0385419406. JH/HS**

When Beauty accidentally time travels to the modern world, she escapes a curse that would put her into everlasting sleep. As Beauty grows up in the contemporary world, she meets several other fairy tale heroines, including Cinderella and Snow White, but Beauty is more concerned with saving the future world from destruction than she is in finding Prince Charming to rescue her. Based on *Sleeping Beauty*. Winner of the 1992 Locus Poll Award.

Keywords: adventure, historical fiction, time travel

Viguie, Debbie

***Midnight Pearls.* Pulse, 2003. ISBN 0689855575. MS/JH**

Pearl is rescued from the sea by a fisherman, who takes her home to raise her as his child. When Pearl is a teenager, she befriends James, the crown prince of Astra. Pearl and James wonder if they might be in love, but before they have a chance to find out, two mysterious strangers threaten to destroy their dreams of a life together. A retelling of the *Little Mermaid*.

Keywords: first love, friendship, princes

Wrede, Patricia C.

***Snow White and Rose Red.* St. Martin's Press, 1989. Reissued by Tor in 1993. ISBN 0812558251. [Adult] JH/HS**

The Widow Arden supports herself and her daughters, Blanche and Rosamund, by selling herbs and healing potions. While searching for herbs it is sometimes necessary for Blanche and Rosamund to cross to the Faerie realm, where they discover magic gone awry among the royal family of Faerie. Prince John seeks the help of Widow Arden and her daughters to make things right again. A retelling of *Snow White and Rose Red*.

Keywords: England, historical fiction, magic, Middle Ages

Myths and Legends

The "Myths and Legends" subgenre, like "Romantic Fantasy," is full of adventure and romance. Familiar lovers are plentiful in romantic myths and legends, including Arthur, Guenevere, and Lancelot, Robin Hood and Marian, and Helen and Paris. And like fairy tales, they may contain recognizable elements. Teen readers may already be as familiar with "Myths and Legends" as they are with popular "Fairy Tales and Fables."

Teens will enjoy stories based on the well-known adventures of the Arthurian myths, such as Rosalind Miles's Guenevere Trilogy, or the Robin Hood legends, such as *Lady of the Forest* by Jennifer Roberson. Readers will also enjoy books based on Greek mythology, including Adele Geras's *Troy* and Caroline B. Cooney's *Goddess of Yesterday*.

Books in the "Myths and Legends" subgenre may appeal more to older teens who already know something about popular myths and legends, and they will be drawn to these books because they can see familiar mythical characters come alive. Stories of myth, legend, love, and adventure can be used to introduce younger readers to the romance and fantasy genres, and because the stories are so satisfying, they will appeal to younger readers who are discovering the myth and legend subgenre for the first time. You may have to do some prompting, but once readers have started this subgenre, you will find they are repeatedly drawn into the romantic myths and legends.

Cooney, Caroline B.

***Goddess of Yesterday.* Delacorte Press, 2002. ISBN 0385729456. MS/JH**

Twelve-year-old Anaxandra is found by Menelaus, the King of Sparta, on a deserted island. Anaxandra informs Menelaus that she is Princess Callisto, the daughter of King Nicander, and she is taken to Sparta to live with Menelaus and his wife Helen. When Paris arrives in Sparta, he and Helen fall madly in love, sparking the Trojan War. Based on Homer's *The Illiad* and the Trojan War myths.

Keywords: Ancient Greece, Trojan War

Geras, Adele

***Troy.* Harcourt, 2001. ISBN 0152164928. [Sexual Content] JH/HS**

The story of the Trojan War is told from the perspectives of two sisters, Xanthe and Marpessa, who are both in love with the young soldier Alastor. All of the Trojan characters are here, including Helen, Paris, Agamemnon, and Achilles, along with the gods and goddesses Aphrodite, Zeus, Ares, Hermes, Eros, and Poseidan; but the story focuses on the events that unfold as a result of Xanthe's and Marpessa's love for the same man. Based on Homer's *The Illiad* and the Trojan War myths. An ALA Best Book for Young Adults.

Keywords: Ancient Greece, goddesses, gods, historical fiction, Trojan War

Levitin, Sonia

***Escape from Egypt.* Little, Brown, 1994. ISBN 0316522732. JH/HS**

Hebrew slave Jesse falls in love with Jennat, another slave who is half Egyptian and half Syrian. The couple's love affair is thwarted by Jesse's betrothal to Talia, the arrival of the Plagues that bring death and destruction, and differences in religion. When Jennat follows Moses in the Exodus, showing a devotion to Jesse's Hebrew God, Jesse believes he might have a future with his true love Jennat. Based on the legends of the Exodus. An ALA Best Book for Young Adults.

Keywords: Egypt, religion, slavery

Llwelyn, Morgan

***The Horse Goddess.* Houghton Mifflin, 1982. Reissued by Tor in 1998. ISBN 0812555031. [Adult] HS**

Epona meets Kazak, a Scythian prince and soldier, and they fall in love. They travel across Europe, running from a Druid priest called the Shapeschanger, who wants to bring Epona home. Based on the legend of Epona. An ALA Best Book for Young Adults.

Keywords: Ancient Greece, religion, shape-shifters

McKinley, Robin

***The Outlaws of Sherwood.* Greenwillow Books, 1988. Reissued by Ace Books in 1989. ISBN 0441644511. HS**

A retelling of the *Robin Hood* legend, *The Outlaws of Sherwood* offers readers a feminist version of the love story of Robin Hood and Maid Marian. The romance only blooms after Robin learns that he cannot tell Marian what to do. An ALA Best Book for Young Adults.

Keywords: England, feminism, historical fiction

McLaren, Clemence

***Aphrodite's Blessings: Love Stories from the Greek Myths.* Atheneum, 2002. ISBN 0689843771. JH/HS**

Three short stories provide feminist revisions of the love stories of women from Greek mythology, including Atalanta, Andromeda, and Psyche.

Keywords: Ancient Greece, marriage, short stories

***Inside the Walls of Troy.* Simon & Schuster, 1996. ISBN 0689318200. JH/HS**

The story of the love affair between Helen and Paris and the Trojan War from a feminist perspective, the story switches from Helen's to Cassandra's point of view. A prophetess, Cassandra foresees the destruction of Troy when her brother Paris returns with his true love, Helen. Based on Homer's *The Illiad* and the Trojan War myths.

Keywords: Ancient Greece, friendship, Trojan War

Miles, Rosalind

The Guenevere Trilogy.

Guenevere, King Arthur's wife, falls in love with his friend Lancelot. Based on Arthurian legend.

***Guenevere: Queen of the Summer Country.* Crown, 1999. ISBN 0609603620. [Adult] HS**

The Arthurian legends are told from Guenevere's perspective in Miles's Guenevere trilogy. In the first book, *Queen of the Summer Country*, Guenevere meets Arthur and they marry to unite their lands. In a twist on the legend, Guenevere is a goddess-worshipping pagan and queen in her own right.

Keywords: Britain, historical fiction, kings, knights

Guenevere: Knight of the Sacred Lake. **Crown, 2000. ISBN 0609606239. [Adult] HS**

Guenevere is confused by her love for Arthur and his knight Lancelot.

Keywords: Britain, historical fiction, kings, knights

Guenevere: The Child of the Holy Grail. **Crown, 2001. ISBN 0609606247. [Adult] HS**

Guenevere is heartbroken by a separation from Lancelot, and she returns to her husband Arthur. But Mordred, Arthur's son, threatens to make Camelot his own. The arrival of Sir Galahad brings the Quest for the Holy Grail and the end of Camelot forever.

Keywords: Britain, historical fiction, kings, knights

Napoli, Donna Jo

Sirena. **Scholastic, 1998. ISBN 0590383884. JH/HS**

Sirena, a mermaid, is granted immortality by the Greek gods after she rescues Philoctetes from the sea. Sirena and Philoctetes fall in love. A revision of the Greek myth of the Sirens. An ALA Best Book for Young Adults.

Keywords: Ancient Greece, mermaids

Roberson, Jennifer

Lady of the Forest. **Kensington, 1992. ISBN 0821739190. JH/HS**

Sir Robery Locksley, a nobleman, begins a dangerous quest for justice in war-torn England. Lady Marian of Ravenskeep, the daughter of a knight, leaves her comfortable life to join Sir Robery and his band of outlaws. During their journey, Sir Robery and Lady Marian fall in love. Based on *Robin Hood.*

Keywords: crime, England, historical fiction

Spinner, Stephanie

Quiver. **Alfred A. Knopf, 2002. ISBN 0375914897. JH/HS**

Atalanta makes a vow of chastity to the goddess Artemis, so she must come up with a plan when her father King Iasus demands that she marry and produce an heir. Atalanta agrees to marry a suitor who can beat her in a race, and everyone but Hippomenes fails the test. Will Atalanta, who has fallen in love with Hippomenes, agree to marry him? A retelling of the Greek myth of Atalanta.

Keywords: Ancient Greece, marriage

Sutcliff, Rosemary

Black Ships before Troy: The Story of the Iliad. **Delacorte Press, 1993. ISBN 0385310692. JH/HS**

The legendary story of Paris's abduction of Helen of Troy and the Trojan War. Based on Homer's *The Illiad* and the Trojan War myths. An ALA Best Book for Young Adults.

Keywords: Ancient Greece, historical fiction, picture books, Trojan War

***Tristan and Iseult*. E. P. Dutton, 1971. Reissued by Sunburst in 1991. ISBN 0374479828. MS/JH**

Irish warrior Tristan meets Iseult, the princess of Ireland, and they fall madly in love. Based on the Celtic myth of *Tristan and Iseult*. An ALA Popular Paperback for Young Adults.

Keywords: adventure, Ireland, princesses

Tomlinson, Theresa

***The Forestwife*. Bantam Doubleday Dell, 1997. ISBN 0440413508. JH/HS**

In this feminist revision of the Robin Hood legend, fifteen-year-old Mary de Holt runs away to Sherwood Forest to escape an arranged marriage. In the forest she finds her nurse Agnes, a skilled healer known as the Forestwife, and a band of outlaws, including a young man named Robert de Loxley. Marian and Robin, as they are known, share romance.

Keywords: crime, historical fiction, magic

Voigt, Cynthia

***Orfe*. Simon & Schuster, 1992. Reissued by Pulse in 2002. ISBN 0689848684. JH/HS**

Orfe's best friend Enny helps her form a popular musical group, the Graces. As Orfe begins to achieve musical success, she is distracted by her obsession with her lover Yuri, a drug addict. The story is narrated by Enny, who watches helplessly as Orfe loses herself in Yuri's problem. A modern-day version of the Greek myth of *Orpheus and Eurydice*.

Keywords: drugs, Greek mythology, music

Romantic Science Fiction

"Romantic Science Fiction" stories appeal to teen readers because these stories combine elements of the romance genre with those of adventure. "Romantic Science Fiction" also includes scientific information or musings that intrigue teens with an interest in science. Like adventures, they are often fast-paced and action filled, and protagonists tend to be heroic. Like "Romantic Fantasy," the stories often involve a battle between good and evil. They also cover themes and topics that appeal to certain teens, including space travel, aliens, space, science, and technology. Teens with an interest in science and technology will especially be drawn to this subgenre. Fans of the Star Wars movie *Attack of the Clones* will find several different versions of the story in book form for readers of all ages. The teen reader who enjoys "Romantic Fantasy" may also like stories that combine romance and science fiction, such as *Dancing with an Alien* by Mary Logue. Readers who want to experience the future of love and romance will enjoy "Romantic Science Fiction" stories.

Gilroy, Henry

***Star Wars Episode II: Attack of the Clones*. Dark Horse Comics, 2002. ISBN 1569716099. JH/HS**

Jedi knight Anakin Skywalker and Senator Padme Amidala fall in love, leading to Anakin's downfall.

Keywords: adventure, first love, graphic novels, space travel

Hesse, Karen

***Phoenix Rising.* Henry Holt, 1994. ISBN 0805031081. MS/JH**

Thirteen-year-old Nyle Sumner, who lives on a sheep farm in Vermont with her grandmother, has survived a radiation leak from a nearby nuclear plant. When Gran allows Miriam Trent and her son Ezra to stay with them, Nyle falls in love with Ezra, despite the fact that he is dying from radiation poisoning. Will Nyle be able to say good-bye?

Keywords: death, environment, first love, illness, science

Hughes, Monica

***Keeper of the Isis Light.* Simon & Schuster, 1981. Reissued by Aladdin Paperbacks in 2000. ISBN 0689833903. JH/HS**

Olwen Pendennis, the Keeper of the Isis Light, lives with her Guardian on the deserted planet Isis. Colonists from Earth arrive and settle in the valleys of Isis, and sixteen-year-old Olwen fears they might ruin her world. Instead, she falls in love with a colonist. An ALA Best Book for Young Adults.

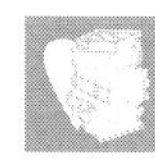

Keywords: first love, space travel

Logue, Mary

***Dancing with an Alien.* HarperCollins, 2000. ISBN 0060283181. [Reluctant Readers] JH/HS**

Branko travels to Earth to find a young woman to bring home to help him repopulate his planet. Seventeen-year-old Tonia's life is changing, and she is not happy about it. When Branko and Tonia fall in love, she must decide if she wants to leave Earth forever. An ALA Best Book for Young Adults.

Keywords: aliens, first love, space travel

Luiken, Nicole M.

"The Eyes Series."

Teens Angel Eastland and Michael Vallant fall in love while they investigate their role in a genetic experiment.

***Violet Eyes.* Pocket Books, 2001. ISBN 0743400771. JH/HS**

Angel Eastland falls in love with her rival, Michael Vallant. When Michael goes missing, Angel learns they are part of a genetic experiment called the Renaissance Children, and she and Michael were designed to become rivals. Will Angel ever see Michael again?

Keywords: first love, science

***Silver Eyes.* Pocket Books, 2001. ISBN 074340078X. JH/HS**

Angel Eastland, the result of a genetic experiment, lives in a world where people are controlled by brain chips and people work on Mars. Angel works as an investigator for a mining company, and an assignment leads her to capture her friend Michael Vallant. Angel and Michael renew their love affair, and Angel must find a way to

protect Michael from her boss and learn why terrorists from Mars are attacking Earth.

Keywords: first love, science, space travel

Pike, Christopher

***The Starlight Crystal.* Pocket Books, 1995. Reissued by Pocket Books in 1996. ISBN 0671550284. JH/HS**

When Paige Christian is invited to join the crew of the Traveler, a spaceship that circles the solar system at light speed, she is thrilled. She will spend two centuries studying Earth. Before Paige leaves, she meets Tem and they fall in love. Paige plans to return to Tem, but a terrible tragedy takes place aboard the Traveler. Will Paige and Tem ever be reunited?

Keywords: first love, science, space travel

Salvatore, R. A.

***Star Wars Episode II: Attack of the Clones.* Ballantine Books, 2002. ISBN 0345428811. [Adult] JH/HS**

In a novelization based on George Lucas's screenplay, Salvatore tells the story of the downfall of Jedi knight Anakin Skywalker, who becomes the evil Darth Vader. Although true love is forbidden to the Jedi, Anakin falls in love with Senator Padme Amidala.

Keywords: adventure, first love, space travel

Shinn, Sharon

***Jenna Starborn.* Ace Books, 2002. ISBN 044100900X. [Adult] HS**

Jenna Starborn is a lonely young woman who was produced in a laboratory. When she goes to work at a nuclear reactor plant owned by Everett Ravenbeck, Jenna and Everett fall in love. But Jenna learns he already has a wife, and Jenna runs away to a remote planet. Will Everett find Jenna in time to save their love? Based on the classic love story *Jane Eyre*.

Keywords: first love, science, technology

Wrede, Patricia C.

***Star Wars Episode II: Attack of the Clones.* Scholastic, 2002. ISBN 0439139287. [Reluctant Readers] MS/JH**

Although true love is forbidden to the Jedi, Anakin Skywalker falls in love with Senator Padme Amidala. For younger readers.

Keywords: adventure, first love, space travel

Alternative Reality Romance Series

"Alternative Reality Romance Series" feature elements of paranormal, fantasy, and horror fiction, combined with stories of love and romance. Teen protagonists in "Alternative Reality Romance Series" must deal with common contemporary social issues, unusual paranormal events, and trouble in their love lives. Most "Alternative Reality Romance Series" books feature continuing characters and story lines, but a few series, like Enchanted

Hearts, introduce new characters and new stories in each book. Settings are usually contemporary, but events in the stories are often influenced by a long history of magic or witchcraft, like in the Sweep series. Several "Alternative Reality Romance Series" are based on popular television shows, such as *Buffy the Vampire Slayer* and *Charmed*. Even when the contemporary issues and paranormal events vary from one series to another, all the series listed here include a strong element of romance.

Books published in each series are listed in publication order. For readers who enjoy these titles, you can also suggest new titles in the contemporary/paranormal Smooch series, found in Chapter 4, "Contemporary Romance Series."

Buffy the Vampire Slayer. Pocket/Pulse, 1997 to Present. [Sexual Content] JH/HS

Written by Various Authors.

Based on the popular television show, which came to an end in 2003. Buffy the Vampire Slayer, watcher Giles, sister Dawn, friends Willow, Xander, Cordelia, and Tara, and boyfriends Angel, Riley, and Spike experience adventure and romance as they fight vampires and demons in Sunnydale.

Keywords: dating, demons, friendship, magic, vampires, witches

1. *The Harvest*
2. *Halloween Rain*
3. *Coyote Moon*
4. *The Night of the Living Rerun*
5. *Blooded*
6. *Visitors*
7. *Unnatural Selection*
8. *Power of Persuasion*
9. *Deep Water*
10. *Here Be Monsters*
11. *Ghoul Trouble*
12. *Doomsday Deck*
13. *Sweet Sixteen*
14. *Crossings*
15. *Little Things*
16. *The Angel Chronicles, Volume 1*
17. *The Angel Chronicles, Volume 2*
18. *The Angel Chronicles, Volume 3*
19. *Child of the Hunt*
20. *Return to Chaos*
21. *The Gatekeeper Trilogy Book 1: Out of the Madhouse*
22. *The Gatekeeper Trilogy Book 2: Ghost Roads*

23. *The Gatekeeper Trilogy Book 3: Sons of Entropy*
24. *Obsidian Fate*
25. *Immortal*
26. *Sins of the Father*
27. *Resurrecting Ravana*
28. *Prime Evil*
29. *The Evil That Men Do*
30. *Paleo*
31. *Spike and Dru: Pretty Maids All in a Row*
32. *Revenant*
33. *The Book of Fours*
34. *The Unseen Trilogy Book 1: The Burning*
35. *The Unseen Trilogy Book 2: Door to Alternity*
36. *The Unseen Trilogy Book 3: Long Way Home*
37. *Tempted Champions*
38. *Oz: Into the World*
39. *The Wisdom of War*
40. *Blood and Fog*
41. *Chaos Bleeds*
42. *Mortal Fear*
43. *The Xander Years, Volume 1*
44. *The Xander Years, Volume 2*
45. *The Willow Files, Volume 1*
46. *The Willow Files, Volume 2*
47. *How I Survived My Summer Vacation, Volume 1*
48. *The Faith Trials, Volume 1*
49. *Tales of the Slayer, Volume 1*
50. *Tales of the Slayer, Volume 2*
51. *Tales of the Slayer, Volume 3*
52. *The Journals of Rupert Giles, Volume 1*
53. *The Lost Slayer Serial Novel Part 1: Prophecies*
54. *The Lost Slayer Serial Novel Part 2: Dark Times*
55. *The Lost Slayer Serial Novel Part 3: King of the Dead*
56. *The Lost Slayer Serial Novel Part 4: Original Sins*
57. *The Lost Slayer Bind Up*
58. *The Watcher's Guide Volume 1: The Official Companion to the Hit Show*
59. *The Watcher's Guide Volume 2: The Official Companion to the Hit Show*
60. *The Postcards*

61. *The Essential Angel*
62. *The Sunnydale High Yearbook*

63. *Pop Quiz: Buffy the Vampire Slayer*
64. *The Monster Book*
65. *The Quotable Slayer*
66. *The Script Book, Season One, Volume 1*
67. *The Script Book, Season One, Volume 2*

68. *The Script Book, Season Two, Volume 1*
69. *The Script Book, Season Two , Volume 2*
70. *The Script Book, Season Two , Volume 3*
71. *The Script Book, Season Two , Volume 4*

72. *The Script Book, Season 3, Volume 1*
73. *The Script Book, Season 3, Volume 2*

Charmed. Pocket/Pulse Books, 1999 to Present. JH/HS
Created by Constance M. Burge; Written by Various Authors.

Based on the television series of the same name, Charmed features adult sisters Piper, Phoebe, and Prue Halliwell. They discover they are the Charmed Ones, the most powerful of witches, and it is their job to protect people from evil. When Prue is killed, half-sister Paige appears so the Charmed Ones can continue to fight evil. Stories feature adventure and romance.

Keywords: angels, dating, demons, family, magic, marriage, witches

1. *The Power of Three.* Eliza Willard
2. *Kiss of Darkness.* Brandon Alexander
3. *The Crimson Spell.* F. Goldsborough
4. *Whispers from the Past.* Rosalind Noonan
5. *Voodoo Moon.* Wendy Corsi Staub

6. *Haunted by Desire.* Cameron Dokey
7. *The Gypsy Enchantment.* Carla Jablonski
8. *The Legacy of Merlin.* E. L. Flood
9. *Soul of the Bride.* Elizabeth Lenhard

10. *Beware What You Wish.* Diana G. Gallagher
11. *Charmed Again.* Elizabeth Lenhard
12. *Spirit of the Wolf.* Diana G. Gallagher
13. *Garden of Evil.* Emma Harrison

14. *Date with Death.* Elizabeth Lenhard
15. *Dark Vengeance.* Diana G. Gallagher
16. *Shadow of the Sphinx.* Carla Jablonski
17. *Something Wiccan This Way Comes.* Emma Harrison

18. *Mist and Stone.* Diana Gallagher
19. *Mirror Image.* Jeff Mariotte
20. *Between Worlds.* Bobbi J. Weiss and Jackly Wilson
21. *Seasons of the Witch, Volume 1.* Various
22. *Truth and Consequences.* Cameron Dokey

Circle of Three. Avon Books, 2001 to 2002. JH/HS
Written by Isobel Bird.

High school sophomore Kate Morgan discovers she has magical powers when she researches witchcraft for a school project. Her love spell does not work out the way she intended, however, and she finds Cooper and Annie, witches who can help her return her life to normal. The series focuses on the growth of the three girls as friends and witches.

Keywords: dating, friendship, magic, witches

1. *So Mote It Be*
2. *Merry Meet*
3. *Second Sight*
4. *What the Cards Said*
5. *In the Dreaming*
6. *Ring of Light*
7. *Blue Moon*
8. *The Five Paths*
9. *Through the Veil*
10. *Making the Saint*
11. *The House of Winter*
12. *Written in the Stars*
13. *And It Harm None*
14. *The Challenge Box*
15. *Initiation*

Daughters of the Moon. Disney, 2000 to Present. JH/HS
Written by Lynne Ewing.

High school sophomore Vanessa Cleveland and her friend Catty discover they have magical powers—Vanessa can make herself invisible, and Catty can shift time. Along with friends Serena and Jimena, they are the Daughters of the Moon, and their task is to use their talents to fight the evil Atrox and its band of Followers. The teens encounter romance as they do battle. One of the few young adult series available only in hardcover.

Keywords: dating, fantasy, friendship, magic, witches

1. *Goddess of the Night*
2. *Into the Cold Fire*

3. *Night Shade*
4. *The Secret Scroll*
5. *The Sacrifice*
6. *The Lost One*
7. *Moon Demon*
8. *Possession*
9. *The Choice*
10. *The Talisman*
11. *Prophecy*

Enchanted Hearts. Avon Books, 1999. JH
Written by Various Authors.

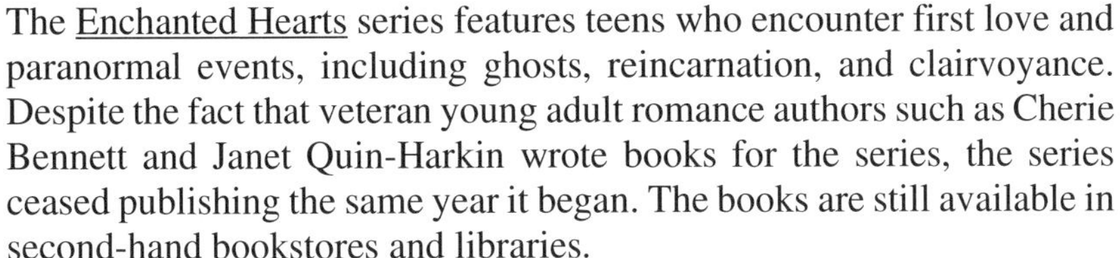

The Enchanted Hearts series features teens who encounter first love and paranormal events, including ghosts, reincarnation, and clairvoyance. Despite the fact that veteran young adult romance authors such as Cherie Bennett and Janet Quin-Harkin wrote books for the series, the series ceased publishing the same year it began. The books are still available in second-hand bookstores and libraries.

Keywords: clairvoyance, dating, ghosts, magic

1. *The Haunted Heart.* Cherie Bennett
2. *Eternally Yours.* Jennifer Baker
3. *Lost and Found.* Cameron Dokey
4. *Love Potion.* Janet Quin-Harkin
5. *Spellbound.* Phyllis Karas
6. *Love Him Forever.* Cherie Bennett

Fear Street. Pocket Books, 1989 to 1999. JH
Written by R. L. Stine.

R. L. Stine's horror series *Fear Street* and its various spin-off series include the element of teen love and romance. While different characters appear in most of the stories, the link that keeps the soap opera going is the evil on Fear Street. Titles such as *First Date, Goodnight Kiss, Broken Hearts, The Perfect Date,* and *The Secret Admirer* are appealing to young adult readers who like their horror stories mixed with a bit of romance.

Keywords: dating, horror, violence

1. *The New Girl*
2. *The Surprise Party*
3. *The Stepsister*
4. *Missing*
5. *Halloween Party*
6. *The Wrong Number*

7. *The Sleepwalker*
8. *Ski Weekend*
9. *The Secret Bedroom*
10. *The Overnight*
11. *Lights Out*
12. *Haunted*
13. *The Fire Game*
14. *The Knife*
15. *Prom Queen*
16. *First Date*
17. *The Best Friend*
18. *Sunburn*
19. *The Cheater*
20. *The New Boy*
21. *Bad Dreams*
22. *The Dare*
23. *Double Date*
24. *The First Horror*
25. *The Mind Reader*
26. *One Evil Summer*
27. *The Second Horror*
28. *The Third Horror*
29. *The Thrill Club*
30. *College Weekend*
31. *Final Grade*
32. *The Stepsister 2*
33. *What Holly Heard*
34. *The Face*
35. *Secret Admirer*
36. *The Perfect Date*
37. *The Boy Next Door*
38. *Night Games*
39. *Runaway*
40. *Killer's Kiss*
41. *All-Night Party*
42. *The Rich Girl*
43. *Cat*
44. *Fear Hall: The Beginning*
45. *Fear Hall: The Conclusion*

Fear Street Super Chiller Series.

1. *Party Summer*
2. *Goodnight Kiss*
3. *Silent Night*
4. *Broken Hearts*
5. *Silent Night II*

6. *The Dead Lifeguard*
7. *Bad Moonlight*
8. *Dead End*
9. *High Tide*

Fear Street Cheerleaders Series.

1. *The First Evil*
2. *The Second Evil*
3. *The Third Evil*
4. *The New Evil*

Fear Street Saga Series.

1. *The Betrayal*
2. *The Secret*
3. *The Burning*
4. *A New Fear*
5. *House of Whispers*
6. *The Hidden Evil*
7. *Daughters of Silence*
8. *Children of Fear*

Ghosts of Fear Street Series.

1. *Nightmare in 3-D*
2. *Stay Away from the Treehouse*
3. *Eye of the Fortuneteller*
4. *Fright Knight*
5. *Revenge of the Shadow People*
6. *The Bugman Lives*
7. *The Boy Who Ate Fear Street*
8. *Night of the Werecat*
9. *Body Switchers from Outer Space*
10. *Fright Christmas*
11. *Don't Ever Get Sick at Granny's*

The Last Vampire. Pocket Books, 1994 to 1999. JH/HS
Written by Christopher Pike.

A series from popular author Christopher Pike, The Last Vampire features a vampire named Sita who wants to know who is stalking her. While she is searching for her stalker, Sita enrolls in high school and falls in love with Ray.

Keywords: dating, Gothic romance, vampires

1. *The Last Vampire*
2. *Black Blood*
3 *Red Dice*
4. *The Phantom*
5. *Evil Thirst*
6. *Creatures of Forever*

Night World. Pocket Books, 1996 to Present. JH/HS
Written by L. J. Smith.

Author L. J. Smith offers readers stories about young women and the vampires who love them. In each book, the vampires offer to rescue the young women with the gift of eternal life.

Keywords: dating, magic, vampires, witches

1. *Secret Vampire*
2. *Daughters of Darkness*
3. *Spellbinder*
4. *Dark Angel*
5. *The Chosen*
6. *Soulmate*
7. *Huntress*
8. *Black Dawn*
9. *Witchlight*

Roswell High. Pulse, 1999 to Present. JH/HS

Based on the popular television show *Roswell*, this series features high school students Liz, Max, Maria, Michael, Alex, and Isabel. Max, Michael, and Isabel are really aliens. The friends experience romance and adventure as they deal with unusual teenage problems. Despite the cancellation of the popular television show in 2002, the story continues in a new Roswell book series.

Keywords: aliens, dating, friendship, science fiction

"The Original Roswell Series."

1. *The Outsider*
2. *The Wild One*
3. *The Seeker*
4. *The Watcher*

5. *The Intruder*
6. *The Stowaway*
7. *The Vanished*
8. *The Rebel*
9. *The Dark One*
10. *The Salvation*

"The New Roswell Series."

1. *Shades*
2. *Skeletons in the Closet*
3. *Dreamwalk*
4. *Quarantine*
5. *Loose Ends*
6. *No Good Deed*
7. *Little Green Men*
8. *A New Beginning*
9. *Nightscape*
10. *Pursuit*
11. *Turnabout*

Sweep. Puffin Books, 2001 to Present. JH/HS
Written by Cate Tiernan.

When witch Cal Blaire arrives at Morgan Rowland's high school, everyone wants to get to know him. Morgan and her friends join Cal in Wiccan ceremonies, and Morgan discovers she has magical abilities. This series focuses on Morgan's growth as a witch, her relationships with family and friends, and her love for Cal and his brother Hunter. The first two books in the series, *Book of Shadows* and *The Coven*, were published first in hardcover without the series name attached to the books, and later they were repackaged in paperback as the first two books in the Sweep series.

Keywords: dating, family, friendship, magic, witches

1. *Book of Shadows*
2. *The Coven*
3. *Blood Witch*
4. *Dark Magick*
5. *Awakening*
6. *Spellbound*
7. *The Calling*
8. *Changeling*
9. *Strife*

10. *Seeker*
11. *Origins*
12. *Eclipse*
13. *Reckoning*
14. *Full Circle*

Sweep Super Specials.

1. *Night's Child: A Sweep Story*

Notes

1. Kristin Ramsdell, *Romance Fiction: A Guide to the Genre* (Englewood, CO: Libraries Unlimited, 1999), 211.

Chapter 7

Romantic Suspense

Stories in the "Romantic Suspense" category feature crime, mystery, suspense, and romance all mixed together. "Romantic Suspense" stories contain adventure and danger that accompany romance in very fast-paced stories. Sometimes the teen protagonists are crime victims; sometimes they are the perpetrators of crime; and sometimes the mystery or crime is peripheral but may affect the romantic relationships in a story. Books in the "Romantic Suspense" category feature both male and female protagonists. Sometimes couples fall in love while solving a mystery, like Noah and Cat in Ellen Wittlinger's *Noticing Paradise*, while in other stories a female protagonist endangers herself and others by falling in love with a criminal. For instance, in Robert Cormier's *We All Fall Down,* Jane falls in love with a boy who injured her sister in a home invasion. Other "Romantic Suspense" stories present political intrigue, such as *For the Love of Venice* by Donna Jo Napoli, or attempted gang rape, like *Crooked* by Laura McNeal and Tom McNeal. Whatever the story is about, the primary element is the suspense that builds throughout the novel.

Book lists in this category include "Contemporary Romantic Suspense"; "Paranormal Romantic Suspense"; and "Historical Romantic Suspense."

Appeal

Mystery and suspense stories are popular with young adult readers, and acclaimed authors such as Lois Duncan, Joan Lowery Nixon, and Robert Cormier created successful careers based on these genres. Because romance fiction is also appealing to teen readers, these readers enjoy the combination of romance and suspense found in the books in the "Romantic Suspense" category. The elements of romance and suspense build upon each other. Suspense adds to the excitement around romance; and romance adds allure to suspense. Young adult authors like Jenny Carroll (Meg Cabot) and Elizabeth Chandler (Mary Claire

Helldorfer) are creating new and popular "Romantic Suspense" stories for teens—with a paranormal twist. The addition of paranormal phenomena gives teen characters special powers to solve mysteries and, at the same time, adds to the building suspense in these stories. Teens who enjoy romance, mystery, and suspense are sure to enjoy the books in the "Romantic Suspense" categories.

Advising the Reader

Following are some tips for advising teen readers about young adult romantic suspense fiction:

- Find out if your patron wants to read "Romantic Suspense" for recreation or for a school assignment. Titles in the "Paranormal Romantic Suspense" book list, like The Mediator series by Jenny Carroll/Meg Cabot or Kissed by an Angel Trilogy by Elizabeth Chandler, may be better choices for recreational reading, while titles from the "Historical Romantic Suspense" list, such as Jennifer Donnelly's *A Northern Light*, may be regarded by parents and teachers as better selections for book reports. The fast pace of "Romantic Suspense" stories might encourage reluctant readers to read a book for a book report!
- If your patron wants to read "Romantic Suspense" stories just for fun, find out which category of the subgenre he or she enjoys reading—"Contemporary Romantic Suspense," "Paranormal Romantic Suspense," or "Historical Romantic Suspense." In order to suggest titles from these categories, you will want to know which elements of "Romantic Suspense" the reader likes—ghost stories, mysteries, political intrigue, exotic locations, historical settings, characters with psychic powers, or protagonists who commit criminal acts. If your patron likes historical and romantic mysteries, then suggest titles from the "Historical Romantic Suspense" book list. The reader who likes stories featuring ghosts and psychics who help solve mysteries will likely enjoy titles from the "Paranormal Romantic Suspense" category. And finally, if your patron likes fast-paced stories with lots of political intrigue and exotic modern settings, he or she will enjoy books in the "Contemporary Romantic Suspense" book list.
- Some teens will be attracted to the mystery and romance elements in the "Historical Romantic Suspense" novels, but they may be less enthusiastic about the history that is included in these stories. If teens are put off by historical elements on the book covers, point out the mystery and romance components and describe the plot. The "Historical Romantic Suspense" subgenre may be a way to hook readers on historical fiction!
- Because this is a relatively small subgenre of young adult romance fiction, you may want to suggest that your customers read "Romantic Suspense" titles written for adults. Authors of historical romantic suspense fiction include Victoria Holt, Mary Stewart, Anya Seton, and Phyllis A. Whitney, while Nora Roberts, Jayne Anne Krentz, and Barbara Michaels write contemporary romantic suspense stories. For more information about the adult romantic suspense genre, see Chapter 6, "Romantic Mysteries," in *Romance Fiction* by Kristin Ramsdell (Libraries Unlimited, 1999).

Contemporary Romantic Suspense

"Contemporary Romantic Suspense" stories for young adults combine mystery and romance in modern-day settings. Books in the "Contemporary Romantic Suspense" category sometimes feature teens who fall in love with criminals, as happens in Robert Cormier's novels *Tenderness* and *We All Fall Down*. Other titles portray characters who fall in love and solve a mystery, such as Noah and Cat in Ellen Wittlinger's *Noticing Paradise* or Rose in *Playing for Keeps* by Joan Lowery Nixon. Exotic locales are sometimes involved, as in Donna Jo Napoli's *For the Love of Venice*, when teen characters go on vacations with family members. These exotic locations will appeal to teen readers who enjoy traveling and learning about cultures new to them. Readers will also enjoy the combination of mystery, romance, and contemporary settings, as contemporary young adult romantic suspense fiction blends familiar surroundings with the exciting unknowns of mystery and first romance.

Cormier, Robert

***Tenderness*. Bantam Doubleday Dell, 1997. ISBN 0385322860. [Reluctant Readers] JH/HS**

Eighteen-year-old Eric Poole has been released from juvenile detention after serving three years for killing his mother and stepfather. Although Eric also killed several young women, he was never charged with their murders, and so he plans to continue thrill-seeking by killing beautiful girls. Lori, a fifteen-year-old runaway who met Eric before he served time, loves and supports Eric, even after she learns his secret—and Lori will do anything to protect Eric. An ALA Best Book for Young Adults.

Keywords: crime, crushes, first love, murder

***We All Fall Down*. Delacorte Press, 1991. ISBN 038530501X. [Reluctant Readers] JH/HS**

When four boys vandalize a home and throw Karen Jerome down the basement stairs, Karen is injured, and the Avenger has seen everything. While Karen lies in hospital in a coma, her sixteen-year-old sister Jane falls in love with Buddy Walker, one of the vandals. The Avenger is distraught when he learns Jane is dating Buddy, and he prepares to take his revenge. An ALA Best Book for Young Adults.

Keywords: crime, dating, first love, mystery

Duncan, Lois

***Don't Look behind You*. Bantam Books, 1989. Reissued by Bantam Books in 1990. ISBN 0440207290. [Reluctant Readers] MS/JH**

High school junior April Corrigan and her family are placed in the Federal Witness Security Program after her father testifies in court against a drug dealer, and April is forced to leave her boyfriend Steve behind. The Corrigan family settles in a new town, where April rebuffs Larry's advances because she misses Steve. However, when April tries to communicate with Steve, she puts her family in jeopardy, and April realizes she must somehow find a way to get over her first love.

Keywords: crime, dating, first love

McNeal, Laura, and Tom McNeal

***Crooked.* Alfred A. Knopf, 1999. ISBN 0679993002. [Sexual Content] JH/HS**

Ninth-graders Clara Wilson and Amos MacKenzie are unhappy teens. Clara's mother has left for a job in Spain, while Amos's father dies unexpectedly during surgery. The two lonely teens find consolation in each other, but they are taunted by bullies who threaten to rape Clara.

Keywords: crime, dating, first love

Napoli, Donna Jo

***For the Love of Venice.* Bantam Doubleday Dell, 2000. ISBN 0440414113. JH/HS**

Percy's family travels to Venice for the summer, where he meets Graziella, a member of an underground political group with plans to save their city from tourists. Despite the fact that seventeen-year-old Percy represents the enemy, Graziella and Percy become romantically involved, and Percy gets caught up in the dangerous plans of a political organization.

Keywords: crime, Italy, politics, vacations

Nixon, Joan Lowery

***Playing for Keeps.* Delacorte Press, 2001. ISBN 0385327595. MS/JH**

When sixteen-year-old Rose Marstead joins her grandmother Glory on a luxury cruise to the Caribbean, Glory plans to set Rose up with her friend's son, Neil. But before the ship even sails, Rose falls in love with Cuban refugee Ricky Diago. Later, Mr. Diago introduces a different boy as his son Ricky, and Rose must find out what happened to her boyfriend.

Keywords: crime, dating, mystery, vacations

O'Rourke, F. M.

***The Poison Tree.* Simon & Schuster, 1996. ISBN 0684802147. JH/HS**

Seventeen-year-old Billy Quinn, who is a member of the Irish Republican Army, travels to Los Angeles to impersonate the grandson of a famous movie director. The move is part of an IRA plot to assassinate British monarch Queen Elizabeth at a reception in L.A. But Billy enjoys life in L.A., where he falls in love with Kelly Huston, and he has a change of heart about being a terrorist.

Keywords: dating, politics, terrorism

Smith, D. James

***Fast Company.* Dorling Kindersley, 1999. ISBN 0789426250. JH/HS**

Fifteen-year-olds Jason and Cat, members of a rollerblading gang, tell their stories of crime and romance in alternate chapters. Jason accidentally kills a boy during a robbery, and the boy's brother seeks revenge on Jason. Meanwhile, Jason's girlfriend Cat learns she is pregnant. After a miscarriage, Cat is confused about her feelings for her criminal boyfriend.

Keywords: crime, dating, gangs, pregnancy

Wittlinger, Ellen

Noticing Paradise. **Houghton Mifflin, 1995. ISBN 0395716462. MS/JH**

Two sixteen-year-olds, Cat and Noah, meet and fall in love on a wildlife cruise through the Galapagos Islands. In a subplot, Cat and Noah solve a mystery.

Keywords: adventure, first love, mystery, vacations

Paranormal Romantic Suspense

"Paranormal Romantic Suspense" stories feature romance, mystery, suspense, and elements of the paranormal, such as ghosts and angels, in contemporary settings. For instance, Suze Simon, the main character in The Mediator series by Jenny Carroll/Meg Cabot, can communicate with ghosts, while angel Tristan must protect his soulmate Ivy from harm in Elizabeth Chandler's exciting Kissed by an Angel trilogy. Other characters in "Paranormal Romantic Suspense" stories are psychic, like the protagonists in Jenny Carroll's 1-800-WHERE-R-YOU series, Liz Berry's *The China Garden,* and Shelley Sykes's *For Mike.* The characters in "Paranormal Romantic Suspense" stories use their powers to solve mysteries. Romance is an important element, however, as the teen protagonists fall in love during their adventures.

Exciting, fast-paced "Paranormal Romantic Suspense" stories like those included in the following book list will hold readers' attention. Teens enjoy reading a thrilling romantic suspense story because they want happy resolutions to both the mystery and the romance. The addition of paranormal phenomena to romantic suspense allows teen characters to obtain the power to find happy resolutions to the mysteries and, it is hoped, their romances, too.

Bell, William

Stones. **Doubleday, 2001. ISBN 038565829X. JH/HS**

When high school senior Garnet Havelock meets Raphaella Skye, he falls in love at first sight. Together Garnet and Raphaella investigate the ghost that hangs around near Garnet's house, and they uncover a buried secret about their community. Winner of the 2002 Young Adult Canadian Book Award.

Keywords: Canada, crime, ghosts, racism

Berry, Liz

The China Garden. **Farrar, Straus and Giroux, 1996. ISBN 0374312486. [Sexual Content] JH/HS**

When Clare and her mother move to Ravensmere, an English estate, seventeen-year-old Clare falls in love with Mark. Clare also discovers she is psychic, and after she learns she and her mother have a link to Ravensmere, Clare uses her psychic powers to solve a mystery. But Clare discovers that Ravensmere is in danger, and saving it will mean risking her future with Mark.

Keywords: clairvoyance, dating, England, mystery

Carroll, Jenny/Cabot, Meg

The Mediator Series.

Meg Cabot, author of The Princess Diaries, offers a paranormal soap opera romance that began under the pen name Jenny Carroll and continues under Cabot's name. High school sophomore Suze Simon moves to California to live with her mother and her stepfamily. Suze is a Mediator, someone who helps ghosts, and she discovers a handsome young ghost named Jesse in her new bedroom. As Suze tries to help Jesse and the other ghosts who seek her help, she falls in love with Jesse.

***Shadowland.* Pulse, 2000. ISBN 0671787918. [Reluctant Readers] MS/JH**

When sixteen-year-old Suze moves to California to live with her mother and her stepfamily, she discovers she is a Mediator, a person who helps ghosts. Suze encounters a ghost at her new school, a student named Heather who killed herself after she was dumped by her boyfriend Bryce. Now Heather's ghost wants revenge on her former boyfriend, and Suze must protect Bryce. Meanwhile, Suze falls in love with Jesse, a teenage ghost who lives in her new bedroom. An ALA Popular Paperback for Young Adults.

Keywords: adventure, crushes, ghosts

***Ninth Key.* Pulse, 2001. ISBN 0671787985. [Reluctant Readers] MS/JH**

When a ghost asks Suze to find her murderer, Suze's investigation leads her to the father of her classmate Tad Beaumont, the first boy to ask Suze out on a date.

Keywords: adventure, crushes, dating, ghosts

***Reunion*. Pulse, 2001. ISBN 0671788124. [Reluctant Readers] MS/JH**

Suze must help the ghosts of four high school students who were killed in a car accident. Suze discovers their deaths were not an accident, and the ghosts want revenge on everyone, including the person responsible for their deaths.

Keywords: adventure, crushes, dating, ghosts

***Darkest Hour*. Pulse, 2001. ISBN 0671788477. [Reluctant Readers] MS/JH**

Suze is spending the summer babysitting young Jack Slater, another Mediator, at a beach resort. While Suze tries to attract the attention of Jack's older brother, Paul, she also has two mysteries to solve: a mysterious grave has been found in her family's backyard and Jesse, the ghost she loves, has disappeared.

Keywords: adventure, crushes, dating, ghosts

***Haunted*. HarperCollins, 2003. ISBN 006029471X. [Reluctant Readers] MS/JH**

The Mediator series continues with *Haunted,* published by HarperCollins under the author's real name, Meg Cabot. While Suze tries to help a teenage boy come to terms with his brother's death, she is caught in a love triangle between Jesse, the ghost who lives in her room, and Paul Slater, the Mediator who tried to kill her last summer.

Keywords: adventure, crushes, dating, ghosts

Carroll, Jenny/Cabot, Meg

1-800-WHERE-R-YOU Series.

A lightning strike gives sixteen-year-old Jessica Mastriani psychic powers. The Lifetime Network television show called *1-800-Missing* is based on this series.

When Lightning Strikes. **Pocket Books, 2001. ISBN 0743411390. [Reluctant Readers] MS/JH**

When sixteen-year-old Jessica Mastriani and her friend get caught in a thunderstorm walking home from school, Jess is struck by lightning. Suddenly Jess is psychic and she knows where missing children can be found. But Jess's new talent doesn't mean she has forgotten about her crush on Rob Wilkins.

Keywords: clairvoyance, crime, crushes, dating

Code Name Cassandra. **Pocket Books, 2001. ISBN 0743411404. [Reluctant Readers] MS/JH**

Jess, now known as "Lightning Girl" by the media and the government, spends the summer working as a camp counselor. When a man needs her help to find his missing daughter, Jess and Rob go in search of the girl.

Keywords: clairvoyance, crime, crushes, dating

Safe House. **Pocket Books, 2002. ISBN 0743411412. [Reluctant Readers] MS/JH**

Jess uses her powers to solve a murder and locate a missing teenage girl, and Rob is there to help her.

Keywords: clairvoyance, crime, crushes, dating

Sanctuary. **Pocket Books, 2002. ISBN 0743411420. [Reluctant Readers] MS/JH**

Jess works with FBI agent Cyrus Krantz to find a missing boy and stop a murderer from killing again. Once again, Jess relies on Rob to help her solve the mystery.

Keywords: clairvoyance, crime, crushes, dating

Chandler, Elizabeth

Dark Secrets Series.

The stories in the Dark Secrets series feature new teen characters involved in mystery and romance.

Legacy of Lies. **Pulse, 2000. ISBN 0743400283. MS/JH**

When sixteen-year-old Megan is invited to meet her grandmother for the first time, she is surprised that she recognizes her grandmother's house—from her dreams. But what Megan can't understand is why her grandmother and handsome cousin Matt do not welcome her into the family, especially since she is so attracted to Matt. Suddenly Megan begins to dream of a life she never lived, and a love she never knew. Now her life is in danger.

Keywords: crushes, ghosts, mystery

Don't Tell. **Pulse, 2001. ISBN 0743400291. MS/JH**

Lauren returns to Wisteria seven years after her mother's mysterious death to visit her godmother, Jule Ingram. Lauren finds the atmosphere at Aunt Jule's house intense. When strange events put Lauren's life in danger, she discovers she can't even trust her childhood friend Nick, whom she believed was more than a friend.

Keywords: crushes, mystery

No Time to Die. **Pulse, 2001. ISBN 0743400305. MS/JH**

Jenny Montgomery registers for the Chase College theater camp under the name of Jenny Baird so she can search for the person who murdered her sister Liza at the camp the previous year. Suddenly Jenny is able to see everything from Liza's perspective. Jenny fights her attraction to Mike, who denies involvement with Liza, but Jenny hopes Mike is not her sister's murderer.

Keywords: crushes, ghosts, mystery

The Deep End of Fear. **Pulse, 2003. ISBN 0689852592. MS/JH**

Seventeen-year-old Kate returns to the Westbrook estate to tutor young Patrick Westbrook. When Patrick informs Kate that he can see and hear the ghost of his sister Ashley, who drowned twelve years earlier, Kate must find out what really happened to Ashley on that deadly night. But everyone, including a handsome young man named Sam, wants Kate to mind her own business.

Keywords: crushes, ghosts, mystery

Chandler, Elizabeth

Kissed by an Angel Trilogy.

Tristan, an angel, must protect his true love Ivy from harm.

Kissed by an Angel. **Archway, 1995. ISBN 0671891456. MS/JH**

When the school swim team star Tristan Carruthers offers to teach Ivy Lyons how to swim, Ivy and Tristan fall in love. On the way to a romantic dinner, Tristan and Ivy have a car accident, which leaves Tristan dead. Tristan returns as Ivy's guardian angel, but Ivy doesn't believe in angels anymore, not since her beloved Tristan died. Will Tristan ever be able to reach Ivy?

Keywords: accidents, angels, dating, death, first love, mystery

The Power of Love. **Archway, 1995. ISBN 0671891464. MS/JH**

Tristan, an angel, realizes the accident that killed him was no accident. Someone wanted to hurt his girlfriend Ivy, and her life is still in danger, but Tristan cannot reach her. Ivy depends on her stepbrother Gregory, who has helped her recover from Tristan's death, and she believes she is falling in love again.

Keywords: angels, crime, dating, death, mystery

Soulmates. **Archway, 1995. ISBN 0671891472. MS/JH**

Ivy regains her belief in angels, allowing Tristan to reach out to her. Tristan and Ivy work together to figure out who wants Ivy dead. But when they solve the mystery, Tristan will have to leave Ivy forever.

Keywords: angels, crime, dating, death, mystery

Sykes, Shelley

For Mike. **Random House, 2000. ISBN 044026937. JH/HS**

When Jeff's best friend Mike disappears early in their senior year of high school, Jeff dreams that Mike is asking for his help. Jeff asks his friend Berry, who knows something about dream interpretation and ESP, to help him figure out what the dreams mean. Soon Jeff and Berry are working together to find out what happened to Mike, and they fall in love. A Delacorte Press Contest Honor Book.

Keywords: dating, dreams, friendship, mystery

Historical Romantic Suspense

Mystery, suspense, romance, and historical fiction blend together to create the small subgenre of young adult "Historical Romantic Suspense" fiction. Stories are usually set in the nineteenth century, like Katherine Kirkpatrick's *Voyage of the Continental*, or the twentieth century, such as *Gentlehands* by M. E. Kerr. It is important to remember that teens regard anything that happened before they were born as history, so some of the titles in this book list are set as late as the 1970s. Most of the stories are set in the United States, although one book, *The Only Outcast* by Julie Johnston, is set in Canada. Sometimes the stories include ghosts, such as Eileen Charbonneau's *The Ghosts of Stony Clove* or Sollace Hotze's *Acquainted with the Night*. While it may seem that the ghost stories belong in the "Paranormal Romantic Suspense" category, all the books on that list are set in contemporary times, and the titles in the following list are distinguished by their sense of time and place in the past.

Teens may find the mysteries and romances, and maybe even the ghosts, in "Historical Romantic Suspense" stories more appealing than the historical settings, so keep this in mind when you are recommending these titles to your patrons. You can play down the historical settings and play up the mystery and romance.

Charbonneau, Eileen

The Ghosts of Stony Clove. **Scholastic, 1988. Reissued by Tor in 1995. ISBN 0812551869. MS/JH**

In 1809, teenagers Asher Woods and Ginny Rockwell investigate stories of ghosts in Stony Clove, a town near the Catskill Mountains. They meet the ghost of indentured servant Sally Hamilton, who helps them solve the mystery of her murder. While chasing ghosts, Asher and Ginny fall in love. Winner of the Romance Writers of America Rita Award.

Keywords: crime, first love, ghosts, mystery

Donnelly, Jennifer

A Northern Light. **Harcourt, 2003. ISBN 0152167056. JH/HS**

Sixteen-year-old Mattie Gokey dreams of going to college, but she is stuck caring for her father and siblings in the Adirondack Mountains in 1906. While Mattie is courted by Royal Loomis, she takes a summer job working at a local hotel. When hotel guest Grace Brown is murdered, it is

up to Mattie to solve the mystery, using letters Grace asked her to destroy. An ALA Best Book for Young Adults and a 2004 Michael L. Printz Honor Book.

Keywords: crime, dating, education, letters, marriage, mystery

Hotze, Sollace

***Acquainted with the Night.* Houghton Mifflin, 1992. ISBN 0395615763. JH/HS**

In the summer of 1970, seventeen-year-old Molly falls in love with her cousin Caleb, who comes to stay with her family to recuperate from injuries sustained in the Vietnam War. The ghost of Evaline Bloodworth appears, to warn Molly away from forming an incestuous relationship with her cousin. Molly and Caleb are determined to learn why the ghost feels so strongly about their love for each other. An ALA Best Book for Young Adults.

Keywords: first love, ghosts, incest, mystery, Vietnam War

Johnston, Julie

***The Only Outcast.* Tundra Books, 1998. ISBN 088776441X. MS/JH**

Sixteen-year-old Fred Dickinson spends the summer of 1904 with his siblings at his grandfather's cottage on Lake Rideau in Ontario. Still grieving the loss of his mother three years earlier, Fred falls in love for the first time, with Nora. He also solves a local murder mystery.

Keywords: family, first love, grief, mystery

Kerr, M. E.

***Gentlehands.* HarperCollins, 1978. Reissued by HarperTrophy in 1990. ISBN 0064470679. JH/HS**

In a modern story of poor boy meets rich girl, Buddy Boyle and Skye Pennington fall in love. But a mystery from the past surrounding Buddy's grandfather threatens to destroy their love. An ALA Popular Paperback for Young Adults and winner of the 1993 Margaret A. Edwards Award.

Keywords: crime, first love, Holocaust, World War II

Kirkpatrick, Katherine

***Voyage of the Continental.* Holiday House, 2002. ISBN 0823415805. JH**

When Emeline McCullough travels on the steamship *Continental* from Massachusetts to Seattle in 1866, she experiences mystery and romance. Emmy hopes she will find her true love in Seattle.

Keywords: diaries, first love, marriage, mystery

Chapter 8

Historical Romance

"Historical Romance" novels can be defined as "love stories with historical settings."[1] In these stories the settings of time and place play a prominent role in the story, and there are plenty of historic details that give readers a sense of another era. However, history is relative. To me, history is anything that happened before 1970. Where teens are concerned, history is anything that happened before they were born. So, for the purposes of this guide, "Historical Romance" fiction refers to love stories set as late as the 1980s. Although this definition theoretically includes classic romances that were written as contemporary romances but are now historical, such as Maureen Daly's *Seventeenth Summer* or Beverly Cleary's *Fifteen*, classic young adult romances have been placed in Chapter 2. Readers who enjoy historical romances may also enjoy historical and modern classics, which is something to keep in mind when recommending titles.

Because historical romances are defined by their settings in time and place, books included in this chapter are arranged by location and time period. The "Historical Romance" book list includes the following sections: "Colonial and Revolutionary America"; "Nineteenth-Century North America" (subdivided into sections "War of 1812"; "Civil War"; "Westward Expansion"; and "Illness and Natural Disasters") ; "Twentieth-Century North America" ("Early Twentieth Century"; "The Forties and World War II"; and "The Fabulous Fifties and Beyond") ; and "Love around the World and throughout Time." "Historical Romance Series" are also noted.

Appeal

What was life like for teens in the past? What would you do about the issue of slavery if you were living in Civil War times? Which side would you have taken in the Revolutionary War? Historical fiction transports readers to other times and places, and gives them a sense of what it might be like to live in different times. Historical fiction can be said to put a face on history, or bring history to life. Readers of this genre often gain new insights or perspectives on historical events.

Like adults, teens enjoy reading "Historical Romance" fiction because they can learn about what life was like in the past. The young adult historical romance reader wants to learn about young people who experience the conflicts and joys of true love in a different environment—a new and exciting setting. Most "Historical Romance" fiction written for young adults is set in nineteenth- or twentieth-century North America, but young adult historical romances may be set in any place during any historical time period.

Historical romances written for teens are usually set against a backdrop of familiar world events, such as wars, the Holocaust, westward expansion, or the sinking of the *Titanic*. Popular settings for historical teen romances published in recent years include well-known American natural disasters, such as the San Francisco earthquake of 1906 or the 1871 Great Chicago Fire. Teens are often already familiar with these historic events from history class and other media, such as movies and television, and the stories allow them to vicariously experience the events, even when the accounts are fictional. Historical fiction can also be very informative, and these titles may be assigned reading.

Authors of young adult novels and series fiction often research their time periods thoroughly, working hard to ensure their historical settings are accurate. Since most teens will read historical romance fiction for the story first and the facts second, it's not the end of the world if the occasional fact is wrong. However, if you are a teacher who wants to use a historical romance book to supplement classroom materials, or a librarian who is recommending books for class assignments, read the book first to see if history is accurately portrayed. Authors sometimes take liberties with history and change facts to suit their stories.

Besides enjoying the historical settings, teens also like to read about the emotions experienced by the heroine and hero in historical romance. The emotions young people experience when they fall in love for the first time or receive their first kiss are always the same, no matter the time period or location of the story. Thus, characterization also becomes important. The lovers in historical romances must prove they are strong enough to survive terrible events, such as wars or natural disasters, in order to be worthy of love. The plots in historical romances are sometimes more complex than contemporary romances, and some young adult readers might enjoy historical romances for this reason.

Advising the Reader

Following are a few points to keep in mind that might be helpful in advising readers about historical romance fiction:

- Find out if your patron wants to read "Historical Romance" fiction for pleasure reading or for a school assignment. This will help you determine if you should suggest a lighter "Historical Romance" novel from the Avon True Romance series or an issue-laden romance story set during World War II, like M. E. Kerr's *Slap Your Sides*. Teachers will likely prefer their students to read historical stories that include facts and timely issues, even when the story includes romance. If your patron has to do a book report, avoid recommending titles in the "Historical Romance Series" section.

- Determine which historical time period(s) your patron is most interested in. If this is for pleasure reading, ask the reader, "If you could choose a time and place to travel to, when and where would it be?" Or, "What periods in history do you enjoy reading about?" Remember, historical romance fiction for teens can be set in any time period, but a lot of historical romance fiction for teens takes place during wars.

- Find out which historical stories your patron has already enjoyed reading and why. This will help you select similar books. Maybe the reader wants to read a romance that includes a specific event in American history or a strong hero or heroine who survives hardship. Refer to the keywords at the bottom of each entry to find issues and important events that apply to each book.

- Find out how much romance your customer requires in a young adult historical romance. Ask, "Do you want to read a historical story with a little bit or a lot of romance?" Some historical romances for young readers focus on the history, with the romance as a subplot. The books selected for this "Historical Romance" book list focus on both history and romance. Read the annotations carefully to identify what else is happening in the story besides romance.

- Historical fiction is often blended with other genre elements. Try to identify which of these elements your reader seeks. Does the patron enjoy a fast-paced, action-filled adventure story? Perhaps a story with a twist of mystery and suspense? Or a gentle romance that affirms core values? Listen for clues about what the reader likes. Describing a book by discussing dramatic events in its story line suggests the patron would be interested in a more adventurous title, while a focus on a nostalgic setting and a virtuous character indicates a different interest. If they are appropriate, do not forget to suggest classic romances included in Chapter 2, historical romantic mysteries included in Chapter 7, or Christian historical romances included in Chapter 9.

- Teens often enjoy reading historical romances written for adult audiences. You might want to suggest younger readers start with books in the Avon True Romance series, which are very similar to adult historical romances. After reading a few books in the series, your patron will be able to tell you if he or she likes Regency, medieval, or Western romances. Reading Avon True Romance will also give your patron the opportunity to sample the writing of authors of adult historical romances, and if the reader likes a particular author or historical subgenre (and is ready for adult content), you can help him or her find similar books. If you are not very familiar with the adult historical romance genres, refer to Kristin Ramsdell's *Romance Fiction* (Libraries Unlimited, 1999), where you will find several chapters discussing historical romances (historical romance, regency period romance, and sagas).

Colonial and Revolutionary America

Young adult romances set in colonial America feature teens who travel to America to live in colonial settlements, where they fall in love for the first time. For instance, the teen protagonist of *Constance: A Story of Early Plymouth* by Patricia

Clapp has several suitors, while Rebekah Hall falls in love with a Native American man in *The Primrose Way* by Jackie French Koller. Love stories set during the Revolutionary War feature teens who fall in love while experiencing the political intrigue, adventure, and devastation of war. Jemima Emerson falls in love with British supporter John Reid in Ann Rinaldi's *Time Enough for Drums*, while British teen Jane Prentice falls in love with patriot Simon Cordwyn in William Lavender's *Just Jane*, and both girls must keep their romances secret so no harm comes to their beloved. Forbidden love is a common theme of romances set in colonial and revolutionary America, and teen readers will be attracted to the titles in this category by the excitement of these illicit romances.

The Revolutionary War and colonial America are two of the periods most studied in school. Teens will already be familiar with some of the events depicted in historical romances set in colonial and revolutionary America, and they will enjoy learning more about historical events while reading a romantic story. Readers will particularly enjoy the stories of secret and forbidden love found here.

Clapp, Patricia

***Constance: A Story of Early Plymouth.* Lothrop, Lee and Shepard, 1968. Reissued by Beech Tree Books in 1991. ISBN 0688109764. MS/JH**

Constance travels to Plymouth on the Mayflower, where she begins her diary. Constance shares with her diary the trials and tribulations of growing up in a colonial settlement, including her feelings about her family, her chores, and her suitors, until she marries at age twenty.

Keywords: dating, diaries, family, marriage, Native Americans

Dokey, Cameron

***Katherine: Heart of Freedom.* Avon Flare, 1997. ISBN 038078565X. [Reluctant Readers] MS/JH**

During the Revolutionary War, Katherine learns that her father is involved in American Patriot activities. After she helps a patriot soldier named Will escape from loyalists, Katherine feels that she too wants to experience adventure. So she disguises herself as a boy and joins the cause. Katherine finds adventure, but she also finds something she didn't expect—that she's fallen in love with Will! A title from the Hearts and Dreams series.

Keywords: family, first love, Revolutionary War, soldiers

Koller, Jackie French

***The Primrose Way.* Harcourt, 1995. ISBN 015200372X. JH/HS**

Sixteen-year-old Rebekah Hall joins her Puritan missionary father on a trip to Massachusetts in 1633. She befriends a Native American girl who teaches her the Pawtucket language so she can act as translator for the missionaries as they work to convert the Native people. Instead, Rebekah comes to appreciate the Native people, and she falls in love with a Native man named Mishannock. Rebekah will have to decide whether to return to England with her father or stay in Massachusetts with the man she loves. An ALA Best Book for Young Adults.

Keywords: first love, Native Americans, religion, travel

Lavender, William

Just Jane: A Daughter of England Caught in the Struggle of the American Revolution. **Harcourt, 2002. ISBN 0152025871. JH/HS**

Fourteen-year-old Lady Jane Prentice, the orphaned daughter of an English earl, travels to South Carolina to live with family in 1776. She finds her family divided by the Revolutionary War, and when she falls in love with patriot Simon Cordwyn, she must keep their romance a secret.

Keywords: first love, Revolutionary War, travel

Rinaldi, Ann

The Fifth of March: A Story of the Boston Massacre. **Harcourt, 1993. ISBN 0152275177. JH/HS**

Fourteen-year-old Rachel Marsh, an indentured servant in the home of John and Abigail Adams, falls in love with British soldier Matthew Kilroy. After Matthew is involved in the Boston Massacre on March 5, 1770, Rachel is torn between her love for Matthew and her loyalty to America.

Keywords: Boston Massacre, first love, soldiers

Finishing Becca: A Story about Peggy Shippen and Benedict Arnold. **Harcourt, 1994. ISBN 0152008802. JH/HS**

Fourteen-year-old Rebecca Syng works as a lady's maid in the Shippen household in Philadelphia. The Shippens socialize with the British soldiers, and Becca watches as flirtatious Peggy Shippen falls in love with British officer John Andre. When the British leave, Peggy falls in love with American soldier Benedict Arnold. Becca has a suitor of her own, Persifor. Will Becca and Peggy find love and happiness?

Keywords: employment, first love, Revolutionary War, soldiers

Time Enough for Drums. **Holiday House, 1986. ISBN 0823406032. MS/JH**

Sixteen-year-old Jemima Emerson, whose New Jersey family members take different positions in the fight for independence as the Revolutionary War approaches, falls in love with her tutor, John Reid. John pretends to support the British, but he is actually a spy for Washington's army. Will John return to Jem after the war? An ALA Best Book for Young Adults.

Keywords: education, family, first love, Revolutionary War

Nineteenth-Century North America

Young adult romances set in "Nineteenth-Century North America" take place with wars, travel, illness, and natural disasters going on in the background. Some love stories are set against the backdrop of wars, such as the War of 1812 and the American Civil War. Some stories feature teens who travel to the western United States in order to survive. Other stories feature characters who are affected by illness and natural disasters, such as blizzards, hurricanes, and fires. Teen readers will learn about the privileges and hardships of life in the nineteenth century, while

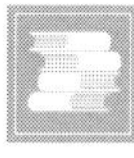

reading romantic and adventurous stories about brave teens who survive adversity and fall in love for the first time. Books in the "Nineteenth-Century North America" book list are subdivided into the following sections: "War of 1812"; "Civil War"; "Westward Expansion"; and "Illness and Natural Disasters."

War of 1812

Several historical romances for teens are set before, during, or after the War of 1812, when the United States battled Britain over maritime practices. The war is sometimes in the background of the story, like in Ann Rinaldi's *The Second Bend in the River*. Although Rebecca Galloway falls in love with Native chief Tecumseh around the same time as the War of 1812, the war has little impact on Rebecca's life. In other stories, the war is more immediate. For instance, when the O'Shea home is occupied by British soldiers in Gloria Whelan's Mackinac Island Trilogy, Angelique falls in love with one of the soldiers. The rest of the trilogy takes place after the war has ended and focuses on young Mary's romances with British Lord James Lindsay and Native American White Hawk.

Readers will be interested in the themes of first love and marriage that permeate the books in this category. By reading books set during the War of 1812, teens can learn about the lives of American settlers and the different kinds of relationships between the settlers and Native Americans.

Dokey, Cameron

Charlotte: Heart of Hope. **Avon Flare, 1997. ISBN 0380785668. [Reluctant Readers] MS/JH**

After being sent to live with family in Baltimore because Native Americans are threatening to attack her home in Indiana Territory, Charlotte finds that life in Baltimore is just as treacherous, with British troops encroaching upon the city. Now Charlotte is not sure whom she can trust, including Matthew, the man she loves. A title in the Hearts and Dreams series.

Keywords: family, first love, Native Americans, War of 1812

Rinaldi, Ann

The Second Bend in the River. **Scholastic, 1997. ISBN 0590742582. MS/JH**

Rebecca Galloway first meets Shawnee chief Tecumseh in 1798, when she is seven years old. Over the years, Tecumseh frequently visits the Galloway farm in the Ohio Territory, and when Rebecca is a teenager, she and Tecumseh fall in love. When Tecumseh proposes marriage, Rebecca must choose between her life as a settler and life as the wife of an Indian chief.

Keywords: family, first love, friendship, Native Americans, War of 1812

Whelan, Gloria

Mackinac Island Trilogy.

Teen orphan Mary O'Shea must choose between Lord James Lindsay and her good friend White Hawk.

Once on This Island. **HarperCollins, 1995. ISBN 0060262486. [Reluctant Readers] MS/JH**

Twelve-year-old Mary O'Shea, her sister Angelique, and her brother Jacques take care of the family farm on Mackinac Island, Michigan, while their father joins American forces fighting the British in the War of 1812. When the family's home is occupied by British soldiers, Angelique falls in love with one of the soldiers. Meanwhile, Mary is upset when her Native American friend Gavin, raised by their neighbors, leaves to live with his Ottawa tribe.

Keywords: first love, Native Americans, soldiers, War of 1812

Farewell to the Island. **HarperCollins, 1998. ISBN 0060277513. [Reluctant Readers] MS/JH**

After her sister Angelique's marriage to a British soldier, Mary visits them in London. When Lord James Lindsay proposes marriage, Mary must decide whether to marry James and stay in England or return home to Michigan.

Keywords: Britain, family, first love, marriage

Return to the Island. **HarperCollins, 2002. ISBN 0064407616. [Reluctant Readers] MS/JH**

Mary O'Shea is back on Mackinac Island in Michigan. She is surprised when Lord James Lindsay shows up, once again requesting her hand in marriage. But Mary's Native American friend Gavin, called White Hawk, also loves her. Mary will have to choose between two very different men and two very different lifestyles.

Keywords: family, first love, friendship, marriage, Native Americans

Civil War

Historical romances for teens are sometimes set during the American Civil War in the mid-nineteenth century. Margaret Mitchell's Pulitzer-winning *Gone with the Wind*, annotated in Chapter 2, is a classic Civil War romance that has thrilled readers for decades. Most of the love stories published in recent years feature teenage girls who fall in love with soldiers involved in the war, such as *Becca's Story* by James D. Forman, *Shenandoah Autumn* by Mauriel Phillips Joslyn, and several of the titles in Cheryl Zach's Southern Angels Saga. Other titles include the Civil War as the backdrop for the love story, like Ann Rinaldi's *The Last Silk Dress*. One title in Zach's Southern Angels Saga, *A Dream of Freedom*, portrays young slaves who fall in love while working on the Underground Railroad. People were working before and during the Civil War to abolish slavery in the United States, and this focus on the Underground Railroad is significant because very few historical romances for young adults feature this setting. Two titles from the Avon True Romance series, Beverly Jenkins's *Belle and the Beau* and *Josephine and the Soldier*, present the Underground Railroad and the Civil War as background. These titles can be found listed in the "Historical Romance Series" book list.

Since the Civil War is an important era of American history, readers may already be familiar with some of the events featured in these stories from their studies. Teens will find Civil War romances appealing because these stories are usually exciting, fast-paced reads with lots of adventure and romance.

Forman, James D.

***Becca's Story.* Simon & Schuster, 1992. ISBN 0684193329. JH/HS**

Fourteen-year-old Becca Case is courted by two best friends, Alex and Charlie, and she is relieved when they enlist in the Union Army because she can delay choosing one of them for her husband. The story includes letters to Becca from Alex and Charlie describing the war, while Becca sends letters detailing the gossip from home. The young men return to Michigan for a time and then they both go back to battle, giving Becca time to make her decision. An ALA Best Book for Young Adults.

Keywords: dating, death, first love, letters, soldiers

Joslyn, Mauriel Phillips

***Shenandoah Autumn: Courage under Fire.* White Mane, 1998. ISBN 157249137X. MS/JH**

Sixteen-year-old Matilda MacDonald, whose father is fighting for the Confederacy in the Civil War, wants to nurse wounded soldiers at a hospital. Mattie's mother, however, will not allow her to leave the farm. When soldier Will Hamilton is brought to the MacDonald farm after being injured in battle, Mattie nurses him back to health. Although Will and Mattie fall in love, he must return to combat, and Mattie wonders if she will ever see him again.

Keywords: first love, soldiers

Rinaldi, Ann

***The Coffin Quilt: The Feud between the Hatfields and the McCoys.* Harcourt, 1999. ISBN 0152020152. JH/HS**

Fanny McCoy remembers the affair between her teenage sister Roseanna and Johnse Hatfield during the 1880s that caused the feud between the Hatfields and the McCoys to escalate to violence. Based on the true story of the family feud between the Hatfields and the McCoys that began during the Civil War. An ALA Popular Paperback for Young Adults.

Keywords: family, first love, violence

***The Last Silk Dress.* Holiday House, 1988. Reissued by Bantam Doubleday Dell in 1990. ISBN 0440228611. JH/HS**

Fourteen-year-old Susan Chilmark and her best friend, Constance, collect silk dresses in Richmond to make a hot air balloon so the Confederates can spy on their enemies. While they work to support the Confederate cause, Susan learns family secrets and falls in love with her brother's friend, Timothy Collier.

Keywords: family, first love, friendship

***Sarah's Ground.* Simon & Schuster, 2004. ISBN 0689859244. JH/HS**

Eighteen-year-old Sarah Tracy is not ready for marriage, so she takes a job as caretaker of Mount Vernon, the family home of George Washington. When the Civil War begins, Sarah influences important people, including soldiers, generals, and President Lincoln. Sarah is not prepared, however, to find true love.

Keywords: Civil War, employment, first love, marriage

Zach, Cheryl

Southern Angels Saga.

Southern teens Elizabeth, Victorine, Hannah, and Rosamund fall in love during the American Civil War.

Hearts Divided. **Bantam Books, 1995. ISBN 0553562177. [Reluctant Readers] MS/JH**

Elizabeth Stafford, the daughter of a Virginia plantation owner, goes to boarding school in Charleston. When Elizabeth meets Union lieutenant Adam Cranfield at the Christmas ball, she falls in love. But she can't marry a Yankee!

Keywords: education, first love, friendship

Winds of Betrayal. **Bantam Books, 1995. ISBN 0553562185. [Reluctant Readers] MS/JH**

Victorine LeGrande goes to New Orleans to marry Andre Valmont in a marriage arranged by their families. When Victorine helps Confederate doctor Brent Whitman tend to injured soldiers, she falls in love with him. Victorine knows her betrothed, Andre, is in love with another woman. Will Victorine do her duty and marry Andre, or will she marry for love?

Keywords: first love, marriage

A Dream of Freedom. **Bantam Books, 1995. ISBN 0553562193. [Reluctant Readers] MS/JH**

Hannah, a slave on the Stafford plantation in Virginia, works on the Underground Railroad. When she falls in love with Joshua, a freed slave, can she keep her promise never to marry until she is free?

Keywords: African Americans, first love, slavery

Love's Rebellion. **Bantam Books, 1995. ISBN 0553562207. [Reluctant Readers] MS/JH**

Rosamund Brigham, a girl from Tennessee, is torn between her love for two soldiers, Union Captain Wesley Harrison and Jonathon Scott, a Confederate soldier.

Keywords: first love, soldiers

Westward Expansion

Titles in the "Westward Expansion" book list are set in America during the nineteenth century, when people were settling in the western United States. "Westward Expansion" love stories combine adventure and romance, portraying teens who fall in love during their travels west. For instance, when Jane Peck travels west to marry her true love in Jennifer Holm's Boston Jane series, she ends up settling in Washington Territory, deciding not to marry her fiancé, and traveling on wilderness adventures with Jehu, a sailor who truly loves her. Other teens travel west for different reasons. Fortune Plunkett travels west with her father's acting troupe in *Fortune's Journey* by Bruce Coville; the protagonist in Cameron Dokey's *Stephanie: Heart of Gold* stows away on a ship to California chasing the man her father

sent away; and Susan Carlisle must take her sheep to California, where she will sell them for a profit, in Theodore Taylor's *Walking up a Rainbow*. During their travels, the girls in these stories all find true love when they least expect it.

Several titles written for adult audiences are also included in this list because they feature teen protagonists, namely Cindy Bonner's DeLony Saga. Several titles in the saga have been selected as American Library Association Best Books for Young Adults, and this made them an appropriate addition to this category. Readers will enjoy the combination of adventure of the American West and romance found in "Westward Expansion" stories. Teens may even learn a little history along the way!

Bonner, Cindy

DeLony Saga.

Teen members of the Texas DeLony family find that falling in love can be complicated. Another title in the saga, *Right from Wrong*, can be found in the "Twentieth-Century North America" book list.

Lily. **Algonquin, 1992. ISBN 0945575955. [Sexual Content, Adult] HS**

Fifteen-year-old Lily DeLony falls in love with outlaw Marion "Shot" Beatty, despite the fact that she is pursued by another man more suitable for marriage. When the Beatty gang is accused of robbery and murder, Marion and his brothers run from the law, and Lily must decide if she should follow the love of her life. An ALA Best Book for Young Adults.

Keywords: American West, crime, family, first love, marriage

Looking After Lily. **Algonquin, 1994. ISBN 1565120450. [Adult] HS**

Marion Beatty is sent to jail for two years, while his younger brother Haywood is released. Marion sends Haywood to take care of his pregnant wife Lily, and Haywood is surprised when he falls in love with his brother's wife. An ALA Best Book for Young Adults.

Keywords: American West, crime, family, marriage

The Passion of Dellie O'Barr. **Algonquin, 1996. ISBN 1565121031. [Adult] HS**

Twenty-year-old Dellie DeLony dutifully marries Daniel O'Barr, the wealthy and well-educated man her sister Lily spurned. When Dellie meets Andy Ashland, a married man with two children and a mentally ill wife, she falls madly in love. When Andy inexplicably disappears after promising to run away with her, Dellie commits a terrible crime on his behalf and flees in search of her lover.

Keywords: American West, crime, family, marriage

Coville, Bruce

Fortune's Journey. **Troll Communications, 1995. ISBN 0816736502. MS/JH**

Sixteen-year-old Fortune Plunkett has inherited her father's acting company, and as they travel West, she falls in love with Jamie, a new member of the acting troupe who joins them in Missouri. While battling natural disasters and fights between troupe members during their travels, Fortune must choose between her new love, Jamie, and her old beau, Aaron.

Keywords: adventure, American West, dating, theater

Dokey, Cameron

***Stephanie: Heart of Gold.* Avon Flare, 1998. ISBN 0380785676. [Reluctant Readers] MS/JH**

Stephanie stows away on a ship bound for California, chasing Maxwell Harrington after her father sends him away. Charlotte Kelly and her son Jack find Stephanie on the ship, and she joins them for the rest of the journey. When Stephanie finally finds Maxwell, she learns why her father sent him away, and she knows she can never truly love him. A title in the Hearts and Dreams series.

Keywords: American West, family, first love, travel

Holm, Jennifer L.

Boston Jane Trilogy.

In 1854, sixteen-year-old Jane Peck travels from Philadelphia to the northwestern United States to marry William Baldt.

***Boston Jane: An Adventure.* HarperCollins, 2001. ISBN 0060287381. MS/JH**

Jane Peck travels by sea to the northwestern United States to marry her fiancé and true love, William Baldt. But William is away when Jane arrives, and she finds herself living with sailors, adventurers, and Chinook Indians who call her "Boston Jane." When William returns, Jane must decide whether her heart belongs to William or Jehu, a sailor who has fallen in love with her.

Keywords: adventure, American West, first love, Native Americans

***Boston Jane: Wilderness Days.* HarperCollins, 2002. ISBN 0060290439. MS/JH**

Jane's plans to return home to Philadelphia come to an end when she learns of her father's death. Jane stays in Washington Territory, even though she has decided not to marry William Baldt. Jane and Jehu experience adventures in the wilderness, and Jane begins to believe the sailor truly loves her.

Keywords: adventure, American West, first love, Native Americans

***Boston Jane: The Claim.* HarperCollins, 2004. ISBN 0060290455. MS/JH**

The arrival of her former nemesis Sally Biddle and ex-fiance Richard Baldt in Shoalwater Bay threatens Jane's happiness in Washington Territory. Jane wonders if Jehu, her true love, will still be able to love her.

Keywords: family, friendship

Taylor, Theodore

***Walking up a Rainbow.* Delacorte Press, 1986. Reissued by HarperCollins, 1996. ISBN 0380725924. MS/JH**

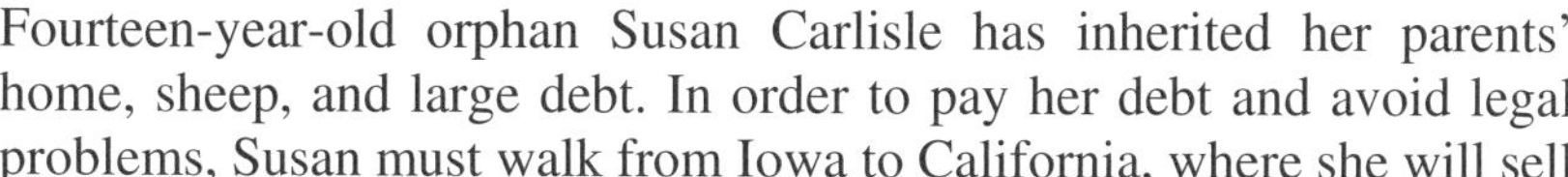

Fourteen-year-old orphan Susan Carlisle has inherited her parents' home, sheep, and large debt. In order to pay her debt and avoid legal problems, Susan must walk from Iowa to California, where she will sell

her sheep. Along the way, Susan falls in love with cowboy Clay Carmer, the man she hires to help her drive the sheep.

Keywords: American West, animals, first love, orphans

Illness and Natural Disasters

A few young adult romance stories set in the nineteenth century feature illness and natural disasters as the backdrop for the love story. Stories featuring natural disasters include Kathleen Duey's *Louisiana Hurricane, 1860*, Dianne E. Gray's *Together Apart*, and Elizabeth Massie's *The Great Chicago Fire, 1871*. Stories featuring illness include Jan Hudson's *Sweetgrass*, where Native Canadian Sweetgrass nurses her family through a smallpox epidemic, and Louis Meyer's *Bloody Jack*, whose young protagonist is orphaned after her family dies from the plague. While most of the stories are set in the United States, Jan Hudson's *Sweetgrass* is set on the Canadian prairies, and Louis Meyer's *Bloody Jack* begins in England and continues on a ship bound for America. Readers will learn about aspects of life in early North America besides settlement and war, such as how people survived terrible illness and natural disasters, including fires, hurricanes, and snowstorms, while enjoying heartwarming love stories.

Dokey, Cameron

Carrie: Heart of Courage. **Avon Flare, 1998. ISBN 0380785692. [Reluctant Readers] MS/JH**

Carrie Kelly falls in love with John Stapleton, but when her friend Jessica also shows an interest in John, Carrie believes Jessica will win his love. Suddenly Carrie, her family, and friends are caught in the Chicago fire of 1871. Carrie wonders if she will ever see her family, her friends, and her true love again. A title in the Hearts and Dreams series.

Keywords: family, fires, first love, friendship, natural disasters

Duey, Kathleen

Louisiana Hurricane, 1860. **Pocket Books, 2000. ISBN 0671039261. [Reluctant Readers] JH**

Madelaine LeBlanc falls in love with Francois Jarousseau, a Cajun farm laborer who helps her father rebuild the farm after a hurricane, and they meet secretly. But Madelaine's father expects her to marry a rich man and live a life of luxury. What will happen when Madelaine's father finds out about her love for Francois?

Keywords: farming, first love, natural disasters

Gray, Dianne E.

Together Apart. **Houghton Mifflin, 2002. ISBN 0618187219. JH**

After surviving a deadly Nebraska blizzard wrapped in each other's arms in 1888, teenagers Hannah and Isaac go to work for Widow Moore, where they can be together without their families' knowledge. Why are Hannah and Isaac hiding their love?

Keywords: first love, natural disasters, winter

Hudson, Jan

Sweetgrass. **Putnam, 1991. ISBN 0399217215. MS/JH**

Fifteen-year-old Blackfoot Indian Sweetgrass is anxious to marry Eagle-Sun, but her father believes she is too young for marriage. During a terrible 1830s winter on the Canadian prairie, Sweetgrass proves her maturity when she nurses her family during a smallpox epidemic. An ALA Best Book for Young Adults.

Keywords: Canada, first love, illness, marriage, Native Canadians

Massie, Elizabeth

***The Great Chicago Fire, 1871.* Pocket Books, 1999. ISBN 0671036033. [Reluctant Readers] JH**

After eighteen-year-old Katina Monroe loses her family in the Civil War, she goes to Chicago, where she disguises herself as a boy actor named "William." When Katina meets a young minister, Russell Cosgrove, he convinces "William" to help him found a shelter for the poor and homeless. When Katina falls in love with Russell, she tells him she is a woman, and they are beginning their life together when fire breaks out in the streets of Chicago.

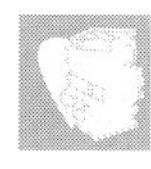

Keywords: fires, first love, natural disasters

Meyer, Louis

Bloody Jack. **Harcourt, 2002. ISBN 0152167315. MS/JH**

After her family dies from the plague in the early nineteenth century, Mary Faber disguises herself as a boy named Jacky and gets a job on a ship sailing for America. "Jacky" falls in love with a boy named Jaimy, who fears he has fallen in love with another boy. Mary tells Jaimy her secret, and they carry on a shipboard romance.

Keywords: adventure, employment, first love, orphans, travel

Twentieth-Century North America

"Twentieth-Century North America" romances are often set against the backdrop of war. Many stories are set during World War II, such as *Pearl Harbor, 1941* by Nancy Holder or *Two Suns in the Sky* by Miriam Bat Ami. Other stories are set in Vietnam War era America, including *Come in from the Cold* by Martha Qualey. War romances set during the twentieth century feature characters whose lives are deeply affected by the violence and turmoil around them. In some stories, the wars serve merely as backdrops for other events, as in the Vietnam War era story *Long Time Passing* by Linda Crew. Other stories, such as *Slap Your Sides* by M. E. Kerr, show the profound and disturbing effects of war on the characters. Characterization is particularly important in these novels, because the lovers must deal with challenges the wars present in their lives, and the young characters are portrayed as strong enough to deal with these challenges. Dealing with the challenges presented by war makes them worthy of love. Coming of age is often a secondary theme in these novels.

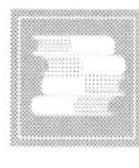

Natural disasters and other world events are other backgrounds used for love stories set in the twentieth century. Examples include Cameron Dokey's *Washington Avalanche, 1910* and Diane Hoh's *Titanic: The Long Night.* Readers enjoy romances set in the twentieth century because they may be familiar with some of the settings and events portrayed in the stories, or may have heard about them from parents and grandparents. Book lists are divided into the following subcategories: "Early Twentieth Century"; "The Forties and World War II"; and "The Fabulous Fifties and Beyond."

Early Twentieth Century

Teen love stories set in "Early Twentieth Century" North America are an eclectic mix of stories. Some stories feature World War I, the Great Depression, and significant events in North American history, including the San Francisco earthquake of 1906 and the sinking of the ship *Titanic* in 1912. These events are the backdrop for breathtaking love stories, such as Kathleen Duey's *San Francisco Earthquake, 1906* and Diane Hoh's *Titanic: The Long Night.* Stories of love relationships gone terribly wrong, including physical and verbal abuse of female characters, are also included here. For instance, Sue Ellen Bridgers's *All We Know of Heaven* portrays Bethany's marriage to the abusive Joel Calder, while Randall Beth Platt's *The Likes of Me* tells the story of Cordelia's relationship with older con man Squirl.

Stories set in the early twentieth century are located all over the United States, including Texas, California, Washington, and North Carolina. While most of the stories are set in the United States, one title, *Mrs. Mike* by Benedict Freedman and Nancy Mars Freedman, is set in the Canadian wilderness. And of course, Diane Hoh's *Titanic: The Long Night,* is set on the infamous ship sailing across the Atlantic Ocean. Teens who enjoy adventure and romance will enjoy this interesting mix of love stories set in different parts of North America in the early twentieth century.

Bonner, Cindy

***Right from Wrong.* Algonquin, 1999. ISBN 156512104X. [Adult] HS**

Teenage cousins Sunny DeLony and Gil Dailey fall in love, despite the fact that their mothers tell them their love is wrong. The couple is separated when Gil leaves to serve in World War I, and Sunny marries another man. When the war ends, it seems Gil and Sunny will be apart forever, trapped in loveless marriages. Another title in Bonner's DeLony Saga; earlier titles can be found in the "Westward Expansion" book list under the "Nineteenth-Century North America" category.

Keywords: American West, family, incest, marriage, World War I

Bridgers, Sue Ellen

***All We Know of Heaven.* Banks Channel Books, 1996. ISBN 0963596748. HS**

Fifteen-year-old Bethany Newell falls in love with Joel Calder, and ignoring her Aunt Charlotte's warnings about Joel's violent past, Bethany marries him. Bethany's happiness is short-lived, despite the birth of her daughter, because Joel becomes violent toward her and baby Caroline. Set in rural North Carolina during the Great Depression.

Keywords: first love, Great Depression, marriage, physical abuse, poverty

Dokey, Cameron

Washington Avalanche, 1910. **Pocket Books, 2000. ISBN 0671036041. [Reluctant Readers] JH**

Eighteen-year-old Ginny Nolan runs away to escape from her brother, who is plotting to marry her off and steal her inheritance. When she meets Virginia Hightower on the train, the girls share their troubles, and they decide to swap identities since they look alike and share a name. Virginia wants Ginny to find out more about the man she is engaged to marry, but when Ginny meets Nicholas Bennett, she falls in love. Then their lives are threatened when their train gets caught in an avalanche.

Keywords: first love, natural disasters, travel

Duey, Kathleen

San Francisco Earthquake, 1906. **Pocket Books, 1999. ISBN 0671036025. [Reluctant Readers] JH**

Eighteen-year-old Sierra O'Nielle works as a housekeeper at San Francisco's Palace Hotel. Joseph Harlan, son of a wealthy cattle rancher, has come to San Francisco to find a wife. When Sierra and Joseph meet, they fall in love, but Joseph's father does not consider Sierra a suitable bride for Joseph, and he tries to keep them apart. Sierra and Joseph are thrown together in a fight for survival when an earthquake hits San Francisco.

Keywords: first love, marriage, natural disasters

Freedman, Benedict, and Nancy Mars Freedman

Mrs. Mike. **Longmans Green, 1946. Reissued by Berkley in 2002. ISBN 0425183238. [Adult] JH/HS**

Katherine O'Fallon, a young woman from Boston, moves to Calgary, Alberta, during the early twentieth century, where she falls in love with police officer Mike Flannigan.

Keywords: adventure, Canada, first love, marriage

Hoh, Diane

Titanic: The Long Night. **Scholastic, 1998. ISBN 059033123X. [Reluctant Readers] JH**

Wealthy Elizabeth Farr, engaged to a man she does not love, falls in love with artist Max Whittaker on the *Titanic*. Third-class passengers Paddy Kelleher and Katie Hanrahan also begin a romance. Though unrelated to the popular movie *Titanic*, the plots are similar.

Keywords: first love, marriage, natural disasters, travel

Namioka, Lensey

An Ocean Apart, a World Away. **Random House, 2002. ISBN 0385730020. JH/HS**

Yanyan leaves her family and her boyfriend Baoshu behind in China, and she travels to the United States to study medicine at Cornell University. As sixteen-year-old Yanyan adjusts to life in 1920s America, she struggles to deal with the racism and prejudice she encounters everyday.

When she finally feels comfortable in the United States, her boyfriend Baoshu pays her a surprise visit.

Keywords: China, dating, education, racism

Platt, Randall Beth

***The Likes of Me.* Delacorte Press, 2000. ISBN 0385326920. HS**

Fourteen-year-old Cordeila Lu Hankins, a half-Chinese albino, falls in love with Washington State lumber camp worker Squirl in 1918. When her father fires Squirl, Cordy runs away to find him, and she winds up working in a carnival with Squirl. Will Cordy ever realize that Squirl is a con man who is taking advantage of her?

Keywords: family, first love, multicultural romance

The Forties and World War II

Many historical romance novels set in the 1940s include World War II as background, and these stories often portray young people from different countries or different backgrounds falling in love. For instance, Yugoslavian Jewish refugee Adam falls in love with Irish-American Christine in Miriam Bat Ami's *Two Suns in the Sky*, religious Quaker Jubal falls in love with Daria, whose family supports the war, in M. E. Kerr's *Slap Your Sides*, and Canadian teen Ellen Logan falls in love with British pilot Stephen Dearborn in Gillian Chan's *A Foreign Field.* Important social issues of the time are included in romances set during World War II—immigration, refugees, conscientious objection to war, and religious and cultural differences between young lovers.

Other love stories set during the 1940s do not feature the war, or its results, so prominently. In Ella Thorp Ellis's *The Year of My Indian Prince*, tuberculosis patient April Thorp is courted by Ravi, an Indian prince who is also recovering at the hospital. Nancy Willard's *Things Invisible to See*, set in the early 1940s, features a couple who fall in love after a terrible accident paralyzes one of them.

Love stories set in the 1940s provide important insight into the lives of people during an important era of history. Readers will find out how people lived and what issues were important to them, and most important, they will learn that true love can survive even the worst hardships, including war, illness, and disability.

Bat Ami, Miriam

***Two Suns in the Sky.* Cricket Books, 1999. ISBN 0812629000. JH/HS**

Adam Bornstein is a Yugoslavian Jewish refugee who lives in a refugee camp run by the U. S. government in Oswego, New York, in 1944. Fifteen-year-old Adam meets Oswego resident Christine Cook, who comes from an Irish-American Catholic family, and the pair fall in love. Adam and Christine take turns telling their love story.

Keywords: immigration, refugees, religion, World War II

Chan, Gillian

***A Foreign Field.* Kids Can Press, 2002. ISBN 1553373499. JH/HS**

Fourteen-year-old Ellen Logan, who lives near a Canadian air base during World War II, falls in love with British pilot Stephen Dearborn.

Keywords: Canada, first love, letters, World War II

Ellis, Ella Thorp

The Year of My Indian Prince. **Random House, 2001. ISBN 038532779X. JH/HS**

When sixteen-year-old April Thorp is sent to recover from tuberculosis at a San Francisco sanatorium in 1945, her boyfriend Mike is not allowed to visit her. April is courted by Ravi, an Indian prince who is also a patient at the hospital. As April gets sicker, she must consider risky surgery to save her life. Will April and Ravi have a future together? Based on the author's real-life experiences.

Keywords: first love, illness, multicultural romance, princes

Freedman, Benedict, and Nancy Mars Freedman

The Search for Joyful: The Story of Mrs. Mike Continues. **Berkley, 2002. ISBN 0425183335. [Adult] JH/HS**

The sequel to *Mrs. Mike* tells the story of Kathy Forquet, the Cree orphan who was raised by the Flannigans. Kathy moves to Montreal, Quebec, to train as a nurse during World War II, where she encounters romance with a Native Canadian man and an Austrian soldier.

Keywords: Canada, first love, Native Canadians, orphans, soldiers, World War II

Greene, Bette

Summer of My German Soldier. **Dial Books for Young Readers, 1973. Reissued by Penguin Putnam in 1999. ISBN 014130636X. MS/JH**

When Patty Bergen, a twelve-year-old Jewish-American girl, meets German prisoner-of-war Anton Reiker in her father's store, she knows she has found a friend. Patty hides Anton in her empty garage when he escapes from the military base, and as Patty takes care of Anton, she falls in love. Can Patty keep Anton safe forever?

Keywords: family, first love, religion, World War II

Holder, Nancy

Pearl Harbor, 1941. **Pocket Books, 2000. ISBN 067103927X. [Reluctant Readers] JH**

After Bekah Martin completes nursing training in San Francisco, she travels home to the Hawaiian Islands, where she plans to marry her dead fiancé's twin brother. But on the trip home, Bekah meets Scott DeAngelo, and they fall in love. When their lives are threatened by the attack on Pearl Harbor on December 7, 1941, Bekah must choose between her love for Scott and keeping her promise to her fiancé.

Keywords: first love, Pearl Harbor, World War II

Kerr, M. E.

I Stay Near You. **HarperCollins, 1985. Reissued by Harcourt in1997. ISBN 0152014209. JH/HS**

Three generations of the Storm family are affected by romances and a ring in three connected stories.

Keywords: family, first love, short stories

Slap Your Sides. **HarperCollins, 2001. ISBN 0060294817. MS/JH**

Thirteen-year-old Jubal Shoemaker's older brother Bud registers as a conscientious objector during World War II because, as a Quaker, he can't support war. Jubal and his family are persecuted by their neighbors in Sweet Creek, Pennsylvania, for Bud's stand against the war. Late one night Jubal catches Daria Daniel, whose brothers are enlisted in the army, vandalizing his father's store. Soon Jubal and Daria become secret friends, and although Jubal knows it is wrong, he falls in love with her.

Keywords: crushes, first love, religion, World War II

Willard, Nancy

Things Invisible to See. **Alfred A. Knopf, 1985. Reissued by iUniverse.com in 2000. ISBN 0595138802. JH/HS**

In the spring of 1941, Clare Bishop is paralyzed when she is hit with a baseball. Ben Harkissian, the boy who hit the baseball, feels guilty and tries to help Clare. As Clare and Ben fall in love, they learn they both have unusual powers. An ALA Best Book for Young Adults.

Keywords: dating, first love, World War II

The Fabulous Fifties and Beyond

Love stories in "The Fabulous Fifties and Beyond" book list are set between the 1950s and the early 1970s. These stories focus on the experience of first love, and they feature important issues in the lives of teens, including death, separation, divorce, homosexuality, physical abuse, rape, sex, and pregnancy. For instance, Martha Brooks's *Two Moons in August* tells the story of Sidonie and Kieran, who fall in love despite the fact that she is grieving her mother's death and he is dealing with his parents' divorce. In Rodger Larson's *What I Know Now*, fourteen-year-old Dave Ryan wonders about his sexuality when he gets a crush on an older, gay man. And in Leslie Wells's *The Curing Season*, misfit Cora Mae Slaughter stays with abusive boyfriend Aaron, even after he rapes her, in the hopes of gaining his love. The books in "The Fabulous Fifties and Beyond" book list deal with serious problems that today's teens can understand, because they are dealing with many of the same issues.

By reading books in this book list, readers will be able to learn what life was like when their parents and grandparents were growing up, while indulging their taste for romance and reading about teens with problems similar to their own.

Book, Rick

Necking with Louise. **Avon Tempest, 2001. ISBN 006447254X. JH/HS**

In seven connected short stories, readers learn about sixteen-year-old Eric Anderson's life on the Saskatchewan prairie in 1965. Eric goes on his first date with Anna Maria, discovers kissing with Louise, and learns the heartache of breaking up.

Keywords: Canada, first love, short stories

Brooks, Martha

 *Two Moons in August.* **Groundwood, 1990. ISBN 0888991231. JH/HS**

Sixteen-year-old Sidonie Fallows is trying to adjust to life after her mother's death, but her grieving family is falling apart, and the hot Canadian summer of 1959 leaves her with too much time on her hands. Then Sidonie meets Kieran McMorran, who is angry because his parents are getting divorced, and she finds herself involved in her first romance. An ALA Best Book for Young Adults.

Keywords: Canada, death, divorce, first love, grief

Clark, Robert

Love among the Ruins. **W. W. Norton, 2001. ISBN 0393020150. [Sexual Content] HS**

When Bill Lowry writes Emily Byrne a love letter in the summer of 1968, he is surprised to receive a response from her. Before long, Bill and Emily are madly in love, and they decide to run away from Minnesota so Bill can escape the Vietnam War draft.

Keywords: dating, family, first love, letters, politics, Vietnam War

Crew, Linda

Long Time Passing. **Delacorte Press, 1997. ISBN 0385324960. JH/HS**

High school sophomore Kathy Shay, who fails in her efforts to join the cheerleading squad, channels her creative energies into folksinging and acting during the late 1960s. When Kathy and James Holderread meet, they fall in love. Their relationship grows until James and his family move away from their small Oregon town, and Kathy is devastated. Will Kathy and James be separated forever?

Keywords: dating, family, first love

Evans, Elizabeth

Rowing in Eden. **HarperCollins, 2000. ISBN 0060195509. HS**

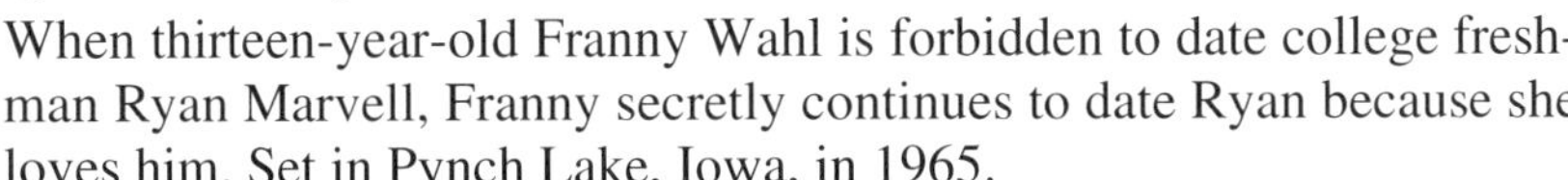

When thirteen-year-old Franny Wahl is forbidden to date college freshman Ryan Marvell, Franny secretly continues to date Ryan because she loves him. Set in Pynch Lake, Iowa, in 1965.

Keywords: dating, first love, vacations

Futcher, Jane

Crush. **Little, Brown, 1981. Reissued by Alyson in 1995. ISBN 155583602X. [Sexual Content] JH/HS**

High school senior Jean "Jinx" Tuckwell attends boarding school in Huntington Hill, Pennsylvania, in 1964. Although Jinx has a serious crush on sophisticated classmate Lexie Yves, she doesn't plan to do anything about it, and she tries to be a good friend to Lexie. But Lexie forces Jinx to publicly admit her love, while denying she ever returned Jinx's affections.

Keywords: crushes, education, friendship, homosexuality, lesbians

Hobbs, Valerie

***How Far Would You Have Gotten If I Hadn't Called You Back?* Orchard Books, 1995. ISBN 0531094804. [Sexual Content] JH/HS**

Sixteen-year-old Bronwyn Lewis moves with her family to California during the late 1950s, where she worries she won't fit in. Instead, Bron has no problem making friends, and she spends her time drag racing with her new friends. Bron likes both Will, a serious boy who plans to attend West Point, and J.C., a wild older man, and she must choose between the two men. An ALA Best Book for Young Adults.

Keywords: death, family, first love

Kincaid, Nanci

***Crossing Blood.* Putnam, 1992. Reissued by University of Alabama Press in 1999. ISBN 0817310096. HS**

During the Civil Rights movement in the southern United States, Lucy Conyers falls in love with Skippy Williams, the black boy who lives next door. But Lucy's family will do anything to keep the young couple apart. An ALA Best Book for Young Adults.

Keywords: African Americans, dating, family, multicultural romance, racism

Larson, Rodger

***What I Know Now.* Henry Holt, 1997. ISBN 0805048693. JH/HS**

When landscape designer Gene Tole arrives in California in the summer of 1957 to help Dave Ryan and his mother with some gardening, fourteen-year-old Dave does not expect to fall in love with Gene. Dave idolizes Gene and wishes the man was his father. But Dave slowly realizes he loves Gene as more than a father figure, and the discovery that Gene is gay makes Dave wonder if he is also homosexual.

Keywords: crushes, first love, homosexuality

Marino, Jan

***Searching for Atticus.* Simon & Schuster, 1997. ISBN 0689800665. JH**

Fifteen-year-old Tessa Ramsey and her family move to Taloosa after Dr. Ramsey returns from a year serving in the Vietnam War. Tess falls in love with wild boy Caleb, and although she knows she should stay away from him, she keeps trying to get his attention until she is successful. But Tess is not ready for what happens next.

Keywords: first love, rape, Vietnam War

Myers, Anna

***Ethan between Us.* Walker, 1998. ISBN 0802786707. JH/HS**

High school sophomore Clare falls in love with Ethan, the mysterious new boy who moves to Collins Creek, Oklahoma, in 1960. Clare tries to help Ethan deal with his secret illness, schizophrenia. When Clare's best friend Liz returns at the end of the summer, she is jealous of Clare's relationship with Ethan, and she prepares to destroy their relationship.

Keywords: first love, friendship, illness

Oughton, Jerrie

Perfect Family. **Houghton Mifflin, 2000. ISBN 0395986680. [Sexual Content] JH/HS**

Fifteen-year-old Welcome O'Neal, who lives in a small town in Northern Carolina in 1955, falls in love with Nicholas Canton, an older boy. After breaking up with Nicholas, who is not ready for a committed relationship, a broken-hearted Welcome loses her virginity with her friend Randy Newsome. Welcome must decide what to do when she discovers she is pregnant.

Keywords: dating, pregnancy, sex

Qualey, Marsha

Come in from the Cold. **Houghton Mifflin, 1994. ISBN 0395689864. JH/HS**

Seventeen-year-olds Jeff and Maud, who live in Minnesota, have both lost siblings to the Vietnam War. Jeff's brother, a Marine, was killed during battle, while Maud's sister died in a bombing during a war protest. When Jeff and Maud meet at a demonstration against the war in 1969, they understand each other, and they soon fall in love. An ALA Best Book for Young Adults.

Keywords: death, first love, grief, Vietnam War

Sparks, Nicholas

A Walk to Remember. **Warner, 1999. ISBN 0446525537. [Adult] JH/HS**

An adult Landon Carter remembers his last year of high school in 1958, when he fell in love for the first time. Landon teased shy Jamie Sullivan, the daughter of a Baptist minister, along with everyone else. But when Landon is desperate for a date for the homecoming dance, Jamie agrees to go to the dance with him. Landon is surprised when he falls in love with Jamie, but Jamie is hiding a terrible secret that will change their lives forever. Also a major motion picture.

Keywords: death, first love, illness

Thomas, Abigail

An Actual Life. **Algonquin, 1996. ISBN 0565121333. [Adult, Sexual Content] HS**

In 1960, Virginia and Buddy got married because she got pregnant the first time they had sex. From Virginia's point of view, readers learn about her unhappy marriage to Buddy. While Virginia is determined to make their marriage work for the sake of their daughter, Buddy is fooling around with his high school sweetheart Irene, who is married to his best friend. Virginia must decide if she will stay in an unhappy marriage.

Keywords: children, marriage

Wells, Leslie

***The Curing Season.* Warner Books, 2001. ISBN 0446526932. [Adult] HS**

Sixteen-year-old Cora Mae Slaughter and her family live on a farm in southern Virginia in 1948. Cora has a clubfoot, and she worries she will never have a boyfriend. Cora is flattered when Aaron Melville, a farm worker, takes an interest in her. When Aaron rapes Cora, she stays with him in the hopes of winning his love. After baby Joshua is born, Aaron continues to physically abuse Cora. Will Cora ever escape?

Keywords: first love, physical abuse, poverty

Love around the World and throughout Time

Books in the "Love around the World and throughout Time" list take readers beyond the borders of the United States. They are set in Europe, Great Britain, Asia, Australia, and the West Indies. Time periods covered by the stories range from Ancient Greece right through to 1980s postwar Vietnam. While teen readers may be familiar with some of the settings and events in these books, like love stories set in Europe during World War II, North American teen readers may find that books in this category feature unknown events and exotic locales. Readers will enjoy the opportunity to learn about events and countries that are new to them. Popular themes include first love, marriage, homosexuality, racism, religion, prejudice, politics, and war. While these novels include familiar themes, the stories give teens a different perspective on those familiar themes as well as world events. For instance, Sherry Garland's *Song of the Buffalo Boy* provides a look at teenage life and love in postwar Vietnam, while Garry Disher's *The Divine Wind* tells the story of World War II from the viewpoint of an Australian teenager who loves a Japanese girl. Readers will gain new insights into world events while reading about familiar emotions of love and romance. Titles here are arranged in roughly chronological/geographical order.

Ancient Greece

Galloway, Priscilla

***The Courtesans' Daughter.* Delacorte Press, 2002. ISBN 0385729073. JH/HS**

Fifteen-year-old Phano, a Greek girl living in ancient Athens, wishes to marry Theo, the man she loves. But her stepmother's enemy spreads rumors that put Phano's parentage in doubt, suggesting she is a slave.

Keywords: Ancient Greece, first love, marriage, politics, slavery

Middle Ages/Europe and the New World

Cushman, Karen

***Catherine, Called Birdy.* Houghton Mifflin, 1994. ISBN 0395681863. [Reluctant Readers] MS/JH**

Thirteen-year-old Catherine, the daughter of a minor English lord in 1290, will do anything she can to keep her father from marrying her off to the richest man who will have her. She tells her diary about her endless chores and her schemes to frighten men away. Can Birdy arrange it so she can marry someone she might be able to love? An ALA Best Book for Young Adults and a 1995 Newbery Honor Award winner.

Keywords: diaries, England, marriage, Middle Ages, religion, saints

Fiedler, Lisa

***Dating Hamlet: Ophelia's Story.* Henry Holt, 2002. ISBN 0805070540. HS**

Ophelia's boyfriend Hamlet is depressed after his father's death, so she pretends to be insane in order to learn who killed Hamlet's father. Will Hamlet and Ophelia have a happy ending this time? Readers will need to be familiar with Shakespeare's play *Hamlet* to enjoy this story.

Keywords: dating, death, ghosts, Middle Ages, Shakespeare

Goodman, Joan Elizabeth

***Paradise: Based on a True Story of Survival.* Houghton Mifflin, 2002. ISBN 0618114505. JH/HS**

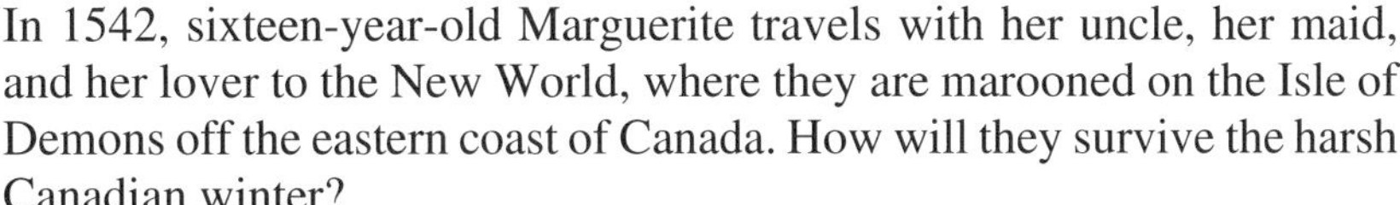

In 1542, sixteen-year-old Marguerite travels with her uncle, her maid, and her lover to the New World, where they are marooned on the Isle of Demons off the eastern coast of Canada. How will they survive the harsh Canadian winter?

Keywords: Canada, first love, France, travel

Skurzynski, Gloria

***Spider's Voice.* Simon & Schuster, 1999. ISBN 0689821492. JH/HS**

A fictional account of the affair between famous twelfth-century French lovers Abelard and Heloise, the story is narrated by Aran, a mute servant who works for Abelard. As scholars, Abelard and Eloise cannot marry, but they carry on a secret liaison, and Eloise bears Abelard's child.

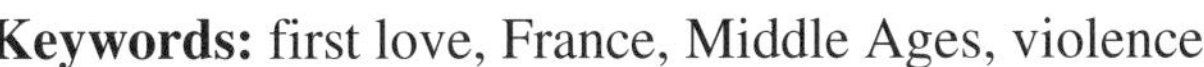

Keywords: first love, France, Middle Ages, violence

Temple, Frances

***The Ramsay Scallop.* Orchard Books, 1994. ISBN 0531068366. JH**

When Elenor's betrothed, Lord Thomas, returns from a crusade to the Holy Land, Father Gregory sends the couple on a pilgrimage to Spain. Elenor and Thomas do not like each other much, despite their impending marriage, and the journey is a chance for them to get to know each other. Set in the fourteenth century. An ALA Best Book for Young Adults.

Keywords: Crusades, marriage, Middle Ages, war

Renaissance/Europe

Napoli, Donna Jo

***Daughter of Venice.* Delacorte Press, 2002. ISBN 0385900368. MS/JH**

Donata, the daughter of a wealthy sixteenth-century Italian nobleman, expects she and her twin sister Laura will enter a convent or remain at home. Donata is desperate to expand her horizons, so she disguises herself as a boy and explores Venice. She meets a young Jewish man named

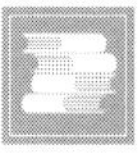

Noe, and although Donata falls in love, she knows religion and tradition will not allow them to marry. While Donata plans to pursue an education, her parents surprise her with an unexpected plan for her future.

Keywords: education, family, first love, Italy, marriage, religion, Renaissance

Eighteenth Century/New World

O'Dell, Scott

My Name Is Not Angelica. **Houghton Mifflin, 1991. ISBN 0395510619. MS/JH**

Raisha, a sixteen-year-old Senegalese girl, is betrothed to her true love, Konje. Before they can marry, they are captured by slave owners and sent to work on a plantation in the Danish West Indies. Konje escapes and leads the slave rebellion of 1733, and Raisha joins him. Will Konje and Raisha ever be free again?

Keywords: Danish West Indies, first love, Haiti, Senegal, slavery

Nineteenth Century/Europe

Peyton, K. M.

Snowfall. **Houghton Mifflin, 1998. ISBN 0395895987. JH/HS**

When Charlotte Campion's grandfather promises she will marry a man she does not love, Charlotte asks her older brother Ben to help her. Ben arranges for sixteen-year-old Charlotte to join his friends on a mountain-climbing expedition in Switzerland. During the trip, Charlotte falls in love with mountain guide Casimir, but he is married. When the trip is over, Charlotte lives with her new friends at Milo's ramshackle country estate, and Charlotte unexpectedly falls in love again. Set in the nineteenth century.

Keywords: adventure, Britain, first love, marriage, Switzerland

Twentieth Century/World War I/Europe

Breslin, Theresa

Remembrance. **Delacorte Press, 2002. ISBN 0385730152. JH/HS**

During World War I, wealthy Scottish teen Charlotte Armstrong-Barnes falls in love with the shopkeeper's son, John Malcolm Dundas, despite their differences. But before long, John Malcolm enlists in the army, and Charlotte signs up for nursing training. Will Charlotte ever see her first love again? An ALA Best Book for Young Adults.

Keywords: first love, Scotland, World War I

Harris, Ruth Elwin

Sisters of the Quantock Hills Quartet.

The orphaned Purcell sisters are left in the care of the Mackenzie family in the Quantock Hills in England. As the sisters grow up, they experience crushes and first love with the Mackenzie brothers during World War I.

Sarah's Story. **Candlewick, 2002. ISBN 0763617075. JH/HS**

In the first book about the orphaned Purcell sisters, the sisters are left in the care of the Mackenzie family in the Quantock Hills in England. The Mackenzie brothers go off to fight in World War I. Youngest sister Sarah has a crush on Gabriel Mackenzie, who loves her sister Frances.

Keywords: Britain, crushes, family, first love, orphans, World War I

Frances' Story. **Candlewick, 2002. ISBN: 0763617040. JH/HS**

Frances, the oldest Purcell sister, falls in love with Gabriel Mackenzie, her guardian's son. Gabriel must leave Frances to fight in the war, but she will wait for his return.

Keywords: Britain, family, first love, orphans, World War I

Julia's Story. **Candlewick, 2002. ISBN: 0763617067. JH/HS**

Julia Purcell falls in love with her guardian's son, Geoffrey Mackenzie. They are separated when they both go off to do their part for the war effort. Julia works as a nurse during World War I in France, until she must return home to a tragedy.

Keywords: Britain, family, first love, France, orphans, World War I

Gwen's Story. **Candlewick Press, 2002. ISBN: 0763617059. JH/HS**

Quiet sister Gwen Purcell is devoted to her family, but her love of gardening and drawing takes her away from their country home. Gwen goes to London, and then to the German Alps, just as Hitler is gaining power in Germany. Will Gwen find love on her journey?

Keywords: Britain, family, first love, Germany, orphans, World War I

Twentieth Century/World War II/Europe

Attema, Martha

When the War Is Over. **Orca, 2002. ISBN 1551432404. JH/HS**

Sixteen-year-old Janke Visser gets involved in Holland's underground resistance during World War II, working as a courier. But to her surprise Janke falls in love with a young German soldier named Helmut, and he loves her, too. Things get complicated when Janke is captured during a courier mission, and Helmut must decide her fate.

Keywords: first love, Netherlands, soldiers, World War II

Chambers, Aidan

Postcards from No Man's Land. **Penguin Putnam, 2002. ISBN 0525468633. [Sexual Content] JH/HS**

Seventeen-year old Jacob Todd travels to the Netherlands to attend a ceremony honoring soldiers who died during World War II, including his grandfather. During his travels, his grandmother's friend Geertrui tells Jacob about her own romantic relationship with Jacob's grandfather during the war. Jacob also experiences first love with a Dutch teen named

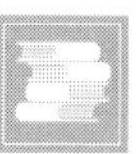

Hille. An ALA Best Book for Young Adults, winner of the 1999 Carnegie Medal, and winner of the 2003 Michael L. Printz Award.

Keywords: family, first love, friendship, Netherlands, World War II

Dokey, Cameron

***Hindenburg, 1937.* Pocket Books, 1999. ISBN 0671036017. [Reluctant Readers] JH**

When Anna Becker's grandfather dies, she takes their tickets for a transatlantic voyage on the *Hindenburg* so she can escape from her brother, who wants to marry her off to a Nazi colleague. During the trip on the *Hindenburg*, Anna is caught in a love triangle between ex-boyfriend Karl Mueller, the man who broke her heart, and a new love, Erik Peterson.

Keywords: first love, Germany, World War II

Huth, Angela

***Land Girls.* St. Martin's Press, 1996. ISBN 031214296X. [Sexual Content, Adult] HS**

Boy crazy Prue, brainy Agatha, and flighty Stella are volunteering as farmhands under England's wartime Land Army plan in 1941. While living on the Lawrence farm, the girls experience adventure, romance, and love. An ALA Best Book for Young Adults. A major motion picture.

Keywords: Britain, friendship, World War II

Mekler, Eva

***Sunrise Shows Late.* Bridge Works, 1997. ISBN 1882593170. [Adult] HS**

When World War II ends, Manya Gerson, a Polish Jew who survived the war working in Warsaw, is sent to a displaced persons camp in Germany. There Manya meets Bolek Holzer, a Zionist who smuggles guns and refugees to Palestine, and Emmanuel Kozek, a scientist, and she is attracted to both men. Manya must choose between a life of danger and excitement with Bolek or a safe and secure life with Emmanuel.

Keywords: first love, Germany, marriage, refugees, religion, World War II

Van Dijk, Lutz

***Damned Strong Love: The True Story of Willi G. and Stefan K.* Henry Holt, 1995. ISBN 0805037705. [Adult] HS**

Based on a true love story, Van Dijk tells the story of Stefan K., a sixteen-year-old Polish boy who falls in love with German soldier Willi G. during World War II. When the Gestapo learns of their affair, Willi is sent to Russia, while Stefan is tortured and sent to a labor camp. An ALA Best Book for Young Adults.

Keywords: homosexuality, Poland, World War II

Twentieth Century/Post–World War II/Australia

Disher, Garry

***The Divine Wind: A Love Story.* Scholastic, 2002. ISBN 0439369150. JH/HS**

After World War II ends, Hartley Penrose remembers what life in Australia was like before the war, before the lives of his family and friends were forever changed, and his Japanese lover was imprisoned in an internment camp.

Keywords: Australia, family, first love, friendship, racism, World War II

Twentieth Century/Asia

Garland, Sherry

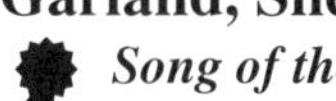

Song of the Buffalo Boy. **Harcourt, 1992. ISBN 0152771077.** <u>**JH/HS**</u>

In postwar Vietnam, seventeen-year-old Loi, a girl of Amerasian heritage, fakes her death to avoid an arranged marriage. She goes to Ho Chi Minh City to meet her true love, Khai, whose family believes she is inferior because of her mixed American and Vietnamese blood. Loi must decide whether she will go in search of her American father and meet other young people of Amerasian heritage, or stay in Vietnam with Khai. An ALA Best Book for Young Adults and winner of the 1993 Romance Writers of America Rita Award.

Keywords: first love, racism, Vietnam

Ho, Minfong

Rice without Rain. **HarperCollins, 1991. ISBN 0688063551.** <u>**JH/HS**</u>

During the 1970s, Jinda's family farms rice in Thailand for a living, but the landlord takes half of their rice crop every year. When a university student named Ned visits their village, he convinces Jinda's father to withhold some of the rice payment in protest. Jinda's father is sent to jail, while seventeen-year-old Jinda follows Ned to Bangkok to join him in political rallies to support the farmers. Can Jinda and Ned's new romance survive the political upheaval that threatens Bangkok?

Keywords: family, first love, politics, Thailand

Murakami, Haruki

Norwegian Wood. **Alfred A. Knopf, 2000. ISBN 0375704027. [Male, Adult]** <u>**HS**</u>

In late 1960s Japan, Toru's best friend commits suicide, and Toru becomes involved with his friend's girlfriend, Naoko. But Naoko is mentally unstable, and she moves to a rest home to recover her health. When Toru falls in love with fellow university student Midori, he wonders what will happen to Naoko if he breaks up with her.

Keywords: death, first love, grief, illness, Japan

Historical Romance Series

"Historical Romance Series" books for teens often span the same time periods and geographic areas mentioned earlier in this chapter. While some stories in "Historical Romance Series" are linked by common characters or themes, these series lack the continuing characters, plots, and cliff-hanger endings of "Contemporary Soap Opera Romance Series." Nevertheless, character is an important element in these novels, as are the continuity and even predictability between titles. Although only a few series are listed, non-romantic historical series for young teens like <u>The Royal Diaries</u>, <u>Dear America</u>, and <u>American Girl</u> are very popular with younger readers, and we may see more historical romance series for young adult readers in the future.

American Dreams. Avon Flare, 1996 to 1997. [Reluctant Readers] JH
Written by Various Authors.

A historical romance series featuring different authors and different American settings.

Keywords: family, first love, marriage

1. *Sarah on Her Own.* Karen M. Coombs
2. *Plainsong for Caitlin.* Elizabeth M. Rees
3. *Into the Wind.* Jean Ferris
4. *Song of the Sea.* Jean Ferris
5. *Weather the Storm.* Jean Ferris
6. *The Innkeeper's Daughter.* Lou Kassem
7. *Reyna's Reward.* Wanda Dionne
8. *Sofia's Heart.* Sharon Cadwallader
9. *Heart of the Hills.* Shelly Ritthaler
10. *With Love, Amanda.* Shelly Ritthaler
11. *Carrie's Gold.* Cheryl Zach

Avon True Romance. Avon, 2002 to Present. [Reluctant Readers] JH/HS
Written by Various Authors.

A new line of innocent historical romance stories featuring catchy titles and attractive cover art, titles in Avon True Romance purportedly "include all the favorite historical periods: Regency, Western, medieval, just to name a few."[2] Well-known authors of adult romance, such as Kathryn Smith, Lorraine Heath, May McGoldrick, Elaine Barbieri, and Beverly Jenkins, along with popular young adult author Meg Cabot, have all written books for the series.

Keywords: family, first love, marriage

1. *Samantha and the Cowboy.* Lorraine Heath
2. *Belle and the Beau.* Beverly Jenkins
3. *Anna and the Duke.* Kathryn Smith
4. *Gwyneth and the Thief.* Margaret Moore
5. *Nicola and the Viscount.* Meg Cabot
6. *Catherine and the Pirate.* Karen Hawkins
7. *Miranda and the Warrior.* Elaine Barbieri
8. *Tess and the Highlander.* May McGoldrick
9. *Emily and the Scot.* Kathryn Smith
10. *Amelia and the Outlaw.* Lorraine Heath
11. *Josephine and the Soldier.* Beverly Jenkins
12. *Victoria and the Rogue.* Meg Cabot

Lorraine Heath, *Samantha and the Cowboy*

Lorraine Heath always knew she wanted to write novels, but she never expected to become a romance writer. In an interview in May 2002, Heath remarked, "I always dreamed of writing a novel but I couldn't quite determine where the stories I wanted to write would fit in. I had a misconception about romance novels, assumed they were mindless stories that held no interest for me. I had to go on a business trip and picked up a book to read on the flight. It was on the *New York Times* list so I figured it had to be a worthwhile read—*Morning Glory* by LaVyrle Spencer. I was halfway through it when I thought, 'I think this is a romance novel.' I was hooked on romance, and I knew the stories I wanted to write belonged in the romance genre."

Lorraine Heath. Photo by Work of Art Studio. Used with permission.

Heath has published many romance novels, including historical and contemporary romance novels for adults such as *The Outlaw and the Lady, Never Marry a Cowboy, Never Love a Cowboy, To Marry an Heiress, The Taming of an Heiress, A Rogue in Texas, Texas Splendor, Texas Glory, Texas Destiny, Always to Remember, The Ladies' Man, Parting Gifts,* and *Sweet Lullaby*. Her work has won numerous awards, including the Romance Writers of America Rita Award.

In 2002, Heath launched her career as a young adult romance writer with several titles in the Love Stories series, using the pseudonym Rachel Hawthorne. She also contributed two books to the Avon True Romance line of historical romances for teens. In *Samantha and the Cowboy*, Samantha Reynolds disguises herself as a boy so she can work on a cattle drive, and then proceeds to fall in love with Matthew Hart. In *Amelia and the Outlaw*, Amelia Harper meets Jesse Lawton, who has come to work on her father's ranch.

When asked how she decided to write romance fiction for a young adult audience, Heath responded, "I have nieces and I wanted to write something for them. I also receive letters from teens who read my adult books. I'm not always comfortable with the younger audience because I know my books were written for adults and contain 'adult content,' so I was thrilled when I heard that HarperCollins was going to launch a new series of historical romances for teens."

Lorraine Heath (*Cont.*)

How does writing romance for young adults differ from writing romance for adults? Heath's reply is simple, "I use a slightly different voice—more upbeat, more excitement about life, a little more innocent. I want teens to be able to identify with the characters, to feel as though they are reading about characters with whom they can identify. In *Amelia and the Outlaw,* the heroine is always bickering with her brothers much as kids do today."

Heath plans to continue writing romance novels for young adult readers using the Rachel Hawthorne pseudonym. Avon Books will publish a new Rachel Hawthorne title, *Caribbean Cruising*, in 2004. Heath has commented, "I really enjoy writing books for a younger audience. I absolutely love writing, telling stories, sharing them with readers. I'm very happy that I've been able to expand my writing to include contemporary romance and stories for a younger audience." She added, "I hope that my stories will continue to please readers. When they finish reading one of my stories, I hope they'll consider it time well spent."

For more information:

Lorraine Heath. 2001. Available: http://www.lorraineheath.com/index.html (accessed September 12, 2002).

Mussell, Kay, and Johanna Tunon, eds. "Lorraine Heath." In *North American Romance Writers*. Lanham: Scarecrow Press, 1999.

Rooney, Terrie M., and Jennifer Gariepy, eds. "Lorraine Heath." In *Contemporary Authors.* Vol. 153. Detroit: Gale Research, 1997.

Wild Rose Inn. Bantam Books, 1994. [Reluctant Readers] JH
Written by Jennifer Armstrong.

Six generations of young women from the McKenzie family live at the Wild Rose Inn in Marblehead, Massachusetts. Each young woman experiences a romance that is affected by critical events in American history.

Keywords: family, first love, marriage

1. *Bridie of the Wild Rose Inn, 1695.*
2. *Ann of the Wild Rose Inn, 1774.*
3. *Emily of the Wild Rose Inn, 1858.*
4. *Laura of the Wild Rose Inn, 1898.*
5. *Claire of the Wild Rose Inn, 1928.*
6. *Grace of the Wild Rose Inn, 1944.*

Notes

1. Kristin Ramsdell, *Romance Fiction: A Guide to the Genre* (Englewood, CO: Libraries Unlimited, 1999), 111.
2. Avon Books, *Avon True Romance: Find True Love.* (New York: Avon Books, 2002).

Chapter 9

Christian Romance

In Christian romance fiction, "Christ is the love interest."[1] Young adult "Christian Romance" fiction, similar to Christian romance fiction written for adults, can be defined as love stories that contain a message of Christian redemption and that affirm Christian values and beliefs. While adult Christian romances often end with the protagonist's love interest converting to Christianity, "Christian Romance" for teens does not always follow this pattern. Sometimes the couple involved in the romance are already committed Christians, while a non-Christian friend or family member converts to Christianity at the end of the story or series. The Christian couple may work together as an evangelical team to help friends, classmates, or family members see the light. Christian teens also struggle with peer pressure to have sex, drink alcohol, or take drugs. In the young adult "Christian Romance," teen protagonists typically struggle with their relationships with God, family, friends, and their love interest. It is often necessary for one or both of the young people involved in the romantic relationship to resolve their relationship with God before the romance can move forward.

The "Christian Romance" generally focuses on teens who are learning how to build strong relationships, based on friendship and faith, with their love interests. Along with the emphasis on Christian values and beliefs, young adult Christian romances feature similar issues and events found in other young adult romance genres, including crushes, dating, first kisses, first love, sex, pregnancy, family problems, drugs, alcohol, and physical abuse. As teens in contemporary Christian romances make plans for their futures, they put their trust in God to help them find the right career and spouse. Unlike Christian romances written for adults, teen "Christian Romance" does not always lead to marriage, but nonetheless, the stories end on a positive note.

While Christian romances for teens tackle some of the same tough issues that contemporary young adult romance addresses, they usually do so without scenes of explicit sex and without using profanity—and problems are always solved through Christian faith and beliefs. Although some Christian romances for teens can be preachy and moralistic, which is a turnoff to many teen readers, other titles present a subtler message of hope and inspiration.

In keeping with Christian values, young adult Christian romances are innocent in nature. Christian romances written specifically for the young adult market are usually targeted at the younger age range of teens. While teen protagonists are involved in committed relationships with members of the opposite sex, there is an emphasis on abstinence from sex until marriage. Affections are generally limited to hand-holding and light kisses. In <u>Christy and Todd: The College Years Trilogy</u>, Christy Miller and Todd Spencer resist temptation and save their passionate kisses for marriage in an imaginary piggy bank. Their friend Doug, who appears in all of Robin Jones Gunn's young adult romance series, saves his first kiss for his wife on their wedding day.

Teen characters in "Christian Romance" fiction must mature in their relationships with family, friends, God, and boyfriends or girlfriends in order to be worthy of love, both from God and from their partners. Characterization is an important element of young adult "Christian Romance" fiction, and teen characters learn how to make good decisions about their lives based on their Christian values. Christian romances are set in historical and contemporary times, but both kinds of stories focus on the strong emotions of the characters as they develop their relationship with God and fall in love with their partners.

The "Christian Romance" subgenre is divided into four categories: "Contemporary Christian Romance," "Contemporary Christian Romance Series," "Historical Christian Romance," and "Historical Christian Romance Series." Most Christian romances today are produced by publishers who specialize in books that promote Christian values and beliefs, such as Bethany House, Moody Press, or W Publishing, but a few books published by mainstream publishers like Bantam Books or Henry Holt also fall into this category. While Bethany House was the largest publisher of "Christian Romance" for teen readers, the publisher recently ceased publishing young adult fiction.

Appeal

The obvious presence of Christian values and beliefs distinguishes Christian romances from other young adult romance fiction. While Christian values and beliefs are prevalent in the stories, some authors choose to emphasize Christianity more strongly than other authors. For instance, Robin Jones Gunn quotes Bible passages extensively throughout her connected <u>Christy Miller</u> and <u>Sierra Jensen</u> series. Gunn's teen characters are actively involved in their churches and overseas missions, and they all attend the same Christian college in <u>Christy and Todd: The College Years</u> trilogy. Laura Peyton Roberts's <u>Clearwater Crossing</u> series also features Christian teens actively involved in church and community events, and by the end of the series, the only atheist active in the youth group decides to join a Bible study class. Judy Baer's <u>Cedar River Daydreams</u> series, on the other hand, includes Christian values and beliefs, but Baer is subtler than Gunn or Roberts.

Either way, it is primarily the Christian message that draws readers to this genre. Teens with religious convictions may wish to affirm their beliefs, and they can do this by reading about characters who share their beliefs; while those struggling with their faith may want to explore spiritual issues.

Other features and characteristics of Christian romances may also appeal to teen readers. Teens uncomfortable with explicit sexual content and profanity can be assured they won't be confronted with language and actions that offend them. And Christian fiction almost always features heroic and virtuous characters who may provide role models and inspiration to teens.

Advising the Reader

Following are some tips for advising readers of the "Christian Romance" subgenre:

- Your patrons who wish to read Christian fiction will usually make their preference known. To determine if readers are seeking Christian fiction, ask about books they have read and enjoyed. The mention of popular titles, such as those in the Christy Miller series, suggests this is the genre for them.

- After you have ascertained that your patron is a fan of Christian romances, find out which "Christian Romance" subgenre your patron wishes to read—"Contemporary Christian Romance" or "Historical Christian Romance." For readers who enjoy "Contemporary Christian Romances," you may also wish to recommend "Inspirational Romances" written for adult audiences. Good choices would be Robin Jones Gunn's Glenbrooke series, which features characters from her teen romance series, or anything written by Janette Oke or Grace Livingston Hill. (*Note:* If you are not familiar with the "Inspirational Romance" genre, refer to the "Inspirational Romance" chapter in Kristin Ramsdell's *Romance Fiction* (Libraries Unlimited, 1999). John Mort's *Christian Fiction* (Libraries Unlimited, 2002) includes two chapters focusing on Christian romances. These books will help you to identify other titles to suggest to your patrons.) Readers who enjoy "Historical Christian Romance" may also like the "Historical Romance" books listed in Chapter 9 as well as those in the "Historical Classics" section of Chapter 2, which usually adhere to many of the same conventions as Christian fiction.

- Although aimed at adult readers, there are several Christian paperback romance series that promote the same Christian values found in young adult Christian romances. Good choices for Christian fiction readers include titles published in various adult Christian romance series, including Harlequin/Silhouette's Love Inspired, Barbour's Heartsong Presents, and Multnomah Press's Palisades Pure Romance.

Contemporary Christian Romance

"Contemporary Christian Romance" features teens striving to build strong relationships with friends, families, boyfriends, girlfriends, and God. "Contemporary Christian Romance" is distinguished from the rest of contemporary young adult romance fiction by the significance the protagonists place on their beliefs and their relationships with God. The protagonists in "Contemporary Christian Romance" must deal with the same issues as teens portrayed in other young adult romance fiction subgenres, such as drugs, alcohol, family problems, first kisses, sex, physical abuse, illness, and death. However, in contemporary Christian romances, the decisions teens make about how to deal with the problems they face are informed by their Christian values and beliefs.

9

Contemporary Christian romances are published by both mainstream and Christian publishers, and both kinds have been successful with teen Christian romances. Robin Jones Gunn, author of the Christy Miller series, the Sierra Jenson

series, and Christy and Todd: The College Years Trilogy, is the most prolific author of Christian romance for teens. Her Christy Miller series has remained popular since it began fifteen years ago, with more than 1 million books in print, and Bethany House printed a revised and updated version of the series in 1998. Lurlene McDaniel, author of popular stories about teens facing life-threatening illnesses published by mainstream publisher Bantam Books, subtly infuses Christian values into her stories as she helps teens learn how to deal with illness, death, and grief. Two of McDaniel's series, The Angels Trilogy and The Barlow Sisters Series, feature teens struggling with their relationship with God and teens who do overseas missions work. These two series also include central love stories, and due to the strong emphasis on Christianity in these series, the books are included in the "Contemporary Christian Romance" category. Teens who enjoy McDaniel's work can find other titles in Chapter 5, "Issues Romance."

Gunn, Robin Jones

Christy and Todd: The College Years Trilogy.

After a year studying in Switzerland, nineteen-year-old Christy Miller returns to California to attend Rancho Corona University with her boyfriend Todd and good friends Katie and Sierra. Features characters from Gunn's popular Christy Miller and Sierra Jensen series.

Until Tomorrow. **Bethany House, 2000. ISBN 0764222724. [Reluctant Readers] JH/HS**

Nineteen-year-old Christy Miller, who is studying in Switzerland, is thrilled when her girlfriend Katie and boyfriend Todd visit. But Christy doesn't get much time alone with Todd, and now she is uncertain about the future of their relationship.

Keywords: college, dating, friendship, Switzerland

As You Wish. **Bethany House, 2000. ISBN 0764222732. [Reluctant Readers] JH/HS**

Christy Miller returns to California to continue college with her friends and boyfriend Todd. When Christy meets old friend Matthew Kingsley, she questions her commitment to Todd.

Keywords: California, college, dating, friendship

I Promise. **Bethany House, 2001. ISBN 0764222740. [Reluctant Readers] JH/HS**

Christy and Todd are engaged to be married when they finish college. But Christy has doubts when she realizes Todd's approach to wedding planning differs from her own, and she wonders if two people who are so different should get married.

Keywords: dating, friendship, marriage, weddings

Robin Jones Gunn, Christy Miller Series

**Robin Jones Gunn.
Photo used with permission.**

No one was more surprised than Robin Jones Gunn when she began writing romance novels for teens in the mid-1980s. Although Gunn had published several children's books, she had no plans to write teen romance novels until girls in a Christian youth group, led by Gunn and her pastor husband, suggested Gunn write Christian romances for them. In an interview in January 2003, Gunn said, "I was challenged by some young teen girls to write novels for them. They were my inspiration. The girls were involved in the development of the first novel, *Summer Promise*, because every week I would read a portion to them and they would tell me everything that was wrong with it and tell me what to change. It took two years and thick skin before that first novel was completed. Ten publishers turned it down, all saying they didn't see a market for novels for that age group. I knew the girls wanted simple, contemporary love stories. . . . I prayed hard for the right publisher."

In the late 1980s Bethany House decided to publish *Summer Promise* as part of a twelve-book series featuring Christy Miller and her friends. The popular series was revised and reissued in 1998, a decade after *Summer Promise* was first published. Gunn stated, "[T]he books had very few references to modern conveniences such as cell phones and the Internet. I went over all the changes with the editor and felt comfortable with how it all came together. We tried to adjust the outfits and hairstyles by taking out specifics in order to keep the stories from feeling dated." Although the series only includes twelve books, the Christy Miller series has sold more than a million copies.

Gunn continued to write about Christy Miller and her friends in the Sierra Jensen series and Christy and Todd: The College Years Trilogy. "I got particularly attached to some of the characters . . . I would think about them long after the book was finished and wonder what they were doing or how they'd changed since I last saw them. Somehow, they'd show up in the book I was currently writing because I wanted to know what was happening to them. I've been told this is a unique style of writing," Gunn said in the same interview. "It's all one big, interconnected story in my mind. Relationships are immensely important to God and I think they're important to me, too . . . even if the relationship is with an imaginary friend!" Some of Gunn's teen characters reappear in her popular Glenbrooke series for women.

Robin Jones Gunn (*Cont.*)

What messages does Gunn offer to her teen readers? "The main characters in all these stories discover something about themselves and about God. They portray believable situations where they see how deeply God loves them and how much he desires to have a close relationship with them. This closeness overflows into their relationships with others in the stories. The common thread through these novels is that God is the Relentless Lover and we are His first love. He never gives up on us because He wants us back," Gunn stated. Gunn's young readers understand these messages. Gunn reported, "Many write to say how they have changed their view of God and His love for them or how they have made important decisions to change areas of their life because they saw a similar decision being played out in the life of one of the characters."

Of a recent fan letter, Gunn said, "One letter that came from Brazil last week was from a sixteen-year-old girl who said, 'We adolescents need explanations of life in a language we understand. Your books give us this language and it goes right into our hearts and stays there.' "

While Gunn doesn't have any current plans to write more teen romances, she continues to write for teenage girls and women. Fans of Gunn's work will be happy to hear she recently completed a new book for younger teens and she has also started a new series for women called Sisterchick*s*. Gunn reported, "*Sisterchicks on the Loose!* will launch a whole new series of fresh stories with a focus on friendship." She hinted that favorite characters from a previous series would reappear in Sisterchicks. Gunn declared, "I love the stories I've been working on lately! I've never had this much fun writing!"

For more information:

Eble, Diane. "Robin Jones Gunn." In *Behind the Stories*. Minneapolis: Bethany House, 2002.

Peacock, Scot, ed. "Robin Jones Gunn." In *Contemporary Authors New Revision Series*. Vol. 101. Detroit: Gale Research, 2002.

Robin Gunn.com. 2003. Available: http://www.robingunn.com/ (accessed January 25, 2003).

Spencer, Paula. "Romance Queens." *Woman's Day* 62, no. 9 (1999): 77–80.

Gunn, Robin Jones, and Wendy Lee Nentwig, Editors

***Departures*. Bethany House, 1999. ISBN 0764222716. [Reluctant Readers] JH/HS**

Short stories feature characters from three popular Christian young adult romance series, including Gunn's Christy Miller and Sierra Jensen series and Nentwig's Unmistakably Cooper Ellis series.

Keywords: dating, short stories

Heynen, Jim

Cosmos Coyote and William the Nice. **Henry Holt, 2000. ISBN 0805064346. [Sexual Content, Male] HS**

After Cosmos DeHaag is arrested a third time, he is sent to live with relatives in rural Iowa, where he attends the Dutch Center Christian Academy. Seventeen-year-old Cosmos puts on his "William the Nice" face for his family and friends, but he fears everyone in the Christian community is trying to convert him, including beautiful and popular Cherlyn Van Dyke. Cosmos and Cherlyn begin a romance that is complicated by her devout faith and his lack of religious beliefs.

Keywords: dating, drugs, religion, sex

McDaniel, Lurlene

The Barlow Sisters Series.

Sisters Heather and Amber Barlow make separate missions trips to Uganda, Africa, where they experience the joys and heartaches of first love.

Angel of Mercy. **Bantam Books, 1999. ISBN 0553571451. [Reluctant Readers] MS/JH**

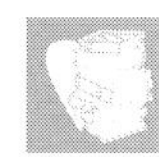

High school graduate Heather Barlow travels to Uganda, Africa, with a Christian mission group, where she falls in love with medical intern Ian McCollum. After Ian dies while rescuing a baby in the Sudan, Heather must complete the rescue mission.

Keywords: death, first love, grief

Angel of Hope. **Bantam Books, 2000. ISBN 0553571486. [Reluctant Readers] MS/JH**

Heather Barlow convinces her mother, a doctor, to travel to Uganda to operate on the baby she and Ian rescued in *Angel of Mercy*. But Heather becomes ill, so her younger sister Amber travels to Africa, where she falls in love with engineering student Boyce. When tragedy strikes the Barlow family, Amber returns to the mission in Africa, seeking love and her purpose in life.

Keywords: death, first love, grief, illness

McDaniel, Lurlene

The Angels Trilogy. Bantam Books, 2002. ISBN 0553570986. [Reluctant Readers] MS/JH

While staying in hospital for cancer treatment, sixteen-year-old Leah Lewis-Hall falls in love with Ethan, her Amish roommate's older brother. Leah and Ethan struggle to maintain their romance despite their religious differences.

Angels Watching over Me. **Bantam Books, 1996. ISBN 0553567241. [Reluctant Readers] MS/JH**

When Leah Lewis-Hall winds up in the hospital alone over Christmas with a diagnosis of cancer, she is supported by her Amish

roommate Rebekah's large, loving family. Before long, Leah falls in love with Rebekah's brother, Ethan.

Keywords: the Amish, family, first love, illness

Lifted Up by Angels. **Bantam Books, 1997. ISBN 0553571125. [Reluctant Readers] MS/JH**

Leah takes a summer job near her boyfriend Ethan's Amish community. But their lives are very different, and Ethan's religion and family obligations threaten their relationship.

Keywords: the Amish, dating, family, first love, illness

Until Angels Close My Eyes. **Bantam Books, 1998. ISBN 055357115X. [Reluctant Readers] MS/JH**

When Leah learns that her stepfather has cancer, she visits her boyfriend Ethan in his Amish community. Ethan moves in with Leah and her family, but Ethan and Leah discover their values are very different, and they are not sure they belong together after all.

Keywords: the Amish, dating, family, first love, illness

Moore, Stephanie Perry

Laurel Shadrach Series.

High school senior Laurel Shadrach, a preacher's daughter, deals with peer pressure to have sex, do drugs, and drink alcohol. Laurel continues to face the same peer pressure when she attends university.

Purity Reigns. **Moody Press, 2002. ISBN 0802440355. [Reluctant Readers] JH/HS**

High school senior Laurel Shadrach wants to remain a virgin until she is married. But when her boyfriend pressures her to become intimate, Laurel is tempted.

Keywords: abstinence, dating, friendship

Totally Free. **Moody Press, 2002. ISBN 0802440363. [Reluctant Readers] JH/HS**

During Laurel Shadrach's second semester of her senior year, she begins dating a Christian boy who doesn't pressure her for sex. But Laurel and her friends experience pressure from their peers to do drugs and drink alcohol, and they must decide if they will give in to temptation.

Keywords: abstinence, alcohol, dating, drugs, friendship

Equally Yoked. **Moody Press, 2003. ISBN 0802440371. [Reluctant Readers] JH/HS**

Laurel Shadrach goes to college, where she meets new friends, including Payton Skky from Moore's Payton Skky series. Laurel continues to deal with peer pressure to drink alcohol and become sexually active.

Keywords: abstinence, alcohol, dating, friendship

Absolutely Worthy. **Moody Press, 2003. ISBN 080244038X. [Reluctant Readers] JH/HS**

Laurel is torn between dating Foster, who is a Christian, and Branson, who pressures her to have sex.

Keywords: abstinence, dating, friendship, sex

Finally Sure. **Moody Press, 2004. ISBN 0802440398. [Reluctant Readers] JH/HS**

In the final book in the series, Laurel Shadrach decides to pursue a Christian lifestyle. While she reevaluates her relationships, Laurel wonders whether she has finally found true, pure love with Charlie.

Keywords: abstinence, dating, friendship

Nentwig, Wendy Lee

Unmistakably Cooper Ellis Series.

Beautiful Cooper Ellis, a high school sophomore, is also a teen model. Although she is very busy, she still finds time for her family, her best friends Claire and Alex, and her new boyfriend Josh.

Tripping over Skyscrapers. **Bethany House, 1998. ISBN 0764220659. [Reluctant Readers] MS/JH**

Cooper Ellis has a good life. She lives in Manhattan, she has two best friends, Claire and Alex, and she has a chance to become a model. Suddenly everything falls apart—Cooper's best friends are busy with new friends, a jealous classmate spreads vicious rumors about Cooper, and her modeling career doesn't seem as glamorous and exciting as it once did.

Keywords: friendship, jealousy

Moonstruck in Manhattan. **Bethany House, 1998. ISBN 0764220667. [Reluctant Readers] MS/JH**

Cooper Ellis is busy juggling high school and a modeling career, and her relationships with her friends and family are strained. When Josh Trobisch asks her out on her first date, she is very happy, but she believes Josh is hiding something from her.

Keywords: dating, friendship

Subway Tokens in the Sand. **Bethany House, 1998. ISBN 0764220675. [Reluctant Readers] MS/JH**

Although Cooper Ellis is pleased to have her first boyfriend, she is unhappy when Josh is invited to join her family on vacation.

Keywords: dating, family, vacations

Cabs, Cameras, and Catastrophes. **Bethany House, 1998. ISBN 0764220683. [Reluctant Readers] MS/JH**

Cooper Ellis's faith is put to the test in a number of situations. She regrets her breakup with boyfriend Josh, and she wonders if there is a chance for reconciliation. Meanwhile, she refuses to pose for a risky photo shoot, putting her modeling career in jeopardy. Can Cooper's friendships and faith sustain her?

Keywords: dating, friendship

Contemporary Christian Romance Series

"Contemporary Christian Romance Series" are set in modern times, and characters deal with contemporary issues. "Contemporary Christian Romance Series" offer continuing stories and characters. Teen readers get to know the characters and follow their development through various episodes. They may even feel that they are "part of the group." Some series offer stronger Christian messages than others, but all the series listed here provide readers with Christian values. The books are usually short, easy reads, aimed at girls on the younger end of the young adult spectrum.

"Contemporary Christian Romance Series" focus on contemporary issues, like much of young adult romance fiction, but Christian series romance addresses issues not found in other series romance fiction. For instance, in the Nikki Sheridan series, Nikki converts to Christianity after a pregnancy leads her to give up her baby for adoption. This unusually serious series ends with Nikki accepting her life choices and making peace with her former boyfriend. Another series, Cedar River Daydreams, features one of the few characters with Down's syndrome found in young adult fiction. Author Judy Baer succeeds in teaching teens to fight their prejudices against people with disabilities.

Readers of these titles, like those who read other series titles, are often very conscious of chronology, so it is important to have the complete series in your collection, and to be aware of the order of titles in the series.

Brio Girls. Bethany House, 2001 to Present. [Reluctant Readers] MS/JH
Created by Lissa Halls Johnson; Written by Various Authors.

While growing up in Colorado, high school students and friends Jacie, Hannah, Solona, Tyler, and Becca face the challenges of remaining true to their Christian faith in their relationships with family, friends, boyfriends, and girlfriends.

Keywords: dating, family, friendship

1. *Stuck in the Sky*
2. *Fast Forward to Normal*
3. *Opportunity Knocks Twice*
4. *Double Exposure*
5. *Good-Bye to All That*
6. *Grasping at Moonbeams*
7. *Croutons for Breakfast*
8. *No Lifeguard on Duty*
9. *Dragonfly on My Shoulder*
10. *Going Crazy Till Wednesday*

Cedar River Daydreams. Bethany House, 1988 to 1999. [Reluctant Readers] MS/JH
Written by Judy Baer.

Sixteen-year-old Lexi Leighton moves to Cedar River, where she has a hard time fitting in with the popular crowd. Her new friends feel uncomfortable around her brother Ben, who has Down's syndrome. Lexi finds real friends in Jennifer, Matt,

Peggy, Chad, and Binky, and she falls in love with Todd Winston, the quarterback on the school football team. As Lexi and her friends grow up, they rely on their Christian faith to help them deal with difficult times.

Keywords: dating, disabilities, first love, friendship

1. *New Girl in Town*
2. *Trouble with a Capital T*
3. *Jennifer's Secret*
4. *Journey to Nowhere*
5. *Broken Promises*
6. *The Intruder*
7. *Silent Tears No More*
8. *Fill My Empty Heart*
9. *Yesterday's Dream*
10. *Tomorrow's Promise*
11. *Something Old, Something New*
12. *Vanishing Star*
13. *No Turning Back*
14. *Second Chance*
15. *Lost and Found*
16. *Unheard Voices*
17. *Lonely Girl*
18. *More Than Friends*
19. *Never Too Late*
20. *The Discovery*
21. *A Special Kind of Love*
22. *Three's a Crowd*
23. *Silent Thief*
24. *The Suspect*
25. *Heartless Hero*
26. *Worlds Apart*
27. *Never Look Back*
28. *Forever Friends*

Christy Miller. Bethany House, 1988 to 1994. Reissued in 1998. [Reluctant Readers] MS/JH

Written by Robin Jones Gunn.

Fourteen-year-old Christy Miller has a summer romance with Todd Spencer during a visit to California, and she is thrilled when her family moves to California. Christy and her friends Todd, Katie, Tracy, Doug,

and Rick experience the joys and heartaches of romantic relationships as they grow up and grow stronger in their faith in God. The series was revised and updated by the author for reissue in 1998.

Keywords: dating, first love, friendship

1. *Summer Promise*
2. *A Whisper and a Wish*
3. *Yours Forever*
4. *Surprise Endings*
5. *Island Dreamer*
6. *A Heart Full of Hope*
7. *True Friends*
8. *Starry Night*
9. *Seventeen Wishes*
10. *A Time to Cherish*
11. *Sweet Dreams*
12. *A Promise Is Forever*
13. *Christy Miller's Diary*

Clearwater Crossing. Bantam Books, 1998 to 2001. [Reluctant Readers] JH/HS
Written by Laura Peyton Roberts.

Best friends and devout Christians Jenna Conrad and Peter Altmann form a youth group called Eight Prime with high school classmates Melanie Andrews, Jesse Jones, Nicole Brewster, Miguel del Rios, Leah Rosenthal, and Ben Pipkin. The members of Eight Prime enjoy friendship and romance while doing good deeds in their community.

Keywords: crushes, dating, first love, friendship

1. *Get a Life*
2. *Reality Check*
3. *Heart & Soul*
4. *Promises, Promises*
5. *Just Friends*
6. *Keep the Faith*
7. *New Beginnings*
8. *One Real Thing*
9. *Skin Deep*
10. *No Doubt*
11. *More Than This*
12. *Hope Happens*
13. *Dream On*
14. *Love Hurts*

15. *What Goes Around*
16. *Tried & True*

17. *Just Say Yes*
18. *Prime Time*
19. *Now & Always*
20. *Don't Look Back*
21. *Clearwater Crossing Special Edition: The Diaries*

Diary of a Teenage Girl. Multnomah Press, 2000 to Present. JH/HS
Written by Melody Carlson.

Sixteen-year-old Caitlin O'Connor becomes a Christian, and although she refuses to date, she forms a strong relationship with Josh Miller. In books 1 through 4, Caitlin struggles with family problems, dating, friendships, peer pressure, and her relationship with Josh. Book 5 introduces Josh's younger sister, Chloe, a musician who forms a girl band called Redemption.

Keywords: dating, diaries, family, friendship

1. *Becoming Me*
2. *It's My Life*
3. *Who I Am*
4. *On My Own*
5. *My Name Is Chloe*
6. *Sold Out*

Holly's Heart. Bethany House, 2001 to Present. [Reluctant Readers] MS/JH
Written by Beverly Lewis.

Holly Meredith's life has changed a great deal—her parents got divorced, her father moved to California, and her mother plans to remarry. When Holly begins junior high school, her life becomes more complicated when she is confused by her feelings for Jared Wilkins and Danny Myers.

Keywords: crushes, dating, family, friendship

1. *Best Friend, Worst Enemy*
2. *Secret Summer Dreams*
3. *Sealed with a Kiss*
4. *The Trouble with Weddings*
5. *California Crazy*
6. *Second-Best Friend*

7. *Good-Bye, Dressel Hills*
8. *Straight-A Teacher*
9. *No Guys Pact*
10. *Little White Lies*

Live! From Brentwood High. Bethany House, 1994 to 1996. [Reluctant Readers] MS/JH
Written by Judy Baer.

The crew of the school radio show *Live! From Brentwood High*, including Darby, Sarah, Jake, Molly, Izzy, and Shane, cover stories about workplace harassment, school violence, discrimination against people with disabilities, graffiti, and problems faced by teenage mothers. While on the job, the friends experience love and romance.

Keywords: dating, first love, friendship

1. *Risky Assignment*
2. *Price of Silence*
3. *Double Danger*
4. *Sarah's Dilemma*
5. *Undercover Artists*
6. *Faded Dreams*

Nikki Sheridan. Bethany House, 1996 to 2000. [Reluctant Readers] JH/HS
Written by Shirley Brinkerhoff.

When sixteen-year-old Nikki Sheridan discovers she is pregnant, she is forced to examine all of her options, including adoption and abortion. After making the most difficult decision of her life, Nikki becomes a Christian. But when her former boyfriend T. J. returns, Nikki must find a way to release her anger at T. J. so she can find true happiness.

Keywords: abortion, adoption, dating, pregnancy

1. *Choice Summer*
2. *Mysterious Love*
3. *Narrow Walk*
4. *Balancing Act*
5. *Tangled Web*
6. *Second Choices*

Payton Skky Series. Moody Press, 2000 to 2002. [Reluctant Readers] MS/JH
Written by Stephanie Perry Moore.

As Payton Skky finishes high school and begins college, she must deal with difficult issues, including peer pressure to do drugs, drink alcohol, and have sex. Her friend Tad Taylor helps strengthen her relationship with God, allowing Payton to avoid temptation. Will Payton's friendship with Tad turn into true love? New cover art, featuring photographs of people instead of crude cartoon drawings, makes this series more appealing.

Keywords: abstinence, African Americans, college, dating

1. *Staying Pure*
2. *Sober Faith*
3. *Saved Race*
4. *Sweetest Gift*
5. *Surrendered Heart*

Sierra Jensen. Bethany House, 1995 to 1999. [Reluctant Readers] MS/JH
Written by Robin Jones Gunn.

High school junior Sierra Jensen returns home from a European missions trip. Before Sierra leaves London, she meets an American boy named Paul, and when she returns to the United States, she meets up with him again. Will Paul ever return Sierra's love?

Keywords: first love, friendship, letters

1. *Only You, Sierra*
2. *In Your Dreams*
3. *Don't You Wish*
4. *Close Your Eyes*
5. *Without a Doubt*
6. *With This Ring*
7. *Open Your Heart*
8. *Time Will Tell*
9. *Now Picture This*
10. *Hold On Tight*
11. *Closer Than Ever*
12. *Take My Hand*

White Dove Romances. Bethany House, 1996 to 1997. JH/HS
Written by Yvonne Lehman.

High school junior Natalie Ainsworth, her boyfriend Scott Lambert, and their friends and family rely on their Christian faith to sustain them as they deal with issues such as alcoholism, accidents, and physical abuse.

Keywords: dating, family, friendship

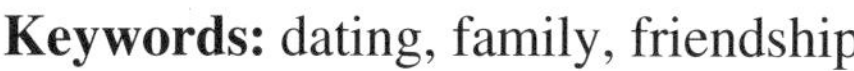

1. *Tornado Alley*
2. *Secret Storm*
3. *Mirror of Dreams*
4. *Picture Perfect*
5. *A Fighting Chance*

Historical Christian Romance

In many ways, "Historical Christian Romance" resembles "Contemporary Christian Romance"; but these novels are set in the past, and the setting of time and place is usually one of the most important features of the stories. Some Christian historical fiction has a nostalgic tone, harking back to more innocent days. Christian historical fiction also has much in common with general historical romance fiction published for young adults, including settings in the American West, the occurrence of natural disasters, and lots of action and adventure. Many historical Christian romances are set in the United States.

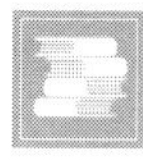

Character also plays an important role in Christian historicals. Like the teen protagonists in contemporary Christian romance, the characters in historical Christian romances deal with significant issues, including dating, family problems, physical abuse, pregnancy, education, careers, sex, and marriage. For instance, Catherine Marshall's protagonists in *Christy* and *Julie* worry about their futures, and they unexpectedly find romance while pursuing their careers.

Janette Oke, a popular author of historical Christian romances, is often credited with creating the genre of commercial Christian fiction. While Oke's books were written for an adult audience, they are suitable for younger readers. John Mort suggests, "All of Janette Oke's titles are excellent for young adults—for girls, at least, because she often uses teenage girls and young women barely out of adolescence for her protagonists."[2] Several of Janette Oke's romantic Women of the West books, including *Roses for Mama* and *A Gown of Spanish Lace,* were recently repackaged as Janette Oke Classics for Girls Series. Oke's Love Comes Softly Series, about the lives and loves of the young women in the Davis family, is also included here.

Readers who enjoy this subgenre may also enjoy titles found in Chapter 9, "Historical Romance," and in the "Historical Classics" section of Chapter 2. Of course, if it is the Christian message they are seeking, titles in the "Contemporary Christian Romance" section of this chapter will also appeal.

Bender, Carrie

Dora's Diary Series.

Set in Amish settlements in Minnesota, California, and Belize in the nineteenth century, Dora's Diary recounts the adventures of sixteen-year-old Dora, the adopted daughter of Miriam and Nate Kauffman from Bender's Miriam's Journal series. Dora falls in love with Matthew, and the couple marries and moves to Belize to start their family.

***Birch Hollow Schoolmarm.* Herald, 1999. ISBN 0836190955. MS/JH**

Dora Kauffman, who lives in Pennsylvania Amish country, often sneaks out of the house at night to see Gideon, the boy she is forbidden to date. When Dora moves to Minnesota to become a schoolteacher, she falls in love with Matthew.

Keywords: the Amish, dating, diaries

***Lilac Blossom Time.* Herald, 2001. ISBN 0836191374. MS/JH**

Dora and Matthew's romance continues, despite the fact that they live in different states. They write letters, Matthew visits Dora, and before long, they are planning a wedding.

Keywords: the Amish, dating, diaries, marriage, weddings

***Beyond Mist Blue Mountains.* Herald, 2003. ISBN 083619165X. MS/JH**

Newlyweds Dora and Matthew go to Belize to work in an orphanage operated by Dora's aunt and uncle. When their prayers for a child of their own go unanswered, they decide to adopt children.

Keywords: the Amish, Belize, diaries, marriage

Coyle, Neva

The Summerwind Trilogy. Bethany House, 1995/1996. Reissued by Galahad Books, 2003. [Adult] HS

Members of Summerwind High School's graduating class of 1957 deal with the consequences of falling in love.

***A Door of Hope*. Bethany House, 1995. ISBN 1556614756. [Adult] HS**

Karissa Hill elopes with Michael Andrews, but when Michael becomes abusive, a pregnant Karissa doesn't know what to do.

Keywords: marriage, physical abuse, pregnancy

***Inside the Privet Hedge*. Bethany House, 1996. ISBN 1556615477. [Adult] HS**

Retta McCarron plans to save the family orange grove from developers, but she didn't expect to fall in love with Alan Conrad, the investor who wants her land.

Keywords: business, family

***Close to a Father's Heart*. Bethany House, 1996. ISBN 1556615485. [Adult] HS**

Amy Weaver is forced to leave college to care for her sick mother. After her mother dies, Amy discovers shocking secrets about her family, and her search for the truth leads her unexpectedly to true love.

Keywords: business, family, mystery

Holmes, Marjorie

***Two from Galilee*. Revell, 1972. Reissued by Bantam Books in 1982. ISBN 0553281003. [Adult] HS**

The love story of Mary and Joseph.

Keywords: children, marriage

Marshall, Catherine

***Christy*. McGraw-Hill, 1967. Reissued by Chosen Books in 2001. ISBN 0800792904. JH/HS**

When nineteen-year-old Christy Huddleston moves to the Smokey Mountains to teach poor children in 1912, she finds herself torn between the love of two men, young minister David Grantland and country doctor Neil McNeil.

Keywords: education, first love, illness

***Julie*. McGraw-Hill, 1984. Reissued by Zondervan in 2002. ISBN 0310246202. JH/HS**

Julie Wallace pursues her dream of becoming a writer by working for her father's Pennsylvania newspaper business in 1934. As a disagreement between local steelworkers and the owners of the steel mills becomes news, Julie's love for two men on different sides of the disagreement is tested.

Keywords: crushes, family, first love, natural disasters

Oke, Janette

Janette Oke Classics for Girls Series.

Classics for Girls is a series from Janette Oke, a popular author of adult Christian romance, aimed at readers ages ten through fourteen. Several of the books in this series, originally published as part of Oke's Women of the West series, portray girls growing up and falling in love on the American frontier during the nineteenth century. While not all of the books in the Classics for Girls series are considered romances, those that are considered romances are included here.

A Gown of Spanish Lace. **Bethany House, 1995. Reissued by Bethany House in 2002. ISBN 0764227114. MS/JH**

Young schoolteacher Ariana Benson is abducted and held captive by outlaws. But her captor's son Laramie helps her escape, and on the trip home, Ariana and Laramie fall in love. After Laramie converts to Christianity, the couple plans a wedding, but secrets from the past threaten their happy union.

Keywords: crime, family, first love, Westward Expansion

Drums of Change. **Bethany House, 1995. Reissued by Bethany House in 2003. ISBN 0764227149. MS/JH**

Running Fawn, a young Native Canadian woman living in southern Alberta, learns to live with the white settlers who want to convert the members of her Blackfoot tribe to Christianity. Running Fawn must choose between the love of Christian missionary Martin Forbes and Silver Fox, the chief's son.

Keywords: Canada, first love, marriage, Native Canadians, Westward Expansion

Roses for Mama. **Bethany House, 1991. Reissued by Bethany House in 2002. ISBN 0764227092. MS/JH**

After their parents' death, seventeen-year-old Angela Peterson and her brother Thomas bear the heavy burden of raising their younger siblings. When new neighbor Carter Stratton begins to court Angela, she wishes her mother was there to guide her.

Keywords: dating, family, first love, Westward Expansion

Oke, Janette

Love Comes Softly Series.

Set on the Iowa prairie in the mid-nineteenth century, this series focuses on the lives, loves, and losses of Marty and Clark Davis and their children. The first title in the series, *Love Comes Softly*, launched Oke's career as queen of the historical Christian romance fiction.

Love Comes Softly. **Bethany House, 1979. Reissued by Bethany House in 1982. ISBN 0871233428. [Adult] JH/HS**

Young newlyweds Marty and Clem Claridge travel West, hoping to claim land. But tragedy strikes, leaving Marty alone on the prairie until she meets widower Clark Davis and his daughter Missie. Has Marty found true love again?

Keywords: children, death, marriage, Westward Expansion

Love's Enduring Promise. **Bethany House, 1980. Reissued by Bethany House in 1982. ISBN 0871233452. [Adult] JH/HS**

Marty and Clark Davis raise their children on their prairie farm and help prepare daughter Missie for marriage.

Keywords: marriage, Westward Expansion

Love's Long Journey. **Bethany House, 1982. ISBN 0871233150. [Adult] JH/HS**

As newlyweds Missie and Willie LaHaye travel West, they must rely on their faith to survive the trip.

Keywords: marriage, Westward Expansion

Love's Abiding Joy. **Bethany House, 1983. ISBN 0871234017. [Adult] JH/HS**

Marty and Clark Davis visit their daughter Missie LeHaye and her happy family on their homestead.

Keywords: children, marriage, Westward Expansion

Love's Unending Legacy. **Bethany House, 1984. ISBN 0871236168. [Adult] JH/HS**

Marty and Clark Davis return home to find Ellie searching for a husband, while Clare and Kate await the birth of their baby. Meanwhile, everyone must get used to Clark's new handicap.

Keywords: children, disabilities, marriage, Westward Expansion

Love's Unfolding Dream. **Bethany House, 1987. ISBN 0871239795. [Adult] JH/HS**

Marty and Clark Davis's daughter Belinda thinks about a career in nursing so she can work with her brother, Doctor Luke. When Belinda's teenage niece Melissa comes to live with the Davis family, Melissa, Belinda, and her friend Amy Jo all fall in love with the same young man.

Keywords: careers, Westward Expansion

Love Takes Wing. **Bethany House, 1988. ISBN 1556610351. [Adult] JH/HS**

Belinda Davis tires of her nursing work with Doctor Luke, and when she is invited to Boston by an elderly woman seeking a nurse, she is excited to have an opportunity to live in the city. But Belinda finds the city lonely.

Keywords: Boston, careers, Westward Expansion

Love Finds a Home. **Bethany House, 1989. ISBN 1556610866. [Adult] JH/HS**

Belinda Davis wants to return home to the prairie, but she inherits a house in Boston. Belinda's choices become even more complicated when she meets Drew.

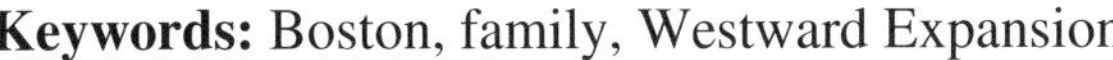

Keywords: Boston, family, Westward Expansion

Historical Christian Romance Series

Very few of the young adult Christian romances have historical settings. One series, Christy, is included here. For more historical young adult romances, see the series listed at the end of Chapter 8, "Historical Romance."

Christy. W Publishing, 1995 to 1997. [Reluctant Readers] MS/JH
Written by Catherine Marshall; Adapted by C. Archer.

When nineteen-year-old Christy Huddleston moves to the Smokey Mountains to teach poor children in 1912, she finds herself torn between the love of two men, young minister David Grantland and country doctor Neil McNeil. Based on Catherine Marshall's classic story *Christy*, originally published in 1967. Cover art features actors from the *Christy* television show that aired in the mid-1990s.

Keywords: education, first love, illness

1. *Bridge to Cutter Gap*
2. *Silent Superstitions*
3. *The Angry Intruder*
4. *Midnight Rescue*
5. *Proposal*
6. *Christy's Choice*
7. *The Princess Club*
8. *Family Secrets*
9. *Mountain Madness*
10. *Stage Fright*
11. *Good-Bye, Sweet Prince*
12. *Brotherly Love*

Notes

1. John Mort, *Christian Fiction: A Guide to the Genre* (Greenwood Village, CO: Libraries Unlimited, 2002), 133.
2. Ibid., 121.

Chapter 10

Research Materials

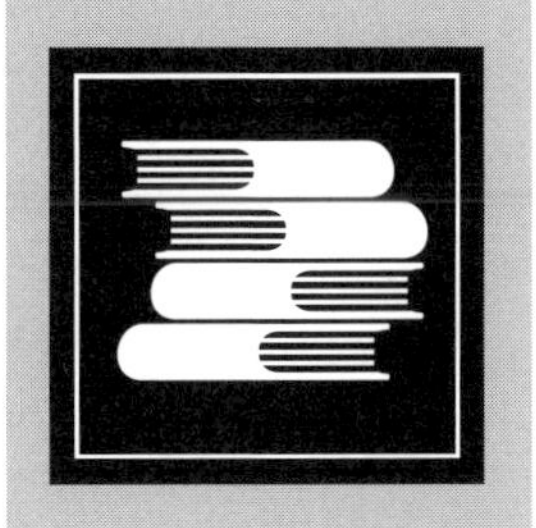

Researchers became interested in studying the young adult romance series novels that proliferated in the 1980s, especially as the decade ended and publishing trends for young adults changed, virtually wiping out the young adult romance series novels. Young adult romance series published in the 1980s were modeled on paperback romance series published for adults. Researchers have been interested in documenting the dramatic abundance and popularity of the young adult romance series during the 1980s, and they want to understand why most of these series failed to remain popular as the decade came to an end. While Linda Christian Smith's book *Becoming a Woman through Romance* is the definitive study of 1980s young adult romance fiction and its readers, other academics and librarians have examined the literary quality of romance novels for young adults, and bibliographers have documented series and titles. Still, very little research has been conducted examining young adult love stories, other than the romance series novels, and this is an area for more research. Researchers interested in studying young adult romance fiction will want to examine the books, articles, and theses listed in this chapter.

Research materials listed below are broken down into the following categories: "Literature Guides"; "History, Surveys, and Criticism"; "Dissertations and Theses"; "Trade and Library Publication Articles"; "Popular Press Articles"; and "Guides for Writing Young Adult Romance." A short list of libraries housing special collections of romance novels or girls' series books is included for researchers or fans who might want to read young adult romance novels, particularly books published in the 1980s.

Literature Guides

Several bibliographic guides to young adult romance literature were published in the 1980s and 1990s. Information about young adult romance series literature can also be found in bibliographies about girls' series books. Both kinds of guides are listed below.

Children's Literature Research Collections. ***Girls Series Books 1840 to 1991.*** **Minneapolis: University of Minnesota Libraries, 1992.**

An extremely thorough bibliography of girls' series books published between 1840 and 1991, this guide is organized alphabetically by series name and includes series and book titles, authors and pseudonyms, and publication dates. The only bibliography to list 1980s young adult romance series such as Sweet Dreams, Wildfire, Sunfire, Windswept, Couples, Cheerleaders, Caprice, Sweet Valley High, and Freshman Dorm by title, the lists are not necessarily complete today, either because of a noted lack of information or because the series were still being published when this bibliography was produced.

Herald, Diana Tixier. "Romance." In ***Teen Genreflecting*****, 101–110. Englewood, CO: Libraries Unlimited, 1997.**

This crisp and concise bibliography provides an overview of the young adult romance subgenres popular in the 1990s. Herald also recommends authors of adult romances whose books teens will enjoy.

Herald, Diana Tixier. ***Teen Genreflecting, 2d Edition*****. Englewood, CO: Libraries Unlimited, 2003.**

In the second edition of Herald's teen fiction bibliography, contemporary romances can be found in the "Contemporary" fiction chapter. This new edition annotates most titles and contains detailed information about characteristics and appeal features of the genres.

Makowski, Silk. ***Serious about Series: Evaluations and Annotations of Teen Fiction in Paperback Series.*** **Lanham, MD: Scarecrow Press, 1998.**

In an extremely useful tool to help librarians learn about the many series of paperback books available for teens in the late 1990s, Makowski provides an evaluation of sixty-two teen series, complete with annotated bibliographies. Some of the series listed have ceased publication, but most of the series should still be available in libraries and, occasionally, in bookstores. Romance series included are Boyfriends, Girlfriends, Cedar River Daydreams, Freshman Dorm, Love Stories, Sweet Dreams, Sweet Valley High, Sweet Valley University, Voices Romance, Wild Hearts, and Wild Rose Inn.

Ramsdell, Kristin. "Appendix 3: Selected Young Adult Romance Bibliography." In ***Romance Fiction: A Guide to the Genre*****, 383–391. Englewood, CO: Libraries Unlimited, 1999.**

An updated version of Ramsdell's previously published bibliography, organized alphabetically by authors' last names. Although a few titles published in the 1990s were added, most of the books listed were published in the 1970s and 1980s.

Ramsdell, Kristin. "Young Adult Romance." In ***Happily Ever After: A Guide to Reading Interests in Romance Fiction*****, 208–230. Littleton, CO: Libraries Unlimited, 1987.**

In a complete annotated bibliography of the popular young adult romance fiction of the 1980s, Ramsdell precedes her bibliography with definitions, reasons for the appeal of young adult romance, tips for advising the reader, and a brief history of the genre. While Ramsdell includes both romance series and individual titles, the bibliography is important because it is the only organized list of the popular young adult romance series of the 1980s to be found.

Society of Phantom Friends. *The Girls Series Companion*. Rheem Valley, CA: SynSine Press, 1997.

In this annotated bibliography organized alphabetically by series name, the authors define girls' series as a group of three or more books with a continuing female protagonist, and therefore, only soap opera romance series, such as Sweet Valley High and Cheerleaders, are included. The annotations provide more information than some of the other published bibliographies, but again, the emphasis is on series published in the 1980s.

History, Surveys, and Criticism

Studies of young adult romance fiction usually focus on the literary quality of romance fiction; romance reading habits of teens; content of the books; messages received by the readers, particularly what readers learn about gender roles in society; and strategies teachers can use to help their students understand young adult romance fiction. A few studies focus on particular young adult romance series, but most of the research examines the general phenomenon of young adult romance series fiction.

Bennett, Susan G., and Alice Kuhn. "Love and Lust in the Secondary Schools: Do Formula Romances Have a Place in the Schools?" *The ALAN Review* 14 (1987): 42–44.

In a later study of 1980s young adult romance fiction, Bennett and Kuhn find the books do not meet acceptable literary criteria, and the authors argue teachers and librarians should not recommend young adult romance novels to young readers.

Cart, Michael. *From Romance to Realism: 50 Years of Growth and Change in Young Adult Literature*. New York: HarperCollins, 1996.

Cart examines young adult literature, beginning with the romance story *Seventeenth Summer* by Maureen Daly in 1942. He follows the growth of young adult literature from romance in the 1940s and 1950s, to realism in the 1960s and 1970s, and back to romance in the 1980s. Cart predicts a new kind of realistic novel for young adults will emerge in the 1990s that presents "hard edged issues" and speaks to readers with "honesty and candor."

Cherland, Meredith Rogers, and Carole Edelsky. "Girls and Reading: The Desire for Agency and the Horror of Helplessness in Fictional Encounters." In *Texts of Desire*, edited by Linda Christian Smith, 28–44. London: Falmer Press, 1993.

In a fascinating study of younger readers, Cherland and Edelsky discover girls who read young adult romance fiction, such as Sweet Valley High, The Babysitters Club, Sweet Valley Twins, and The Nancy Drew Files, do not passively accept the prescribed femininity in the texts. Instead, girls use their reading of fiction to explore other kinds of agency and to imagine themselves as powerful young women.

Christian Smith, Linda K. *Becoming a Woman through Romance*. New York: Routledge Kegan Paul, 1990.

In the consummate study of young adult romance fiction published to date, Christian Smith examines young adult romance fiction published between 1942 and 1982. Christian Smith studies the messages readers receive from young adult romance fiction about love, romance, femininity, and gender roles, and she concludes that young adult romance readers learn about a narrow and outdated feminine ideal that is unrealistic in today's world. Christian Smith has also published numerous articles based on this study.

Daly, Brenda. "Laughing *With*, or Laughing *At*, the Young Adult Romance." *English Journal* 78 (October 1989): 50–60.

In a unique study, Daly investigates the relationship between the lack of humor in romance fiction and the problems of body image and eating disorders among young adult romance readers. Daly suggests humor is an important coping mechanism, and she believes young adult romance readers are not learning the positive roles humor can play in life. She recommends teachers help young women romance readers learn about the myriad choices they have before them, including humor.

De Jesus, Melinda L. " 'Two's Company, Three's a Crowd?': Reading Interracial Romance in Contemporary Asian American Young Adult Fiction." *LIT: Literature Interpretation Theory* 12 (2003): 313–334.

De Jesus examines the portrayal of interracial romance in young adult romance novels, including *Yang the Second and Her Secret Admirers, Tae's Sonata, If It Hadn't Been for Yoon Jun, Name Me Nobody*, and one title from the Love Stories series, *The Language of Love*. De Jesus concludes these novels are limited to heterosexual romances between Asian-American girls and white boys. She encourages young adult authors to write "beyond the ending of the interracial romance triangle" to include homosexual relationships and relationships between Asian-American teens and "other kids of color."

Dickson, Cheryl L. "A Psychological Perspective of Teen Romances in Young Adult Literature." *The ALAN Review* 28 (Spring–Summer 2001): 44–48.

In this study, Dickson analyzes the portrayal of teen romance in two novels, *Hard Love* by Ellen Wittlinger and *A Walk to Remember* by Nicholas Sparks, and she compares her findings to the portrayal of teen relationships in two books in the Love Stories series. Dickson concludes that novels and series romances provide teens with realistic models of teen love relationships.

Gilbert, Pam. "*Dolly* Fictions: Teen Romance Down Under." In *Texts of Desire*, edited by Linda Christian Smith, 69–86. London: Falmer Press, 1993.

Australian researcher Gilbert studies the Dolly Fiction romance series books published in 1988 and 1990 to determine how gender roles and love relationships are portrayed. She discovers earlier books show narrow characterizations of young women and an innocent love relationship, while later books portray a broader range of characterizations, settings, and opportunities for the heroine, including sex. Despite these changes, however, Gilbert concludes gender roles are narrowly constricted by the young adult romance genre.

Kaye, Marilyn. "The Young Adult Romance: Revival and Reaction." ***Top of the News*** **38 (Fall 1981): 42–47.**

In a defense of light romance fiction for young adults, Kaye describes the revival of the genre and the reaction against this revival. Kaye responds to an article written by Elaine Wagner for *Bulletin of the Council on Interracial Books for Children*, where Wagner discusses her campaign to end the publication of Scholastic's *Wildfire* magazine. Kaye objects to Wagner's efforts to censor children's reading material, and she concludes libraries should carry some young adult romance series books since young adults wanted to read the books.

Kundin, Susan G. "Romance versus Reality: A Look at YA Romantic Fiction." ***Top of the News*** **41 (Summer 1985): 361–368.**

In an interesting study, Kundin compares the kinds of problems included in young adult romance fiction to problems found in mainstream young adult fiction. She finds similar problems were covered in equal amounts by both kinds of fiction. Kundin concludes that young adult romance fiction in small doses will not harm teen readers and that libraries should provide young adult romance fiction to readers.

Litton, Joyce. "Double Date to Double Love: Female Sex Roles in Teen Romances, 1942 to 1985." ***The ALAN Review*** **14 (Spring 1987): 45–46, 55.**

Litton compares young adult romance novels published between 1942 and 1963 and 1980 and 1985 to determine how girls and women are portrayed in the innocent teen romance novel. Litton found several significant changes in the 1980s, including women who work outside the home and desires on the part of female protagonists to attend college, work, and have a boyfriend. Litton concludes, despite differences between the earlier and later books, 1980s romances may be harmful to readers because the books reinforce stereotypes of women and offer an unrealistic picture of daily life.

Litton, Joyce. "Dreams, Guys, Lies, and Occasionally Books: The Young Women of the ***Freshmen Dorm*** **Series."** ***The ALAN Review*** **22 (Winter 1995): 10–13.**

Focusing on the Freshmen Dorm series, Litton examines the first fourteen books in the soap opera romance series. Litton argues the series shows a fairly realistic view of college life, strong role models are provided in the characters, and treatment of serious issues such as sex and alcohol is superficial. Litton concludes the Freshmen Dorm series, despite its flaws, is preferable to the popular Sweet Valley High series.

Litton, Joyce. "The Sweet Valley High Gang Goes to College." ***The ALAN Review*** **24 (Fall 1996): 20–24.**

Litton examines the content of the first fourteen books in the Sweet Valley University series. She finds the series tries to deal with serious issues such as premarital sex, date rape, and alcohol abuse, but the ways these issues are portrayed send conflicting messages to teen readers. Litton concludes the series does not have a "well defined social conscience."

Litton, Joyce. "The Wild West, Wars, and Boys: *Sunfire* Historical Romances for Young Adults." *The ALAN Review* (Fall 1991): 22–23, 25.

Litton examines twelve titles in the Sunfire historical romance series and determines that the Sunfire series shows readers strong and intelligent protagonists, and therefore in her opinion, it is the best young adult romance series on the market. Unfortunately, the series is out of print.

Mitchell, Diana. "If You Can't Beat 'em, Join 'em: Using the Romance Series to Confront Gender Stereotypes." *The ALAN Review* 22 (Winter 1995): 8–9.

Mitchell suggests classroom activities and questions teachers can use to get their students thinking about the content of romance series books.

Motes, Julia. "Teaching Girls to Be Girls: Young Adult Series Fiction." *The New Advocate* 11 (Winter 1998): 39–53.

In a study examining the content of popular young adult series books, Motes read titles in the Sweet Valley High, Clueless, and Fear Street series to discover the messages readers receive about female identity and gender roles. Motes found that female characters are obsessed with beauty and body image, that they are in constant competition with each other for boys and popularity, and that having a boyfriend symbolizes a young woman's success in life. She suggests activities teachers can use to help their students negotiate the gendered texts of young adult series fiction.

Parrish, Berta, and Karen Atwood. "Romantic Fiction Revisited." *The ALAN Review* 13 (Spring 1986): 53–56, 74.

In a gentle defense of young adult romance fiction, the authors review the literature to define young adult romance fiction, discover the appeal of young adult romance fiction, determine whether adults should encourage young adults to read these books, and figure out how teachers can use young adult romance fiction as a tool in the classroom. Parrish and Atwood surveyed 250 teens to learn their reading interests. Their findings show that teens read books in many genres, and therefore, adults need not be concerned about young adult romance novel reading.

Willinsky, John, and R. Mark Hunniford. "Reading the Romance Younger: The Mirrors and Fears of a Preparatory Literature." In *Texts of Desire*, edited by Linda Christian Smith, 87–105. London: Falmer Press, 1993.

Inspired by Janice Radway's study of adult romance readers, Willinsky and Hunniford studied forty-two readers of young adult romance series fiction to learn the appeal of the genre. They discovered that young readers are using romance fiction to help prepare them for real life. The authors encourage parents and teachers to talk to young adults about what they are learning from romance series fiction.

Dissertations and Theses

Academic researchers became interested in the young adult series romance phenomenon, and as it began to wane in the late 1980s, several master's theses and doctoral dissertations were written examining the fiction and its readers.

Bereska, Tami M. "Adolescent Romance Novels: Changes over Time." Master's Thesis, University of Alberta, Edmonton, Canada, 1990.

In a timely study, Bereska examines the decline in publishing and popularity of 1980s young adult romance series fiction. She found that adult romances and young adult soap opera romances kept pace with changes regarding attitudes toward sexuality in society by including sex in their stories, but the young adult category romance series generally failed to include sex in their books, and they became outdated.

Hurley, Frances K. "In the Words of Girls: The Reading of Adolescent Romance Fiction." Ed. D. Dissertation, Harvard University, Cambridge, Massachusetts, 1999.

Using Brown and Gilligan's research findings, which indicate that failure to meet the cultural ideal of being perfect, passive, selfless, White, and thin causes young women psychological distress, Hurley examines the treatment of female characters in the Sweet Valley High series. She found that readers aspire to be like Elizabeth, the perfect, introverted, studious twin, rather than Jessica, who is wild and extroverted. Hurley concludes that the waning popularity of young adult romance series fiction indicate the books are less likely to be influential in young women's lives.

Irvine, Carolyn L. "An Analysis of Attitudes, Values and Literary Quality of Contemporary Young Adult Romance Series Novels." Ph.D Dissertation, Florida State University, Tallahassee, Florida, 1999.

Irvine examines the content of twenty popular young adult romance series to determine attitudes, values, and literary quality. Her findings reveal positive attitudes, and the books studied rated high as literary choices. Irvine concludes that romance series novels could be included in the English curriculum, with teachers guiding students' reading.

Lam, M. "Reading the Sweet Dream: Adolescent Girls and Romance Fiction." M.Ed. Thesis, University of Melbourne, Australia, 1986.

Rampoldi Hnilo, Lynn A. "The Effects of Romance in Young Adult Fiction on Pre-Adolescent African American Females." Master's Thesis, Michigan State University, East Lansing, Michigan, 1996.

Using Bandura's social learning theory, Rampoldi Hnilo analyzes themes in young adult romance fiction to determine their effects on young African-American women. She discovered themes of love and romance transcend cultural boundaries. She concludes social learning theory can be used as a predictor of the adoption of attitudes and beliefs, and therefore, girls will adopt the attitudes and beliefs they learn from young adult romance novels.

Uddin Kahn, Evelyne A. "Gender, Ethnicity and the Romance Novel." Ed. D. Dissertation, Columbia University Teacher's College, New York City, New York, 1995.

In a study of immigrant and American young women, Uddin Kahn found that young immigrant and American women read romance novels to learn about social situations, dating, and relationships, while young immigrant women also read the novels to help them learn

the English language. Uddin Kahn concludes that reading romance may be harmful to young women if they perpetuate the models of behavior found in romance novels.

Trade and Library Publication Articles

Much has been written about young adult romance novels in the library and trade publications. Most of the articles focus on the poor literary quality of the books, and the authors recommend that librarians not purchase the books or that they be selective in their choices of young adult romance fiction. A few guides to romance literature and strategies for evaluating young adult romance fiction are offered.

Charles, John, and Shelley Mosley. "Getting Serious about Romance: Adult Series Romances for Teens." ***Voice of Youth Advocates*** **25 (June 2002): 87–93.**

In a useful article that demystifies adult series romances, Charles and Mosley define series romances as "shorter romances released in order and by month, with a series number on each title." They discuss the significance of series romances, highlight important collection development issues, and provide a list of reference resources, including books and Web sites. The authors present an annotated bibliography of "100 Series Romances That Teens Will Love," recommending titles published by Harlequin and Silhouette between 1990 and 2002.

Charles, John, Shelley Mosley, and Ann Bouricius. "Romancing the YA Reader." ***Voice of Youth Advocates*** **21 (February 1999): 414–419.**

In an excellent and concise guide for librarians who want to direct their young adult readers to adult romance titles, the authors also recommend Internet resources and print reference sources to help librarians advise romance readers. The authors won the 2000 Veritas Award from the Romance Writers of America for their article.

Fong, Doris. "From Sweet Valley They Say We Are Leaving . . . " ***School Library Journal*** **36 (January 1990): 38–39.**

Fong provides librarians with strategies for evaluating young adult romance series fiction and suggests tips for advising readers of the genre.

Harvey, Brett. "Sweet Dreams: Virtue Rewarded with the Right Boy." ***Interracial Books for Children Bulletin*** **12 (1981): 13–14.**

Harvey argues the Sweet Dreams romance series from Bantam Books teaches readers to value superficiality, and after learning a moral lesson, the main character is rewarded with the "right" boy who makes her life worthwhile. Young women learn that a boyfriend is the reason for living.

Harvey, Brett. "Wildfire: Tame But Deadly." ***Interracial Books for Children Bulletin*** **12 (1981): 8–10.**

Harvey criticizes the content of the Wildfire romance series published by Scholastic, arguing the series fails to provide racial diversity among the characters in the stories. She concludes the series is dangerous because the primary message girls get from the series is that they must have a boyfriend.

Huntwork, Mary M. "Why Girls Flock to Sweet Valley High." *School Library Journal* 36 (March 1990): 137–140.

Huntwork recounts the findings of her research into the appeal of young adult romance series *Sweet Valley High*. While Huntwork describes young adult romance series as "skillfully marketed junk food," she also recognizes their value in encouraging young adult (females) to read.

Jenkinson, Dave. "The YA Romance: A Second Glance (Sigh!)" *Emergency Librarian* 11 (May–June 1984): 10–13.

In an effort to help librarians understand the appeal of young adult romance series fiction, Jenkinson discusses cover art, titles, logos, and content of the books. Jenkinson suggests librarians use standard reviewing sources to identify the better titles in the romance series and purchase only those books for their libraries.

Lanes, Selma. "Here Come the Blockbusters—Teen Books Go Big Time." *Interracial Books for Children Bulletin* 12 (1981): 5–7.

In the opening article to an issue of *Interracial Books for Children Bulletin* devoted to the subject of young adult romance series, Lanes describes the development of the young adult romance series in the early 1980s.

Peters, Mike. "Sweet Hearts and Couples: Teen Romances and the School Library." *School Librarian* 38 (August 1990): 92–95.

Peters analyzes the content of three American young adult romance series, including Sweet Dreams, Sweet Valley High, and Couples, and he compares them to the British series Heartlines and Tender Hearts. Peters identifies three common themes among the series: fear of male sexuality, peer pressure, and the contrast between home and the outside world. He finds these problems are confronted and resolved in young adult romance series fiction.

Pisik, Betsy. "In This Valley It's Always Sweet 16." *Insight on the News* 6 (January 15, 1990): 62–63.

Pisik reports on the popularity of the Sweet Valley High series and the various kinds of merchandise tied to the series, such as dolls, games, puzzles, date books, and a possible television show.

Pollack, Pamela D. "The Business of Popularity: The Surge of Teenage Paperbacks." *School Library Journal* 28 (November 1981): 25–28.

In an early look at 1980s young adult romance fiction, Pollack describes the new paperback romance series for young adults, focusing on the cover art, marketing of the books, and content of the stories. She reviews criticisms of the formula young adult romance novel and predicts that if the romance series become popular with teen readers, librarians won't buy them because romance fiction is not "great literature."

Ramsdell, Kristin. "Young Adult Publishing: A Blossoming Market." *Top of the News* 39 (Winter 1983): 173–181.

Ramsdell provides a succinct and focused history of book publishing for young adults leading to the development of the new original paperback romance novels created, written, and published especially for teen readers.

Smith, Wendy. "An Earlier Start to Romance." ***Publisher's Weekly*** **220 (November 13, 1981): 56–61.**

Smith describes the birth of the young adult romance series in the early 1980s, providing information about series such as Scholastic's Wildfire, Wishing Star, and Windswept; Dell's Young Love; Bantam's Sweet Dreams; and Silhouette's First Love. Justifications for these new publishing ventures are offered, and predictions suggest the books will be very popular.

Sutton, Roger. "Girls Just Want to Have Fun." ***School Library Journal*** **31 (May 1985): 52.**

Sutton compares the young adult romance novel to the adult romance novel, finding significant differences between the genres. He describes young adult romance novels as "developmental fantasies" and argues they are rather unromantic.

Sutton, Roger. "Hard Times at Sweet Valley." ***School Library Journal*** **(November 1990): 50.**

Sutton discusses the introduction of real-life problems such as racism, violence, and suicide into young adult romance series fiction. While young adult romance series are attempting to address serious issues, Sutton argues that mainstream young adult fiction is trying to avoid important social issues.

Sutton, Roger. "Librarians and the Paperback Romance: Trying to Do the Right Thing." ***School Library Journal*** **32 (November 1985): 25–29.**

In response to the uproar by librarians about the quality of young adult romance series fiction, Sutton argues that librarians are spending too much time and energy worrying about young adult romance series. He suggests librarians stock some titles for their libraries and continue to suggest quality literature to teen readers.

Van Vliet, Virginia. "Young Love on Fantasy Island." ***Emergency Librarian*** **11 (May–June 1984): 6–9.**

Van Vliet discusses the lack of literary quality of the young adult paperback romance series, but she recommends libraries stock them, along with quality literature.

Watson, Emily Strauss. "Wishing Star: Hiding Trash with a Veneer of 'Reality.' " ***Interracial Books for Children Bulletin*** **12 (1981): 11–12.**

Watson argues that Scholastic's Wishing Star series fails to provide readers with realistic solutions to problems, and as a consequence, the series is destructive.

Wigutoff, Sharon. "First Love: Morality Tales Thinly Veiled." ***Interracial Books for Children Bulletin*** **12 (1981): 15–17.**

Wigutoff contends that Silhouette's First Love series is promoted as recreational, escapist reading, but in fact the series teaches outdated stereotypes regarding gender roles, family structures, racial diversity, and socioeconomics.

Popular Press Articles

A few informational and promotional articles about young adult romance fiction have been published in the popular press.

Brockway, Laurie Sue. "The Thrills and Spills of Romance Novels." ***Young Miss*** **31 (September 1983): 80, 89.**

Brockway encourages readers to take advantage of the benefits of reading young adult romance novels, including escape from problems, entertainment, lessons learned from the books, and the fact that romance gets young women to read.

Dougherty, Steve. "Heroines of 40 Million Books, Francine Pascal's ***Sweet Valley*** **Twins Are Perfection in Duplicate."** ***People Magazine*** **30 (July 11, 1988): 66–68.**

A profile of Francine Pascal, creator of the Sweet Valley High series.

Harvey, Brett. "Boy Crazy: How Far Can You Go in a Teen Romance?" ***The Village Voice*** **(February 10–16, 1982): 48–49.**

Harvey suggests 1980s young adult romance series fiction was created to counter the frank depictions of love and romance found in young adult fiction in the 1970s. She argues the young adult series romance stories are morality plays, rather than love stories, and their purpose is to instruct young women to be good girls.

Jefferson, Margo. "Sweet Dreams for Teen Queens." ***The Nation*** **234 (May 22, 1982): 613–617.**

Jefferson criticizes popular young adult romance series of the 1980s for their unrealistic and nostalgic portrayal of the lives of teens.

"Romance Novels: Why You Can't Put Them Down." ***Teen*** **30 (February 1986): 8, 11, 83.**

A promotional article highlighting the appeal of the formula young adult romance novel.

Guides for Writing Young Adult Romance

When the young adult romance series were proliferating in the 1980s, guides began to appear to help authors learn how to write the formula for the romance series.

Cavanagh, Helen. "Cooking Up the Teen Romance Novel." ***Writer's Digest*** **62 (May 1982): 43–45.**

Cavanagh, the author of several books in the Wildfire young adult romance series, describes her experiences as a new novelist. She uses episodes from her books to illustrate the formula for writing the young adult romance novel.

Lowery, Marilyn M. "The Young Adult Romance." In ***How to Write Romance Novels That Sell*****, 151–160. New York: Rawson Associates, 1983.**

Lowery outlines the requirements for a category young adult romance novel published in the 1980s, citing examples from the popular Sweet Dreams and Wildfire series.

Miner, Jane Claypool. "Writing Teen Romances." *The Writer* 95 (July 1982): 18–20.

Miner, author of several books in the Wildfire and First Love from Silhouette lines, highlights key elements necessary for a successful young adult romance novel, including characterization, themes, setting, and rules of the young adult romance.

Library Research Collections

A few research libraries specializing in popular culture materials have collected young adult romance novels and series books. Young adult romance books collected were generally published between 1942 and the 1980s. These books are usually housed in special collections that can only be used in the libraries.

Bowling Green State University

The Popular Culture Library features Romance Collections, which include 10,000 volumes of category romance series and the Romance Writers of America Archives. The collections include a few titles from some of the popular 1980s young adult romance series, such as Wildfire, Sweet Dreams, Sweet Valley High, Sunfire, First Love from Silhouette, Caprice, Caitlin, and Seniors. The library also has titles by popular young adult authors who frequently incorporate the romance element into their work, such as Rosamund Du Jardin, Maureen Daly, and Judy Blume.

Michigan State University

The Russell B. Nye Popular Culture Collections include a Romance Fiction collection and a Juvenile Series Fiction collection. Holdings in the Juvenile Series Fiction collection include titles from many of the 1980s young adult romance series, including Sweet Valley High, Sweet Dreams, Wildfire, First Love from Silhouette, Cheerleaders, The Girls of Canby Hall, Seniors, and Sweet Valley University.

University of Minnesota

The Hess Collection at the University of Minnesota's Children's Literature Research Collections features dime novels and popular literature. Young adult romance series included are Sweet Dreams, Sweet Valley High, and Caitlin.

Appendix A

Sample Core Collection

The sample core collection is a list of young adult romance novels you should have available in your library. At the time of this writing, all of the titles on this list were in print and, therefore, available for purchase. The titles selected for this sample core collection were chosen either because they are award winners or because they are very popular with readers, or both. Some titles have remained popular with readers over time, while particular current titles are extremely popular with teen readers and therefore can't be excluded from the list. Many award-winning titles, including titles selected by the American Library Association as Best Books for Young Adults, are included on this core list. Award winners are denoted with a symbol.

If you are unable to purchase all the books on this list for your library, the top twenty-five young adult romancces you should buy for your collection are identified in boldfaced type. The sample core collection is organized to match the overall themes of the book lists found here so that you can turn quickly to a particular chapter to learn more about the titles in this sample core collection.

Chapter 2: Classic Romance

Blume, Judy

***Forever.* Bradbury Press, 1975. Reissued by Pocket Books, 1996. ISBN 0671695304.**

Cleary, Beverly

***Fifteen.* William Morrow, 1956. Reissued by HarperTrophy in 2003. ISBN 0060533005.**

***Jean and Johnny.* William Morrow, 1959. Reissued by HarperTrophy in 2003. ISBN 0060533013.**

***The Luckiest Girl.* William Morrow, 1958. Reissued by HarperTrophy in 2003. ISBN 0060532998.**

***Sister of the Bride.* William Morrow, 1963. Reissued by HarperTrophy in 2003. ISBN 006053298X.**

Daly, Maureen

***Seventeenth Summer.* Dodd, Mead, 1942. Reissued by Simon & Schuster in 2002. ISBN 0671619314.**

Greene, Bette

***Summer of My German Soldier.* Dial, 1973. Reissued by Penguin Putnam in 1999. ISBN 014130636X.**

Zindel, Paul

My Darling, My Hamburger. Harper & Row, 1969. Reissued by Bantam Starfire in 1984. ISBN 0553273248.

Pardon Me, You're Stepping on My Eyeball. Harper & Row, 1976. Reissued by Bantam Starfire in 1983. ISBN 055326690X.

Chapter 3: Contemporary Romance

Cabot, Meg

The Princess Diaries Series.

***The Princess Diaries.* HarperCollins, 2000. ISBN 0380978482.**

The Princess Diaries Volume II: Princess in the Spotlight. HarperCollins, 2001. ISBN 0060294655.

***The Princess Diaries Volume III: Princess in Love.* HarperCollins, 2002. ISBN 0060294671.**

The Princess Diaries Volume IV: Princess in Waiting. HarperCollins, 2003. ISBN 006009608X.

The Princess Diaries Volume IV and a Half: Project Princess. Harper Trophy, 2003. ISBN 0060571314.

Dessen, Sarah

***This Lullaby.* Penguin Putnam, 2002. ISBN 0670035300.**

Hidier, Tanuja Desai

***Born Confused.* Scholastic, 2002. ISBN 0439357624.**

Korman, Gordon

Son of the Mob. Hyperion Books, 2002. ISBN 0786807695.

McCafferty, Megan

"The Diaries of Jessica Darling".

***Sloppy Firsts.* Crown, 2001. ISBN 0609807900.**

Second Helpings. Crown, 2003. ISBN 0609807919.

Rennison, Louise

The Confessions of Georgia Nicolson.

***Angus, Thongs and Full Frontal Snogging: Confessions of Georgia Nicolson.* HarperCollins, 2000. ISBN 0060288140.**

Spinelli, Jerry

Stargirl. Alfred A. Knopf, 2000. ISBN 0679886370.

Van Draanen, Wendelin

Flipped. Alfred A. Knopf, 2001. ISBN 0375811745.

Whelan, Gloria

Homeless Bird. HarperCollins, 2000. ISBN 0064408191.

Wilson, Jacqueline

The Girls Quartet.

Girls in Love. Delacorte Press, 2002. ISBN 038572974X.

Girls under Pressure. Delacorte Press, 2002. ISBN 0385729758.

Girls out Late. Delacorte Press, 2002. ISBN 0385729766.

Girls in Tears. Delacorte Press, 2003. ISBN 0385730829.

Wolff, Virginia Euwer

True Believer. Simon & Schuster, 2001. ISBN 0689828276.

Chapter 4: Contemporary Romance Series

Luna Bay. Harper Entertainment. Written by Fran Lantz.

Mary-Kate and Ashley Sweet 16. Harper Entertainment. Written by Various Authors.

Smooch. Dorchester. Written by Various Authors.

Chapter 5: Issues Romance

Bechard, Margaret

Hanging on to Max. Millbrook Press, 2002. ISBN 0761315799.

Cart, Michael (Editor)

Love and Sex: Ten Stories of Truth. Simon & Schuster, 2001. ISBN 0689832036.

Dessen, Sarah

Dreamland. Penguin Putnam, 2000. ISBN 0670891223.

Someone Like You. Viking, 1998. ISBN 0670877786.

Flinn, Alex

Breathing Underwater. HarperCollins, 2001. ISBN 0060291982.

Freymann-Weyr, Garret

My Heartbeat. Houghton Mifflin, 2002. ISBN 0618141812.

Garden, Nancy

Annie on My Mind. Farrar, Straus & Giroux, 1982. ISBN 0374303665.

Koertge, Ron

Stoner and Spaz. Candlewick, 2002. ISBN 0763616087.

Sanchez, Alex

<u>**"Rainbow Series"**</u>.

 ***Rainbow Boys.* Simon & Schuster, 2001. ISBN 0689841000.**

Wittlinger, Ellen

 *Hard Love.* Aladdin, 1999. ISBN 0689821344.

Chapter 6: Alternative Reality Romance

Block, Francesca Lia

<u>**Weetzie Bat Saga**</u>.

 *Weetzie Bat.* HarperCollins, 1989. ISBN 0060205342.

Cherokee Bat and the Goat Guys. HarperCollins, 1992. ISBN 0060202696.

Missing Angel Juan. HarperCollins, 1993. ISBN 006023007X.

Cooney, Caroline B.

<u>**Time Travel Quartet**</u>.

Both Sides of Time. Delacorte Press, 1995. ISBN 0385321740.

Out of Time. Bantam Books, 1995. ISBN 0385322267.

Prisoner of Time. Bantam Doubleday Dell, 1998. ISBN 0385322445.

For All Time. Delacorte Press, 2001. ISBN 0385327730.

Klause, Annette Curtis

 ***Blood and Chocolate.* Bantam Doubleday Dell, 1997. ISBN 0385323050.**

***The Silver Kiss.* Delacorte Press, 1991. ISBN 038530160X.**

Levine, Gail Carson

 ***Ella Enchanted.* HarperCollins, 1997. ISBN 0060275103.**

McKillip, Patricia A.

 *The Forgotten Beasts of Eld.* Atheneum, 1974. Reissued by Magic Carpet Books in 1996. ISBN 0152008691.

McKinley, Robin

 ***Beauty: A Retelling of the Story of Beauty and the Beast.* HarperCollins, 1978. Reissued by HarperCollins in 1993. ISBN 0064404773.**

Chapter 7: Romantic Suspense

Carroll, Jenny/Cabot, Meg

<u>**The Mediator Series.**</u>

 *Shadowland.* Pulse, 2000. ISBN 0671787918.

Ninth Key. Pulse, 2001. ISBN 0671787985.

Reunion. Pulse, 2001. ISBN 0671788124.

Darkest Hour. Pulse, 2001. ISBN 0671788477.

Haunted. HarperCollins, 2003. ISBN 006029471X.

Carroll, Jenny/Cabot, Meg

1-800-WHERE-R-YOU Series.

When Lightning Strikes. Pocket Books, 2001. ISBN 0743411390.

Code Name Cassandra. Pocket Books, 2001. ISBN 0743411404.

Safe House. Pocket Books, 2002. ISBN 0743411412.

Sanctuary. Pocket Books, 2002. ISBN 0743411420.

Cormier, Robert

Tenderness. Bantam Doubleday Dell, 1997. ISBN 0385322860.

We All Fall Down. Delacorte Press, 1991. ISBN 038530501X.

Chapter 8: Historical Romance

Chambers, Aidan

***Postcards from No Man's Land*. Penguin Putnam, 2002. ISBN 0525468633.**

Cushman, Karen

***Catherine, Called Birdy*. Houghton Mifflin, 1994. ISBN 0395681863.**

Rinaldi, Ann

The Coffin Quilt: The Feud between the Hatfields and the McCoys. Harcourt, 1999. ISBN 0152020152.

Historical Romance Series

Avon True Romance. Avon, 2002 to 2003. Written by Various Authors.

Chapter 9: Christian Romance

Gunn, Robin Jones

Christy and Todd: The College Years Trilogy.

Until Tomorrow. Bethany House, 2000. ISBN 0764222724.

As You Wish. Bethany House, 2000. ISBN 0764222732.

I Promise. Bethany House, 2001. ISBN 0764222740.

Contemporary Christian Romance Series

Christy Miller. Bethany House, 1988–1994. Reissued in 1998. Written by Robin Jones Gunn.

Appendix B

Romance Readers' Advisor Resources

Although resources on young adult romance are not plentiful, there are a few resources that every teen readers' advisor should have. The following list of resources includes books, reviewing sources, and listservs.

Books

The following books offer more readers' advisory tips that can help you work with the young adult romance reader. Bibliographies in these books will also help you identify romance novels to recommend to your patrons.

Benedetti, Angelina. "Leading the Horse to Water: Keeping Young People Reading in the Information Age." In *The Readers' Advisor's Companion*, edited by Kenneth D. Shearer and Robert Burgin. Englewood, CO: Libraries Unlimited, 2001.

A concise article outlining key issues librarians need to consider when providing readers' advisory services to their teen customers.

Bouricius, Anne. *The Romance Readers' Advisory: The Librarian's Guide to Love in the Stacks.* Chicago: American Library Association, 2000.

A lively overview of the romance genre focusing on romances written for adult audiences.

Gillespie, John T., ed. *Best Books for Young Teen Readers Grades 7–10.* New Providence, NJ: R. R. Bowker, 2000.

This extensive bibliography includes an annotated bibliography of young adult romances.

Herald, Diana Tixier. *Genreflecting: A Guide to Reading Interests in Genre Fiction.* 5th ed. Englewood, CO: Libraries Unlimited, 2000.

A guide to genre fiction that includes a concise chapter about romance novels aimed at adult audiences.

Herald, Diana Tixier. *Teen Genreflecting.* 2d ed. Englewood, CO: Libraries Unlimited, 2003.

This guide to young adult fiction, organized by genre, includes a guide to young adult romance fiction in the chapter about "Contemporary Fiction."

Holley, Pam Spencer. *What Do Young Adults Read Next?* Vol. 4. Detroit, MI: Gale Research, 2002.

An annotated bibliography of young adult fiction, including love stories and romances written for teen readers.

Makowski, Silk. *Serious about Series: Evaluations and Annotations of Teen Fiction in Paperback Series.* Lanham, MD: Scarecrow Press, 1998.

This selective guide to teen paperback series fiction includes summaries and bibliographies of several popular romance series. It is necessary, however, to read the entries to determine if the series are romances.

O'Dell, Katie. *Library Materials and Services for Teen Girls.* Greenwood Village, CO: Libraries Unlimited, 2002.

Includes a brief bibliography on current fiction featuring romance and sexuality.

Ramsdell, Kristin. *Romance Fiction: A Guide to the Genre.* Englewood, CO: Libraries Unlimited, 1999.

The most complete guide to romance fiction available, it is organized by subgenre and includes definitions and history of subgenres, readers' advisory tips, and bibliographies of romance fiction aimed at adult audiences. Also has an appendix listing young adult romances.

Ramsdell, Kristin. *What Romance Do I Read Next?* 2d ed. Detroit: Gale Research, 1999.

An annotated romance bibliography that includes a few young adult titles.

Saricks, Joyce G. *The Readers' Advisory Guide to Genre Fiction.* Chicago: American Library Association, 2001.

An essential tool for readers' advisors, this book includes chapters on the romance and romantic suspense genres. Saricks explains the important elements of the romance genres, and she suggests valuable tips for the romance readers' advisory interview.

Reviewing Sources

There are no reviewing sources solely devoted to young adult romance fiction. Popular reviewing sources such as *Booklist, Library Journal,* and *Publisher's Weekly* all review young adult fiction, including romances. *Booklist* also publishes an annual column in September reviewing young adult romantic fiction, which is particularly useful. Other journals devoted to reviewing young adult fiction, including books in the romance genre, are listed below.

Periodicals

The ALAN Review
National Council of Teachers of English
1111 W. Kenyon Rd.
Urbana, IL 61801

Reviews new young adult fiction. Also offers articles about teaching young adult literature, interviews with authors, reports on publishing trends, and current research on young adult literature.

KLIATT
33 Bay State Rd.
Wellesley, MA 02481

Reviews hardcover, paperback, and audio books written for young adults.

School Library Journal
245 W. 17th St.
New York, NY 10011

Reviews fiction written for both children and young adults.

VOYA: Voice of Youth Advocates
Scarecrow Press
4720A Boston Way
Lanham, MD 20706

Besides reviewing books, VOYA also includes articles about young adult genre fiction. Young adult romances are regularly reviewed in the column about young adult paperback fiction.

Listservs

Listservs are online discussion groups focused on a particular topic, and anyone with an e-mail account can join these discussion groups. Two listservs for youth librarians are PUBYAC and YALSA-BK.

PUBYAC

PUBYAC is an online discussion group focusing on issues related to library services for children and young adults. To subscribe to PUBYAC, send an e-mail message to listproc@prairienet.org. Leave the subject line blank. The message should say: subscribe pubyac.

YALSA-BK

YALSA-BK, hosted by the Young Adult Library Services Association of the American Library Association, is an online discussion group about books for young adults. Young adult romance fiction is often a topic of discussion. To subscribe to YALSA-BK, send an e-mail message to listproc@ala.org. Leave the subject line blank. The message should say: "Subscribe yalsa-bk first name last name."

Author/Title Index

Subject Index

About the Author

CAROLYN CARPAN, Reference Librarian of Olin Library in Winter Park Florida, and Assistant Professor at Rollins College, is an avid romance reader. She has published a number of journal articles in such publications as *YA Hotline* and *Bulletin of Bibliography*.